Principles and Techniques of
Effective Business Communication

A Text-Workbook
Isabelle A. Krey / Bernadette V. Metzler

Principles and Techniques of

Effective
Business
Communication
A Text-Workbook

Principles and Techniques of

Effective Business Communication

A Text-Workbook

Isabelle A. Krey
Kingsborough Community College

Bernadette V. Metzler
Hunter College

Harcourt Brace Jovanovich, Inc.

New York / Chicago / San Francisco / Atlanta

ISBN: 0-15-571310-8
Library of Congress Catalog Card Number: 75-45520

Printed in the United States of America

PREFACE

The ability to communicate accurately and effectively is the most important step to success in today's fast-moving, fast-changing business world. Since more than 90 percent of all office jobs require communication skills, it is essential that students learn and master the principles and techniques of effective business communication. This text-workbook aims to help them achieve that requisite goal.

In *Principles and Techniques of Effective Business Communication* we have adopted a modified case approach and an informal style in order to involve students directly in the business writing process. We try to *show* students, not merely *tell* them, what to do by providing examples that are within their range of experience—not hypothetical business cases far beyond the comprehension of those who have never worked in an office. Interspersed throughout are many models of good business writing, side by side with samples of what *not* to do, and the reasons why.

Part I, "Elements of Effective Writing," offers a thorough discussion of general principles: how to put a letter together, how to choose the appropriate style, and, most important, how to compose a message that will reach the reader. We emphasize how crucial it is for the writer always to keep the reader in mind, to tailor the message to fit its purpose, and to use clear, effective language. These principles are then reiterated throughout the book.

In Part II, "Social- and Personal-Business Writing," we discuss various types of communication—for example, the simple request, the invitation, the order letter, the letter of inquiry, the claim letter, and the series of letters involved in applying for a job. Here, as in other parts of the book, we have attempted to use the student's own needs and experiences to give him or her an introduction to basic business procedures and to illustrate the importance of written communication in the business world.

The chapters in Part III, "Writing on the Job," stress the unique purpose of each type of business communication—from the interoffice memorandum to claim and adjustment letters, credit, sales, and collection letters, and, finally, to the report itself. In this last chapter, we present a sample report, with marginal annotations that point to its strengths and weaknesses.

In our presentation of principles, we have drawn on discussions that appeared in our previously published *Effective Writing for Business*

(Harcourt Brace Jovanovich, 1968). This new book, however, integrates text and workbook materials in a combination text-workbook format. Among the distinctly new features of *Principles and Techniques of Effective Business Communication* are:

- The inclusion of performance goals and sub-goals—an integral part of the book—that enable students to know what their objectives are at each stage of their study.

- The provision for immediate evaluation of student performance and progress—instructor, peer group, or self-evaluation—based on specific criteria incorporated in the objectives.

- The Skills Activities, with accompanying goals and criteria for evaluation, that require students to apply the principles and techniques they have learned in each unit of each chapter.

- The "Focus on Language" sections in each chapter, also with accompanying goals and criteria for evaluation, that concentrate on common problems in grammar, vocabularly, spelling, punctuation, and proofreading.

- The inclusion, at the back of the book, of a complete answer key to the Skills Activities and "Focus on Language" sections to encourage student self-checking and to provide immediate reinforcement.

Because we believe that strong language skills are essential for effective communication, we have emphasized points of grammar and usage throughout the book; marginal glosses are used to highlight these points. In addition, the grammar and usage entries in the Index are set off in italics for the student's ease of reference.

We wish to thank our colleagues, friends, and, most particularly, our students at Kingsborough Community College and Hunter College for their constructive criticism and their many fine suggestions. We are grateful to Ms. Dorothy Snowman for her extraordinary skill and patience in editing our manuscript, and to the editorial and production staffs of Harcourt Brace Jovanovich for their care and concern in solving a myriad of problems and in shepherding this book through to publication.

A final word of thanks to our friend and teacher, Dr. Estelle L. Popham, for her interest, encouragement, and counsel. Her expertise and acumen contributed enormously to the development of this book.

Isabelle A. Krey
Bernadette V. Metzler

CONTENTS

I
ELEMENTS OF EFFECTIVE WRITING

1

WHY WRITE BUSINESS COMMUNICATIONS?

deluged: flooded; over-whelmed

Every business firm, government office, and service organization is deluged with typed and duplicated materials—house organs, bulletins, government reports, handbooks, instruction leaflets, letters, interoffice memorandums, manuals, minutes of meetings, and proposals. Higher and higher builds the paper mountain! However, through these materials flows the lifeblood of business. Without written communication, orders would not be filled, supplies would not be received, credit would not be established, new techniques would not be devised, research would be slow and plodding, and management's decisions would be based on in-adequate information. Without written communication, our economy could not have expanded so rapidly. Over the past two decades alone our gross national product (the total value of all final goods and services produced in the economy in one year) has nearly quadrupled.

received

The quality of communications can speed up the service you or your company gives or receives. Your ability to communicate in writing will enable you to run your own personal- and social-business life more effi-ciently. It is a skill that business firms need in their personnel, from clerks to top excecutives. Do you know how much it costs to write a business letter? A survey by a team of management consultants showed that today's letters cost anywhere from $1.37 to $3.79. The good letter costs no more than the poor one, but it gets better results. Management seeks results.

management

Your performance objective for the first unit is:

Given a question of why communications in a business situation should be written,

You will clearly state four principal reasons for putting the message in writing.

UNIT 1 WHY WRITE IT DOWN?

Why write that letter? Why not communicate directly over the telephone or by a personal visit? It's faster, and you get the answer right away. True, but face-to-face conversation is not always feasible, practical, or efficient as a means of contacting another person.

it's: contraction of "it is"; not the possessive "its"
feasible: suitable   efficient

Economy

Distance, with the resulting expense of a toll call, is one deterrent to telephone conversation. It is less expensive to write to someone in another state or in another country than to telephone and wait for an answer while the minutes tick away on that toll call. And you may save only a little time, since the answer may not be available at once and may have to be sent through the mails anyway. Also, it is more economical to write when hundreds, thousands, or tens of thousands of people must receive the same information—think of the letters inviting charge customers to a private sale at a leading department store.

deterrent: something that prevents

Efficiency

It is impractical in today's business world to interrupt a customer by telephoning to say "thank you" for an order and to state the date the shipment will arrive. Just as annoying would be the department-store call to your home in the middle of a luncheon or a bridge game to tell you that delivery of the rug you had ordered would be delayed until the end of the month. A card would suffice.

suffice: satisfy; be enough

```
November 19, 19--

Dear Mrs. Jones,

The trucking strike is over, and your 9 x 12
foot Karastan rug will be delivered on Monday,
November 25.

We are sorry for the delay.

Sincerely,

GROSS DEPARTMENT STORE
```

In determining the most efficient means of communicating, letter writers must think not only of themselves but of the persons to whom they are writing.

Accuracy

The major determinant of the method of communication is, of course, the type of information to be transmitted or requested. Detailed, intricate information requires the written word to ensure accuracy and correct understanding. Would you call your showroom to make ten changes in a price list? How would you get the proposal for a new program of in-service training before the personnel manager? Can you rely on a telephone conversation to get the breakdown of individual item charges for your automobile insurance? What about that yearly schedule of club

determinant: that which influences; a cause
ensure: make certain

schedule

activities? How would you like to take the information in this letter over the telephone?

> Your automobile-insurance policy No. 01-GA24-3234 covers: bodily injury of $100/300,000 for a premium of $103; property damage of $25,000 for $33; comprehensive fire and theft, according to value, for $21; collision, with $50 deductible, for $68; towing up to $25 for $2.

collision; deductible

These items must be in written form. Word-of-mouth communication can often result in error, such as a transposed figure, an incorrect date or address, or a misheard phrase; but a carefully written communication ensures accuracy.

Official Record

Finally, a written communication becomes part of the record—it becomes official. For this reason, corporations, prior to their annual meetings, send out written proxies for their stockholders' signatures. So that they can give thoughtful consideration to new ideas, executives ask you to "write it up" when you offer a proposal for a change in office procedure, a change in letter style, or an office bowling competition or picnic. Giving your supervisor a good written proposal can win a promotion for you; mentioning it in passing can consign your idea to oblivion.

proxies: power to act for another

competition

consign: turn over
oblivion: state of being forgotten

The mail clerk who wrote this memorandum received a promotion in a growing advertising agency:

> Date: August 9, 19--
>
>   To: Mr. Peters
>   Office Manager
>
> From: I. Smart
>   Chief Messenger
>
> Subject: Handling Incoming Mail
>
> When the mail comes into the office each morning, it is delivered unopened to the departmental secretary, who must then process it.
>
> I propose that the following procedure be considered for all departmental offices.

```
The mail clerk:

     Opens all pieces of mail.
     Time stamps each individual communication.
     Checks for enclosures.
     Indicates on letter special notations from
        envelope such as special delivery, certi-
        fied mail, registry.
     Sorts by departments.
     Assigns office messengers to deliver.

This procedure would necessitate the purchase
of the following equipment:

     mail-opening machine
     date-and-time stamping device


Because our mail volume has now increased to
more than a thousand letters daily, this pro-
cedure would effect a more rapid and efficient
handling of incoming mail.
```

necessitate

The person with ideas who has the ability to put those ideas in writing scores. The worker who generates ideas for others to "write up" under their own names remains obscure.

obscure: hidden; unnoticed

Most businesspeople, in responding to an invitation, request the invitation in writing. You may call Mr. Patrick, the vice-president of a department store in your community, to ask him to speak at your retailing club's annual dinner the following month. "I'll be glad to be your guest speaker next month," he says, "but will you write me a note on it? And please be sure to include your suggestions for a topic."

In your personal-business life, too, you write notes for the record—as, for example, when you write that you have already paid a bill for which you have just received a dunning letter.

dunning: pertaining to a demand for payment

Now you are ready for Skills Activity 1.

SKILLS ACTIVITY 1

Do you know why you write instead of telephoning or meeting face-to-face?

1. _____

2. _____

3. _____

4. _____

<table>
<tr><td colspan="2">Given a question on the reasons for writing instead of using oral communication, list four reasons correctly.</td></tr>
<tr><td>Excellent</td><td>4</td></tr>
<tr><td>Good</td><td>3</td></tr>
<tr><td>Fair</td><td>2</td></tr>
</table>

Check the key on page 509. If you fall below Fair, review the answers and be sure you understand them before you continue.

Name_____ Date_____

UNIT 2 PURPOSES OF BUSINESS WRITING

Your performance objective is:

Given the problem of identifying the reasons for written communications,

You will clearly describe the three principal purposes.

Business firms use written communication for these same reasons of economy, efficiency, accuracy, and record-keeping. At least 85 percent of business is conducted either completely or partially by mail. The more than thirty billion first-class letters mailed annually in the United States alone attest to the importance of written communication. These letters are written for a variety of purposes: to get information or materials; to answer a request; to volunteer information; to observe the amenities of expressing thanks, congratulations, and condolences—and thus to build goodwill.

attest: confirm as true or genuine

amenities: courtesies

Requesting and Furnishing Information and Materials

If you had lived several centuries ago, you, as the sole owner of your business, would have supervised all your work and would have been in touch with your suppliers and customers personally. Except for keeping records, you would have had little need for the written word. However, today's improved methods of transportation enable businesses to operate farther from their markets and from their sources of supply. Letters assist business in bridging these distances. Air mail and Mailgrams are so rapid today that your letter with vital information can be received in an office across the country the next morning; your request for information can be answered and received the following business day.

farther: greater space or distance
Mailgrams: communications sent by telegram to nearest post office and then delivered as first-class mail.
enabling

These letters sped across the country within two days, enabling the distributor in Boston to get a prompt answer to a request for information:

```
Ladies and Gentlemen:

Please quote your terms on 100 redwood picnic
sets (table and four chairs), No. 5522, for
delivery by March 15.

We are considering featuring these sets in the
opening of our outdoor furniture department at
the end of March.

                        Sincerely,

                        J. J. Greenwood
                        Manager
```

Mr. Greenwood received his answer from the supplier as follows:

supplier

Dear Mr. Greenwood:

The 100 redwood picnic sets, No. 5522, can be delivered by March 12 at the cost of:

Quantity	Item	Unit	Total
100	Redwood picnic set #5522	$20	$2,000

Our terms are 2/10, n/30.

As soon as we hear from you, we will ship your order.

We are pleased that you are considering the California redwood picnic sets as a feature in the opening of your outdoor furniture department.

Thank you.

                      Sincerely yours,

That is, the buyer may take a 2 percent discount if payment is made within 10 days or pay the full amount within 30 days.

Building Goodwill

You buy in Smith's market rather than in Brown's. Why? One reason could be that Smith's clerks greet you with a friendly "Good morning. How are you today?" and always remember to say "Thank you." Smith's employees create goodwill for the business, so when you need something you think of Smith's.

While businesspersons may do many other things to build goodwill and hold it, they realize that their letters are particularly important in creating a favorable image of the company. Every letter—of sales, adjustment, credit, request—presents an opportunity to develop this tremendously important intangible asset. Many people to whom you write never see you, never talk to you. Their impressions of you and your business and their attitudes toward you are formed entirely through the letters they receive. When you direct your writing to the reader's viewpoint, you build goodwill for your business. To do this, you must have an understanding not only of business operations but of human nature. The importance of letters as goodwill ambassadors or human-relations tools cannot be exaggerated.

intangible: can't be perceived by touch

exaggerated

Consider the action taken in the following situation. Mr. Jonas, a client of an auto-rental company, had parked his rented car on an out-of-town city street while he called upon a customer. When he returned to the car, there was a dent in the rear fender. The client reported the damage to the rental agency immediately and was told that there would be no problem in handling the case because he was not at fault. He was further told that the rental agency's insurance would cover the damage. A few days after he returned to his home office, he received the following letter:

Re the damage to our rented car in Cincinnati (Rental Number 64325) on July 6:

Cincinnati

According to the scant information you supplied us at the time of the accident, you are completely at fault, and we will not accept any responsibility for your negligence, which obviously caused the damage to said car.

negligence: carelessness

Under the terms of the insurance covering the car, Contract 105558, you must pay the entire bill. Please send your check for $89.38 immediately.

Should you have anything further to say on this subject, you can write to Mr. Sidney Martinson in our Cincinnati office.

What is your reaction to the letter? Should the client have requested a release from the rental agency? Did this letter create goodwill? Would you write a letter like this? What would you do if you received it?

Now turn to Skills Activity 2.

SKILLS ACTIVITY 2

Do you know the main purposes of business communications?

1. _____

_____

2. _____

_____

3. _____

_____

> *Given a question on why business communications are written, describe clearly three purposes.*
>
> *Peer judgment:*
>
> *Excellent   3*
> *Good   2*

As soon as your instructor signals you to stop, form into groups of five or six. The group will listen to each student's answer and will rate the answer according to the scale in the margin.

If you achieved Good or Excellent, you are ready to go on. If you did not achieve at least Good, review, rewrite the answers, and ask your instructor to judge your rewritten answers. Then go on to the Summary and Focus on Language.

Name _____ Date _____

SUMMARY

permanent

In your personal-business life as well as in your business career, you will write letters that request or furnish information. You will find that written communication is more effective than spoken communication in terms of economy, efficiency, and accuracy and that it provides a necessary permanent record. No matter what the purpose of a letter may be, the way it is written can either build or destroy goodwill. It is important, therefore, that you learn to use written communication effectively.

Now you are ready for Focus on Language. In these exercises, you will cover the 31 spelling and vocabulary words spotlighted in the chapter; and you will check your ability to catch all the errors in a proofreading exercise.

FOCUS ON LANGUAGE

Spelling

Its said that he recieves several offers of employment each week. Although we know that he is a responsible, eficient worker and that compitition for such employees is keen, we believe he has exagerrated his importance. He says it would not be feasible for him to accept an offer in Cincinati because his scedule will not allow him to travel further than 20 miles each day. But managment wants him to accept, for they feel his refusal will necesitate a switch in supplyers. They are offering him a large salary increase, a consinement of top quality merchandise, and a permenant position on the staff. And, of course, his added expenses would be deductable.

Given a paragraph containing misspelled words, write the correct spelling of each of these words directly above it.

Excellent	*14*
Good	*13*
Fair	*12*

Check the key on page 509. If you achieved Fair or above, go on to Vocabulary. If you scored below Fair, review the spelling words spotlighted in the chapter.

Vocabulary

Here are some of the vocabulary words that were spotlighted in the chapter you have just read. Make them part of your everyday vocabulary.

1. feasible   a. impractical   b. useless   c. suitable   d. forceful
2. dunning   a. asking for payment   b. fearing   c. losing
   d. running
3. amenities   a. disagreements   b. courtesies   c. endings
   d. paintings
4. deterrent   a. determining   b. helpful   c. a tool   d. preventive
5. collision   a. accident   b. helpful   c. subterfuge   d. violent
   hitting together

Given 15 vocabulary words with a choice of four meanings each, circle the letter of the word or phrase you believe is nearest in meaning to the numbered word.

Excellent	*15*
Good	*14*
Fair	*13*

Name _____ Date _____

6. intangible   a. easily reached   b. not perceived by touch
   c. machinery   d. intelligent

7. negligence   a. caution   b. carelessness   c. attentive   d. law
   case

8. determinant   a. holding back   b. effect   c. deterrent
   d. influence

9. enabling   a. making possible   b. not capable   c. using well
   d. enduring

10. obscure   a. definite   b. open   c. hidden   d. clear

11. proxies   a. laws   b. legal papers empowering one to act for
    another   c. lengthy books   d. stockholders meeting

12. attest   a. disprove   b. disagree   c. confirm   d. sign

13. suffice   a. satisfy   b. insufficient   c. disagree   d. take
    action

14. deluged   a. flooded   b. undermined   c. raced   d. forced

15. oblivion   a. prominence   b. remembrance   c. forcefulness
    d. forgetfullness

Check the key on page 509. If you scored Fair or above, go on to the next exercise. If you scored below Fair, review the definitions of the words you had incorrect and then use these words in a sentence. Ask your instructor to evaluate the sentences and to discuss the evaluation with you.

---

its, it's

Let's look at the difference between two troublemakers—*it's, its. Its* is the possessive form of the third-person neuter pronoun *it*. It is used to modify or show possession. Note that you never use an apostrophe in the possessive forms of pronouns such as *ours, yours, hers, theirs, its.*

Given 10 sentences which require the use of its *or* it's, *underline the correct word or words in each sentence.*
Excellent   10
Good   9
Fair   8

Each car is parked in its assigned place.

The book had its pages in an incorrect order.

Theirs is not to question his opinion.

It's is the contraction of *it is.*

It's a beautiful day.

Ms. Perez thinks it's too early to file the papers.

Now that you are certain of the correct use of these words, try these sentences.

1. General Air is planning to release (*its, it's*) earnings statement shortly.
2. (*Its, It's*) important to assign the best programmers to this job.
3. This book is well regarded for (*its, it's*) diverse selection of alternative styles and problem solutions.

4. (*Its, It's*) good to know that (*yours, your's*) is the best report.
5. Although the Council has agreed to a price increase, (*its, it's*) too late to have an effect on holiday business.
6. (*Its, It's*) difficult to know whether the idea is (*theirs, their's*) or (*ours, our's*).
7. The department is planning to review (*its, it's*) auditing procedures.
8. Our office staff has developed (*its, it's*) own methods for handling absenteeism.
9. Management feels that (*its, it's*) time to plan a sale.
10. The alumni group is conducting a campaign to increase (*its, it's*) membership.

Check the key on page 509. If you achieved Fair or above, go on. If you scored below Fair, review the definitions above. Write two sentences using *its* and two using *it's*. Ask your instructor to check them and to discuss any problems with you.

---

further, farther

Farther refers to space or distance.

   We shall walk farther than they did.

   She is standing on the farther shore.

Further refers to a greater degree.

   He gave a further explanation of his plans.

See how well you can apply these definitions in the following sentences.

> *Given 10 cases that call for the use of* further *or* farther, *write the correct word in the space provided.*
>
> | | |
> |---|---|
> | *Excellent* | *10* |
> | *Good* | *9* |
> | *Fair* | *8* |

1. The distance between the two cities was _____ than we had expected.

2. Therefore, we had to borrow _____ funds to pay for the additional fuel.

3-4. We cannot acquire _____ evidence without _____ study.

5. Our company has developed _____ plans for working with the community.

6-7. She told me, _____, that I had walked _____ than all the others.

8-9. We had _____ information, which confirmed that we had traveled _____ than was necessary.

Name _____ *Date* _____

10. _____ progress has been made in moving to the metric system.

Check the key on page 509. If you were able to achieve Fair or above, go on to the proofreading exercise. If you did not score Fair or above, review the definitions.

Proofreading

Given a proofreading exercise with 17 spelling and punctuation errors, write your corrections directly above the mistakes.

Excellent	*17*
Good	*16*
Fair	*15*

If you buy your cloths at the Smyth Store you cannot

only save money but earn valuble trading stamps as

as well. You will find that shoping at Smith's is

all ways a interesting expereince. At Smyth

you will find the last styles in mens and womens

clothing at prises that will apeal to you.

Stop in soon; well be looking for you.

Check the key on page 509. If you achieved Fair or above, you have completed Chapter 1, Focus on Language. If you did not, discuss your score with your instructor.

2

APPEARANCE COUNTS

After a long walk down a well-polished corridor, the young job applicant finally found the room to which she had been referred by the college placement director. She introduced herself to the woman executive who had been watching her through the open door. The applicant had the job the moment she walked into the office—the appraisal had been made during that long walk. Yes, appearance does count. Think of the many times you have become interested in someone because of the way that person looks. Think, too, of the millions of dollars business spends in packaging its products, and you will acknowledge the importance of outward appearance.

> **well-polished:** Hyphenate compound adjectives.

> **appraisal:** official valuation; judgment

The same is true of the letters you write. What the reader sees—from the address on the envelope to the last initial on the letter itself—*is you.* Be sure the impression you make is a good one.

To make that good impression, in the following units you can review:

Unit 3   Letter Styles
Unit 4   Parts of the Letter
Unit 5   Envelope Address

UNIT 3   LETTER STYLES

Your performance objective for this unit is:

Given the problem of determining when to use the official business letter form, the interoffice memorandum form, and the personal- and social-business letter form,

You will select the correct style for a specific situation, follow the appropriate style, and correct errors in style.

Style, of course, is important. It characterizes you as an up-to-date, behind-the-times, or avant-garde individual. But before we can proceed to discuss style, you must be able to identify the parts of a letter. Figure 2–1 shows what these parts are called and where they are usually placed.

> **avant-garde:** Avant-garde means in the vanguard; most advanced in new ideas.
> **proceed** (but procedure)

Now let's look at four of the business styles currently in use so that you can get an idea of the style you would choose. Remember, however, that the office in which you work will probably make that decision for you, until you achieve the kind of position that gives you

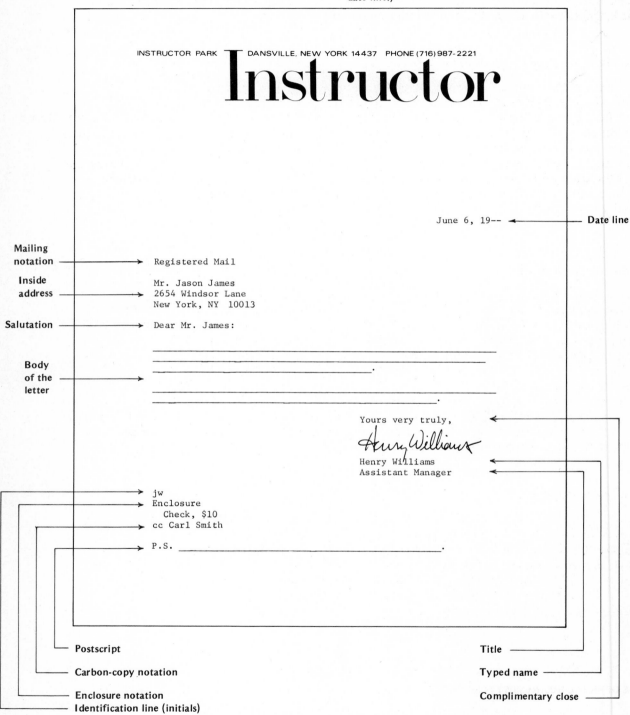

Figure 2-1
Parts of the Letter

the authority and responsibility to choose the style you prefer. The office manager, the executive secretary or administrative assistant, or sometimes the employer makes that decision.

The four main business-letter styles we will discuss are the modified-block, the semiblock, the full-block, and the simplified.

Hint for good human relations in the office: Don't make a decision that isn't yours to make.

The Modified-Block and Semiblock Styles

The two most popular business letter styles today are the modified block (Figure 2–2) and the semiblock (Figure 2–3). Of the two, the modified block is the more clean cut, and it is gradually replacing the semiblock. Every part of the letter in the modified-block style begins at the left margin except the date and the closing. Notice the type of punctuation used in both styles. It is *mixed punctuation*: colon after the salutation and comma after the complimentary close.

clean cut: Don't hyphenate predicate adjectives.

Mixed punctuation.
complimentary

The semiblock differs in only one way—the paragraphs are indented, usually five spaces.

The Full-Block Style

The up-and-coming advertising executive, the publicity director, the business educator, the business publisher often select the next style—the full-block (Figure 2–4). More and more business firms are adopting it. Every part of the letter begins at the left margin. This style saves time in typing, offers less opportunity for error, and is therefore more efficient. Of course, this style cannot be used if it does not blend with the company's letterhead.

adopting: taking as one's own

Do you notice the innovation in punctuation used in this style? This is *open punctuation*: omission of the colon after the salutation and of the comma after the close. Open punctuation is modern, too, to conform with the modern full-block style.

Open punctuation.
omission

The Simplified Style

Next is the simplified style (Figure 2–5). Contrast it to the full-block. The differences are obvious: the simplified style omits the salutation and closing and includes a *subject line* in capital letters. These changes make this style closer to ordinary conversation. After all, no one greets you with "Dear Sir" or ends a conversation with "Sincerely yours." The Administrative Management Society has endorsed this style, but business has not yet popularized it.

Other Styles

THE OFFICIAL-BUSINESS STYLE

You may need to write to the president of the local Rotary Club, the pastor of your church, the rabbi of your synagogue, or a city, state, or federal official, requesting that person to speak or to lend support to an activity, or you may thank him or her for assistance. This type of letter requires a more formal style than those we have been discussing.

Spacing: single
Margins: 17—67 pica;
20—80 elite*

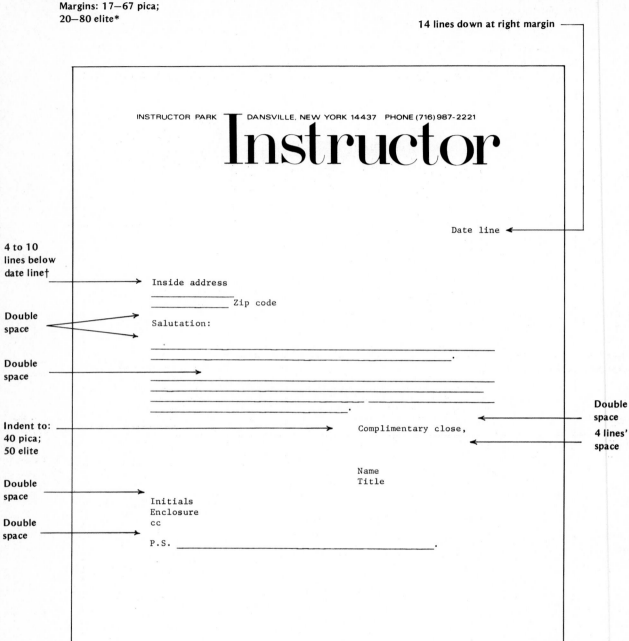

14 lines down at right margin ─────────┐

INSTRUCTOR PARK ❙ DANSVILLE, NEW YORK 14437   PHONE (716) 987-2221

Instructor

Date line ◄──────────────

**4 to 10
lines below
date line†** ──────────► Inside address

_____
_____ Zip code

**Double
space** ──────────► Salutation:

**Double
space** ──────────►

Complimentary close, ◄────────── **Double
space**

**Indent to:
40 pica;
50 elite** ──────────►

Name
Title

4 lines'
space

**Double
space** ──────────► Initials
Enclosure
cc

**Double
space** ──────────► P.S. _____ .

*Margins given (for all styles) are for medium-sized letter (100–200 words); they can be adjusted somewhat for longer or shorter letters.

†Space above inside address depends on length of letter.

Figure 2–2
The Modified-Block Style

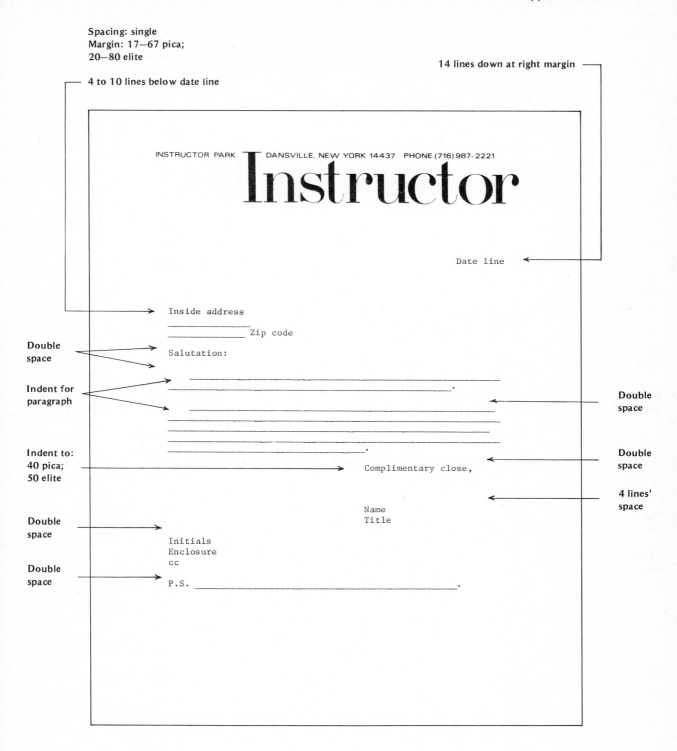

Spacing: single
Margin: 17—67 pica;
20—80 elite

4 to 10 lines below date line

14 lines down at right margin

INSTRUCTOR PARK   DANSVILLE, NEW YORK 14437   PHONE (716) 987-2221

Instructor

Date line

Inside address
_____ Zip code

Double space
Salutation:

Indent for paragraph

Double space

Indent to: 40 pica; 50 elite
Complimentary close,

Double space

4 lines' space

Name
Title

Double space
Initials
Enclosure
cc

Double space
P.S. _____.

Figure 2–3
The Semiblock Style

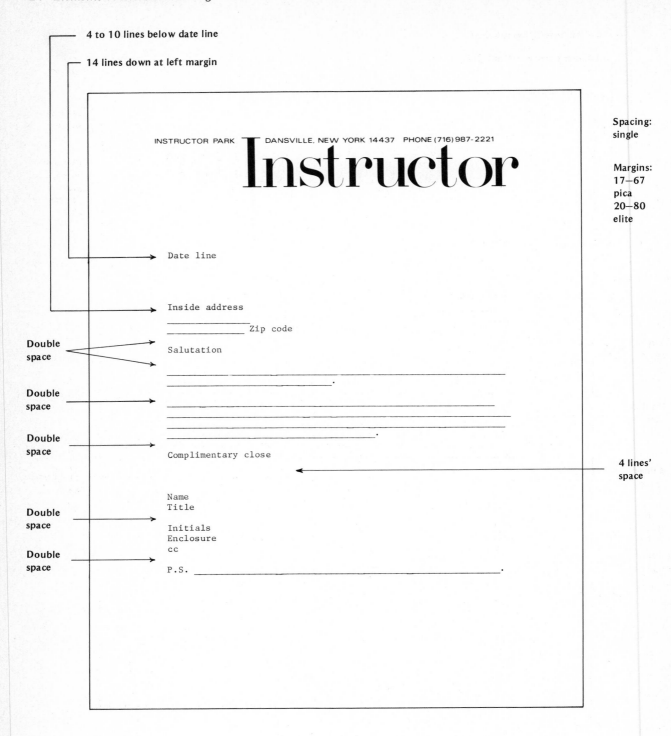

4 to 10 lines below date line

14 lines down at left margin

INSTRUCTOR PARK   DANSVILLE, NEW YORK 14437   PHONE (716) 987-2221

Instructor

Spacing: single

Margins: 17–67 pica 20–80 elite

Date line

Inside address
_____Zip code

Double space
Salutation

Double space

Double space
Complimentary close

4 lines' space

Name
Title

Double space
Initials
Enclosure
cc

Double space
P.S. _____.

Figure 2-4
The Full-Block Style

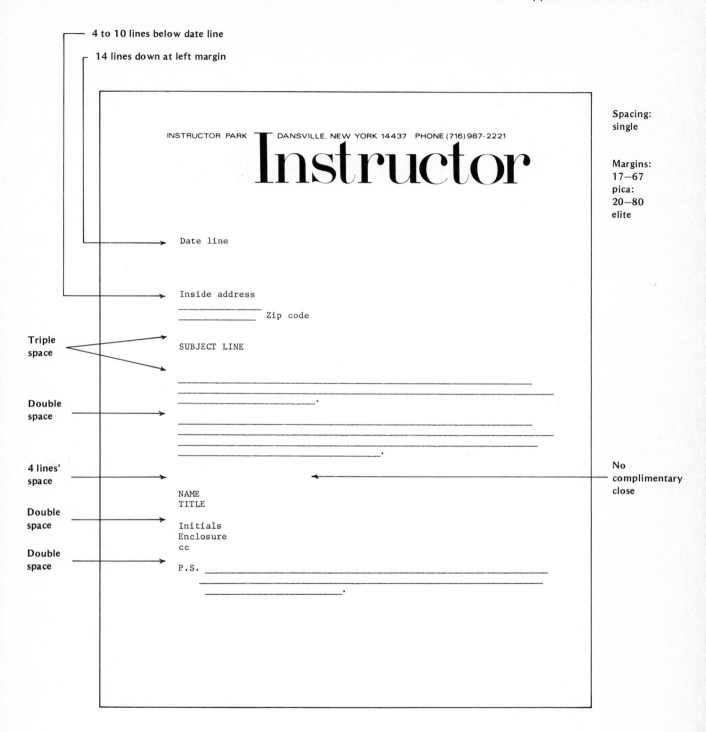

4 to 10 lines below date line

14 lines down at left margin

INSTRUCTOR PARK   DANSVILLE, NEW YORK 14437   PHONE (716) 987-2221

Instructor

Spacing:
single

Margins:
17—67
pica:
20—80
elite

Date line

Inside address
_____ Zip code

Triple space

SUBJECT LINE

Double space

4 lines' space

No complimentary close

NAME
TITLE

Double space

Initials
Enclosure
cc

Double space

P.S. _____

Figure 2–5
The Simplified Style

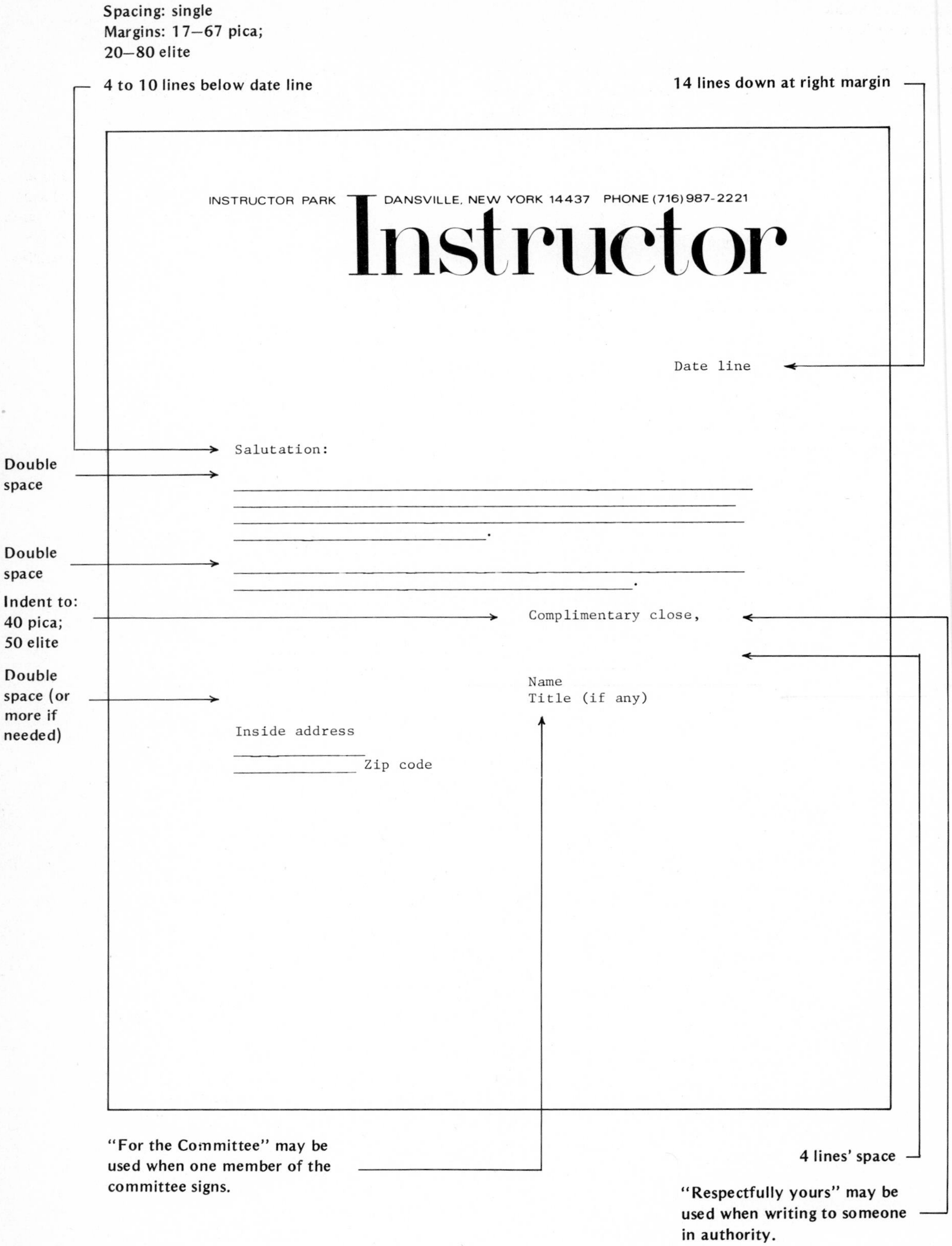

Spacing: single
Margins: 17—67 pica;
20—80 elite

4 to 10 lines below date line

14 lines down at right margin

INSTRUCTOR PARK   DANSVILLE, NEW YORK 14437   PHONE (716) 987-2221

Instructor

Date line

Salutation:

Double
space

Double
space

Indent to:
40 pica;
50 elite

Complimentary close,

Double
space (or
more if
needed)

Name
Title (if any)

Inside address

_____ Zip code

"For the Committee" may be
used when one member of the
committee signs.

4 lines' space

"Respectfully yours" may be
used when writing to someone
in authority.

Figure 2-6
The Official-Business Style

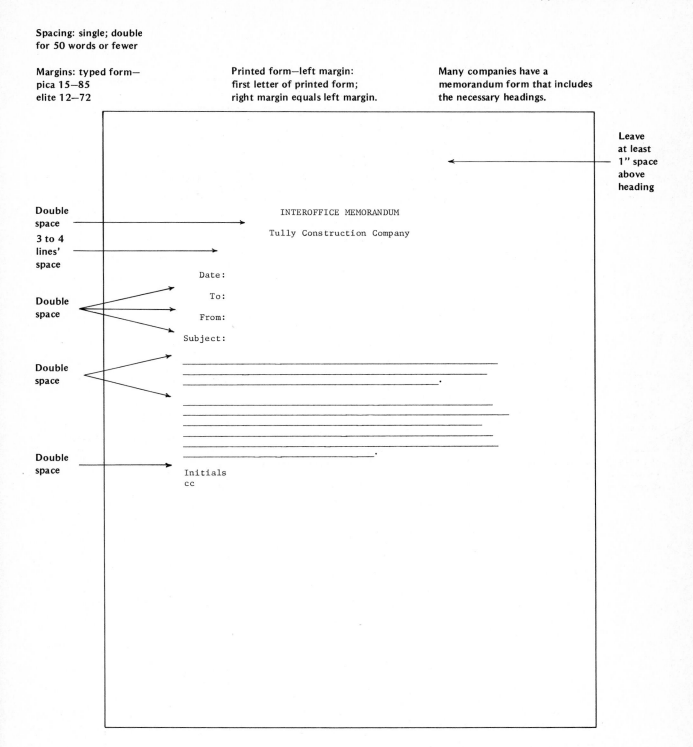

Spacing: single; double
for 50 words or fewer

Margins: typed form—
pica 15—85
elite 12—72

Printed form—left margin:
first letter of printed form;
right margin equals left margin.

Many companies have a
memorandum form that includes
the necessary headings.

Leave
at least
1″ space
above
heading

Double
space

3 to 4
lines'
space

Double
space

Double
space

Double
space

INTEROFFICE MEMORANDUM

Tully Construction Company

Date:

To:

From:

Subject:

Initials
cc

Figure 2-7
The Interoffice Memorandum

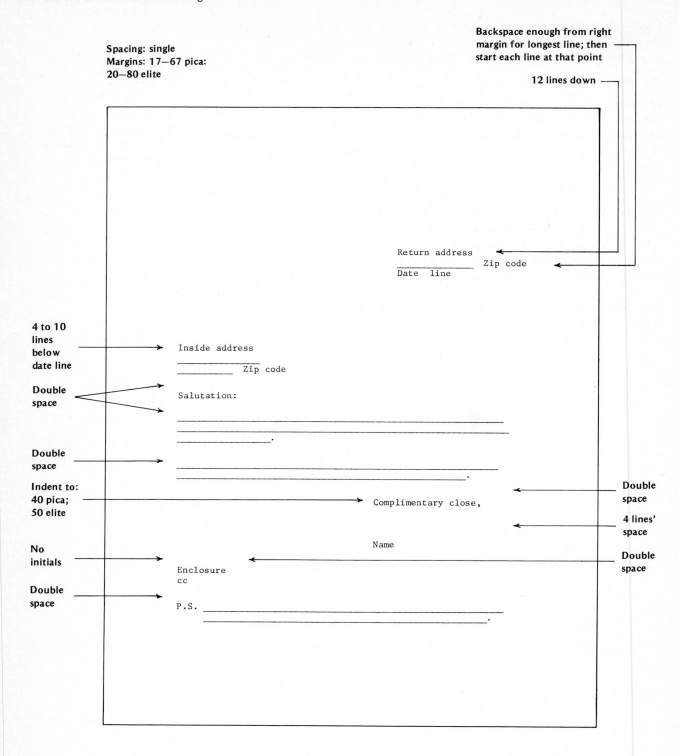

Figure 2–8
The Personal-Business Letter

Figure 2-6 illustrates the proper style of letter for such an occasion. (Notice that mailing notations—such as special delivery—are omitted, as are typist's initials. Note, too, the placement of the inside address.)

occasion

THE INTEROFFICE MEMORANDUM

When you write to another employee in your office, the proper form is the interoffice memorandum (Figure 2-7). You save time and effort by omitting an inside address, a salutation, and a complimentary closing. If you use a printed memorandum form, the heading includes these essentials, as well as a subject line.

interoffice: Many common prefixes, such as inter, non, pro, and semi, are joined to the following word without a hyphen. When in doubt, check your dictionary.

THE PERSONAL-BUSINESS LETTER

The letters you type for a business firm and those you type for yourself differ slightly in style. Since you usually do not have personal letterhead paper and must use plain bond paper, you must include your return address. And, as it is assumed that the typist is the writer, initials are not typed after the closing. (See Figure 2-8.)

Try Skills Activity 3 to put your knowledge of the styles of business letters to work in the business office.

SKILLS ACTIVITY 3

What style would you choose if—

1. You are secretary to an advertising executive._____

2. Your employer is an established attorney working for a prestigious law firm._____

3. You work for the personnel director in an insurance office.
   _____

4. You are secretary to the vice president of a bank._____

5. You are writing to request a state senator to speak at a meeting of the Business Club of your college. _____

6. You are writing a letter of application enclosing a data sheet.
   _____

7. You are secretary to an officer of the Administrative Management Society._____

8. You are secretary to the principal of a high school.
   _____

9. You are executive secretary to the chairperson of the Business Education Department of the college.._____

10. You are writing to a co-worker in your company about a meeting on personnel practices to be held in the director's office.
    _____

Check the key on page 509. If you did not score Fair or above, discuss the answers with your instructor.

> Given 10 cases in which you must choose the style of a communication, write the name of the appropriate style in the space provided.
>
> | | |
> |---|---|
> | Excellent | 10 |
> | Good | 9 |
> | Fair | 8 |

Name_____ Date_____

UNIT 4 PARTS OF THE LETTER

Now that you have seen the picture of the letter as a whole, let's examine the individual parts separately.

Your performance objective for this unit is:

Given problems that require the use of 15 parts of the business letter,

You will correctly place each part of the business letter in each letter style: letterhead or return address, date, inside address and attention line, subject line, salutation, body of the letter, complimentary close, typed name, title, initials, and notations for enclosure, carbon copy, postscript, and special mailing.

Stationery and Letterhead

Standard-size paper for most business letters measures 8½ by 11 inches. Smaller sizes (baronial and executive) lose themselves in the files and cost extra money in time wasted in locating them. While there is a trend toward color in paper, white is generally used.

Letters should be typed on a good quality, watermarked, rag-content paper of 20-pound weight. It has a clean, crisp feel, and your typing stands out more clearly. Furthermore— and you will agree that this is important—it is easiest to make neat corrections on paper of good quality.

watermarked: having translucent lines in the paper, from processing while in the pulp stage.

Every business has a printed letterhead. In good letterhead design, simplicity is imperative. Important information must be supplied within the top fifth of the page. This information includes the company name, address, telephone number, and (if there is one) cable address. To indicate the nature of the firm, an emblem or trademark is often incorporated in the design. That design must reflect the company image forcefully. See Figure 2–9 for some examples of good letterhead design.

imperative: urgent; very necessary.

When you do not have a printed letterhead, you must use a personal heading, which includes your return address (don't forget the zip code) and the date of the letter. (Look at the personal-business letter, Figure 2–8.) Start your heading two inches from the top of the page, and use single spacing. The longest line of this heading should end at the right margin (unless you are using the full-block style, in which case you will begin the inside address at the left margin). Below are some correct return addresses:

Rural route

```
Route 3
Torrance, CA  90506
November 7, 19--
```

Post-office box

```
P.O. Box 250
Riverside, CA  92502
November 7, 19--
```

Street address

```
6648 Dawes Street
Oakland, CA  94615
November 7, 19--
```

Where would you position the date line on these letterheads?

Cambridge School of Business INC.

ADMINISTRATION • 219 EAST 42nd STREET, NEW YORK, N. Y. 10017 • (212) 490-0865

Newsweek

444 MADISON AVENUE • NEW YORK, N.Y. 10022 • (212) 350-2000

𝕿𝖍𝖊 𝕹𝖊𝖜 𝖄𝖔𝖗𝖐 𝕿𝖎𝖒𝖊𝖘

229 WEST 43 STREET
NEW YORK, N.Y. 10036

CBS

CBS Inc., 51 West 52 Street
New York, New York 10019

DANA **DANA CORPORATION** • WORLD HEADQUARTERS
P.O. BOX 1000 • TOLEDO, OHIO 43697 • CABLE: DANA

NUS CORPORATION

4 RESEARCH PLACE
ROCKVILLE, MARYLAND 20850
301 948-7010

Figure 2-9
Business letterheads

Notice that abbreviations are not used except for the name of the state (which is abbreviated according to the latest rules of the Postal Service) and for "P. O. Box." Some firms prefer not to follow this style, as you see in Figure 2-9. Letterheads also vary in their treatment of numbers in street names. Notice that the up-to-date writer omits *st, rd, nd, th* after the date of the month. However, in the body of the letter, when the day precedes the month or the month is not named, these ordinal endings are used, or the date is spelled out: "the 5th of December," "the 5th," "the fifth of December," or "the fifth." Also notice that two spaces are left before the zip code.

precedes: goes before
ordinal: showing position in an order.

Inside Address

This part of the letter identifies the name and address of the person or company receiving the letter. Single spaced, it begins at the left margin of the letter, from four to ten lines below the date line (depending on the length of the letter).

Names of individuals should be preceded by *Mr. Ms., Mrs., Miss* or by a title, such as *Dr., Reverend, Professor.* Use *Ms.* when you are in doubt as to whether a woman is married, or if she prefers its use regardless of her marital status. The following are common forms:

```
Mr. Paul Chivers        Miss Alice Mackey       Messrs. Thomas Jay
Dr. John Nelson         Mrs. Alan Michel           and James Sims
Professor David Dunn    Ms. Eileen Nolan        Misses Alice and Jane Clark
                                                Mr. & Mrs. Edwin Slade
```

Several items should be noted: *Professor*, like *Reverend* and *Honorable*, is generally spelled out. When addressing two married women or an unrelated man and woman, each name is given its proper title, and one name is listed below the other. Also, watch your spelling of the plural of *Mr.* One inaccurate typist wrote "Messes," which caused no little embarrassment. Be sure you use *Messrs.*

embarrassment
Messrs.

A person's title in an organization may be used after the name. To maintain uniformity of line length, the title may be typed on either the first or the second line:

```
Ms. Leona L. Whitford, Manager      Mr. James L. Farmingdale, III
Industrial Exhibitors Mart          President, Ace Company
```

If the title is more than one word—as, "General Manager"—place it on a separate line.

```
Ms. Leona L. Whitford
General Manager
Industrial Exhibitors Mart
```

Use abbreviations sparingly in the inside address. Except for *Mr., Messrs., Mrs., Ms., Jr., Sr., Esq.,* and *Dr.,* write out all words and titles. Note that the abbreviation *Esq.* may be used following the names of attorneys, judges, members of congress, and other government officials. Some women attorneys now use *Esq.* after their names. When it is used, no other title or degree may be used with it:

Esq. is the abbreviation for Esquire.

*Don't be redundant
(using two titles for
the same name).*

                        Mr. Philip King
        or   Philip King, Esq.
        not   Mr. Philip King, Esq.

The same is true when you use academic degrees:

                        Dr. Marian Jason
        or   Marian Jason, M.D.
        not   Dr. Marian Jason, M.D.

Numerical street or avenue names up to and including ten are spelled out. Some offices still use the ordinal endings—*st, nd, rd, th*--after street and avenue names, but many are omitting them:

                795 Fifth Avenue

                55 25th Street
        or   55 25 Street

                396 East 116th Street
        or   396 East 116 Street

Cooperate with the Postal Service: Use those zip codes! Remember to allow two spaces after the state abbreviation before you type the zip.

Salutation

Type the salutation two lines below the last line of the inside address. A colon follows it if you use mixed punctuation (see Figure 2–2); the colon is omitted in open punctuation (see Figure 2–4).

The salutation agrees with the first line of the inside address. In the singular, the preferred salutation is *Dear Mr., Mrs., Miss, Ms. Smith.* "*Dear Sir*" and "*Dear Madam*" are considered too stiff for good public relations. In the plural, use *Gentlemen* for several men, and use *Ladies* or *Mesdames* for several women. (*Ladies* is more commonly used today.)

What salutation do you use when you do not know whether you are writing to a man or a woman? Standard practice is now in transition, and you will find several forms in use:

        Dear Sir or Madam   Dear Resident
        Dear Friend   Dear Reader
        Dear Person   Dear Customer

When the addressee is a company, you can use one of these forms: *Ladies and Gentlemen, Dear People, Dear Friends*, and so on. Of course, this question can easily be answered by the use of the simplified style (Figure 2-5) in which the salutation as well as the closing is omitted.

Following are some typical addressees with accompanying salutations.

Stack Supply Store	Ladies and Gentlemen <u>or</u> Dear People
Floridale Women's Club	Ladies
Miss Margaret Murn	Dear Miss Murn <u>or</u> Dear Ms. Murn
Mrs. Jack Barnes	Dear Mrs. Barnes <u>or</u> Dear Ms. Barnes
Mr. Wilson Hathaway	Dear Mr. Hathaway
Box 564, Fresno Times	Ladies and Gentlemen <u>or</u> Dear People
Professor Frank Statler	Dear Professor Statler
Dr. Martin James	Dear Doctor James
Messrs. Swift and Throne	Gentlemen
Ms. Catherine Block	Dear Ms. Block
Misses Marie and Dora Smith	Ladies

Note that *Doctor* is written out in the salutation, where the given name is not used.

When you are writing to a company but know that your letter will be serviced more rapidly by a specific individual, you direct the letter to that person's attention. In that case, because the first line of the inside address is plural, the salutation must be plural:

Acceptable	Better
Glen Service Center	Mr. Arnold Pope
Attention Mr. Arnold Pope	Glen Service Center
1215 Trane Road	1215 Trane Road
Omaha, NE 68112	Omaha, NE 68112
Dear People	Dear Mr. Pope

If you do not know the name of the person who will act on your letter but must address a department only, use one of these forms:

Scovill Manufacturing Company	Service Department
Attention Service Department	Scovill Manufacturing Company
Scovill Square	Scovill Square
Waterbury, CT 06708	Waterbury, CT 06708
Ladies and Gentlemen:	Dear People:

Try Skills Activity 4 to check your ability to use the correct salutation in business letters.

SKILLS ACTIVITY 4

You are writing letters to the following. What salutation would you use?

1. Box 143, *New York Times* _____

2. Hopedale College Alumnae (Alumnae are female graduates; *alumni* denotes male graduates or graduates of both sexes.) _____

3. Messrs. Wright and Clark _____

4. Professor Milton Frye _____

5. Mr. Robert Brown _____

6. Mrs. Otto Eckner _____

7. Dorothy Hart, Ph.D. _____

8. Irma Morton _____

9. Reverend Arthur Starbuck _____

10. Kenneth Hammer Associates _____

Check the key on page 510. If you achieved Fair or above, go on to Body of the Letter. If you did not achieve Fair or above, discuss the problem with your instructor.

Name _____ *Date* _____

Body of the Letter

The body—that is, the content—of the letter begins two lines below the salutation. Single space the letter, but double space between paragraphs.

   Some correspondents use a special line to precede the body of the letter. We call this the *subject line.* It identifies the message—it gives it a title. The use of the subject line enables you to begin your letter directly and to avoid dull beginnings.

correspondents

Modern treatment

Dear Mr. Harnack

Request for Credit Information

Body of Letter

A little old-fashioned

Dear Mr. Harnack:

Subject: Request for Credit
           Information

Body of Letter

Complimentary Close

Refer to Figures 2–3 and 2–4. Notice that the closing line is written two spaces below the body of the letter, either at the left margin or right of center, according to the style you use. Be consistent in punctuation and style. Place a comma after the complimentary close when a colon follows the salutation; omit it when no punctuation follows the salutation.

   The usual business letter ends with one of these closing lines:

Yours very truly
Very truly yours
Sincerely yours

Only the first word is capitalized.

Custom, more than anything else, dictates the use of these closing lines. But the tone of the letter or the relationship between the writer and the addressee may call for other terms, such as *Cordially* or *Respectfully yours.* A formal salutation, such as *Ladies and Gentlemen,* takes an equally formal *Yours truly.* Many correspondents feel that both the salutation and the complimentary close are trite and outmoded; they simply omit both of them, as illustrated in the simplified style (Figure 2-5). But, as we have already noted, this style has not yet gained wide business acceptance.

Make the closing fit the situation.

Match the closing to the salutation.

Try Skills Activity 5 to check your ability to use the correct complimentary close.

SKILLS ACTIVITY 5

Here are some situations you may encounter in your letter-writing. You want to be sure to match your salutation and complimentary close with the tone of the letter. Would you make any changes in the following?

1. You are writing a fourth letter trying to collect a long-overdue bill from Henry Agar.

    Dear Henry: Cordially yours,

    _____   _____

2. This letter is to a customer, Harold Lowery, who is also a good friend.

    Dear Mr. Lowery: Yours very truly,

    _____   _____

3. Here is one to the president of your college, whom you would like to interview for your club newsletter.

    Dear Mr. Dewey: Sincerely yours,

    _____   _____

4. You are writing to the Cornwall Paper Company to ask about their new paper products.

    Dear Sirs: Very truly yours,

    _____   _____

5. You are writing to Mrs. Mary Gray to ask her when she plans to visit your college on her annual recruitment drive.

    Dear Miss Grey: Respectfully yours,

    _____   _____

Check the key on page 510. If you achieve Good or Excellent, go on to Signature. If you scored below Good, discuss the problem with your instructor.

Name_____ Date_____

Signature

After you have typed the complimentary close, leave four lines for the writer's signature. Type the name, followed on the next line by the person's title.

The writer usually signs his or her full name, but many sign only the first name if the reader is a friend or a familiar correspondent. However, the typed signature must include the full name. A married woman may indicate her status (Mrs.) preceding her typed signature. In social-business usage, she may type her married name in parentheses beneath her written signature. It is acceptable for any woman, if she wishes, to use her first and last names only, with no title. Here are the usual forms:

preceding

Business usage

Sincerely yours

Michael L. Story

Michael L. Story
Personnel Manager

Sincerely yours   or

Mary Murphy

(Mrs.) Mary Murphy
Credit Division

Sincerely yours

Mary Murphy

Mary Murphy
Credit Division

Social-business usage

Sincerely yours

Michael L Story

Michael L. Story

Sincerely yours   or

Janet Hardy

(Mrs. Frank J. Hardy)

Sincerely yours

Janet Hardy

Janet Hardy

Identification Line

"Who typed this letter?" said the boss to the supervisor of the typing group. "It's beautifully done." Flush with the left-hand margin, two spaces below the last line of the signature section, Mary Jones' initials told the tale. Because the writer's name had already been typed on the signature line, only the typist's initials appeared. However, many companies prefer to use both the writer's and typist's initials. Either form is acceptable.

Sincerely yours,

Alfred Hossler

Alfred Hossler
Transfer Department

or

Sincerely yours,

Alfred Hossler

Alfred Hossler
Transfer Department

mj

AH:mj

Other Notations

In addition to the items we have just discussed, some letters require one or more further notations.

SECOND-PAGE NOTATION AND CLOSING

If the second page of a letter is misplaced, it must find its way back to the first page—of the correct letter. Therefore, careful identification is needed. Nine lines from the top edge of each page after the first one (using plain bond paper, not letterhead), you should type the name of the addressee, the page number, and the date:

addressee: person to whom a letter is sent.

```
Ms. Helen Hickman              -2-                June 6, 19--
```

Or you may type these items one beneath the other, with the first line placed nine lines from the top and beginning at the left margin:

```
Ms. Helen Hickman
Page 2
June 6, 19--
```

Allow three lines below the second-page notation before continuing the body of the letter.

You must also remember to carry over at least two lines of a paragraph to the second or succeeding page. Since you cannot leave fewer than two lines of a paragraph at the bottom of the preceding page, you may not break a three-line paragraph. Place it entirely on one page or the other.

The closing changes somewhat on the two-page letter. Because the letterhead is not used, the name of the company is included in capitals two lines below the complimentary close. Then the writer's name and title are typed as usual.

```
Very truly yours,

APEX CORPORATION

Myra Starris
Myra Starris
Credit Manager
```

Try Skills Activity 6 to check your ability to handle second-page headings, continuation of the body of the letter, and complimentary closes.

SKILLS ACTIVITY 6

How would you handle these problems?

1. You are 1¾ inches from the bottom of the page. You must still type a three-line paragraph to complete your letter. Which of the following would you do?
    a. Complete the paragraph on page 1; place the closing lines on page 2.
    b. Type the entire paragraph and closing lines on page 2.
    c. Break up the paragraph with two lines on page 1 and one line on page 2, or vice versa.
2. You are 1½ inches from the bottom of the page. You have a four-line paragraph to type to complete the letter. Choose your course of action.
    a. Complete the letter on page 1.
    b. Break up the paragraph with two lines on each page.
    c. Complete the paragraph on page 1 and place the closing lines on page 2.
3. You are at the end of the final line of page 1 of a two-page letter. The bell rings when you type the *re* in "recapitulation." What would you do?
    a. Finish typing the word.
    b. Type the entire word on page 2.
    c. Hyphenate the word and finish it on page 2.
4. Your company uses plain bond paper for the second page of its two-page letters. Choose from the following the preferred closing lines for the two-page letter.

```
        a.  Very truly yours,


            Personnel Manager


        b.  Very truly yours,

            SCOTT & COMPANY


            Personnel Manager
```

c.   Very truly yours,

SCOTT & COMPANY

Lydia Colon
Personnel Manager

5.   You are ready to begin the second page of a two-page letter. From the following, which heading would you select.

a.   Page 2
September 16, 1977
Rita Watson

b.   Ms. Rita Watson
Page 2
September 16, 1977

c.   Watson
P. 2
Sept. 17, 1977

Check the key on page 510. If you achieved Fair or above, go on to Enclosure Notation. If you did not score Fair or above, discuss the problem with your instructor.

Name_____ Date_____

ENCLOSURE NOTATION

The enclosure notation has two purposes: It enables you to check quickly to see that you have included the items mentioned in the letter. And the addressee can quickly ascertain whether the materials were enclosed as noted.

When extra material accompanies a letter, make the notation immediately below the typist's initials. The usual method is to type the word *Enclosure*; then describe the enclosed item. If there is more than one enclosure, use the plural, and list them.

ascertain: learn with certainty

Spell with an "e." Do not abbreviate.

One enclosure	More than one enclosure
jfb	jfb
Enclosure	Enclosures
Check $10	Check $10
	Signed contract

CARBON-COPY NOTATION

Very often you want to send a copy of the letter that you are typing to a third party for information. Make a carbon-copy notation following the identification line or the enclosure line (if there is one). Use the initials *cc* with no punctuation.

With enclosure

Very truly yours,

Herbert Jones

Herbert Jones
Manager

In the full-block style, of course, the closing and signature are also typed at the left margin.

ji
Enclosure
   Check $10
cc Mr. Patrick Downes

Without enclosure

Very truly yours,

Herbert Jones

Herbert Jones
Manager

ji
cc Mr. Patrick Downes

POSTSCRIPT

omitted

As an added note to attract special attention, to add an explanation, to mention an idea unrelated to the letter, or to include information that was omitted from the body of your letter, you use a postscript. Type it following the carbon-copy notation, if there is one. The initials P.S. are used to indicate a postscript.

Double space.

```
ji
Enclosure
   Check $5
cc Ms. Maria Peters, Accounting
```

calendar

```
P.S.    Remember to circle that date on your
        calendar -- Monday, September 5.
```

MAILING NOTATIONS

When a letter is sent by a special mail service, type *Special Delivery, Certified Mail, Registered Mail,* or *Insured Mail* on the envelope and on the letter itself so that the information is available for possible reference.

```
Certified mail
```

Inside address.

```
Mr. John Starkweather
224 West Ninth Street
New York, NY   10038
```

Try Skills Activity 7 to set up five different letters with special instructions.

SKILLS ACTIVITY 7

Use sheets of plain paper for these problems. Set up the parts of each letter, including the current date, in their proper positions. Capitalize and punctuate; spell out abbreviations except where abbreviations are approved. You may choose modified- or full-block style and open or mixed punctuation. Label the style and punctuation form for each problem.

> *Given cases requiring you to set up parts of the letter, write or type the correct forms, according to the special instructions listed.*
>
> *Excellent   5*
> *Good   4*

Special instructions: Use correct salutation and complimentary close.

Dictated or written by	Transcribed by	Sent to
john f gersten president	ella gibbins	mrs leonard houghton 9907 engels dr bethesda, md 21811

Special instructions: Attention of mr alfred charlton; carbon copy to edward cusack.

michael f thomas sales dept	gerald turman	gibbs construction co 735 s jackson st denver, co 80210

Special instructions: A check for $10 is being sent with the letter. The subject is order 5670.

norma timms purchasing agent	ann massey	frances lockwood 1347 shady ave pittsburgh, pa 15217

Special instructions: Certified mail.

peter knight general mgr	florence egan	bruce lineman treasurer national optical co 2000 penn ave ann arbor, mi 48103

5.   *Special instructions*: You are writing about a legal case, *Prentis v. Hill.*

you   you   messrs klein & smith
                                                                 attorneys at law
                                                                 1545 dickens st
                                                                 sherman oaks, ca
                                                                 95681

Check the key on page 510. If you were not able to score Good or above, discuss the problem with your instructor.

UNIT 5   ENVELOPE ADDRESS

Since your addressee sees the envelope before seeing the letter, you must pay as much attention to it as to the letter itself. The address on the envelope must agree exactly—in wording, spelling, and so on—with the inside address of the letter.

Your performance objective for this unit is:

Given the problem of typing business- and legal-size envelopes, including all parts,

You will type the envelope in correct form, using the required parts.

For a letter typed on regular 8½ by 11 paper, the business-size envelope may be used (Figure 2-10). If there is an enclosure or if your letter is more than one page, use a legal-size envelope (Figure 2-11). Many companies are now using the legal-size envelope only. Study the illustrations to learn correct placement of items included on an envelope.

Because the Postal Service is expanding its use of automated equipment, following the points listed in Postal Service publications will help the mail to move efficiently. These practices are recommended:

1. Use single space and block addresses on envelopes of all sizes.

2. Type the zip code two spaces after the state abbreviation.

3. List apartment numbers or building room numbers on the same line as the street address.

4. Type the "Attention" line, if used, as the second line of an address.

5. Be sure to use the state abbreviations prescribed by the Postal Service. They are as follows:

Alabama	AL	Montana	MT
Alaska	AK	Nebraska	NE
Arizona	AZ	Nevada	NV
Arkansas	AR	New Hampshire	NH
California	CA	New Jersey	NJ
Colorado	CO	New Mexico	NM
Connecticut	CT	New York	NY
Delaware	DE	North Carolina	NC
Florida	FL	North Dakota	ND
Georgia	GA	Ohio	OH
Hawaii	HI	Oklahoma	OK
Idaho	ID	Oregon	OR
Illinois	IL	Pennsylvania	PA
Indiana	IN	Rhode Island	RI
Iowa	IA	South Carolina	SC
Kansas	KS	South Dakota	SD
Kentucky	KY	Tennessee	TN
Louisiana	LA	Texas	TX
Maine	ME	Utah	UT
Maryland	MD	Vermont	VT
Massachusetts	MA	Virginia	VA
Michigan	MI	Washington	WA
Minnesota	MN	West Virginia	WV
Mississippi	MS	Wisconsin	WI
Missouri	MO	Wyoming	WY

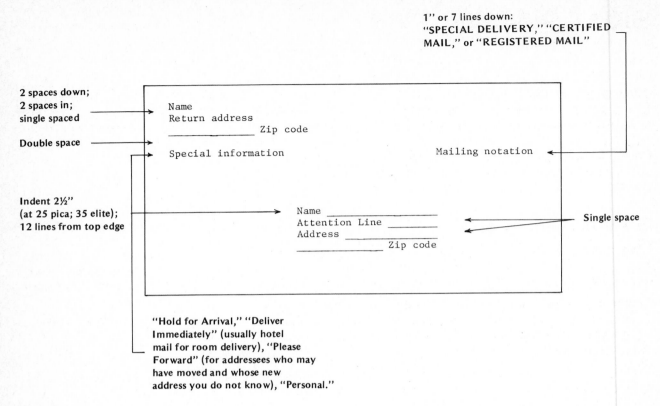

1" or 7 lines down:
"SPECIAL DELIVERY," "CERTIFIED MAIL," or "REGISTERED MAIL"

**2 spaces down;
2 spaces in;
single spaced**

```
Name
Return address
_____ Zip code
```

Double space

```
Special information                    Mailing notation
```

**Indent 2½"
(at 25 pica; 35 elite);
12 lines from top edge**

```
Name _____
Attention Line _____
Address _____
           _____ Zip code
```

Single space

"Hold for Arrival," "Deliver Immediately" (usually hotel mail for room delivery), "Please Forward" (for addressees who may have moved and whose new address you do not know), "Personal."

Figure 2–10
The Business-Size Envelope

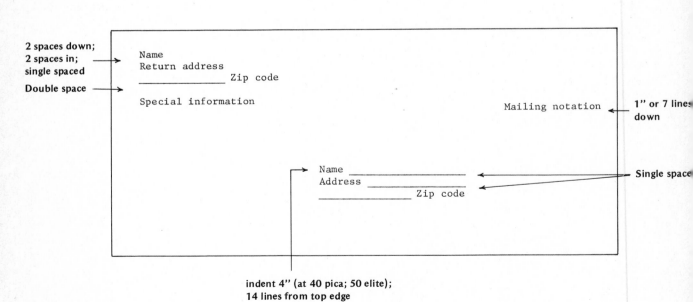

**2 spaces down;
2 spaces in;
single spaced**

```
Name
Return address
_____ Zip code
```

Double space

```
Special information
                                        Mailing notation
```

1" or 7 lines down

```
Name _____
Address _____
           _____ Zip code
```

Single space

**indent 4" (at 40 pica; 50 elite);
14 lines from top edge**

Figure 2–11
The Legal-Size Envelope

SKILLS ACTIVITY 8

Type envelopes (business size) for each case in Skills Activity 7. Be sure to include all the necessary information. Assuming that all companies have printed envelopes, you need use a return address in only one case.

Check the key on page 511. If you achieved Fair or above, continue. If you did not achieve Fair or above, retype the envelopes correctly before going on.

Given cases in which envelopes, involving specific problems, are to be typed, prepare the envelopes correctly.

Excellent   5
Good   4
Fair   3

Be Your Own Severest Critic

Your letter, in addition to being correct and up to date in style and form, must be a model of accuracy and neatness. It must look professional. To judge your letter's appearance, answer these questions:

1. Where you made a correction, does your correction show? If it is obvious, it is still an error even though you tried to erase and hide it. Did you strike that key so hard when you corrected the error that you spotlighted the correction?

2. How about your touch? The electric typewriter must be on the correct pressure if you are to have even type. The manual typewriter needs your even touch to obtain sharp, clear letters.

3. How about the condition of your typewriter? Are you maintaining a clean machine free from grime and eraser particles? Look at the individual letters. If they are filled in, blurred, crowded, spread, your machine should be serviced. Keep it clean and in optimum working condition. If your type is faded, change your ribbon.

4. How is the placement of your letter? Check the space from the top of the page to the date line. Now check the space between the last line of the letter and the end of the page. Is there about half an inch more space at the bottom? Are the left and right margins even, or is one much wider than the other? (The left margin may be one or two spaces wider.) Have you been able to maintain a fairly even right margin? Are the parts of the letter correctly spaced?

Try Skills Activity 9 to see if you can correct the errors.

up to date
No hyphens are used when compound adjective follows the noun.
Make corrections neatly.

Use your typewriter skillfully.

Help your typewriter help you.

Check the overall appearance of your letter.

SKILLS ACTIVITY 9

Given a letter with numerous errors, write your corrections directly above each error.

Excellent	18
Good	17
Fair	16

Read carefully the following letter, which has at least 18 errors in placement, form, spelling, and punctuation.

July 7, 19--

Ms. Ethel Baker

23 2 Ave.

New York, N.Y.   10007

Dear Miss Baker:

We were certainly embarrased to learn that

our maintainance staff has been so negligent in

servicing your air conditioner.

Mr. Swan has proceeded to assign some one to

service your equipment tomorrow at 8:30 a.m..

If you cannot be in youre apatement then, will you

please leave your key in the inclosed envelope

with the building suprintendent.

We hope that you air conditioner will be back in

service without any further delay.

Sincerely yours;

Anita Farrar

Anita Farrar

Manager

AF;jb

Check the key on page 511. If you achieved Fair or above, go on to the Summary. If you did not, note your errors, review your work, and discuss any problems with your instructor.

Name_____ Date_____

SUMMARY

We have now described the four letter styles businesses most commonly used. When you write a business letter in an office, you will probably use either the modified-block or the semiblock style, the most popular styles today. Many firms, however, are now adopting the newer, time-saving full-block style, and others are accepting the simplified style. It will be to your advantage to know each of them.

You have also learned how to handle special situations. For the formal letter of invitation, thanks, or congratulation, you will find that the official-business style adds dignity to the communication. For the innumerable times that you write to other members of your company, the interoffice memorandum provides an efficient form. And there is the personal-business letter, for which you usually do not use letterhead paper. You include your return address above the date, and you omit the typist's initials.

congratulation

Your punctuation form must also be correct and consistent. The two forms most often used are open and mixed.

The purpose and prescribed form of each part of the letter should now be familiar to you: letterhead, date line, special mailing notations, inside address and attention line, salutation, subject line, body of the letter, second-page notation, complimentary close, typed signature and title, and closing notations (initials, enclosure, carbon copy, and postscript).

prescribed: set down as rules

The envelope, too, must receive your careful attention. There is one correct form for business-size and legal-size envelopes. Remember to include all the information required for rapid delivery.

Before you mail your letter or interoffice memorandum, check it carefully for correctness of style and professional appearance.

Double checking always pays.

You are now ready for Focus on Language. You will cover 26 vocabulary and spelling words and three rules for hyphenation.

FOCUS ON LANGUAGE

Spelling

Do you know when to use one "e" and when to use two? It's easy to spell words ending in -sede, -ceed, or -cede. Why?

Only ONE word in the English language is spelled with -sede: *supersede*, meaning to take the place of because of superior worth or right; to supplant; to set aside.

Only THREE words are spelled with -ceed: *exceed, proceed, succeed*. The rest are spelled with -cede. Easy, isn't it? But watch procedure!

Do you use *correspondents* and *correspondence* correctly? Correspondents are persons who communicate by means of letters; they are also people who are employed to report news. Correspondence is communication by letters, or the letters actually written. Correspondents write correspondence.

The following paragraph contains 16 misspelled words.

To our embarassment, it seems we omited your new calenders from our

preceeding shipment. We hope that you will acceed to letting us send

them seperately to Misses Smith and Richards. Thank you for your

curtesy in calling our attention to this ommission. May we take this

ocasion to send you a complementary copy of our poplar "Congradula-

tions to Charlie" cartoon cards? If you succede in selling them, they

would superceed those you now sell. The price should not exseed 50

cents each.

We hope that there will be no need for further correspondents about

this shipment.

Given a paragraph with misspellings, write the correct spelling directly above each misspelled word.

Excellent   16
Good   15
Fair   14

Check the key on page 511. If you achieved Fair or above, go on to Vocabulary. If you did not score at least Fair, review the spelling hints above and the corrections in the paragraph. Ask someone to read the words you had incorrect as you type or write them. Check again. List any incorrect words. Repeat this procedure until you can spell every word correctly.

Name _____ Date _____

Vocabulary

The underscored words have been used in this chapter. Let's see if you really know their meanings.

1. a. His avant-garde ideas show that he is a leader in his field.
    b. In adopting old ideas, he shows that he is avant-garde.
2. a. The assessor will make an appraisal of the property to determine the taxes to be paid.
    b. He studied his appraisal last week.
3. a. The company will be adopting many of these principles as its own.
    b. He is adopting to a new situation in his business.
4. a. Watermarked paper is considered to be the poorest grade of paper.
    b. Letters typed on watermarked, rag-content paper make a good impression.
5. a. It is not imperative to arrive on time if you wish to see the entire performance.
    b. It seemed imperative to assure the people that their government was telling them the truth.
6. a. Endings such as *th, st,* and *nd,* are called ordinal endings because they show the order of a unit in a series.
    b. *One, two, three,* and so on are called ordinal numbers.

7. a. Major headings on term papers are usually typed in lower case.
    b. Nearly all printed material is in lower case except for the first letter in a sentence and proper nouns.
8. a. You may ascertain when the plane leaves if you read the flight schedule.
    b. They may ascertain the letter.
9. a. The person who writes a letter is called the addressee.
    b. The person to whom a letter is written is called the addressee.
10. a. The registrar will prescribe the program to be followed.
    b. We shall prescribe to the three business magazines.

Check the key on page 511. If you achieved Fair or above, go on to Hyphenation. If you fell below Fair, review the meanings of the words in the chapter. Compose a sentence using each word you had incorrect. Ask your instructor to check your sentences and to discuss any errors with you.

Hyphenation

In a number of places in this chapter, two or more words were hyphenated to form a compound adjective. Do you know when to use a hyphen? Here are some general rules:

Rule: *When two or more words having the force of a single modifier precede the noun, they are hyphenated.*

two-page letter   personal-business letter
well-polished corridor   up-to-date writer

Rule: *But, when such words are used as a predicate adjective—when they follow the noun—they are usually not hyphenated.*

a letter of two pages   a letter of personal business
a corridor that is well polished   the writer who is up to date

Rule: *When the first of two words is an adverb ending in* ly, *the hyphen is omitted.*

a truly good man
his fairly interesting report

Although you should learn these rules and follow them, it is always a good idea to have a dictionary handy. Some prefixes, such as *self* and *quasi* are hyphenated, while others are part of the word that follows and take no hyphen—for example, *anti, non,* and *semi.* Always check your dictionary when you aren't sure about hyphenating prefixes.

Correct the hyphenation in the following paragraph. You will have to add hyphens in some places and remove them in others. (Some hyphens in the paragraph may be correct.)

A well known business executive delivered a first rate speech on the impact of the income tax law on the spending habits of individuals. He mentioned that the post war era has brought many changes in tax laws. Middle-income people have seen how their money making plans have benefited the tax-collector. As a result, they have had to forgo non-essential items. Many reasonably-intelligent people do not realize that it is after-tax income that really counts. This well known executive further stressed the importance of keeping up-to-date where taxes are concerned.

> Given a paragraph containing hyphenated words, write the correct forms above the errors.
>
> | | |
> |---|---|
> | Excellent | 10 |
> | Good | 9 |
> | Fair | 8 |

Check the key on page 511. If you did not score Fair or above, review the rules for hyphenation, and then correct the paragraph again. Discuss any problems with your instructor.

Name _____ *Date* _____

3

ORGANIZE YOUR THINKING

Now that you have seen how business letters are put together, let's turn to the body of the letter, the message itself. In this chapter you will cover—

Unit 6   Outline Your Plan

Unit 7   Get to the Point Immediately

Unit 8   Use the Right Word

Unit 9   Use the Tools of the Trade

Unit 10   Form Sentences

Unit 11   Paragraph to Facilitate Reading

Unit 12   Check the Accuracy of Facts, Figures, and Details

UNIT 6   OUTLINE YOUR PLAN

The planning of letters—organization—is one of the most difficult tasks for you as a novice to learn. Your performance objective for this unit is:

novice: beginner

Given the problem of planning a message,

You will jot down the ideas to be included, carefully consider whether you have omitted any needed item of information, check to be sure no unnecessary details are included, then put all points in the order in which you should cover them.

Businesspeople who answer many letters a day too often feel that it is not necessary to plan each letter. Their return mail is filled with requests like these for follow-up material:

```
I do not understand why my new automobile
casualty-insurance policy AF12403657 does not
include towing service as my previous policy
did. Will you please add this to my policy and
bill me for any additional charges.
```

casualty: serious accident

The red-faced insurance broker.

liability: that for which
one is responsible, as a
debt

I am also interested in increasing my liability
coverage to $100,000–$300,000. Please tell me
the difference in the premium.

*Lack of service from a
service organization.*

Thank you very much for the information on job
opportunities in the field of social work. Have
you forgotten to include the list of accredited
schools that offer degrees in social work?

*The slipping office man-
ager.*

Of course we will route all orders through the
new agency in Dallas, as you request. Can you
tell us the name of the person who will take
charge of our account?

Don't let this happen to you.

Even the expert letter writer will take the time to outline difficult
letters. Mr. Espersen, the vice president of a leading bank, did not finish
his working day at five o'clock. After dinner, he reviewed a financial

judgment
copious: plentiful

problem that required his judgment. He made copious notes to be incorporated in a report he planned to dictate the next morning, showing
the step-by-step reasoning behind his decision to refuse a $150,000 loan
to an expanding industrial firm in the community. Then he listed the
points he would include in his letter to the head of the firm. He planned
his reports, his letters, his memos; that was one reason for his success.

List Points to Include

Follow this procedure.
irrelevant: not related

Let's try organizing responses in several business situations. Remember
the procedure: List the ideas, check for completeness, eliminate
irrelevant information, arrange in logical sequence.

catalogs
brochures: pamphlets

In the first case, assume you are employed as a clerk in a college
during the summer months to fill requests for catalogs and brochures
on special programs, adult-education courses, and foreign-student guidance. The requests for the brochures on the Certified Professional
Secretarial Examination have been so heavy that you have run out of
them. You have 25 requests you cannot fill. What will you do? If you
wait until the new supply is received, you will be getting second requests; so you decide to write to the 25 secretaries. What will they
want to know?

*Put yourself in the reader's
position.*

This is easy for you to answer if you put yourself in the place of the
person writing the original letter. Answer the question: "What would I
want to know if I did not receive this brochure?" You must tell the
secretaries:

The request has been received.

The delay is temporary.

The brochure will be sent by a specific date.

You are sorry for the delay.

Now consider the order in which you will use these ideas in writing the letter. The principle of "first things first" will prompt you to re-arrange the ideas this way:

The brochure will be sent by a specific date.

You are sorry for the delay.

The delay is temporary.

Omit the fact that the request has been received. (You wouldn't be answering if it had not been received.)

As a beginning worker or a part-time summer clerk, of course, you would not send this letter until you had checked with your supervisor. Only after receiving approval would you prepare the form letter to be mailed to all those for whom brochures were not available.

A similar situation arises in this next position. You are a clerk in the office of a local repair shop, and a customer expects an electric broiler to be repaired and ready for pickup the following Saturday. Unfortunately, the original distributor has gone out of business. You are trying to locate the needed part at one of the other dealers' shops. Rather than wait for Saturday, you anticipate the customer's irritation and decide to write a note. Does this list cover the points you need to make?

Hint for good human relations in the office.

similar: alike in substance or essentials

distributor

customer's: Note how possessive of a singular noun is formed.

The repair has not been made.

Why?

What is being done about it.

A definite follow-up is set.

Apology.

Your next position is a more demanding one, with greater responsibility. You are a full-time employee in the Exchange Import Company, a small company in which you handle the cash sales, the accounts, and the billing as well as the mail. You receive a package from Mr. Frisbee containing a walkie-talkie on which the antenna has been broken. He wishes to have it repaired free under his one-year guarantee. You know that the guarantee covers any defect of workmanship within a year of normal use, but it is obvious that the antenna was snapped off by force. Repairs will cost $13, including return postage. You need part payment of $5 in advance. Before reading further, organize your thoughts; write down the ideas you must include in your letter to Mr. Frisbee; then check your list against these suggestions:

guarantee: formal promise that something will meet stated standards

The antenna can be replaced without difficulty.

The guarantee covers faulty work or materials.

The antenna was snapped off, probably accidentally.

The repair will take three days after the order is placed.

The repair will cost $13, and part payment of $5 must be made in advance.

The repair will put the walkie-talkie in operating order.

Workmanship is guaranteed for 90 days.

accidentally

Check for Completeness

stationery: spelled with an *e*.

It is important to include all the necessary facts in your letters. If you were a secretary in a stationery-supply company, how would you react to this order letter?

```
Gentlemen:


I am starting my own business as a consulting

engineer.  I would like to order my stationery

from you.  Enclosed you will find the letterhead

I have designed.


Will you quote me a price on a thousand letter-

heads with envelopes to match?


                              Sincerely yours,

                              Sam Enterline

                              Sam Enterline
```

quotation: Note that you "submit" a quotation.

Can you submit a quotation on the basis of the information in the letter? Did Mr. Enterline tell you anything about the size, quality, color of the paper and the envelope, or the color or colors of the printed letterhead? He did not, and you will have to request that information from him.

delete: to take out

Delete the Unnecessary

Clear organization demands that you exclude nonessential information, which not only takes time to write and to read but clouds the essentials. The reader wonders why you put that sentence or phrase in the letter. Is he or she missing the point or failing to see an implication? Be careful to include only relevant information and to delete the extraneous facts that detract from the unity of your communication.

relevant: related
extraneous: not related
digress: to turn aside from main subject

Stick to the objective of the letter. Don't digress; don't tell too much. This letter to a stationery-supply company has included information that is not necessary to achieve the objective of the message:

> Mr. Silvers is no longer working for us and
> has accepted a controller's job with another
> company. Therefore, remove his name from our
> letterhead.

Do you agree that the first sentence is unnecessary? The letter can be
revised efficiently to:

> Please remove Mr. Seymour Silvers' name from
> our letterhead and include the name of Mr.
> Morris Eisman. Mr. Eisman will take Mr. Silvers'
> place as treasurer.

When a name ends in s, form the possessive by adding an apostrophe and s if name has only one syllable; add apostrophe only if name has two or more syllables.

Put Your Outline to Work

Once you have completed the first three steps (listing your points,
checking for completeness, deleting unnecessary details), you are ready
to write your letter. Think back to the clerk in the repair shop. Here is
a letter you might write to the customer whose electric broiler needed
repair. To be sure you did not omit anything the customer should know,
check your letter against the list of points you made.

> Please give us one more week to repair your
> broiler. The Acme Company, who made this
> broiler, has gone out of business, and we are
> trying to locate a new kolar unit at one of
> the other dealers' shops.
>
> We will let you know by the end of this week
> whether or not the part is available.
>
> We are sorry this repair is taking so long.

dealers': Note how possessive of a plural noun is formed.

Now consider the case of Sam Enterline, who requested a price for his
new letterhead. Suppose you made these notes to reply to his letter:

Give quotes on all qualities from the least to the most expensive, and
include brochure.

Enclose samples.

Recommend 8 1/2 x 11, but say that any size is available.

Ask whether printing is to be in one or two colors; give price for the
second color.

Set delivery time for two weeks after the order is placed.

Say that terms are 30 days net.

Thank him for asking.

30 days net: The full amount must be paid within 30 days of the billing date.

Is everything necessary included? Is irrelevant information excluded?
Are the points in a logical sequence? Before writing, you might re-
arrange them this way:

Thank him for asking.

Give quotes on all qualities from the least to the most expensive, and include brochure.

Ask whether printing is to be in one or two colors; give price for second color.

Recommend 8 1/2 x 11, but say that any size is available.

Enclose samples.

Set delivery time for two weeks after the order is placed.

Say that terms are 30 days net.

Now let's check your ability to outline your message effectively. Try Skills Activity 10.

SKILLS ACTIVITY 10

Take five minutes to add the essentials that are missing from the following statements.

1.   March 1, 19--

   Gentlemen:

   Please send me Guide to Income Tax Deductions.

   which you advertised in the Sunday Times.

   Thank you.

                                      Mary Smith

> Given messages with incomplete information, add the essential information in the space provided.
>
> Excellent   6
> Good   5
> Fair   4

Missing _____

2. Please send me at the above address the blue

   sport shoes advertised in the magazine Sartorial

   Elegance, page 152. Here is my check for the

   full amount, plus $5 for shipping and insurance,

   as you requested in the advertisement.

Missing _____

3. Please tell me whether or not I can obtain

   credit for an English course taken at another

   school last summer.

                                      Davis Scott

Missing _____

Name _____ *Date* _____

4. Please deliver 1000 gallons of heating oil to our new residence at 555 Steuben Street, Newtonville, New York, at the beginning of next month.

Missing _____

5. (Listing of business reference)

Ms. Thelma Thompson

234 Western Boulevard

Elizabeth, NJ   07208

Missing _____

6. We cannot pay our bill for $2500 at this time because we are financially strapped.

Missing _____

Check your answers with the key on page 511. If you are below Fair, be sure you understand the explanations. Discuss any problems with your instructor. Then try Skills Activity 11.

SKILLS ACTIVITY 11

You are ready to check your ability to outline your message, include the essentials, delete the unnecessary, and arrange the items in logical sequence. Take five minutes to delete the unnecessary parts in the following statements by drawing a line through the words to be taken out:

1. Please send me 12 dozen No. 2 Clarilead pencils; our stock is now low.

2. The weather caused five major accidents, each involving three to seven cars of various makes and colors.

3. The applicant for the position wanted career information concerning fringe benefits, salary raises, the tuition remission plan, and the marital status of the supervisory personnel.

4. As an excellent transportation center, this city offers rail, air, and shipping facilities, as well as spacious, well-constructed buildings for the automobile plant.

5. I have been interested in Jonny Singingstar since I was thirteen and buy every one of his records. Please send me his new album, "Bright Clouds." Here is my check for $6.95.

6. We have one of the finest concerns in the chemical industry. We employ over 10,000 workers and have three locations in this area. Please send us a reference for Miss Mary Peters, who has applied for a position as secretary in our personnel office.

7. Vacation schedules are again being determined by seniority. Those who have worked for the firm for the longest time will get their first choice. For example, one of the employees of long standing, the president's secretary, who has been with the firm for sixteen years (and who has already purchased her airline ticket to Paris), will get her first choice, the last three weeks in July.

Check your answers with the key on page 511. If you are below Fair, be sure you understand the explanations. Then try Skills Activity 12.

Name _____ Date _____

SKILLS ACTIVITY 12

Now we are ready to move up the organizational ladder to a more difficult task. You will be placed in situations which you may meet in your personal business and in your professional life. See how well you meet the demands of effective business communication.

A. You are a member of the "Protect Our Environment" Club in your town and have been on the Arrangements Committee for the past year. Today you received a note from the president of the club asking you to take over the chairmanship of the committee. She asks that you let her know your decision in writing before the end of next week.

> Given a case in which nine ideas are listed for an answer to a letter of invitation, list the major item that is missing.

   You jot down your ideas as follows:

1. Yes, I will accept.
2. Was this appointment a decision of the Executive Board or of the president?
3. Who are the new members of the committee?
4. What are the addresses and phone numbers of all members?
5. Is my understanding correct—the Executive Board plans the program for the year at its opening meeting, which I attend; and the Arrangements Committee carries out the plans for meetings, dinners, seminars, conferences, on-site visits with the approval of the Executive Board?
6. As Committee Chairman, am I the direct liaison to the Executive Board?

liaison to: contact with

7. Do I have an expense account?
8. Are there special plans this year that would take more time than was required by the committee last year?
9. Last year we met in the chairman's home. Since my home is in the suburbs, is there a meeting place in town?

Missing _____

Check with the key on page 511 before going on with the rest of the problem.

Name_____ Date_____

> *Given a list of points to be considered for inclusion in a message, list those to be communicated by telephone and by written communication, and cross out the items you would exclude.*

As you are reading over these notes, do you think that some questions should be discussed in a telephone conversation with the president of the club? If so, list their numbers below in order of importance. You may wish to omit some items. If you do, cross them out. Then list the numbers of the items you would include in your written reply in order of importance.

Discuss by telephone: _____

Include in letter: _____

Check page 511 to see how closely you agree with the authors. Discuss major disagreements with your instructor.

> *Given a situation in which 10 items are listed for answering an irate letter, add to and/or delete from the items listed, and arrange them in a logical sequence.*
>
> | | |
> |---|---|
> | Excellent | 8–10 items |
> | Good | 6–7 items |
> | Fair | 5 items |

B. You are the administrative assistant in the Alumni Office of Bedford College. You receive the following letter written by Dick Baer, an irate alumnus.

> I heard from a friend that our semiannual dinner was held last month. I never received a notice of the meeting and I've been a dues-paying member of the alumni for 15 years.
>
> The school surely must have gone down since my time. Nothing gets done right any more. Drop my name from the roster.

After checking Mr. Baer's file, you see that notice was sent to him and returned because he had moved a year ago without leaving a forwarding address. The returned notice is in the files.

Here are the notes you may have jotted down before answering his letter:

1. It's his mistake; don't blame us.
2. You're glad to have his new address.
3. You're sorry he missed the meeting.
4. You hope to see him next time.
5. The returned notice is enclosed as proof.
6. You commend him on his long membership.
7. You advise him to leave a forwarding address and to notify you when he moves.
8. You inform him that his name will be kept on the roster.
9. A copy of the dinner program is to be sent to him.
10. You advise him to be more careful.

Is there anything you would like to add? _____

_____

Is there anything you would like to delete? _____

_____

Arrange the ideas in logical order by number._____

_____

Check page 511 to see how closely you agree with the authors. Discuss major disagreements with your instructor.

C. List the points you would include if you were to write a letter under the following circumstances: You hold a position in the admissions office of Valley Military Academy, a secondary boarding school for boys. You receive this inquiry from a Ralph Trainor—the father of a prospective student.

> My son Colin will be eligible to attend second-
> ary school in September of 1980. I have heard
> about the excellent reputation of Valley
> Academy, and I would like him to attend school
> there.
>
> Please send me a brochure showing the course of
> study at the Academy.
>
> Is it possible to pay the annual tuition in
> installments? Must my son take the SAT examina-
> tion in order to qualify for entrance, or will
> his school grades be accepted? Is there an
> opportunity to have an interview before he
> applies to Valley Academy?
>
> Thank you for your help.

Given the problem of answering an inquiry, list the items essential for the written answer.

Excellent	*9–10*
Good	*7–8*
Fair	*5–6*

---

1. _____
2. _____
3. _____
4. _____
5. _____
6. _____
7. _____
8. _____
9. _____
10. _____

Check page 511 to see how closely you agree with the authors' answer to this situation. If you have attained the performance objectives at any level listed, you may skip D and E and continue with Unit 7 of this chapter.

Given a problem of writing about payment of a bill, list the essential items to be included in the letter.	
Excellent	*4-5*
Good	*2-3*
Fair	*1*

D. Outline the points your letter would cover in this situation: On March 30, you receive a second invoice for $1250 from Prebilt Corporation for five filing cabinets. You have already paid for the cabinets, and you have your canceled check to prove payment.

1. _____
2. _____
3. _____
4. _____
5. _____

Check page 511 to see how closely you agree with the authors' answer to this situation. Discuss major disagreements with your instructor.

Given a problem of writing to request a contribution, list the essential items to be included in the request.	
Excellent	*9–10*
Good	*7–8*
Fair	*5–6*

E. You are secretary of your high school alumni organization. Outline the points you would include in your letter to the group asking them to contribute to a fund for construction of a new swimming pool at the school.

1. _____
2. _____
3. _____
4. _____
5. _____
6. _____
7. _____
8. _____
9. _____
10. _____

Check page 512 to see how closely you agree with the authors' answer to this situation. If you have attained Fair or above in planning your message, you can move on to the next section, in which you will find the answer to writing that first sentence. If you did not achieve Fair or above, discuss the problem with your instructor.

UNIT 7 GET TO THE POINT IMMEDIATELY

Your performance objective for this unit is:

Given the problem of communicating a business message,

You will compose an opening sentence (or sentences) stating your reason for writing.

How will you begin your letter? Don't hesitate; let the opening sentence tell the reader why you are writing. A long or short introduction is not necessary in a business letter; in fact, it detracts from the letter. In one such letter, a personnel manager wrote two pages about the company before asking for a reference for a young person who was applying for a position. How annoying to the reader!

personnel: not a "personal" manager.

All of us get into habits of doing things, and it is difficult to change. One habit many businesspeople have acquired is starting a letter with—

```
Re your letter of the fifteenth . . .

This is in answer to your letter of July 15.

We have received your letter of the fifteenth.
```

Remember, when the date stands alone or precedes the month, spell it out or use figures with ordinal endings.

How unnecessary! You must have received the letter or you would not be writing the answer. Compare these beginnings with this first sentence:

```
It is a pleasure to send you a copy of
Cleaning Your Rugs.
```

This gets to the point immediately and avoids the unnecessary sentence.
   Even the "no" letter should include its negative reply in the opening paragraph. You may want to start positively; but, if your objective is to say that you cannot do something, say so in the first or second sentence. The answer to your request for a convention speaker is quickly and efficiently given in this first paragraph:

```
Thank you very much for inviting me to be the
banquet speaker at your November convention. I
am unable to accept because I will be speaking
at the University of Hawaii on that date as part
of my fall lecture series.
```

Your personal letter in answer to an invitation to a dinner party could say:

```
I wish I could be with you at your dinner party
on Friday, the fifteenth; but I must be at the
twenty-fifth anniversary celebration of my
parents' wedding.
```

parents'

Don't waste your reader's time with a long preliminary discussion. Remember to reply to a request in your first or second sentence.

Study these opening statements. Note how the revised sentences get to the point at once.

Original	Revised
We thank you for your letter of the third in which you placed an order for 500 barrels of No. 40 oil.	The 500 barrels of No. 40 oil were shipped today. Thank you for this order.
Referring to your letter of October 10, we have sent the report you requested on "Health Insurance Under Social Security."	"Health Insurance Under Social Security" was mailed to you today.
In reply to your letter of the first, we regret the error made in your last order, in which we inadvertently neglected to include two gross of ball-point pens.	We mailed two gross of ball-point pens by special delivery today. We are very sorry that we made this error.
Ms. Esther Barnes has applied to us for a charge account. She has given us your name as a reference. Will you be good enough to give us a credit rating on her?	Please complete the enclosed credit report form on Esther F. Barnes. Ms. Barnes gave your name as a business reference when she applied for a charge account with us.
The Federal Deposit Insurance Corporation has recently increased the amount of insurance to depositors in member banks. Heretofore, individual depositors were insured in a single capacity to a limit of $20,000. Now, the limit has been raised to $40,000.	The Federal Deposit Insurance Corporation now insures your account in our bank to a limit of $40,000. (The previous limit was $20,000.

Put this strategy to work in the following Skills Activity.

SKILLS ACTIVITY 13

1. a. This is in answer to your inquiry of June 10.
   b. The answer to your inquiry of June 10 is "yes."

2. a. Our most recent price list has been mailed to you today.
   b. We have noted your request for our most recent price list.

3. a. Could you please give me the credit rating of Donald Brown, who has an account with you?
   b. Donald Brown has applied for a charge account at our store. He has given your name as a reference.

4. a. We hope that you have enjoyed reading the books you purchased two months ago. However, do you realize that you have not yet sent us your check in payment of your account?
   b. May we remind you that we have not yet received your check for $8.69, which was due us last month?

5. a. Your account at the Fulton Bank now earns 5 percent interest.
   b. If you have been following the financial news, you realize that the State Banking Department has given permission for mutual savings banks to pay a maximum of 5 percent on all savings deposits, an increase from the 4½ percent interest formerly paid.

6. a. We're planning to build a new office building in Akron, so we would like to have your bid for the job.
   b. This letter is being sent to all local contractors who may be interested in placing bids for our new office building, which is to be built in Akron.

7. a. We have received your letter of September 15, in which you inquire about the basketball schedule for the coming season.
   b. Here is the complete schedule of basketball games for the coming season, which you asked about in your letter of September 15.

8. a. We are very sorry to read in your letter of February 1 that your orders have not been delivered on time because we have been addressing the packages incorrectly.
   b. You have every reason to complain about your orders arriving late because of our incorrect method of addressing the packages.

9. a. In this rapidly changing world, it is essential that a young man have adequate training before he applies for an accounting job. I am that young man.
   b. Will you consider my qualifications for a position in your accounting department? I have a B.S. in Accounting and have completed 16 credits toward my M.A.

> *Given 10 problems offering a choice of two opening sentences, select the more effective opening sentence in each by circling the appropriate letter.*
>
> *Excellent   9-10*
> *Good   8*
> *Fair   7*

Name _____ Date _____

10. a. In recent months, there have been many changes in the various health plans offered to the public. You may be interested to know that a major change is the increase in the allowable number of days of hospitalization from 14 to 21 days completely paid up.

b. Health plans now offer 21 days of completely paid-up hospitalization—an increase of 7 days over previous plans.

Check your answers with the key on page 512. If you have not succeeded in attaining Fair, review Unit 7. Discuss any problems with your instructor. If you scored Fair or above, move on to Unit 8.

UNIT 8   USE THE RIGHT WORD

Your performance objective is:

Given the problem of selecting effective words in writing your communications,

You will avoid superlatives and relative terms, give specific information, and use general terms with care.

Your choice of words and the way you use them affect the clarity of your communication and determine what effect it will have on your reader.

affect
effect

Avoid Superlatives

So often a salesperson will say, "This is perfect for you." Such a remark makes many people's sales resistance zoom—they prefer to make their own decision. And this principle is important to remember in letter-writing. When a letter states, "This is the best investment on the market for you," the reader will probably comment, "Prove it."

How would you react to these statements? Our opinion is given in the margin.

> This article will surely give you a very clear understanding of all the issues.

This is for the reader to decide.

> We are proud of our exceptionally prompt and most efficient service.

"Prompt service" is enough.

> Use of our system will produce a tremendous and outstanding improvement in the handling of incoming mail in your office.

Implication of current inefficiency is offensive.

> We are really extremely sorry for the delay.

Sounds false; omit "really extremely."

> Our company is most delighted with your fine and welcome order.

Sounds like a social butterfly answering an invitation to tea.

> This model is the best television set ever produced.

At any price?

The business letter and the personal-business letter are written to comparative strangers. Keep these letters free of superlatives that give a false tone to the writing or tend to draw conclusions for the reader.

comparative: resulting from a comparison

Choose Words for Clarity

How can you write so that your reader knows at first reading what you want to say?

RELATIVE TERMS ARE AMBIGUOUS

Words such as *late, early; high, low; good, bad; productive, nonpro-*

ductive; expensive, inexpensive are relative terms. They mean one thing to the writer but may mean something else to the reader. To you, "Don't be late" may mean to be home at midnight, but to someone else it may mean to be home at 10 p.m. "My son spent his savings on this expensive car." How much is "expensive"? $10,000? $3,000? $2,000? It varies from person to person and from item to item. A father may consider $3,000 expensive for his son but not for himself. Government control of utilities may be considered "good" by some. But in the opinion of many United States citizens government control of utilities is "bad."

advertisement

An advertisement for a famous perfume read: "Great savings! Buy now at 20 percent off list price." The customer, not knowing the list price, is unaware of the exact cost or how great the saving actually is. Similarly, when the college newsletter states that a student needs a "high average" for the scholarship grant, a student may wonder whether 85, 90, or 95 is needed. What does "high" mean? Does he or she qualify?

Don't waste the reader's time with relative terms. Note that the ambiguity of the sentences on the left can easily be clarified with exact data.

Ambiguous	Clear
Compared to 1975, the tax rate is high this year.	In 1975, the tax rate was 50 cents per $100 value; this year, it is 75 cents on every $100 value, an increase of 50 percent.
We will follow up on your request late in the year.	We will follow up your request on November 30.
Amair has a daily early flight to Paris.	Amair has a daily 10 a.m. flight to Paris.
The crew discovered a productive oil well.	The crew discovered an oil well that produced 750 barrels a day.

GIVE SPECIFIC INFORMATION

mortgage: contract specifying pledge of property as security for repayment of loan

A letter from a bank denying a mortgage of $40,000 on a $50,000 house contains the suggestion that the amount of the mortgage be reduced: "If you can put more money down and carry a lower mortgage, we can process your application immediately." That letter should have stated:

"Percent" should usually be spelled out.

```
If you can see your way clear to a mortgage
of $25,000, at 8 percent, for 25 years, we can
process your application immediately. To obtain
approval for a $40,000 mortgage in your case,
at this time of tight money and high interest
rates, may mean a delay of six months.
```

These precise figures enable the hopeful mortgagor to make a decision.
  Which one of the following expressions gives you specific information? You are told to come in for an appointment—

mortgagor: one who
mortgages property to
another as security for a
loan
*Type "a.m." and "p.m."
as shown here.*

        early Monday morning, July 18

        on Monday, July 18, in the morning

        at 9:30 a.m., Monday, July 18

The first two lines leave you wondering when to arrive. And they make
an unfavorable impression, because they convey the idea that you may
have to wait—that no one is expecting you at a special time. The last
line sets a definite appointment and gives the impression that you will
receive prompt attention at 9:30 a.m.

convey: to make known

USE GENERAL TERMS WISELY

It is easy to be specific about dates and prices and other numerical
information. But you can also pinpoint your meaning by being careful
in your use of such general terms as *matter, situation, area, problem,
field, subject, issue, action.*

Vague	Specific
He is an excellent man in his field.	He is an excellent electronics engineer.
Help us in this matter.	Help us locate the error in the account.
We ask your assistance in this situation.	Please extend our credit for 30 days.
Salesmen will visit your area soon.	Salesmen will visit Chicago on August 1.
We shall discuss the issue with you when we meet.	We shall discuss your application when we meet on Saturday.
We will confer about the subject.	We will discuss employment opportunities.
This material will explain the action of the Board.	The enclosed minutes will explain the Board's opposition to the dividend increase.

Of course, you don't want to repeat yourself constantly. Sometimes,
general words such as those listed above are useful and even necessary.
The key to wise use of general terms is *context.* For instance, take the
final sentence about the Board's action in the list above. Suppose the
sentences directly preceding that one had read:

*The clarity of words is af-
fected by the company
they keep.*

preceding: going before

> In its March 15 meeting, the Board voted not to
> increase the company's dividend. A copy of the
> minutes of that meeting is enclosed.

redundant: more than
required

In this case, using the specific sentence (shown above on the right) would be redundant; the left-hand sentence—"This material will explain the action of the Board"—would be more suitable.

Context, then, can make an otherwise vague sentence precise or a precise sentence redundant. But remember that it is better to err on the side of too much clarity than to leave your reader wondering what you are talking about.

To check your ability to write with clarity, try Skills Activity 14.

SKILLS ACTIVITY 14

Would you change any of these sentences?

1. The meeting of shareholders takes place on Monday morning at the Grange Hall in Springfield. _____
_____

2. The holiday shopping season began early this year. _____
_____

3. How can you resist such an inexpensive coat? _____
_____

4. We have the finest display of radios in the entire world. _____
_____

5. Do not worry about the bill. The cost of repairing your watch will be nominal. _____
_____

6. Our area has tallied up the highest dollar volume of Christmas sales in history. _____
_____

7. This is an issue that will come up at the next meeting of the committee. _____
_____

8. Your savings account at the Dollar Bank earns money at the rate of 6 percent. _____
_____

9. Your welcome order arrived at our office today, and we were very delighted to receive it. _____
_____

10. We expect to raise some money to send several boys and girls to camp next summer. _____
_____

> Given 10 sentences containing generalities, vague terms, and superlatives, rewrite the sentences where necessary, using exact data, definite terms, and realistic comparisons.
>
> Excellent   10
> Good   8–9
> Fair   7

Check page 512 to evaluate your responses. If you do not receive a rating of Fair or above, reread this section. Discuss your score with your instructor. If you have attained a rating of Fair or above, move on to Unit 9.

Name_____ Date_____

UNIT 9 USE THE TOOLS OF THE TRADE

Your performance objective is:

Given situations in which you need assistance in spelling accurately and using vocabulary correctly,

You will use the dictionary and thesaurus to find correct spellings and the right words to express your meaning.

Use a dictionary and a thesaurus to help you choose the right words to express your meaning exactly. By skillful use of these aids, you can develop the ability to select words and to combine them so that they will give you the meaning you desire.

thesaurus: a book of words and their synonyms

The Dictionary Can Help You

When you look up a word, do you give its meaning only a glance? Take the word *premium*. To the insurance broker, it means the money paid for a contract of insurance. But if you do not read beyond the first meaning of the word in your dictionary, you may think that a premium is only a reward or a prize. Are you speaking the same language as your insurance broker when you consider your insurance premium a reward or a prize?

Many words have more than one meaning.

The word *premium* has other meanings. The personnel manager may offer employees premium pay to work on a late shift. To the manager it is a bonus offered to induce the staff to work at odd hours. When the broker sells a $10 par value stock at a market value of $25, the stock is sold at a premium of $15. In this case, the premium represents the sum above the nominal or par value of the stock. The jeweler sells only premium merchandise—that which has an exceptionally high value.

nominal: existing or being something in name or form only

Most words in our language can be interpreted in different ways. And words may be used as more than one part of speech. *Well*, for instance, has several meanings as a noun; it is also a verb; it is also an adverb.

Many words have more uses as any of several parts of speech.

Aside from the meanings of words, what other information will you find in your dictionary?

1. The correct spelling of a word—such as *phlegm* or *queue.*

2. Preferred spelling when more than one spelling is correct—such as *judgment* or *judgement, advertise* or *advertize, enclose* or *inclose.*

3. Grammatical information:
   a. The part of speech.
   b. Irregular plurals—such as *foot, feet; notary, notaries.*
   c. Principal parts of verbs—such as *give, gave, given.*
   d. Comparison of adjectives and adverbs—such as *good, better, best; well, better, best.*
   e. Cases of pronouns—such as *I, my* or *mine, me; we, our* or *ours, us.*

4. Syllabication.

5. Pronunciation.

6. Whether to use a hyphen with a prefix or suffix or to join it to the word—such as *self-interest, selfish, businesslike.*

7. Whether a term is one word, two words, or hyphenated—such as *openhearted, open-air, open house.*

8. Synonyms. (These are not given for all words.)

9. Capitalization of proper nouns and adjectives.

10. The origin (etymology) of the word.

11. Examples of uses of the word.

Each dictionary has its own way of showing this material; to get the most from yours, you should read carefully the explanatory notes at the front.

consistent (used as an adjective): Look it up.

A dictionary, like any reference book, is no better than your ability to use it correctly. Get yourself a good dictionary, study its method of presenting its information, and then be consistent in using it. Develop the look-it-up habit.

The Thesaurus Can Help Too

When you are trying to find exactly the right word, or a synonym for a word you are using too often, or perhaps the opposite of a word, turn to a thesaurus for help. Here you will find many more synonyms than the dictionary provides, and you can discover antonyms as well.

Finding a more precise word.

For example, you want to say that John is a skillful politician, but you have used "skillful" in the preceding sentence. So you make use of your thesaurus, where you find numerous synonyms, among them:

dexterous, adroit, expert, apt, handy, quick, deft, ready, smart, proficient, good at, master of, a good hand at, masterly, accomplished

Now you can choose among other words to describe John, and you find that "adroit" not only replaces "skillful" but, in this instance, even improves upon it.

Avoiding a colloquialism.

Sometimes you may want to replace a phrase that is too colloquial—for instance, "in a jiffy." If you look in the index under "jiffy," you will be referred to a section that gives you such substitutes as these:

moment, instant, second, minute, twinkling, flash, breath, crack, burst, flash of lightning, stroke of time

Finding an antonym.

Still another way to use your thesaurus is to find antonyms. Since words are usually grouped in a thesaurus according to ideas (rather than alphabetically), you can find contrasting words in adjacent entries. If you look up "attraction," for instance, you might find that the next entry is "repulsion."

If you will get into the habit of utilizing your dictionary and thesaurus, you'll find your vocabulary expanding and your writing skills improving rapidly.

Can you make the dictionary and thesaurus work for you so that you can achieve correct spelling and correct usage? Try Skills Activity 15.

SKILLS ACTIVITY 15

A. The endings *ence, ance, ent,* and *ant* often give us trouble. Can you fill in the correct letter in the following words?

extravag__nt   irrelev__nt   resid__nt

independ__nt   accept__nce   acquaint__nce

superintend__nt   defend__nt   consist__nt

abund__nt   recurr__nce   inherit__nce

> *Given 21 partially spelled words commonly used in business, using a dictionary, complete the spelling of the words within 10 minutes.*
>
> *Excellent   21*
> *Good   20*
> *Fair   19*

B. The *er, ar, or* endings are another source of frequent spelling mistakes. Which is the correct ending for each of these words?

calend__r   counsel__r   vend__r

mortgag__r   distribut__r   simil__r

endeav__r   competit__r   less__r

If you are unable to complete A and B in 10 minutes or if you cannot spell the words correctly, practice with five words each day, reviewing the words you practiced the day before until you complete the list.

C. The dictionary lists preferred spellings for the following words. Circle the preferred spelling.

labor   labour   acknowledgement   acknowledgment

judgement   judgment   theater   theatre

enclose   inclose   counsellor   counselor

> *Given nine words with more than one spelling, using the dictionary, identify the preferred spelling within three minutes.*
>
> *Excellent   9*
> *Good   8*
> *Fair   7*

If you are unable to complete the task in three minutes, check yourself on the time it takes you to find the word "capitalization" in the dictionary. Are you taking more than 30 seconds? If so, ask your instructor to review with you the steps for finding a word in the dictionary. After this review, try to find the preferred form of *honor/honour* in the dictionary. Did you succeed in finding it in 30 seconds?

Name _____ *Date* _____

SKILLS ACTIVITY 16

To ensure your success in working on problems A–E, consult your dictionary for the correct definitions of the words in question.

A. As you know from the discussion of *premium* in the chapter, many words have more than one meaning. Look back at the chapter to see how the words *liability* and *quotation* were used (the words in the margin will help you find them). Is this the way you would usually use these words? See if you can give another definition for each word. Use the space below.

liability _____

_____

quotation _____

_____

> Given two words used in a specific way, find and write another meaning for each in the dictionary, within an allotted time period.
>
> Excellent   4 minutes
> Good   5 minutes

B. Let's try it again. This time you'll try finding three words: *extraneous, nominal, novice.* Write definitions to fit the way the words were used in this chapter.

extraneous _____

_____

nominal_____

_____

novice _____

_____

> Given three words used in this chapter, using the dictionary, write definitions for the way each word was used, within an allotted time period.
>
> Excellent   5 minutes
> Good   6 minutes

C. Sometimes a word can be used as any of several parts of speech. *Drink,* for example, can be a noun ("Have a drink") or a verb ("I drink tea"). The words *requisite* and *antecedent* can be used as nouns or adjectives. Write two sentences in the space below for each word, using it first as a noun, then as an adjective. (If you aren't sure of the different meanings of these words, check your dictionary before you begin.)

> Given two words that can be different parts of speech, using a dictionary, write four sentences that use each word as a noun and as an adjective, within seven minutes.
>
> Peer group or instructor evaluation:
>
> Excellent   4
> Good   3

Name _____ *Date* _____

requisite

as noun _____

_____

as adjective _____

_____

antecedent

as noun _____

_____

as adjective _____

_____

If you did not achieve Good or above, discuss your score with your instructor.

D. Let's make the dictionary work for you in finding synonyms (words having the same meaning) for the words below. (If you know some of them but cannot think of a one-word synonym, you may use two or three words.) Be sure your synonym is the same part of speech as the original word.

Given nine words, using a dictionary, write synonyms for these words, within five minutes.
Peer group or instructor evaluation:

Excellent   9
Good   8
Fair   7

1. casualty _____

2. cursory _____

3. digress _____

4. ambiguous _____

5. facilitate _____

6. convey _____

7. marginal _____

8. denote _____

9. criterion _____

Discuss your score with your instructor if it is below Fair.

E. Have you ever used a thesaurus? The next task will show you just how easy it is to use a thesaurus to find other words and phrases to express your ideas.

You have used the term *get ahead* quite frequently in a report you are writing. For variety you would like to find some other words to express that idea. Using the thesaurus, list below the synonyms which can be used to express this same idea.

Given three terms, using a thesaurus, find three other ways of expressing each term, within an allotted time period.

Excellent   9 minutes
Good   10-11 minutes

get ahead _____

Now look up synonyms for two more terms. (Look under *use* to find *be of use*.)

stop _____

be of use _____

Discuss any problems with your instructor.

UNIT 10   FORM SENTENCES

Your performance objective for this unit is:

Given the problem of writing effective sentences in business messages to convey exact meanings to the reader,

You will form simple, compound, and complex sentences, skillfully using clauses, placement, parallel construction, and correct grammar.

Simple, Compound, Complex

Choosing the right words is only the first step. In order to communicate ideas to the reader, you must combine words into sentences. What is a sentence?

"I cashed my check" is a *simple* declarative sentence. The doer of the action, "I," is the subject. The action, "cashed," is the verb. And the thing acted upon, "my check," is the object.

The simple sentence

Now let's add a qualifying word, an adjective. "I cashed my *first* check." You immediately picture a new employee happily counting his or her first salary payment—an important occasion. Or we can add an adverb—"I *quickly* cashed my check." What picture does this call to mind? Qualifying words (modifiers) help make your writing more specific and more interesting.

qualifying: modifying

Here are two simple sentences:

```
I cashed my check.

I paid the bill.
```

There can be no question that the two thoughts are closely related. So we can make an improvement here if we add the coordinating conjunction "and" and delete the period. See how much more smoothly the sentences read when they are combined:

```
        I cashed my check, and I paid the bill.
```

Note use of comma between clauses.

Whenever two clauses are closely allied, you can use a *compound* sentence to add variety to your style and to help your reader understand relationships between thoughts.

The compound sentence

The other coordinating conjunctions—*but, or, nor, for*—can also be used to connect two thoughts. Which would you choose to connect these sentences?

coordinating conjunction: word joining words of equal rank.

```
The president of the company wishes to appoint
Ms. Dorothy James head of the Advertising
Department. The Board of Directors has not yet
acted on his proposal.
```

Use but

Use for	These data will provide the basis of his report. They show future trends in sales.
Use or	Will you join the group in Hawaii? Will you catch up with them in the Philippines?

Now look at this sentence:

> Because I needed money, I cashed my check.

The complex sentence

Here we have combined two related thoughts in a different way. Instead of a compound sentence (two simple sentences joined by a coordinating conjunction such as "and"), we now have a *complex* sentence. It is composed of an independent clause—"I cashed my check"—and a dependent clause—"because I needed money."

A dependent clause is simply one that cannot stand alone—it leaves the reader waiting for the rest of the sentence to follow. Read the following dependent clauses. Do you notice that you are waiting for something else to follow each of them, that you have a feeling of incompleteness?

After reading this,	You remark:
If you cannot pay your bill by the end of the month	What will happen?
As I have already said	Something is coming that I should know.
Because the capital-investment tax refund has been temporarily suspended	What will result?
When you apply for a position	What should I do?

These clauses need the support of an independent clause because they do not contain a complete thought when they stand alone. Here they are with an independent clause, giving them full status as complex sentences:

> If you cannot pay your bill by the end of the month, your phone service will be discontinued.

> As I have already said, you are making progress.

> Because the capital-investment tax refund has been temporarily suspended, many companies are not putting in new machinery.

> When you apply for a position, bring your résumé with you.

In the examples above, *if, as, because,* and *when* are subordinating conjunctions. You can see that a subordinating conjunction is what makes a clause dependent; you use it when you want to write a complex sentence. (Other commonly used subordinating conjunctions are: *after, although, before, since, unless, until,* and *while*.)

You have now seen how conjunctions can be used to connect whole clauses to make your writing smoother. But you may also use the conjunctions *and, or,* and *nor* to connect parts of a clause—verbs, adjectives, nouns, or phrases.

> You should <u>take</u> the initiative and <u>see</u> the job through to completion.

Verbs

> The student is <u>industrious</u>, <u>efficient</u>, and <u>alert</u>.

Adjectives

> This subject is not taught <u>in the high schools</u>, <u>in the colleges</u>, or <u>in the universities</u>.

Phrases

> Neither <u>Professor Cooper</u> nor his <u>assistant</u> can speak to the group.

Nouns

Although these sentences have compound elements (verbs, adjectives, nouns, and phrases), they are not compound sentences, for they do not have two parts that can stand alone with full meaning.

For and *but* are also used as prepositions:

> Do this for him.

> All but the last figure have been checked.

Can you identify sentences and clauses? Check your ability to do so in Skills Activity 17. Can you improve your writing and make your message clearer by putting the right conjunction in the right place? Try it in Skills Activity 17.

subordinating conjunction: word joining clauses of minor rank to principal clauses.

SKILLS ACTIVITY 17

A. Identify each sentence: **S**—Simple; **CD**—Compound; **CP**—Complex.

1. The president and the treasurer held a special meeting in the conference room.   S   CD   CP

2. Mr. Barnes authorized the payment of the invoice, and the accountant issued the check.   S   CD   CP

3. Because the bill was already overdue, the company could not take the 2 percent discount.   S   CD   CP

4. The project was approved after it was reviewed by the committee.   S   CD   CP

5. These desks may be repaired and painted, or we can purchase new ones.   S   CD   CP

6. The company will be forced into bankruptcy unless management revises its methods.   S   CD   CP

7. As the cost of living rises, Social Security payments will also increase.   S   CD   CP

8. Reputable retailers try to provide a broad selection of merchandise, to sell it at reasonable prices, and to service the goods sold.   S   CD   CP

Check your answers against the key on page 512. If you achieved Fair or above, continue. If you were below Fair, review Unit 10 and the explanations in the key; discuss any problems with your instructor.

B. Very often, combining two sentences helps to make the meaning clearer and also provides a more flowing style of writing. What coordinating conjunction (*and, or, nor, for, but*) would you choose to place after the first sentence in each of the following cases? Write the conjunction in the space provided.

1. Mr. Watkins wrote the check for $75. His bookkeeper cashed it.

_____

2. The brochures arrived today. We will not mail them until next week.

_____

3. Do you wish to pay your union dues through a payroll deduction plan? Do you prefer to pay annually by check? _____

4. Take the correspondence to the file clerk. Ask him to file it.

_____

Name _____ Date _____

5. The orientation of new employees is done in the Sales Department.

It really should be done in the Personnel Department. _____

Check the answers on page 512. If you were correct in four out of five sentences, move on to the next section. If you were not able to achieve the goal, review the explanations in the key. Discuss any problems with your instructor.

Use the Independent Clause for Emphasis

While you are organizing your thoughts, consider the point you want to emphasize. In the following sentences the emphasis shifts as the topic of the independent clause shifts.

```
I did my assignment while watching television.

I watched television while doing my assignment.
```

In the first sentence, doing the assignment is more important. In the second sentence, the emphasis is on watching television.

Another way to spotlight a word or idea is to make it the first or last word in the sentence. Conversely, burying it in the middle of the sentence will often keep it from attracting attention. After reading this sentence, what do you remember?

conversely: on the contrary

```
In the job interview, you will want to find out
the job responsibilities, the hours, the size of
the office in which you will be working, the
salary, and the training program, if any.
```

Do you notice that *salary* is buried in the list?

You can't miss the word *profit* in the next sentence.

```
Profit, not charity, is the motive in this
venture.
```

If we change this sentence—

```
According to the present plans, metric measure-
ments will be in use in a short time.
```

to read—

```
Measurements will soon be made by the metric
system.
```

the focus will be on *the metric system.*

Parallel Construction Aids Equal Emphasis

There are times when each unit of a sentence or paragraph is of equal importance. Using a sentence whose parts are parallel in construction will show this equality. For example, when you receive the following information from the admissions office of the college to which you are applying, you realize the importance of each of the three requirements:

parallel: corresponds to or closely resembles

To be considered for matriculation at Wooley
College next February, you must complete the
following requirements before November 15:

1. Complete an Admission Form.
2. Have a transcript of your record
   sent from your high school.
3. Take the College Entrance Examination.

requisites: necessities

What do we mean by parallel construction? If you look at the example,
you will see that equal units are presented identically. Each unit starts
with the same part of speech—in this case a verb—and is followed by a
similar construction—in this case a direct object. To neglect any one of
the three requisites would deny you the chance to be considered for
entrance to the college. The three are equal in importance, and parallel
construction is used to make this clear to you.

But parallel construction is more than a matter of equal emphasis; it is
part of adherence to correct grammar. Coordinating conjunctions must
connect parts that are parallel in form. They should connect noun with
noun, verb with verb, phrase with phrase, clause with clause, and so on.

Clause with clause

If you select a gift and if you pay for it now,
it will be shipped today.

Phrase with phrase

We are concerned about taxes, about crime, and
about inflation.

Verb with verb

Select your material, take it to the desk, and
pay your bill.

Noun with noun

The treasurer and the president prepared the
statement.

Note how the following revised sentences correct the errors in parallel
construction in the original sentences:

Nonparallel	Revised
Landing on a carrier for the first time and to cope with a defective engine upset the young pilot.	Landing on a carrier for the first time and coping with a defective engine upset the young pilot.
We plan to build fine homes, to pave highways, and develop educational systems.	We plan to build fine homes, to pave highways, and to develop educational systems.
His notes read: Attend the meeting of the board on the tenth, contact AMS for convention information, plan sales analysis report, and presentation of merit award at the sales conference.	His notes read: Attend the meeting of the board on the tenth, contact AMS for convention information, plan sales analysis report, and present merit award at the sales conference.

It is important to enlist the
seniors, juniors, sophomores, and
the freshmen in student government.

Keep the motor in tiptop condition,
good tires, and a tankful of high
test.

It is important to enlist seniors,
juniors, sophomores, and freshmen
in student government.

Keep the motor in tiptop condition,
equip the car with good tires, and
fill the tank with high test.

This paragraph shows how a former President made effective use of parallel construction:

In a land of wealth, families must not live in hopeless poverty. In a land rich in harvest, children must not go hungry. In a land of healing miracles, neighbors must not suffer and die untended. In a land of learning, young people must be taught to read and write.

Lyndon B. Johnson
Inaugural speech, January 20, 1965

In forming sentences, do you get your meaning across by emphasizing the important points clearly for your reader? Can you use parallel construction to show that ideas have equal value? Find out by trying Skills Activity 18.

SKILLS ACTIVITY 18

A. The important point (underlined) is not emphasized in the following sentences. How would you correct them?

1. I believe that <u>your plan</u> will be accepted by the committee. _____

_____

2. We will respond <u>by telegram</u> as soon as we receive your request. _____

_____

3. It was announced that new <u>fringe benefits</u> would be included in the contract. _____

_____

4. It will be necessary that <u>the plans</u> for the next meeting be changed.

_____

_____

5. If all of us work together, a <u>clean environment</u> can be achieved.

_____

_____

6. The quarterly statement will show <u>a profit</u>, which will <u>please the shareholders</u>. _____

_____

7. There were a <u>number of people</u> in the audience who <u>disagreed</u> with the speaker. _____

_____

Check your answers with the answers on page 512. If you agree with the ideas presented in the key for five of the seven sentences, go on to the next activity. If you scored below Fair, review the answers and discuss your score with your instructor.

B. Are there errors in parallel construction in the following sentences?

1. I want to take this opportunity to remind you of the annual campaign of the City College Fund, which is now under way, and urging you to renew your generous support.

_____

_____

_____

Given seven sentences with problems in emphasis, rewrite the sentences to emphasize the underlined words.

Excellent   7
Good   6
Fair   5

Given eight sentences with problems in parallel construction, rewrite the sentences correctly.

Excellent   8
Good   6–7
Fair   5

Name _____ *Date* _____

2. Your thoughtful response in the past has enabled the Fund to open new avenues of opportunity for our students and provided direct financial aid for young men and women in need who would not otherwise have been able to continue their education.

_____

_____

_____

_____

3. Won't you take a moment to read it and send your check today to the City College Fund?

_____

_____

4. We offer attractive rates, steady employment, and our working conditions are pleasant.

_____

_____

5. We find that the Wick Investing Corp. incorporated under the laws of this state on June 21, 1970, filed a Certificate of Amendment with change of name, on September 2, 1974, name changed to Mountain Equities Inc.

_____

_____

_____

_____

_____

6. They must not only rewrite the material but the figures need to be verified.

_____

_____

7. We can either call a general meeting next month, or the committee can assume the responsibility for making the decision.

_____

_____

8. He is not only an excellent salesman but also has accounting skills.

_____

_____

If you achieved Fair or above, go on to the next part of the text. If you did not achieve Fair, discuss the problems with your instructor.

Avoid Fractured English

Correct use of antecedents, participles, and tenses and proper agreement of subject and verb are essentials of good, clear writing. If you break the principles of grammar, you are fracturing the English language.

ANTECEDENTS

> The teacher told the student that he would be
> finished at three.

Who would be finished at three—the teacher or the student?

> Mr. Johnson explained to the salesman that he
> would attend the sales conference in October.

Would Mr. Johnson attend the conference, or does "he" refer to the salesman?

By placing the pronoun near the antecedent to which it refers and by planning carefully that the pronoun cannot refer to anything else in the sentence, you will keep your message clear.

Check the revised sentences to see how they clarify the meaning:

Unclear	Clear
The teacher told the student that he would finish work at three.	The teacher said the student would finish work at three.
When Mr. Smith spoke to the treasurer, he told him that the figures were incorrect.	Mr. Smith spoke to the treasurer and told him that the figures were incorrect.

The word "this" in the second sentence of each of these reports is ambiguous:

Unclear	Clear
The president and the board of directors felt that the dispute between labor and management could be resolved quickly. This kept them in a relatively good frame of mind.	Because the president and the board of directors felt that the dispute between labor and management could be resolved quickly, they were in a relatively good frame of mind.

(Does "this" refer to the feeling or to the possibility of resolving the dispute?)

During the dissolution proceedings, the partners agreed to equal distribution of assets. This surprised their business associates.	Their business associates were surprised when, during the dissolution proceedings, the partners agreed to an equal distribution of assets.

(What surprised the associates? Was it the fact that the partners could agree on anything? Was it that the assets were to be distributed equally?)

Watch your antecedents; unclear reference can make your writing ambiguous. To check your ability to use antecedents correctly, try Skills Activity 19.

ambiguous: not clear in meaning

SKILLS ACTIVITY 19

Are the antecedents clear in these sentences? If not, correct the sentences.

1. When Mr. Saxon handed Mr. James the award, he smiled. _____
_____

2. Because John's father is a lawyer, he chose this as a profession. _____
_____

3. The managers told the foremen that they would make the decisions.
_____
_____ _____

4. The treasurer spoke to the bookkeeper who did not know what he was talking about. _____
_____

5. The auditor told the accountant that she could prepare the statements. _____
_____

6. The committee asked the group to meet tomorrow and to consider the possibility of weekly meetings hereafter. This is not possible.
_____
_____

7. The computer terminal is located in another building and is available only during certain hours. This slows our progress. _____
_____
_____

Given sentences with ambiguous antecedents, rewrite the sentences using the antecedents correctly.

Excellent   7
Good   6
Fair   5

Check your answers against the key, page 513. If you succeed in getting Fair or above, move on. If you fall below Fair, reread "Antecedents," and review the answers. Discuss any problems with your instructor.

Name_____ Date_____

PARTICIPLES

Did you ever read a sentence like this?

```
While walking down the street, a car hit the
man.
```

Obviously, the phrase "while walking down the street" is intended to refer to "man," but it actually modifies the subject—"car." Since a car cannot walk down the street, this construction is clearly an error. It is a common one in writing as well as in speaking.

You can solve the problem in several ways. Notice how each of the following revisions avoids the ambiguity of the original sentence:

```
While walking down the street, the man was hit
by a car.
```

```
As the man was walking down the street, a car
hit him.
```

Here is another example. Note the different meaning that is conveyed in the correct sentence.

```
When applying for a position, the
personnel director requires the
completion of an application blank.
```

```
When applying for a position, an
applicant is required to fill out an
application blank for the personnel
director.
```

(Is the personnel director applying for the position?)

A participle usually modifies the noun that it is closest to. Participles that do not sensibly belong to the noun they modify are called *dangling participles*. This error is common in business writing. To be sure that you can use participles correctly, practice in Skills Activity 20.

SKILLS ACTIVITY 20

Are the participles in these sentences dangling?

1. Flying high in the sky, I saw the plane. _____

   _____

2. Realizing that the report was late, it was filed with an explanation.

   _____

   _____

3. Reacting quickly to the crisis, the fuel allocation was increased.

   _____

   _____

4. Opening his remarks with a question, the audience listened attentively

   to the President. _____

   _____

5. Reviewing carefully the consumer reports on refrigerators, the C & D

   brand was bought. _____

   _____

6. Answering the letter, the book was sent by Ms. Miller's secretary.

   _____

   _____

7. When taking telephone messages, careful notes were typed by the

   secretary. _____

   _____

Check your answers against the key on page 513. If you achieve Fair or above, move on. If you are below Fair, review the answers carefully and reread the text on Participles. Discuss any problems with your instructor.

Name _____ *Date* _____

AGREEMENT

You know that the verb must agree with its subject. You say: *I do, you do, they do;* but *he does;* and *I am, you are, he is, they are.* Finding the subject sometimes requires special care. If you are aware of the most common difficulties, you can learn to solve them. For example, in the sentence, "I will buy one of the suits that are on sale," *that* refers to *suits* and takes the plural verb *are.* However, in this sentence, "In this scene Joe is the only one of the students who escapes," *who* refers to *one* and takes the singular verb *escapes.* Which verb is correct in each of these sentences?

> You are the only one of the many applicants who (has, have) been appointed.

> You are one of the many who (has, have) applied for federal jobs.

In the first sentence, since the antecedent of *who* is *many,* the verb must be *have.* You are correct if you picked *has* in the second sentence, because *who* refers to *one.*

Another problem you may have is distinguishing the subject from intervening additions. Note the subjects and verbs in the sentences below:

intervening: coming between

> The president, as well as the board members, <u>agrees</u> to this statement.

> The students, in cooperation with the teacher, <u>plan</u> the field trips for the class.

The subject is students.

> The society, in association with the business firms in the community, <u>sponsors</u> a yearly conference in retailing.

The subject is society.

> Mr. Richard Peters, together with his wife and family, <u>was invited</u> to join the club.

The subject is Mr. Peters.

You will check your ability to maintain agreement of subject and verb in Chapter 3, Focus on Language. Now go on to Tense.

TENSE

You know that verb tenses denote the *time* of an action, and you can choose easily among the past, present, and future tenses. But what do you do when you want to show whether one past action has preceded, occurred at the same time as, or followed another past action? Look at the following example:

denote: show; indicate

> At the end of the month, I paid my bill for everything I had bought during that month.

In this sentence, the writer has indicated that the action of buying preceded the action of paying the bill. This is shown by the use of the past tense—*paid*—and the past perfect tense—*had bought.*

Using the past perfect

Compare these sentences:

The student corrected all the errors that the instructor <u>marked</u> on the theme.	The student corrected all the errors that the instructor <u>had marked</u> on the theme.

Which action came first? Obviously, the instructor must have marked the errors before the student corrected them. To show this sequence, you must use the past perfect tense for the instructor's action.

The present perfect tense is useful for a different purpose. It enables you to show an action started in the past and completed at any unspecified time up to the present. Here are two sentences:

Prices <u>rose</u> on the stock exchange today.	Since January, when we sent you our estimate, prices <u>have risen</u>.

How the present perfect differs from the past

Both sentences speak about an action that was started and completed in the past—that is, before the moment at which the sentence was written. However, the sentences are different. The first sentence, which uses the past tense, indicates a *specific* time during which the action took place. By contrast, the second sentence, which uses the present perfect tense, indicates only that the action happened *sometime between January and now*.

Progressive forms

But what if you want to go further and say that prices are still going up? They went up this morning, they have gone up since this morning, and they are continuing to go up as you write the sentence. To show this sort of *continuing* action, you must use one of the *progressive* forms of the verb *rise*.

Prices <u>are rising</u> on the stock exchange today.

If you suspect that prices will stop going up shortly—or if you aren't sure—you might say:

Prices <u>have been rising</u> on the stock exchange today.

Forming the progressive

There are also other progressive forms: *will be rising* shows continuing action in the future; *had been rising* shows sustained action in the past.

You can see from these examples that the progressive forms are made by using some form of the verb *be* plus the present participle (the *ing* form) of the main verb.

Be sure that you understand these verb forms. If you use them properly, they will contribute to the precision of your writing and facilitate your reader's comprehension of it.

Can you use the correct tense to tell the reader what you mean? You will check this ability in Chapter 3, Focus on Language.

UNIT 11   PARAGRAPH TO FACILITATE READING

Your performance objective for this unit is:

Given the problem of structuring the complete message of the letter,
You will paragraph to facilitate the reader's comprehension.

You have learned the importance of choosing the right words and of forming them correctly into sentences. But there is another step you must take to write a good letter: paragraphing. Paragraphing facilitates the reader's comprehension of your message; it says, "Here are the organized parts of the whole." The unparagraphed letter appears as a mass of information that he will have to take apart to understand.

facilitates: makes easier

No formula determines how many paragraphs you should have or how long a paragraph should be, but the most important criterion is meaning. Each paragraph should have its own central idea or topic; a new topic usually calls for a new paragraph. Compare the unparagraphed and paragraphed forms of the letter shown in Figures 3–1 and 3–2.

criterion: standard or rule

Many business letters, however, are short and concern only one main topic, so a single paragraph should suffice. However, appearance is a second criterion of paragraphing. Even a short letter looks better if it contains more than one paragraph. In addition, you should try to keep your paragraphs short, since the eye is attracted to shorter units. This is especially true of the first paragraph; a long first paragraph is an obstacle the reader hesitates to encounter. When you paragraph correctly, you will like the break that white space gives, and so will your reader.

Try Skills Activity 21 to get some practice in paragraphing.

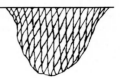

simms, inc.

896 Brattleboro Avenue
Boston, Massachusetts 02111
(617) TR 6-6700
showrooms: Middlebury, Vt. / Pittsfield, Mass.

May 15, 19--

Mr. James S. Johnson
70 Lincoln Street
Martins, VT 05201

Dear Mr. Johnson:

You and your friends are cordially invited to visit the new Simms
Showroom in Middlebury, Vermont, which was built in 1976 to celebrate our 100th anniversary. It is a red building of modern
architecture with casting pool and is located directly on U. S.
Route 7. Many visitors have commented, "It's the finest in the
East." The interior of the building is attractively paneled with
striated plywood, and it is uniquely lighted from overhead as well
as from wall showcases, the design of which came from England. A
large fireplace and confortable chairs make you feel at home.
Needless to say, we have a wide variety of the finest in fishing
tackle, including all the rods Simms makes, for your inspection
and actual trial in our pool outside; but, in addition to this,
the showcases are filled with a great assortment of imported
items. Country clothes and specialities -- collectors' items
such as Gibbs' minature birds and rare crystal jewelry -- will
keep your interest high as you look around. Right off this main
showroom is a new women's shop in which the women in your party
can browse. They will see beautiful imported sweaters, skirts,
and jackets. Our showroom has something to interest and please
the whole family. We are open Monday through Saturday all year
'round. Come to see us.

Cordially yours,

Frank Stampler
Showroom Manager

hf

Figure 3-1
A Mass of Information Is Uninviting

simms, inc.

896 Brattleboro Avenue
Boston, Massachusetts 02111
(617) TR 6-6700
showrooms: Middlebury, Vt. / Pittsfield, Mass.

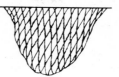

May 15, 19--

Mr. James S. Johnson
70 Lincoln Street
Martins, VT 05201

Dear Mr. Johnson:

You and your friends are cordially invited to visit the new Simms
Showroom in Middlebury, Vermont, which was built in 1976 to cele-
brate our 100th anniversary. It is a red building of modern
architecture with a casting pool and is located directly on U. S.
Route 7. Many visitors have commented, "It's the finest in the
East."

The interior of the building is attractively paneled with striated
plywood, and it is uniquely lighted from overhead as well as from
wall showcases, the design of which came from England. A large
fireplace and comfortable chairs make you feel at home.

Needless to say, we have a wide variety of the finest in fishing
tackle, including all the rods Simms makes, for your inspection
and actual trial in our pool outside; but, in addition to this, the
showcases are filled with a great assortment of imported items.
Country clothes and specialities -- collectors' items such as
Gibbs' minature birds and rare crystal jewelry -- will keep your
interest high as you look around.

Right off this main showroom is a new women's shop in which the
women in your party can browse. They will see beautiful imported
sweaters, skirts, and jackets.

Our showroom has something to interest and please the whole family.
We are open Monday through Saturday all year 'round. Come to see
us.

Cordially yours,

Frank Stampler
Frank Stampler
Showroom Manager

hf

Figure 3-2
The Value of Paragraphing

SKILLS ACTIVITY 21

Here is a letter which was sent to a client of a brokerage firm.

It is with great pleasure that we announce to our clients that as of January 2, 1978, our firm will join the well-known New York Stock Exchange member firm Halsey and Moore. Our headquarters will be at a new branch office of the firm of Halsey and Moore at 535 Madison Avenue; our telephone number will be 753-4300. We plan to occupy this space on January 3, 1978, or as soon thereafter as practicable. Your representatives and the present senior partners, who will become limited partners of Halsey and Moore, will handle your accounts and will continue to provide all the services we have provided in the past. Our research and floor partners will be general partners at the main office of Halsey and Moore at 30 Broad Street. We hope that the confidence you have shown in us for 30 years will continue, and we wish to extend to you at this time the season's greetings and our best wishes for a healthy, prosperous, and happy New Year.

Name_____ Date_____

Check the key on page 513. Note the explanations. Do you agree with the authors? If you did not agree on three of the four paragraphs, discuss your problems with your instructor.

UNIT 12 CHECK THE ACCURACY OF FACTS, FIGURES, AND DETAILS

Your performance objective for this unit is:

Given the problem of ensuring the accuracy of business communications,

You will check to make sure that dates, figures, and facts are accurate, and that grammar, spelling, and punctuation are correct.

Business demands accuracy. Writing letters entails the responsibility of checking every fact, every figure, every word. Develop the habits of careful proofreading, of looking up information, of confirming figures and dates. For you to *think* it's correct indicates that you are a marginal employee, the first to go when your employer can find someone better. The worker who *knows* the work is right has reached a level of competence that leads to positions of higher responsibility.

marginal: lower limit of qualification, acceptability, or function

Errors may be expensive—a misplaced decimal point or comma can cost your employer many hundreds of dollars. The secretary who wrote "1,000 barrels of oil" instead of "100 barrels" could hardly believe that one little zero could so disrupt the plant's operations. There was no place to store the extra 900 barrels. The company's fire-insurance policy would not cover an accidental fire under these conditions. The delivery was made on Friday, and a regular pickup could not be made until the following Monday morning. What happened? The extra 900 barrels were returned at the expense of a special trucking service at overtime pay.

decimal point: dot at left of a decimal fraction

With modern data-processing, errors are even more costly; that same misplaced decimal point can cause millions of other complications at the flick of a switch. How can you avoid errors? Simply make it a habit to check your facts and figures carefully. When you enclose a check for $65.56, compare that figure with the original bill. You can easily reverse figures without knowing that you did it.

Always double check figures.

Another common error is the day-date mixup. The invitation to the office party read, "Be sure to come on Friday, December 12." The phone rang all morning, and important tasks had to be put off. The frantic secretary should have made a tape recording of the answer that had to be given to all callers: "Sorry, the date is *Thursday*, December 12, same time, same place." Add to the cost of the office party the time, the phone calls, the irritation, and the work interruption caused by that simple error.

An incorrect letter of the alphabet can change the meaning of a phrase. Take the embarrassment caused by the letter sent to a group of experienced reporters who were honoring a colleague at a dinner. The man to be feted was described as: "A reformed actor, bon vivant, and raconteur, and a degenerate city editor." Several hundred letters were mailed before someone caught the mistake. The typist should have typed "regenerate city editor." But this was a word he did not know. What should he have done? Because he was in doubt, he should have looked it up; and, if he was still unsure, he should have asked his supervisor. Why don't you check the meaning of those two words? Would you have been embarrassed?

colleague: fellow worker; associate

Always check your spelling.

A cursory reading will not always catch the misuse of a word. Catch this one if you can:

cursory: brief or hasty

> The members were invited to attend an
> an open meeting of the board.

If you were alert, you saw the two *an*'s, one at the end of the line and the other at the beginning of the next line.

A professor affixed her signature to a letter in which her secretary failed to correct this sentence:

> The event has past, and we must move forward to
> better things.

The verb *passed* should have been used. *Past* is either a noun ("His *past* came before him") or an adjective ("*Past* events proved this to be true").

You must check grammar, spelling, punctuation, and usage as you write. You must double check all facts and figures. And you must always proofread carefully. Be sure that your written communications are correct in every way.

Are you alert? Can you correct the errors that occur in business letters and correct them? First read the Summary, then check your success in Focus on Language.

SUMMARY

You will be on your way to successful letter-writing if you will spend some time in thought before you sit down at the typewriter. Your preliminary work must include a careful outlining of the points you wish to discuss so that you will be certain to include all necessary information and to exclude extraneous material.

Then, when you write the first sentence, get to the purpose of the letter immediately.

Next, choose words and phrases that have precise meanings, and avoid generalities that keep your reader guessing. If you rely on the dictionary and thesaurus, you will use your words correctly and add variety to your language. And remember, you can make context work with you to achieve clarity and brevity.

Use simple, compound, and complex sentences not only to add variety to your style but also to enhance the meaning of the message itself.

As you write, organize your sentences into one-idea paragraphs to aid your reader's understanding.

Before you mail anything you have written, check the accuracy of facts, figures, and details. So important is accuracy in the business world that you must make checking and proofreading one of the integral parts of writing. No letter should be signed and mailed unless you are certain that it is correct.

Now you are ready for Focus on Language. You will review 49 vocabulary and spelling words, formation of possessives, agreement of subject and verb, and tense. You will also check your ability to proofread accurately.

FOCUS ON LANGUAGE

Spelling

1. comparitive _____
2. judgment _____
3. delete _____
4. accidently _____
5. colleague _____
6. laison _____
7. decimal _____
8. parellel _____

9. qualifying _____
10. consistant _____
11. garantee _____
12. advertisment _____
13. copous _____
14. redundent _____
15. catologs _____

> *Given 15 words, some of which are misspelled, write the misspelled words correctly.*
>
> *Excellent   14–15*
> *Good   12–13*
> *Fair   10–11*

Check the key on page 513. If you achieved Fair or above, go on to the next exercise. If your score was below Fair, review the spelling of the words you missed. Have someone read these words to you as you write or type them. Check. Repeat the procedure until you can spell every word correctly.

Vocabulary

You used the following words in this chapter. Can you identify their meanings?

1. novice   a. idea   b. distributor   c. quotation   d. beginner
2. liability   a. criterion   b. antecedent   c. disadvantage   d. requisite
3. copious   a. plentiful   b. ambiguous   c. redundant   d. marginal
4. digress   a. stray   b. denotes   c. digest   d. claim
5. relevant   a. comparative   b. related   c. revealing   d. elevated
6. extraneous   a. qualifying   b. more   c. within   d. unrelated
7. facilitate   a. convey   b. fascinate   c. make easy   d. hasten
8. nominal   a. slight   b. coordinating   c. decimal   d. careful
9. colleagues   a. friends   b. co-workers   c. socialites   d. college students
10. cursory   a. definite   b. careful   c. hasty   d. curving

> *Given 10 words with a choice of four meanings each, circle the letter of the word that is closest in meaning to the first word.*
>
> *Excellent   10*
> *Good   9*
> *Fair   8*

Check the key on page 513. If you achieved Fair or above, go on to the next exercise. If your score was below Fair, review the meanings of the words you missed. Write a sentence using each word you missed. Ask your instructor to evaluate your sentences and to discuss any errors with you.

Name _____ Date _____

Sound-Alikes

Words that sound alike often trouble us. As we go along, we will be checking on a number of these bothersome terms. The four pairs for this chapter are:

principle, principal

stationery, stationary

affect, effect

personnel, personal

Study their meanings below before you do the exercises.

principal

1. a man or woman
   The principal of the school is the person in charge.
   A principal can appoint an agent—someone to act for him or her.

2. an amount of money
   You put an amount of money in your savings account. This principal earns interest for you.

3. an adjective meaning "main"
   What is the principal city in Nebraska?

principle

This word means only one thing: "rule."
   What principle guides your life?
   This principle of law protects women and minorities.
(One way of remembering these words is to think of the *a* in the last syllable of princip*a*l and the *a*'s in m*a*n, wom*a*n, *a*mount, and m*a*in. Think of the *le* at the end of princip*le* and of ru*le*.)

stationery

letter paper. (Note the *e* near the end of station*e*ry and the *e*'s in l*e*tt*e*r.)

stationary

standing still. (Note the *a* at the end of station*a*ry and the *a* in st*a*nd.)

affect

to produce a change. (Note the *a* in *a*ffect and in ch*a*nge.)

effect

1. as a noun, as a result.

2. as a verb, to bring about a result. (Note the *e* in *e*ffect and in r*e*sult.)

personnel

1. as a noun, persons employed in a business.

2. as an adjective, pertaining to persons employed in a business.

personal

private; individual; belonging to one person.

Can you use the following sound-alikes correctly?

1. Interest of 4 percent is earned on the (*principal, principle*).
2. The (*principal, principle*) spoke to the senior class.
3. Do you think we can (*affect, effect*) some changes in procedure during the next month?
4. A (*personal, personnel*) letter to your representative in Congress may (*affect, effect*) his or her vote on the amendment.
5. This is the (*principal, principle*) reason for our writing.
6. The appearance of your (*stationary, stationery*) (*effects, affects*) the reader.
7. The new revenue law may (*affect, effect*) the outcome of the election.
8. The (*personal, personnel*) manager explains the (*principals, principles*) of management to the audience.
9. Their position remained (*stationary, stationery*) for three years.
10. The (*stationary, stationery*) department in their Pittsburgh store has been their (*principal, principle*) source of revenue.
11. Our class president is a young man of high (*principal, principle*).
12. An agent has the power to make contracts for his (*principals, principles*).

> Given pairs of words that sound alike, underline the correct word in each sentence.
>
> Excellent   15-16
> Good   13-14
> Fair   11-12

Check the key on page 513. If you did not achieve Fair or above, review the definitions. Write each word that you had incorrect in a sentence. Ask your instructor to correct your sentences and to discuss any errors with you. If you achieved Fair or above, go on to the next exercise.

Agreement of Subject and Verb

Let's clear up some of the common difficulties concerning agreement. The "heart" of a sentence is the agreement of the subject and the predicate. Your first step is to identify the subject. Is it singular (one) or plural (more than one)? A singular subject takes a singular form of the verb; a plural subject takes a plural form of the verb.

Rule: *Words that come between the subject and the predicate do not affect the number of the verb.*

The men who play on the team are our employees.

The subject is *men*; therefore, the verb must be plural—*are*.

The manager, together with his assistants and advisers, has written the report.

The subject is *manager*; therefore, *has*, the singular verb, is needed.

Name _____ *Date* _____

Rule: *When two or more subjects are joined by* and, *whether the subjects are singular or plural, they form a* compound subject *which is always plural.*

Mary and Jack have formed the new club.

More than one has formed the club; therefore use the plural verb.

Let's apply these rules. How well can you achieve agreement between your subject and verb in these sentences?

1. The proposal to offer stock options to all officers of the company (*was, were*) opposed by minority shareholders.

2. The file on James and Smith (*doesn't, don't*) seem to be in the proper place.

3. The retention of a major portion of our earnings (*has, have*) helped build the new factory.

4. The engineer, as well as the superintendent, (*was, were*) present at the meeting.

5. One of the senior accountants employed at the company headquarters (*has, have*) prepared these reports.

6. Mr. Jones, accompanied by his secretary, (*has, have*) arrived at the office.

7. The report and the statements of the people involved in the accident (*has, have*) been studied.

The answers are on page 513. Evaluate your success. If you achieve Fair or above, continue with the activity on tense. If you fall below Fair, reread the material on Agreement and review the answers in the key. Discuss any problems with your instructor.

Tense

Remember that the dictionary, which gives the principal parts of verbs, can be of help in writing the correct tense.

1. Watch me. First I (place) the cup on the table. _____

2. Yesterday, he (interview) the applicant. _____

3. Last night the temperature (drop) 20 degrees. _____

4. At this time, the snow (fall) for four hours. _____

5. As I am writing, prices (rise). _____

6. Yesterday when the rain (stop), I (go) home. _____

7. Last Monday, when I (take) the employment test, the personnel director (interview) me. _____

8. Whatever errors he (make) up to this time, he (make) up for them now. _____

Check the key on page 513. If you achieved Fair or above, go on to Possessives. If you did not achieve Fair or above, discuss your problems with the instructor.

Possessives

In Unit 6, we noted the use of singular and plural possessives. Can you form possessives correctly? Remember these simple rules:

Rule: *Add 's to the singular noun if it ends with any letter but* s, *or if it is a one-syllable noun ending in* s. *To nouns of more than one syllable that end in* s, *you need add only an apostrophe.*

woman's heart; dealer's stock; boss's desk; James's office; Jonas' kitten

Rule: *Add only an apostrophe to plural nouns ending in* s. *Add 's to plural nouns not ending in* s.

collectors' coins; parents' attitudes; the Jamesons' house; women's shop

Revise the following sentences so that they use the possessive case, as in the following example:

The books of the girls are in the library.
The girls' books are in the library.

> *Given sentences in which the possessive case is to be used, write the correct form in the space provided.*
>
> | | |
> |---|---|
> | *Excellent* | *7* |
> | *Good* | *6* |
> | *Fair* | *5* |

1. The library of the children is open during the afternoon.

   _____

2. The fur of the fox has a glossy sheen.

   _____

3. They had a special sale on hats for women.

   _____

4. The son of Mr. Jones spent several days in Canada.

   _____

5. Inventories of the dealers must be reduced.

   _____

6. The boss of Miss Simmons offered her a promotion.

   _____

7. The statement of the accountant had an error in addition.

   _____

Name _____ Date _____

Check the key on page 513. If you achieved Fair or above, note the errors and go on to the next activity. If you fell below Fair, review the rules above and review the answers. Discuss any problems with your instructor.

Given an exercise with errors, identify and correct them by writing in the space directly above the error.

Excellent	*10-12*
Good	*7-9*
Fair	*6-8*

Proofreading

The following memo has been typed for the president to send out to his employees. You are to check it for accuracy before it is duplicated and distributed. Use your dictionary if you need it.

To the Members of the Staff:

Once more it is my privilidge and obliation to report to you the results of our operations during the passed year as they effect our Profit-Sharing Plan.

The too categories of principle interest to you involve the following figures:

1. a payment to you Fund for the year of 15% of 1974 compensation;

2. a dollar value per unite as of November 30, 1975, of $18.08.

Evaluate your success in proofreading by checking the key on page 513. If you achieved Fair or above, go on to Chapter 4. If you fell below Fair, discuss your work with your instructor.

4

YOUR READER'S RESPONSE

A good business letter does not merely transmit information; it begins or continues a relationship between you and your reader. Of course, you want your reader to understand your message; but you want to accomplish more than that. You intend your letter to arouse the reader's interest and to elicit a positive response from him or her. You want the reader to act on your proposal, buy your merchandise, accept your apology. Whether or not you are successful depends on the impression your words make. Ideas cannot always speak for themselves; the way you present your message, the point of view from which you write, and the impression of you that your words evoke—all these play a part in the success of your communication.

elicit: draw out

evoke: to call forth; to bring out

The chapter breaks into two units:

Unit 13   Spotlight the Reader

Unit 14   Choose Your Language with a Purpose

UNIT 13   SPOTLIGHT THE READER

Your performance objectives for Unit 13 are:

Given problems of emphasizing the reader's point of view in writing business messages,

You will use four approaches to write effective sentences that focus on the reader.

First, and most important, write with the reader in mind. We all see from our own point of view. We may be influenced by others, pressured by circumstances, tamed by culture; we may be sympathetic and altruistic, but we are each the center of our own world. So, too, the reader is the core of his or her world. To get your message read and acted upon, put the reader in the center of the stage—tell what your message can do for him or her, answer questions, use language that is meaningful.

altruistic: concerned with the well-being of others; benevolent

Address Yourself to Your Reader's Interests

Use *you* and *your*, not *I, we, my, our*. This puts you and the reader in the right frame of mind. Notice how the sentences at the right improve the original sentences at the left:

We are delighted to have customers write us to ask about our personal bank loans.	You may take out a personal bank loan up to $1,000 by visiting us tomorrow.
We appreciate the order for one dozen blue plaid shirts and will be pleased to send them immediately.	Your order for one dozen blue plaid shirts is on its way to you today. Thank you.

Remember, your letter will get a better response if it impresses the reader with his or her importance and with your concern for him or her.

benefit; benefited

Also, show your readers how you are serving them. You write to benefit yourself and your business; but you will be benefited most if you can convince your readers that what you propose is to their advantage. For example, compare the following approaches to the dunning notice. Which message would get your vote?

We wish to have a check to meet your overdue account so that we can bring our books into balance for our annual audit.	Your check in the mail before June 30 will maintain the sound credit rating of your business. Of course, your credit reputation is a valuable asset that you want to preserve; but your account is now three months past due. Please don't delay another day.

audit: to examine and certify accounts

The businessperson in financial difficulty would not care whether or not the creditor's annual audit was taking place. But a firm cannot afford to lose its own credit standing—it could mean loss of business. Credit allows a firm to stock what is needed and to pay for it later, out of the income from future sales. The second approach would get our vote. Did it get yours?

Now consider this paragraph from a sales letter:

The new Scout is the best car we have ever made. We know that it is better than any other car on the market today. We are offering a special trade-in on your old Scout and a low price on the new model.

Your boast certainly doesn't interest the reader. How about this instead?

Give yourself the pleasure of driving the new
Scout. As the owner of a 1976 Scout, you will
realize the greater efficiency, finer performance, and improved safety of the new model. By
trading your old Scout this month, you will get
the highest price toward purchasing the new
safer Scout with the high gas mileage.

Greater safety, more effective performance, special trade-in bonus are
all available to the new Scout owner.

   What would you do with this opening to redirect the major interest
to the reader?

The enclosed brochure, <u>Priceless Holidays</u>,
contains 42 pages describing exciting travel
adventures, including trips to many world capitals, priced as low as $599 for 15 days.

*Underline titles of pam-
phlets and brochures (or
type in capital letters).*

One answer might be:

See the capitals of the world. You've begun your
trip when you read <u>Priceless Holidays</u>. From 42
pages of travel adventures, you will be able to
select a tour that excites the imagination. Just
think -- you may choose a vacation trip of 15
days for as little as $599.

capitals

Now that you have gained some insight into the importance of focusing
on the reader, can you identify sentences that do not do so, can you
state why they fail, and can you rewrite them? Try Skills Activity 22 to
check your success.

SKILLS ACTIVITY 22

Do these sentences focus on the reader?

_____ 1. We are happy to send our new price list to all our customers.

_____

_____ 2. This new model is our latest in a long series of "firsts" in the industry. We were first in producing a low-cost radio. We made the first portable television. Now we are first in portable color television.

_____

_____ 3. _Good Times_ has been read by thousands of people who have benefited from its excellent suggestions. They have always found dozens of ideas for making their money stretch by reading our fine publication.

_____

_____ 4. I am applying for the position of junior accountant in your office. I feel that my grades prove that I am intelligent and capable, and I know I can do a good job for you.

_____

_____ 5. We are happy to send the claim payment within ten days of the receipt of your claim. This proves just how great our service is.

_____

_____ 6. Our car gives you the best gas mileage, the smoothest ride, and the best service contract of any car on the market.

_____

_____ 7. I know this trip to Paris will be the high point of your life.

_____

> _Given seven business messages, identify accurately those that do not focus on the reader by placing O next to the number and stating your reasons in the space after the sentence._
>
> | | |
> |---|---|
> | _Excellent_ | _7_ |
> | _Good_ | _6_ |
> | _Fair_ | _5_ |

Check your answers with the key on page 513. Note differences and evaluate your score. If it was below Fair, discuss any problems with your instructor. Now go on to the next part.

In the space below, rewrite the sentences that do not focus on the reader to make them more effective.

Name _____ _Date_ _____

Given sentences that do not focus on the reader, rewrite them so that they achieve this objective.

Peer judgment or instructor evaluation:

Excellent   7
Good   5–6
Fair   4

_____
_____
_____
_____
_____
_____
_____
_____
_____

A committee of four or five students working together in class can judge each other's work. The instructor's judgment may be substituted.

If you score Fair to Excellent, continue with the second approach to spotlighting the reader. If you scored below Fair, review Unit 13 and the answers to Skills Activity 22 before continuing. Discuss any problems with your instructor.

Enter the Reader's World

This second approach to spotlighting the reader relates the message directly to the reader's interest in order to obtain a positive response.

How do you know what the reader wants to know, how he or she feels about price, what is the best way to serve him or her?

Look through former correspondence with this reader if there is any. Is this an old customer or a new one? Is your customer a man or woman? Engaged in what business or profession? Does the style of writing give you any clues to the individual's personality? Is it usual for this customer to delay in paying bills?

engaged

Take the case of Paula, a clerk who was hired for the summer months and therefore did not know the business or its customers. Trying to impress Mr. Richards, her employer, with her efficiency, she mailed out second notices at the end of a ten-day waiting period with a typed remark: "Did you forget? Your bill is overdue!" One customer of 20 years' standing, piqued by this, sent in a check, the second notice, and a note addressed to the owner that read: "No, I did not forget, but you can forget to include me in your list of customers for the fall season." The owner immediately called to apologize to this good customer, who had been one of the first buyers of this neighborhood store. He knew that she was away during the summer months, but the new clerk had not checked with him.

immediately

Anticipate your reader's reaction to your statements. How can you do this? Write as if you were looking at the reader. Will you get a smile or a frown? Will you get cooperation or a rebuff? Will you get action or delay?

rebuff: an abrupt refusal

Reach into your own experience to develop an understanding of your reader's reaction. If you remember how you felt when you did not receive one of your textbooks on time, you will know how to answer the angry complaint you receive as part-time assistant in the college bookstore. You would not irritate the student with a postcard saying:

```
The textbook you ordered has not come in. The
expected delivery date is February 15.
```

February

You would assuage the customer with the message:

assuage: soothe

```
You can pick up your textbook on February 15.
Your instructor knows that the book will not be
available until that date.
```

Another part of writing from the reader's point of view is awareness that his or her background and interests may be different from yours. Your business, like every other field of endeavor, has its own specialized vocabulary. Will your reader understand that vocabulary? As a stockbroker, for instance, would you write this letter to a beginning college student?

We recommend the purchase of Ajax common stock
for long-term capital gains. The stock has a 4:1
ratio by 1976 projections, a low evaluation by
historical standards. A capital expenditure of
$900 million to develop new energy products
suggests a base adequate to support a doubling
of the price of Ajax within the next two years.

*Note that "million" is usu-
ally written out to avoid
many zeros.*

If you did, it might not make much sense to the student. To the
sophisticated investor, this language is clear; but the college student
would better understand the language of the following letter:

Begin your investment program with the purchase
of shares of Ajax, a stock that should make
your money grow. The currect price of the stock
is low in comparison to the firm's probable
earnings this year. In addition, Ajax is introducing many new energy products that will have
broad appeal to customers. Sales and profits
should increase enough to cause the price of
Ajax to double within the next two years.

Thus, the stockbroker must write different letters to the international
banker and the inexperienced student, to the new investor and the active
customer. So you, too, must use your own experience and your knowledge of people's reactions to meet them at their level of interest. Can
you enter the reader's world and rewrite a letter that addresses itself to
the reader's interests? Let's try it in Skills Activity 23.

SKILLS ACTIVITY 23

Here is a letter to a college student who wrote to a broker to ask about buying ten shares of Goode Electric Power Company stock. Does it enter the reader's world?

Yes _____   No _____   Partly _____

What changes, if any, would you make in it?

Dear Harold:

Thank you for your letter asking our opinion about your purchasing ten shares of Goode Electric Company stock.

The performance of the stock has been rather erratic of late. Undoubtedly it has been subjected to selling pressure by people taking tax losses.

However, its P/E ratio is now only 15 to 1, which we consider to be quite favorable under the circumstances. We do not foresee that the stock should decline much more. As a matter of fact, our projections indicate that the company has an excellent future.

Congratulations on wanting to buy stock for your future. But if you are a minor, you cannot purchase the shares yourself. An adult will have to open a custodial account for your benefit. We will be glad to help you in any way.

Sincerely yours,

Name _____ Date _____

Check with the key on page 514 to see how closely you agree with the authors. Discuss any disagreements with your instructor.

In the space below rewrite the letter.

_____

_____

_____

_____

_____

_____

_____

_____

_____

_____

_____

_____

_____

_____

_____

_____

_____

_____

_____

_____

_____

_____

_____

_____

_____

_____

_____

_____

_____

Given a letter in which parts of it do not enter the reader's world, rewrite the sentences that need improvement and list sentences to be omitted.

For a check with the author's point of view, see page 514. If you have scored Fair to Excellent according to the key and your instructor's judgment, go on to the next section. If you scored below Fair, discuss your problem with your instructor.

To Your Reader Be True

This is the third approach in writing business messages that keep the reader in focus.

When you write that an order will be shipped next week, is this just a delaying action to keep your customer from going to your competitor? Are you planning to write again next week to say that there has been an unfortunate delay for another week? How would you feel if someone played this game with you? Such a lack of integrity causes loss of respect for your company. It also takes away your customer's right to make a decision that may be urgent; through subterfuge, you have forced the customer to wait two weeks for an order.

integrity: honesty

subterfuge: strategem to avoid unpleasantness or difficulty

When Joe Clark, the new clerk, received this order letter, he was concerned because the delivery could not be made:

```
Please send the electric clock radio No. 6680
for $22.95 which is advertised in your Christmas
brochure on page 16. Here is my check for $22.95.
```

What should Joe tell the customer? This was his answer:

```
Dear Madam:

Your order for the elctric clock radio and your
check were received today.

The order will be filled as soon as possible.

                    Very truly yours,
```

The clerk submitted the letter to his supervisor, who suggested the following:

```
Dear Mrs. Jones:

Thank you for your order for the electric clock
radio.

Unfortunately, there has been a delay in our
shipment. We will notify you as soon as the
order goes out, which should be within a week
or two.

We are sorry for this delay.

                    Very truly yours,
```

Notify customer of delay.

Apologize.

Before the letter was mailed, Sheila Ross, the sales manager, made a special request to the office manager. Noting that the shipment had been hijacked and that the order was to be duplicated, she requested all clerks to refer orders for the electric clock radio to her. This was her answer to Mrs. Jones:

Dear Mrs. Jones:

Your electric clock radio No. 6680 will be shipped on December 20.

Give explanation whenever possible.

The hijacking of our truck on December 10 prevented your receiving the radio on time, but the manufacturer is duplicating the shipment immediately. We are sorry for this delay.

We shall not cash your check for $22.95 until the order is shipped.

Sincerely,

The third letter gives the reader a clear understanding of the situation and the reason for it. She can accept the delay or cancel her order.

You must believe that what you are writing is true—that the car will give safety and top performance at a low price, that you will pay on August 31, that the order will be shipped on December 20. If it is not true, the deception will soon be discovered; and the relationship between you and your reader will be destroyed.

Use semicolon before a conjunction when a comma is used in either independent clause of a compound sentence.

For example, when a businessperson purchases something on credit, he or she has established a relationship with the creditor that is important to the business. If he or she cannot pay the bill on time, how can that good relationship be preserved? What about this letter?

Please give us an extension of 60 days on our account. We have run into a serious problem. As you know, tight mortgage money has slowed down construction of new homes in Allentown, so that our heating units have remained unsold.

We expect to be able to pay our account in full by August 31.

incurred

Think of the angry collection letters that need not be written, the expense of writing them that will not be incurred, and the reassurance the creditor now has that the customer is honest and is not merely trying to avoid payment.

Truthfulness goes hand in hand with sincerity. The following sentence from a form letter is an insult to the reader's intelligence:

> I am writing this letter to you personally to give you an opportunity to subscribe to our magazine, <u>News from the Capitol</u>, at a reduced rate.

capitol

The reader knows that thousands of copies of this letter are being mailed. Therefore, he or she will ascribe to everything that follows the same lack of sincerity found in this first sentence. Interest in the reader must be genuine, or it will backfire.

ascribe: consider as belonging

Now that you have some understanding of the ways in which the relationship between the writer and the reader can deteriorate through lack of integrity, you will be able to judge competently messages that exaggerate the truth and to improve these messages to maintain the reader's belief in the integrity of the writer. Check your competence in Skills Activity 24.

SKILLS ACTIVITY 24

Do these statements ring true? Place 0 at the left of each sentence that does *not* sound true and + at the left of each sentence that does sound true.

_____ 1. Although delays in shipment are normal at this time of the year, we will see to it that your orders are the first to leave our shipping room.

_____ 2. Yours is the first complaint our store has ever received.

_____ 3. Place your account with Withers and Company, and watch your money grow. We don't make mistakes.

_____ 4. You can borrow up to $25,000 with no problems.

_____ 5. Our shoes outlast all others in comfort and durability.

_____ 6. We can give you the job of your choice. Apply.

_____ 7. You will be entitled to a 2 percent discount if you pay before the tenth of the month following the date of the bill.

> *Given seven sentences that may or may not exaggerate the truth, judge accurately the sentences that do and do not.*
>
> *Excellent 7*
> *Good 6*
> *Fair 5*

Check the key on page 514. Note any differences of opinion between you and the authors, and discuss major disagreements with your instructor. Now, in the space below, rewrite five of the sentences that did not sound true.

_____

_____

_____

_____

_____

_____

_____

_____

> *Given five sentences that do not sound true, rewrite them so that they maintain the integrity of the writer.*
>
> *Peer judgment or your instructor's evaluation:*
>
> *Excellent 5*
> *Good 4*
> *Fair 3*

If you scored Fair to Excellent, continue with the fourth approach to focusing on the reader. If you scored below Fair, reread To Your Reader Be True and review Skills Activity 24 before continuing with the fourth approach. Discuss any problems with your instructor.

Name _____ *Date* _____

Remember the Amenities

This is the fourth and final approach to keeping your attention on the reader.

How do you react to these commands?

Pick up the papers on the floor.

Answer the phone.

Close the file drawer.

Do you feel that the person issuing such orders is imposing on you? These peremptory statements can be softened by the addition of "please" or "will you."

peremptory: commanding

In your business communications, too, you must preface your request with the magic word "please." No matter how interested you are in brevity, this word may not be omitted.

Courtesy also requires an apology for an oversight, a late response, a negative reaction, or an error. The customer's anger is dissipated with "I am sorry" or "I apologize."

dissipated: dissolved

Finally, include a "thank you" for your reader's assistance, for the action that was taken, for the time and attention that was given to a proposal. Otherwise, you will be guilty of being discourteous.

To be courteous is easy, but it's also easy to forget. Let's check ourselves in Skills Activity 25.

SKILLS ACTIVITY 25

If you remember the amenities, you can make these messages sound friendlier.

1. Send me the travel folder you advertised in *This Week.*

_____

2. We have received your order of February 20.

_____

3. Will you consider my application for employment?

_____

4. Your account is now up to date.

_____

5. Return the questionnaire to us soon so that we can publish our findings early next year.

_____

6. Don't forget to order soon.

  ,_____

7. Your materials have been located in another department. This will cause some delay in checking their suitability.

_____

> Given seven sentences that do not contain the amenities, include them in the space beneath each sentence.
>
> | | |
> |---|---|
> | Excellent | 7 |
> | Good | 6 |
> | Fair | 5 |

Check yourself with the key on page 514. If you scored below Fair, review the worksheet carefully and discuss your score with the instructor.

Name _____ *Date* _____

UNIT 14 CHOOSE YOUR LANGUAGE WITH A PURPOSE

This unit is divided into two parts:

Language that gives a picture of you, and

Language to create interest.

At the completion of the unit, you will achieve the following performance objectives:

Given business communications that contain outmoded, trite expressions,

You will recognize such expressions and revise each by using correct modern, updated language.

Given sentences and paragraphs that are weak in the mechanics of language (sentence length, varying sentence structure, continuity, verbs of being or action, active and passive voice, concrete expressions versus abstract statements),

You will identify the weaknesses and rewrite such sentences and paragraphs using correct language to attain reader's interest.

Language That Gives a Picture of You

You have learned the importance of writing from the reader's point of view. Even when you do that, however, your letter will give the reader a picture of you. What kind of impression will that be?

Recently the director of a large summer resort catering to varying age groups received this letter and assigned the three vacationers to Cottage 148 on the far side of the lake.

```
                         386 East Avenue
                         Aro, Wisconsin    53289
                         July 30, 19--


Winnebago Resort
Fond du Lac
Wisconsin    53276

Dear Sir:

     Re your advertisement on Vacation Lakes in
the travel section of the Times, I would like to
reserve a cottage on the lake for the two weeks,
August 15th to August 31st. The cottage must
have at least three bedrooms, inasmuch as there
will be three of us renting it.
```

Would you write Wisconsin or WI?

Would you use this salutation?

Would you use re*?*

15th; 31st
inasmuch

*pursuant; stated require-
ments; remainder*

I remain

> Pursuant to the stated requirements, I am enclosing my check in the amount of $50.00 as down payment and will pay the remainder upon our arrival on August 15th.
>
> Looking forward to a delightful vacation, I remain,
>
> Very truly yours,
>
> *Ilka Krauss*
>
> Ilka Krauss

The three occupants of Cottage 148 were surprised to find that they had been placed with the more mature vacationers—those 60 years old and older. But the director of the resort was even more startled to see three unhappy young 20-year-olds crossing the bridge as they made their way into the office to complain about their assignment to the quiet side of the lake. But the letter had been written in language of the nineteenth century—surely no modern young woman would have used such outdated expressions, such old-fashioned form. Red-faced, Ilka realized that she had followed the pattern used by her own employer.

trite: made commonplace by repetition

The business world is populated by many Ilkas who imitate the past and by many employers who make frequent use of outdated, trite expressions. These expressions tell the reader that he or she is communicating with an old, staid stick-in-the-mud. What do you think of these expressions taken from typical business letters? Would they be used in face-to-face conversation? What improvement in language can you suggest?

Worn-out expressions	Suggested revisions
Re your letter of the tenth, I would like to order the textbook.	Please send the textbook.
inasmuch as	because _or_ since
in accordance with the requirements	as required
I am enclosing herewith	here is
thanking you in advance, I remain	thank you
In reply to your letter, I believe that we can make an adjustment forthwith.	Your account was adjusted today. (We adjusted your account today.)
We acknowledge the receipt of your check for $10.	Thank you for your check for $10.

We are in receipt of your order.	You will receive the calculator in ten days.
you will please find enclosed	here is
due to the fact that	because
in accordance with the	according to
We would like to express our appreciation.	Thank you.
prompt consideration of the matter	Please let us know what you think of this plan.
pursuant to	according to
We value your patronage.	Thank you for your business.

You can easily avoid these clichés by "talking" your letter. Would you say what you have written in a telephone conversation? If the answer is no, then rewrite it. Replace those expressions that have worn thin with the easier, shorter, more pointed language of today.

But avoiding the outdated expressions of the past does not mean selecting the jargon of the present. Our everyday talk is peppered with such expressions as: "Oh, yeah!" "I don't get it." "Come again?" "He's a right guy." A student can be heard suggesting that another student "con" the teacher into giving a better grade. Slang is appropriate in conversations with friends, but it is out of place in business correspondence. It characterizes you not as modern but as nonprofessional and flippant.

flippant: lacking respect

Consider the suggestions at the right to replace the slang expressions at the left:

He's a right guy.	Mr. Jones gets along very well with his co-workers as well as his supervisors.
We're hitting on all cylinders.	Every worker is reaching his or her production level.
We've made it now.	We have achieved success.
The Democrats are in.	The Democrats have been elected.

Successful letter writers do not lean on the clichés of the past or the jargon of the present; they choose their own expressions.

Can you recognize outmoded expressions in business messages and rewrite sentences containing them in modern language? Try Skills Activity 26.

SKILLS ACTIVITY 26

A. Too much writing is marred by old-fashioned expressions. Below are sentences taken from an 1880 publication that employ expressions still in use today.

1. Enclosed please find a check for $10.
2. Please be advised that your order will be shipped within a short period of time.
3. I enclose herewith an order to which you will please give your earliest attention and forward, with as little delay as possible, as per shipping instructions attached.
4. Your letter dated July 25th has been duly received and noted.
5. Referring to your letter of the 5th, we beg to state that there has been no error in your statement.
6. With reference to your letter of the tenth instant, we wish to state that there will be no interference with the affairs of your department.
7. Thanking you in advance for your consideration, I am . . .

Check with the key on page 514. Note the differences of opinion, and resolve disagreements by discussing them with your instructor. Now, in the space below, correct the outmoded expressions.

If you scored Fair to Excellent, continue with the second part. If you scored below Fair, discuss your problem with your instructor.

Name_____ Date _____

B. Identify the slang expressions in the following sentences.

1. We goofed! We charged you $15.75 for the radio when it should have been $50.75.
2. You'll have a ball when you shop at Tracey's.
3. Why don't you get with it? Join the crowd. Buy this new outdoor pool.
4. If you can grant me the interview, we can rap a bit about my qualifications.
5. If you feel ripped off at the supermarket, just call your consumer advocate for advice.

Check the key on page 514. If you scored below Fair discuss the problem with your instructor. If you achieved Fair or above, go on to the next problem.

In the space below, rewrite the five sentences in correct language.

_____
_____
_____
_____
_____
_____
_____
_____
_____

If you scored Fair to Excellent, go on to the second part of Unit 14, Language to Create Interest. If you scored below Fair, discuss the problem with your instructor.

Language to Create Interest

If you can approach your readers on their own level and can leave a good impression of yourself as a businessperson, you're off to an excellent start. But your messages themselves must also leave a favorable impression. Let's look at some ways to accomplish this.

ELASTIC SENTENCE LENGTH

The length and complexity of your sentences should be tailored to the type of message you are writing. If your objective is rapid understanding, keep your sentences short enough to be absorbed at a glance. In a sales letter, for instance, you must catch the reader's attention and get your message across before that attention wanes.

tailored: fitted

wanes: fades, declines

In a different situation, you might use a series of short, declarative sentences to show a cold analysis of facts:

> You charged $520 worth of goods in October. However, you have not yet paid your bill or contacted us. Thus you have delayed payment for three months without any explanation.

The technical writer—the scientist or mathematician—might also use this staccato effect. You can see each arrow hitting the mark in this series:

staccato: marked by abrupt sharp emphasis

> The fourteen patients were given the drug. Seven patients showed marked improvement. These seven patients had a common form of the disease. The drug is likely to be effective against one form of this disease.

Complex and compound sentences, on the other hand, enable you to qualify your statements, to add nuances that broaden and deepen your meaning, to bring clearer understanding. (Review Chapter 3 on compound and complex sentences.) For example, the answer "I will" may be qualified by the clause "if it doesn't rain." Or, the cold statement "you have delayed paying your account for three months" can be softened by the addition of "although you have been one of our best charge customers over the past five years." The student who reads "your application for matriculation in January 1976 has not been accepted" knows he or she has been rejected—but does not know why. The clause "since it was not filed before the November 1 deadline" clarifies the student's understanding of the situation.

nuances: fine variations as in color or meaning

Flowing thoughts and lively writing usually call for a variety of sentence lengths. In most situations, a mixture of short, simple sentences complemented by longer ones will best hold your reader's attention. You should remember, however, that too long a sentence is burdensome. It usually requires rereading, and that is a waste of the reader's time. Just try this for sentence size:

complemented: note the *e,* in the middle; compare with *complimented* with an *i.*

Use numerals for percents.

Although there has been a tremendous drive by
our employees to improve production quotas, and
although production has been increased by 10
percent, it is imperative that, in an attempt
to meet the new request by management for production to be increased another 25 percent, an
extra shift of 50 men be added between the hours
of 8 p.m. and 2 a.m. for the months of October,
November, and December.

Did you grasp the meaning of the sentence the first time you read it?
Break it down to shorter units of thought for quick, easy reading:

The cooperation of our employees in improving
quotas increased production by 10 percent. To
meet the new 25 percent increase set by management, we should add another shift of 50 men. We
can schedule the shift from 8 p.m. to 2 a.m. for
the months of October, November, and December.

The average sentence contains between 16 and 22 words. If you find
that your sentences consistently go beyond this average, you will certainly want to cut them. In the following activity you will check your
ability to keep sentences within reasonable lengths.

SKILLS ACTIVITY 27

Are the following sentences too long?

1. When your insurance representative discusses your automobile insurance with you, he or she can also discuss your life insurance, tell you about health insurance, and also explain insurance protection on your boat and personal property.
2. We would like to know whether, during the several weeks in which you have been considering our estimate to paint and refurnish your office, you have made any decision to go ahead with the work.
3. Since I am delighted to accept your kind invitation to speak at your club meeting on Monday, January 5, at 8 p.m., on any topic I deem advisable, I have decided to say a few brief words on that ever-increasing hazard to our national physical health—air pollution.
4. Since we do not have a large-enough work force, we cannot bid on this job but ask you to ask us again when you have another job for which we may be able to bid at a later date.
5. The sales report indicates an increase in sales in certain areas of the country and a decrease in others, with higher increases in the East than in the West, and greater decreases in the North Central area than in the South Central area.

Given five lengthy sentences, rewrite them in the spaces provided below, breaking them into shorter effective sentences.

Peer judgment or instructor evaluation:

Excellent	*5*
Good	*4*
Fair	*3*

Name_____ Date_____

Varied Approaches

In addition to varying the length of your sentences, you can add interest to your letter by varying sentence structure.

Personnel directors are accustomed to receiving letters of application that begin:

>   I would like to apply for the position of

and continue in the second paragraph with:

>   I was graduated from Long Beach High School in
>   June, 1976. I had a B average. I was also active
>   in school affairs.

and repeat the ubiquitous "I" even in the final paragraph with:

ubiquitous: existing every-
where at once; omni-
present

>   I will be glad to come in for an interview. I
>   have listed my phone number on my data sheet.

The repeated subject-verb beginning dulls any message. You get the feeling that you are back in elementary school reading that first primer. To add a vital touch to your written communications, vary the beginnings of your sentences.

Don't begin each sentence with a noun or pronoun.	Try these ideas.
The company wishes to order a transistor for its specially designed machine.	verb: Please send transistor No. 17 for our automated drill press.
Transistor No. 17 is no longer being produced.	conditional clause: Because we have replaced it with another type, No. 17 is no longer being produced.
The increase in voltage output will increase the efficiency of the machine.	prepositional phrase: In fact, with the increase in voltage output, the drill press will operate more efficiently.
Reactions that are quick and alert can save your life.	adjective: Quick, alert reactions can save your life.
The key to high production is selecting personnel carefully.	adverb: Carefully selecting personnel is the key to high production.
The ability to write clear effective messages requires organized thinking.	gerund: Writing clear, effective messages requires organized thinking.

We can only hope than an individual live life to its fullest
degree.

It is a trying problem for the
youth of today to choose the right
vocation.

The secretary opened the mail as he
was waiting for his employer.

<u>noun clause</u>:   That an individual
live life to its fullest capacity is
all that we can hope.

<u>infinitive</u>:   To choose the right
vocation poses a trying problem for
the youth of today.

<u>adverbial clause</u>:   While the secre-
tary was waiting for his employer,
he opened the mail.

Nothing about your writing should happen accidentally. You must work
at it. Planning for variety in your sentence beginnings will give your
communication vitality.

Can you vary your sentence beginnings to compose a more interesting
business message? Try Skills Activity 28.

SKILLS ACTIVITY 28

Given three sentences
with suggestions for
varied beginnings, re-
write them effectively
and correctly.

Excellent   9
Good   7–8
Fair   6

1. I would like to have an interview at your convenience.

   Verb _____

2. It is difficult to complete the arrangements without further help from you.

   Gerund _____

   _____

   Infinitive _____

   _____

   Noun _____

   _____

   Prepositional phrase _____

   _____

   Conditional clause _____

   _____

3. It was his primary duty to improve the company's profits.

   Gerund _____

   Infinitive _____

   Noun _____

Check your answers with the key on page 514. If you scored Fair or above, go on to the next section. If you scored below Fair, review and study the answers. Discuss any problems with your instructor.

Name_____ Date_____

Continuity

In the credits for motion pictures, you often see the listing "Continuity." If one scene does not lead smoothly into the next, confusion results. The same is true in business communication. Without continuity, your writing lacks punch. It jerks along, forcing the reader to expend extra effort in jumping the hurdles between ideas, as you will notice in the following paragraph:

> The modern version of <u>Carmen</u> is receiving rave reviews. It opened in New York in November. Tickets are to be ordered for any Friday in December. The tickets cost $6 each. The Business Club is going. The cost of the tickets is high for college students. Twenty-five tickets will be ordered. Student Council is asked to make a loan of $150 for the purchase of tickets. This has been the procedure in the past.

With a little organization and with the use of transitional phrases, the same report reads:

> The Business Club selected the modern version of <u>Carmen</u> for its theater party in December. Since the critics gave this production rave reviews, the members are willing to purchase tickets for $6.
>
> Following the procedure last year, the Business Club asks Student Council to extend a loan of $150 for 25 tickets at $6 each so that the Club can order the tickets immediately. Repayment of this loan will be made within two weeks.

Organization, as we said in Chapter 3, has much to do with continuity; the simple technique of using transitional words keeps the reader with you. Such expressions as these will bridge the gap:

> in the second place, finally, of course
>
> however, nevertheless, therefore
>
> as you see in the attached memorandum, in Section II
>
> when I telephoned you
>
> after that

expend: to use up

For amounts of money, use figures. Omit decimal and zeros.

Use words, not figures, at beginning of sentence.

Underline titles of plays, operas, ballets.

Use figures for numbers over ten.

```
            in reviewing the first case

            to summarize
```

Without such transitions, readers lose time in reading and comprehending your ideas; with them, they read easily and smoothly.

In Skills Activity 29 you will have an opportunity to see the importance of continuity and transitions.

SKILLS ACTIVITY 29

Dear Customer:

The "new" United States Postal Service was created on July 1, 1971. It was created by Act of Congress. Service to the customer is basic to the founding principles of the new organization. That is what its name implies.

Many of our customers have told us they would like to know more about our services. They would like to know about our products. We think we can meet this need and help you get the most for your postage. We are publishing a new Postal Information pamphlet to do the aforesaid.

                    Sincerely yours,

Given a letter of two paragraphs with poor continuity and transition, rewrite the letter effectively. (Submit your revision on a separate sheet.)

Peer judgment or your instructor's evaluation:

Excellent	*5*
Good	*4*
Fair	*3*

Some hints: Combine sentences 1 and 2. Combine sentences 3 and 4 starting with an introductory clause. In paragraph 2, use a transition word in your second sentence. Combine sentences 3 and 4.

If you were able to rewrite the letter effectively, according to peer judgment or the evaluation of your instructor, go on to the fourth way to create interest in your writing for business—choosing words for added effect. If you were unable to rewrite the letter effectively, discuss the problem with your instructor.

Name_____ Date_____

VERBS OF BEING AND ACTION VERBS

This is a fourth technique you may use to make your language interesting. Verbs and nouns can increase the vitality and punch of your writing or make it dull; they can keep a moderate tone or introduce a note of harshness. As always, choosing the right word for the right purpose enhances your communication.

enhances: increases, as in reputation or quality

Verbs such as *seem, feel, am, was, were, are,* and *is* assume a condition or state of being:

> I am tired.
>
> They feel that it is not true.
>
> We are right.

These "being" words are useful when you want to speak generally or to make a statement without emphasis. For these purposes, they are important. Usually, however, you want to *add* action and life to your writing, and overuse of verbs of being slows your business writing to a crawl. Compare the pairs of sentences below:

"Being" verb	Action verb
Being there is a balance of $87 due on your account.	You owe $87 on your account.
We are the largest manufacturers of ski equipment in this country.	Our company manufactures more ski equipment than any other company in the United States.
This is your opportunity to buy at low prices.	Now you can buy at low prices.
It is my opinion that I can help you increase your profits.	I believe that I can help you increase your profits.
There is evidence that Mr. Jones is a reliable credit risk.	We rate Mr. Jones a reliable charge customer.

Notice how changing the verb converts a quiet, lifeless sentence into an active, emphatic one. Action verbs bring your sentence right to the point and tell the reader just where responsibility for the action lies. When you have completed a letter, count the number of times you used *it is, there is,* or *there are.* Did you mean to write this kind of letter? Or can you add power to your letter by eliminating these drowsy words and phrases?

Let's put this fourth technique to work in Skills Activity 30.

SKILLS ACTIVITY 30

Can you substitute action verbs for is/are verbs?

1. A result of inflation is an inefficient redistribution of our national resources.

   _____

   _____

2. This is an opportunity you should not miss.

   _____

3. In my opinion, it would be better to keep costs down than to increase our prices.

   _____

   _____

4. There are several choices which you have in selecting courses.

   _____

5. The course will be of benefit to her in her business writing.

   _____

6. Safety is a factor to be considered in the installation of that machine.

   _____

7. It is necessary to the success of the peace settlement to keep communication lines open.

   _____

   _____

> Given seven sentences using is/are verbs, enliven the sentences by substituting action verbs in the space provided.
>
> Excellent   7
> Good   6
> Fair   5

Check with the key on page 515. If you scored Fair or above, go on with the fifth language technique, Passive Voice versus Active Voice. If you scored below Fair, review before continuing. Discuss any problems with your instructor.

Name_____ Date_____

PASSIVE VOICE VERSUS ACTIVE VOICE

Do you like the straightforward person who always gives you a direct answer and who does not hedge? If your answer is "yes," you will want to exhibit this same straightforward approach in your own writing. To do so, use the active voice. When you make the subject of your sentence the doer of the action, you employ the active voice. When you make the subject the receiver of the action, you use the passive voice.

hedge: to avoid a forthright statement of action

Passive voice	Active voice
```I was made a better letter-writer by taking this course.```	```I write better letters because I took this course.```

In the first sentence, you passively accept what is being done to you; in the second, you actively participate in achieving writing skill.

Now look at the sentences below. Notice the vagueness and lack of directness of those at the left. Do you see how the active voice in the sentences at the right emphasizes the doer and adds forcefulness to the sentence?

Passive voice	Active voice
```The figures have been checked by the auditor.```	```The auditor has checked the figures.```
```It is noted that your business is improving.```	```The Board noted the improvement in your business.```
```Your assistance is appreciated by us.```	```We appreciate your assistance.```
```The procedures manual has been prepared by the personnel department to help new employees.```	```The personnel department has prepared the procedures manual to help new employees.```

Under certain circumstances, however, the passive voice can be useful. If, for instance, you don't want to place specific blame in a given situation (or if you don't know who is to blame), the passive voice will shift the onus from a person or company—as in the following sentences:

onus: burden or responsibility

```The company was forced to close its doors.```

[*Not:* Misuse of funds forced the company to close its doors.]

```John was not permitted to attend the conference.```

[*Not:* The sales manager did not permit John to attend the conference.]

permitted
When the accent is on the last syllable, form the past tense by doubling the final consonant and adding ed.

Or perhaps you must tell your reader that he or she is at fault, but you want to keep his or her good will. By using the passive voice, you can avoid a clear-cut, definite statement that gives offense. Compare the following answers to the housewife who complained about her malfunctioning washing machine:

Active voice	Passive voice
Because you have made unauthorized adjustments on your Speedex, we cannot service your machine under the guarantee.	Because unauthorized adjustments have been made on your Speedex, your guarantee has been invalidated.

Remember, the active voice is direct, specific, and positive; and it keeps your writing moving. In most cases, these are the values for which you strive. The passive voice, on the other hand, is indirect and general, and it removes the emphasis from the doer of the action. Limit its use to the times when these are your goals.

SKILLS ACTIVITY 31

Can you achieve a straightforward, direct style of writing by using the active voice?

1. Your letter of the fifth has been read, and the order will be shipped immediately. _____

_____

2. These fabrics have been produced by Glenn Company for the past 75 years. _____

_____

> Given seven sentences using the passive voice, rewrite them in the active voice.
>
> Excellent 7
> Good 6
> Fair 5

3. Your itinerary will be carefully drawn up by one of our experts, and all details will be handled by him. _____

_____

4. Our report was considered by the board, but no definite decision was made. _____

_____

5. It was noticed that an error was made by us on your statement. _____

_____

6. A careful analysis of the sales report was made by the vice-president.

_____

_____

7. The sales manager's recommendations were submitted to the vice-president. _____

_____

Check the key on page 515. If you achieved Fair to Excellent, go on to the sixth and last part of the section on language to create interest. If you scored below Fair, review and discuss any problems with your instructor.

Name_____ Date_____

THE LONG-WINDED ABSTRACTION

Many writers try to impress their readers with abstract words and long-winded phrases. In most writing, however—and especially in business letters—the best way to say something is usually the simplest way, and the most suitable word is frequently the shortest one. Compare the following sentences:

Analysis of the situation indicated the ineffectiveness of his plans in ameliorating the food shortage for a thousand people.	His plans had not included transportation for the hundred tons of rice; without it, a thousand people starved.
Try to effectuate some changes in your plans so that we can utilize these tickets.	Try changing your plans so that we can use these tickets.
The exigencies of the situation demand that the government decrease its monetary expenditures.	The financial crisis makes it necessary to cut government spending.
We anticipate that the optimum remuneration we can offer you is $8,000 per annum.	The best salary we can offer you is $8,000 a year.
We are in a position to assist you without further delay.	We can help you now.

Notice how difficult it is to understand the sentences on the left. Formless, abstract words and convoluted phrases detract from the clarity and force of your writing. They obscure your meaning; in some cases they may lose it entirely.

convoluted: twisted

It is important to build an extensive vocabulary—the more words you know, the more precisely you will be able to express yourself. However, you must remember that the major purpose of your business writing is to communicate with your reader; and that means choosing the clearest words, not necessarily the longest ones. Save the "big" words for those cases where a simpler word will not do.

Build your vocabulary— then use it well.

Can you use short, specific, concrete words and phrases in business messages? Try Skills Activity 32.

SKILLS ACTIVITY 32

Be sure to check your dictionary if you don't understand the meaning of any of the words in the following sentences.

1. In this report, we are offering our recommendations of five preferred stocks.

   _____

   _____

2. They suggest that you make additions to your portfolio.

   _____

3. We should like to know if there is a confirmation of all of our purchases.

   _____

   _____

4. There has been some substantiation by economists of the fact that profits have declined in the past quarter.

   _____

   _____

5. The conclusion ascertained from a cursory reading of the income statement was that for the preceding period the business had sustained a substantial deficit.

   _____

   _____

   _____

6. Proofread carefully your typed letters. Letters that are inadvertently erroneous may cost you a lucrative contract.

   _____

   _____

7. In the course of this dissertation, I hope to clarify the reasons why our organization failed to amass a profit last year.

   _____

   _____

Given seven sentences using abstract and wordy phrases, rewrite the sentences eliminating the abstract.

Peer judgment or instructor evaluation:

Excellent	*7*
Good	*6*
Fair	*5*

If you achieved Fair to Excellent on this worksheet, go on to the summary. If you did not score Fair or above, discuss the problem with your instructor.

Name_____Date_____

SUMMARY

A powerful dimension of your business-letter writing is the relationship created between you and your readers. Focus on them as individuals by appealing to their interests, by showing them that you want to serve them, by placing yourself in their positions, and by being honest with them.

Your readers should get a picture of you as an up-to-date writer. Don't let them find you trapped in the dead language of the past. "Talk" your letters to give them a natural tone. Vary the length and construction of your sentences to retain interest, and make your thoughts flow smoothly with transition words. Pack power into your writing by using action verbs, the active voice, concrete words, and short, specific words and phrases.

Develop a positive attitude toward your readers; then you will gain their positive reactions.

FOCUS ON LANGUAGE

In Focus on Language you will review spelling, vocabulary, and sound-alike words; agreement, punctuation (comma), and parallel construction.

Spelling

1. a. concede b. Febuary c. vertical

   d. independent _____

2. a. comparative b. privileged c. imediately

   d. accidentally _____

3. a. procedure b. tailered c. similar

   d. delete _____

4. a. onas b. parallel c. guarantee

   d. catalogs _____

5. a. integrity b. benifit c. consistent

   d. separately _____

6. a. permitted b. benefitted c. audited

   d. incurred _____

7. a. inasmuch b. nevertheless c. engaged

   d. rebuf _____

Given a list of spelling words, identify the mis-spelled words and write them correctly.

Excellent   7
Good   6
Fair   5

Check the key on page 515. If you scored Fair to Excellent, go on to Vocabulary. If you did not succeed in achieving Fair or above, review the words that you missed. Ask a friend to read them to you as you write or type them. Check again. Repeat the procedure until you can spell every word correctly.

Vocabulary

1. elicit a. give help b. evoke c. render d. pay
2. altruistic a. selfish b. benevolent c. stingy d. happy
3. evoke a. call forth b. outrage c. tunnel d. operate
4. peremptory a. soft-hearted b. decisive c. judgment d. perceived
5. ubiquitous a. far off b. dissipated c. useful d. omnipresent
6. staccato a. abrupt b. slow c. sluggish d. vague
7. nuances a. changes b. variations c. works d. news
8. enhance a. hurt b. improve c. run d. wane
9. convoluted a. conscience b. flying c. twisted d. converged
10. trite a. genuine b. short c. monotonous d. commonplace
11. wanes a. attributes b. owns c. subscribes d. grows smaller

Given 15 words spotlighted in the chapter, circle the letter of the word or phrase that is closest in meaning to the first word.

Excellent   14-15
Good   12-13
Fair   10-11

Name_____ Date_____

12. expend   a. give   b. translate   c. elicit   d. spend
13. hedge   a. think   b. avoid decision   c. work   d. release statistics
14. audit   a. treat   b. interpret   c. examine   d. control
15. assuage   a. persuade   b. soothe   c. convert   d. gauge

Check the key on page 515. If you achieved Fair or above, go on to Sound-Alikes. If you did not achieve Fair or above, review the definitions of the words you missed. Use each word in a sentence. Ask your instructor to check your sentences and to discuss any errors with you.

Sound-Alikes

Be sure you know the difference between *accede* and *exceed*, *complement* and *compliment*, *capital* and *capitol*. Now get a perfect score on the sentences below.

Accede means to give one's consent or agreement (used with *to*).
Ms. Pilgrim will accede to the wishes of her friends.

Exceed is to surpass, as in quantity or quality; or to go beyond the limit.
You can save energy if you do not exceed the 50 mph limit.

Complement is that which completes. (Note the *e* in the middle of *complement* and *complete*.)
The ship has its complement of men.

Compliment is a flattering comment; or, as a verb, to flatter.
The teacher paid a compliment to Elisa.
Mr. Towne wishes to compliment his students on their good work.

Capital is a word with a number of meanings, the most important of which are:
the capital city of a state or country; as
Lisbon is the capital of Portugal.
the total amount of money or property owned by an individual or business; as
The capital of this business amounts to $5 million.

Capitol refers to the building in which a legislative body convenes.
The Capitol is an outstanding building in Washington, D.C.

Given sentences using words that sound alike, underscore the correct word in each case.

Excellent	10–11
Good	8–9
Fair	6–7

1. Please accept our (*complements, compliments*) on your excellent display.
2. If he (*accedes, exceeds*) to our request, we'll have our full (*complement, compliment*) of engineers.
3. There is not sufficient (*capital, capitol*) to finance the proposal.
4. The direct object is a (*complement, compliment*) of the verb.
5. If your debts (*accede, exceed*) your assets, we cannot (*accede, exceed*) to your request for credit.
6. The (*capital, capitol*) in most state (*capitals, capitols*) is an impressive building.

7. The Police Department sent a small (*complement, compliment*) of men to guard the (*capital, capitol*) building.

Check the key on page 515. If you achieved Fair to Excellent, move on to More on Agreement. If you scored less than Fair, write a sentence for each sound-alike word you missed. Ask your instructor to check your sentences and to discuss any errors with you.

More on Agreement

In Chapter 3, you learned not to be confused by words that intervene between subject and verb. Here are some hints for solving other agreement problems.

Rule: *When the subject is one of the following words (or is modified by one of them), the verb must be singular:* every, each, everybody, everyone, every one, anybody, anyone, any one, nobody, everything, anything, somebody, something, someone, some one, many a, more than one, no one, nothing.

> Everyone misses a class from time to time, but no one skips an exam.
> Many an idea is lost in the discussion.
> No one is above suspicion.

Even when *each* or *every* is part of a compound subject, the subject is considered singular:

> Each student and each teacher keeps his or her own records.

Collective nouns (that is, nouns, such as *committee* or *group* or *audience*, that refer to several individuals together) also confuse many writers.

Rule: *Treat the collective noun as a singular if it refers to a group acting as a unit; treat it as plural if it is a group whose members are acting as individuals.*

> The committee has announced its decision.
> The committee have left for their homes.

Be sure you understand these rules; then try your hand at these sentences:

1. Every one of the men (*wishes, wish*) to order (*his, their*) own stationery.
2. Each of the sorority members (*is, are*) obliged to sign (*her, their*) name.
3. The audience (*has, have*) given (*its, their*) approval of the performance.
4. Every regional director and supervisor (*has, have*) sent in a work report.
5. More than one of the workers (*has, have*) gone home.
6. Our team (*is, are*) going to play tomorrow.
7. None of the boys (*is, are*) leaving.
8. Many a miracle (*has, have*) been wrought.

> *Given 13 problems concerning agreement, underscore the correct word in each case.*
>
> | | |
> |---|---|
> | *Excellent* | *12–13* |
> | *Good* | *10–11* |
> | *Fair* | *8–9* |

Name_____ Date_____

9. Somebody among us (*knows, know*) the answer.

10. (*Does, Do*) each student and each teacher get tickets?

Check yourself; the key is on page 515. If you achieved Fair or above, go on to Punctuation. If you scored below Fair, discuss the problem with your instructor.

Punctuation: Comma

The comma is the punctuation mark that gives many people the most trouble. Let's look at two rules for using it.

Rule: *Use a comma between the independent clauses of a compound sentence.* (An independent clause is one that can stand alone as a sentence; a compound sentence is one in which two or more independent clauses are joined by one of the coordinating conjunctions—*and, but, or, nor, for.*)

Interest in our new product is high, and sales have doubled.

Remember, a clause has both a subject and a verb. Don't be fooled by sentences like the one below. It has only one clause since there is only one subject; therefore, it has no comma.

Roger went fishing with his father last week and brought home seven bluefish.

Rule: *Use a comma following introductory clauses or phrases.*

When John finished eating, he went out to find Dave.
Of all the possibilities, you had to choose this.
If I didn't know better, I'd say you did that one.

Given 10 sentences which contain compound clauses and introductory clauses and phrases, punctuate them accurately.

Excellent	10
Good	9
Fair	7–8

1. Since you are learning to write correctly you will be a successful correspondent.

2. The secretary called the meeting to order at noon and read the minutes immediately.

3. Attend the stockholders' meeting and write me a complete report of the day's activities.

4. When Sally and Jo finished riding Sam applauded them.

5. The case has closed but our lawyer has not yet received his fee.

6. The editor read the copy quickly and made the necessary changes.

7. If I were to go he would surely recognize me.

8. Either James went to the conference or he got news of the decision from Henry.

9. When the economy functions smoothly employment is high.

10. You may file the report on schedule or you may request an extension.

Check the key on page 515. If you score above Fair, go on to Parallel Structure. If you score below Fair, review the rules. Discuss disagreements with your instructor.

Parallel Structure

Remember our discussion of parallel structure in Chapter 3? Review it if you need to; then rewrite the following sentences to make them conform to the rules of parallelism.

1. Our new dacron shirts wash easily, drip dry quickly, and you can wear them right away.

   _____

Given seven sentences with errors in parallel construction, rewrite the incorrect parts in the space below each sentence.

Excellent	*7*
Good	*6*
Fair	*5*

2. Come join our company, where the pay is high, working conditions are pleasant, and to succeed is possible.

   _____

3. The mechanics are trained in repairing all makes of domestic cars and in foreign-car repairs.

   _____

4. The personnel manager said that this employee is intelligent, alert, and has been a capable worker.

   _____

5. Trying to get ahead in business is not necessarily to succeed in it.

   _____

6. If you would like additional copies of this report, mail the enclosed form or you can call us by phone.

   _____

7. Professor Lowell asked her students to read the chapter, write answers to the questions, and she asked them to comment on the chapter.

   _____

Check answers on page 515. If you achieve Fair to Excellent, you have completed Chapter 4. If you fall below the level of Fair, review and discuss your work with your instructor.

Name_____ Date_____

II

SOCIAL-BUSINESS AND PERSONAL-BUSINESS WRITING

5

CONCISE COMMUNICATIONS

discrete: separate (not *discreet*)

You have reviewed and mastered discrete principles of business writing. Now let's integrate these principles into the complete business communication. In Units 15 and 16, you will write a simple personal-business request and a social-business invitation to a speaker.

UNIT 15   THE SIMPLE REQUEST

Your performance objective for Unit 15 is:

Given the situation in which you must write a simple request,

You will use the correct form, get to the point immediately, include all the necessary information, exclude the unnecessary information, organize the message, and maintain good human relations.

Suppose we start with a simple written communication typical of our normal personal-business life. While reading the *Times* last Sunday, you clipped this item:

McDONNELL & COMPANY
REPORTS ON
TRANS-AMERICA CORPORATION

To receive your copy,
just send a postcard to us at
228 Vista View Road
San Francisco, CA   94102

---

pertinent: related to matter at hand; relevant

This report may contain some data pertinent to your economics project, so you have decided to send for it.

This is a simple problem, but you must organize your thoughts to be sure that you receive the report quickly. Remember that a postcard is requested; don't burden the mail room with a letter that must be opened and then routed.

Now let's read a few of the requests received by McDonnell & Company the next morning. The first was this postcard:

When a firm uses an ampersand (&) in its name, type the symbol, not the word "and."

186

```
        Dear Sir:

        Send me your report advertised in Sunday's
        newspaper.

                              Yours truly,

                              Bert Jones
                              Bert Jones
```

Sad to say, Bert never received the report. Of course, you know why—he did not include his return address. Is that unusual in personal communications? Not at all. Ask any radio or newspaper advertiser how often he receives requests he cannot answer because of lack of a return address—and sometimes even of a name.

Although Bert's one-sentence request was short and to the point, it certainly did not include all the facts. First, there was no date. In personal-business communications, as well as in regular business correspondence, the first thing you must remember is to include the date. Second, the phrase "your report" is not specific enough; "the report on Trans-America Corporation" would have indicated clearly which report Bert wanted. This is especially important if McDonnell & Company is distributing other companies' reports. Third, do you know what paper Bert was referring to? Would it not have been just as easy for him to say "Sunday's *Times*"?

Include all the facts.

Be specific.

companies': *Remember how to form the possessive of a plural?*

Yes, Bert omitted many facts in this simple communication. Have you noticed other errors? What about the salutation? Do you address a company as "Dear Sir"? The salutation should be "Ladies and Gentlemen" or "Dear People." Finally, what is the word that must precede the command "send me"? You're right—that word is "please."

Use correct mechanics.

Remember the amenities.

Can you rewrite Bert's one-sentence postcard to make it a more effective personal-business communication?

Here is another card received by McDonnell & Company:

```
                              585 Benefit Street
                              San Jose, CA  95127
                              October 6, 19--

        Gentlemen:

        I have seen your ad in Sunday's Times of October
        5 re Trans-America Corp. I would appreciate it
        if you would send me a copy of this report. I
        must write a paper for my course in economics,
        and having this report should be a great help
        to me.
```

Thanking you in advance, I am

Yours truly,

Sheila Kissel

Sheila Kissel

Sheila Kissel did get the report because she included all the information that McDonnell & Company needed. But her communication, too, could be improved. She took too long to write something simple, which wasted her own time and that of the person receiving the message. Her organization was poor because she included unnecessary information concerning the use of this report in writing her economics paper.

Include only the necessary facts.

In addition, anyone receiving this communication would believe that the writer was an older person. Can you see why? Who else would use such outmoded expressions as "re" and "thanking you in advance, I am"?

Use up-to-date language.

Sheila has another common problem: "I" trouble. Just count the number of sentences beginning with that pronoun.

But all in all, her communication was more effective than Bert's. Why? She received the report.

The third request received by McDonnell & Company on Monday morning was superior to the first two:

717 Depot Street
Santa Clara, CA   95060
October 6, 19--

Gentlemen:

Get to the point in the first sentence.

Please send me a copy of the report of Trans-America Corporation that you advertised in the *Times* on October 5.

Thank you.

Yours truly,

Patrick Muskie

Patrick Muskie

Notice that Patrick made his point immediately; he included the facts necessary to obtain his request, but no others; and he built good human relations by remembering to say "please."

Would you choose Patrick's postcard as the one you would send? Can you make any improvement? If you are eliminating unnecessary elements, you can also omit the salutation and the closing. And, by moving the return address to a position under your name, you make it easier for the typist at McDonnell & Company to address that report to you.

```
                          October 5, 19--


    Please send me a copy of the report on the
    Trans-America Corporation, as advertised in the
    Times of October 2.

    Many thanks.
                          Robert Newriter
                          Robert Newriter
                          225 North Avenue
                          Los Angeles, CA  90021
```

Can you identify the most effective simple personal-business message, and can you compose an effective order reqeust? Try Skills Activity 33.

SKILLS ACTIVITY 33

A. Poor & Rich placed an ad in the *Wall Street Journal* of January 9, saying that a brochure, "Timely Investments," would be sent to anyone requesting it by postcard. The following three cards were received by Poor & Rich.

1.

```
    Sir:

    Send me my copy of the brochure you advertised.
    Thanks a lot.
                        Ted Thewes
                        Ted Thewes
```

2.

```
                        January 9, 19--

    Please send me the brochure, "Timely Invest-
    ments," which you offered in today's Wall Street
    Journal.

    Thank you.

                        Meg Horne
                        Meg Horne
                        15 River Road
                        Dubuque, IA  52001
```

3.

Box 747
Manchester Center, VT   05255
January 9, 19--

Sirs:

Please send me the brochure, "Timely Investments," which you advertised in today's Wall
Street Journal.

Thank you in advance,

Yours truly,

Michael Gonzalez

Michael Gonzalez

The most effective postcard is ＿＿＿＿＿＿.

My choice is based on the following:

＿＿＿

＿＿＿

The least effective postcard is ＿＿＿＿＿＿. My decision is based on

＿＿＿

＿＿＿

＿＿＿

Check the key on page 515. Do you agree with the authors' reasons for their choices? Discuss any disagreements with your instructor.

B. Tramp Trips offers a free Caribbean travel folder if you will write a postcard to Air and Sea Travel Service, Hudson Avenue Hotel, 228 West 56 Street, New York, NY 10019.

Write a postcard requesting this folder. Refer to this checklist to be sure you have included everything. Starred items must be included. Can you add something to the checklist?

1. *Correct address on address side of card
2. *Return address (Remember correct state abbreviation and zip.)
3. Date
4. *Please and Thank You
5. *Title of material requested

*Given the problem of re-
questing a travel folder,
compose an effective re-
quest in postcard form.*

*Peer judgment or instruc-
tor's evaluation:*

Excellent   7
Good   6
Fair   5

6. *Your name

7. Correct salutation and complimentary close if used

C. Let's try another simple request. Let's see if you can compose this one in ten minutes.

Station WROY offers a free sample of Lazy Day Soap Powder to anyone who sends a postcard requesting it to Lazy Day Soap Powder, 250 Barome Street, New Orleans, LA 70116. Write for your sample.

If you have achieved Fair or above, go on to the Unit 16. If you fell below Fair, discuss the problem with your instructor.

Given a problem of requesting a free sample, compose an effective request in postcard form.

Peer judgment or instructor's evaluation: (See checklist for preceding problem.)

Excellent	7
Good	6
Fair	5

Name_____ Date_____

UNIT 16   THE NOTICE OF A MEETING

Adding Some Complications

Now we are ready to go on to a more difficult problem—one that involves more data.

In Unit 16 you will strive for the following performance objective:

Given the social-business situation in which the membership of an organization is to be invited to a meeting,

You will write a notice that uses the correct form, gets to the point immediately, includes all the necessary information, excludes the unnecessary information, is well organized, persuades the reader to act, and makes it easy to answer.

The situation you will experience concerns the newly-elected secretary of the Cap-it Bowling Club, John Foresight. He must prepare the notices for the first fall meeting of the club to be held at the Arbor Avenue Alleys on Friday, September 15, at 8 p.m. All members and their guests are invited to be present. Refreshments will be served.

Let's work through this problem with the secretary. Not only must he contact each of the 25 members, but he must reactivate their interest in the club after the summer respite. The success of the year's activities really depends on the turnout for the opening meeting, and getting a good turnout is John's responsibility.

respite: delay; rest

In outlining his plan, he realizes that he does not have all the information. First, he must look up the exact address of the Arbor Avenue Alleys. Second, he must ascertain from the Arbor Avenue Alley's manager the deadline for reservations. Alleys must be reserved, and refreshments must be ordered. One more item remains—the fee. The officers tell him that the cost of refreshments will come out of the club dues, but each person who attends will be asked to pay $2 in advance or at the door for use of the bowling facilities.

ascertain: *Remember this word?*

And now an insistent voice should be saying, "Mr. Secretary, don't slip up on checking the date. Be sure that Friday is September 15 and that the date and time have been reserved at the alleys for your club." Checking must be an integral part of a writer's planning.

insistent: urgent
Check accuracy of dates.

The secretary has collected and verified all the pertinent facts. What form of communication will he use? Will a postcard do? How will he get the RSVP's? He decides that a mimeographed card would be most economical. Therefore, he presents this card to the vice-president for his suggestions before duplicating it for the membership:

integral: essential
verified: checked for accuracy

Omit th, st, rd, nd when date follows month.

Use figures before a.m. and p.m.

Use figures for amounts of money. Omit decimals and zeros for amounts in dollars.

September 1, 19--

Dear Member:

The Cap-It Bowling Club is holding its first fall meeting on Friday, September 15th, at 8 p.m., at the Arbor Avenue Alleys, 251 Arbor Avenue, Beverly Hills.

Since this is our first meeting, we are planning to serve refreshments. Wives and guests are invited. The price is $2.00 per person, payable in advance or at the door.

Please let me know by September 12th if you are coming.

Yours truly,

John Foresight

John Foresight
Secretary

Mr. Foresight has included almost all the necessary information, but *almost* is not enough. He may not get many responses, for he has made it difficult to answer by omitting his address and telephone number. The vice-president advises that he add his address and asks him to highlight the date and time. He rewrites the card to read:

advises

September 1, 19--

The Cap-It Bowling Club is holding its first fall meeting on FRIDAY, SEPTEMBER 15, at 8 p.m., at the Arbor Avenue Alleys, 251 Arbor Avenue, Beverly Hills.

Refreshments will be served. Guests may be invited by members. The prices is $2 per person.

Please let me know by September 12 the number of reservations you wish to make. You may send a check or pay at the door.

John Foresight
John Foresight, Secretary
228 Fourth Street
Beverly Hills, CA 90212

Telephone: (213) 385-4789

Avoid passive voice; use "You may invite guests."

At this time, the president joins the other two officers and comments, "For this first meeting of the fall season, why don't we send a letter?" (How wise he is to consider the reaction of the membership. A card would detract from the importance of this first meeting.) "Wouldn't a tear-off form at the end of the letter and a self-addressed, stamped envelope make it a cinch for our members to answer?" (In this case the president is not concerned with economy; the difference in postage will amount to only a few dollars. The purpose is to make it easy for members to say "yes.")

detract: take away a part

The secretary is quick to accept these suggestions, for he knows of the president's past success as secretary of the college's intramural sports program. Together they rewrite the announcement (Figure 5–1), which is then mimeographed and mailed to the members on September 1.

intramural: taking place within a school
mimeographed: stencil duplicator
already

Three days later, an amazed John Foresight reports to the president and vice-president that 30 of the 50 members have already answered and that 10 of them plan to bring one or two guests. The members must have mailed back their forms the day they received them or the following day. The president had been correct in making it easy for members to respond. Only two or three minutes were needed to complete the form, and it was all ready to be inserted in the envelope and mailed back to the secretary. In arranging this, the president had also made it easier on John, who was now thinking of a follow-up. On the twelfth, he would telephone every member who had not responded. There would be very few, if any.

received: *Remember this word?*

all ready

Thus, John Foresight had learned from his first experience as secretary. For the first postcard he wrote he had made every effort to gather all the information he would need; but, like Bert Jones in his request for the Trans-America report, John made a glaring omission—he did not include his return address.

Did you notice, however, that John did exclude the unnecessary information that the cost of refreshments was to come out of club dues?

Of course, John's major misconception was his preoccupation with economy. The objective was not to inform the members of the meeting in the most economical way; it was to get the total membership out to the first meeting. He had forgotten to put himself in the reader's place. Besides, the difference in cost between 25 postcards and 25 first-class letters (including stamped return envelopes) was minimal.

misconception: mistaken idea
preoccupation: being fully absorbed

John quickly accepted the president's advice, however, and was very glad he had done so when he realized how good the response was and how much easier the follow-up would be.

advice

Skills Activity 34 will give you an opportunity to compose a more detailed request, write an announcement of a meeting, and make decisions on the best way to communicate in specific situations.

```
        T H E   C A P - I T   B O W L I N G   C L U B
_____

                                    BEVERLY HILLS, CA  90212

                                    September 1, 19--


        TO ALL MEMBERS:

        Our first fall meeting has been scheduled:

                    Date:   Friday, September 15
                    Time:   8 p.m.
                   Place:   Arbor Avenue Alleys
                            251 Arbor Avenue
                            Beverly Hills
               Admission:   $2 per person

        Don't miss this opportunity to get together after our two-month
        summer vacation.  If you wish, you may invite guests to this
        first meeting.  Refreshments will be served at 10:30 p.m.

        Your Executive Committee has been busy setting up the team
        schedule and the final tournament for the year.  You may pick up
        copies of their proposals at the meeting.  They will be discussed
        at the October meeting.  This promises to be a great year!

        Please make your reservations by September 12.  Just complete the
        form below, and send it to me in the enclosed envelope.  We're
        hoping that every member will come.

                            Sincerely,

                            John Foresight
                            John Foresight
                            Secretary

- - - - - - - - - - - - - - - - - - - - - - - - - - - - - - - - - - - - - - - -

        Please detach and mail by September 12 to:  Mr. John Foresight
                                                    228 Fourth Street
                                                    Beverly Hills, CA  90212


        I ___ will (___ will not) attend the September 15 meeting and
        will bring ___ guests.

        ___ My check for $___ is enclosed.  (Please make check payable
            to the Cap-It Bowling Club.)
        ___ I will pay at the door.


                            _____
                                      Name
```

Figure 5-1
A Good Letter Suits Its Purpose

SKILLS ACTIVITY 34

A. As the elected secretary of the safety squad in your office, you are asked to send an announcement to all members of the squad of a meeting for Friday, January 17, at 2 p.m. in the employees' dining room. The group will discuss the need to educate employees to use safety devices which the company supplies for their protection. There have been ten accidents in the office within the past month because employees neglected to follow safety regulations.

Before beginning to write, let's answer some questions.

1. What form will you use—a card, a letter, an interoffice memorandum, or perhaps a phone call?

2. What are the objectives of the communication—
   to supply information?
   to persuade members of the squad to come?
   to get maximum participation?

3. What information do you want to include?

4. How will you know who is coming?

5. What can you do to make the meeting successful?

After you have answered these questions, write the communication. Again, check your message against the performance objective on page 195. Now ask for peer or faculty judgment or both. Rewrite if necessary. If you succeeded, go on to B.

B. Check the method of communication you would use for each of the following situations.

	Letter	Phone	Postcard
1. Your utility bill shows that your meter has been read incorrectly and you are being charged for 100 kilowatt hours more than you have consumed.			
2. You wish to remind 20 members of your executive board of their regular monthly meeting at your home on Friday, May 18, at 8 p.m.			
3. You are calling a meeting of the by-laws committee at your home tomorrow at 6 p.m.			
4. You want to receive several publications of the Federal Reserve System relating to monetary policy, the operations of the Federal Reserve System, financing of foreign			

Given the problem of sending an announcement of a meeting to members of a committee, choose the correct style and compose an effective message.

Peer judgment or your instructor's evaluation.

Excellent	*7*
Good	*6*
Fair	*5*

Given seven sentences with spelling errors, identify each incorrectly spelled word and write the correct spelling directly above it.

Excellent	*7*
Good	*6*
Fair	*5*

Name_____ Date_____

	Letter	Phone	Postcard
trade, and the history of the Federal Reserve System.			
5. Your new TV set is to be delivered in two days but you will be on a business trip.			
6. You have been notified that you owe $20 for a mail-order purchase you made two months ago. You paid the bill when you placed the order.			
7. You wish to know if there is a position for an accountant with IBM.			
8. You wish to receive a copy of *Colorful South America* which costs $1.			

Check with the key on page 516. Note the reasons given. Evaluate the differences of opinion, if any, and discuss problems with the instructor.

SUMMARY

When writing your business communication, choose the form that suits the situation. Use a postcard for a short notice or request, a form letter for large mailings, and an individually typed letter for more personal communications. In deciding which form to use, consider the purpose of your letter and the reaction you want from your reader. Individually typed letters are not a suitable way to send sale notices to hundreds of charge-account customers, but they are the only correct way to request an extension of credit from two or three of your suppliers.

Whatever the form, follow the correct writing procedures. Include all the necessary facts, be specific and to the point, use correct mechanics, keep your language natural, and by all means remember the amenities. Before you sign and mail your card or letter, read it through carefully to verify its accuracy. No matter how short or simple the communication is, following these procedures saves time and trouble.

Now you are ready for Focus on Language. You will check your mastery of 19 spelling and vocabulary words, review and apply two more principles of agreement, add another comma rule, continue with your use of parallel structure, and check your ability to proofread carefully.

FOCUS ON LANGUAGE

Spelling

1. If I could acertain its meaning, I could chose the right answer.

2. Please send the members mimiographed copies of the letter.

3. He was very insistant, so I chose one of the magazines.

4. Have you recieved a parcel recently?

5. Action on tax reform should supercede all other legislation.

6. We are priveledged to offer a permanent settlement in this contract.

7. The company has choosen the new method of valuing inventory.

Given seven sentences with spelling errors, identify each incorrectly spelled word and write the correct spelling directly above it.

Excellent   7
Good   6
Fair   5

Check the key on page 516. If you achieve Fair or above, go on to Vocabulary. If you score below Fair, review the spelling you missed. Ask someone to read these words to you as you write or type them. Check again. Repeat the procedure until you can spell every word correctly.

Vocabulary

1. a. The pertinent facts in the case showed that he had not made a mistake.
   b. He is a pertinent individual who pushes others aside.
2. a. The intramural sports program sponsored a contest between Hanes College and Bates College.
   b. The sophomores, juniors, and seniors took part in intramural football at Hanes College.
3. a. Steel has been an integral part of every automobile for many years.
   b. His truthfulness and integral are well known to his friends.
4. a. We expect to buy a respite for our correspondence.
   b. Following the summer respite, classes will be resumed.
5. a. His preoccupation has been to learn effective business writing.
   b. He has worked five years in this preoccupation.
6. a. We do not wish to detract from your achievements by talking about one small error.
   b. If we detract five from ten, the answer is five.
7. a. Because of a misconception, the adviser gave the student incorrect advice.
   b. Such a misconception will help us greatly.

Given seven pairs of sentences, choose the sentence that shows the more effective or correct use of the underlined word.

Excellent   7
Good   6
Fair   5

Check with the key on page 516. If you achieved Fair or above, go on to the next activity. If you scored below Fair, review the meanings of the vocabulary words you missed. Use each of these words in a sentence. Ask your instructor to mark and to discuss any errors with you.

Name_____ Date_____

Sound-Alikes

In reading this chapter, you should have learned the difference between *all ready* and *already, discreet* and *discrete, advice* and *advise.* You can review the definitions below.

all ready—Use these words when the meaning is "ready" as
  We are all ready to go to the game.

already—before or by this time; as,
  They have already completed the project.

discreet—tactful and judicious; careful not to say or do the wrong thing; as,
  Mary is a discreet person.

discrete—disconnected from others; separate or distinct; as,
  The programmer will study several discrete systems.

advice—a noun meaning counsel given to encourage or dissuade; as,
  The lawyer will offer advice to the client.

advise—a verb meaning to give advice to; to notify; to recommend; as,
  The lawyer will advise the client.

Let's see if you can select the correct sound-alike in the following sentences.

Given ten problems in the use of six sound-alikes, underline the correct word.

Excellent	10
Good	9
Fair	8

1. When the meeting began, the directors were (*already, all ready*) to answer questions.

2. A (*discreet, discrete*) person would never make an insulting remark about someone's intelligence.

3. We have (*already, all ready*) sent the check to pay the premium.

4. The teacher's (*advise, advice*) was to use several (*discreet, discrete*) steps in solving the problem.

5. We knew the plans were (*already, all ready*), but we had to be (*discreet, discrete*) in speaking about them.

6. The Constitution requires that the President get the (*advise, advice*) and consent of the Senate.

7. It's time to take a (*farther, further*) look into his actions to see whether he has acted in a (*discrete, discreet*) manner.

Check the key on page 516. If you achieved Fair to Excellent, continue. If you fell below Fair, review the definitions. Discuss the problem with your instructor.

More on Agreement

Occasionally the structure of a sentence may mislead us into thinking of the wrong word as the subject. As we saw previously, this can occur when words intervene between subject and verb. It also happens when the verb precedes the subject.

Are the file cabinet and the duplication equipment in the same room?

The compound subject—"cabinet and equipment"—takes a plural verb —"are."

Clearly visible on the desk were the statements for the past five years.

The subject is "statements," so the verb is "were."

Rule: *When the sentence begins with* there *or* here, *locate the true subject and make the verb agree with it.*

Here is an idea that should be accepted.
Here are several ideas that should be considered.
There is, in Salt Lake City, a beautiful capitol.
There are, in Salt Lake City, many private gardens.

Rule: *The expletive* it *requires a singular verb, even when the real subject is plural.*

It is the blue and green copies that belong there.
It is the figures we are questioning.

1. There (*is, are*) some meetings to be held in the president's office.
2. Included in his baggage (*was, were*) a tape recorder, a sheet of instructions, and a reel of tape.
3. To all the scientists and engineers who worked on the project (*go, goes*) our appreciation.
4. It (*is, are*) our systems and procedures that we must overhaul.
5. During the early hours (*is, are*) the best time to get work done.
6. Here (*is, are*) the opportunity you have been seeking.
7. There (*is, are*) the letters you requested.

> *Given seven sentences involving agreement of subject and verb, underline the correct verb.*
>
> | | |
> |---|---|
> | *Excellent* | 7 |
> | *Good* | 6 |
> | *Fair* | 5 |

Check the key on page 516. If you achieved Fair to Excellent, go on to the next activity. Otherwise, review the rules and discuss your score with your instructor.

Punctuation: Comma

Rule: *Use commas to set off items in a series.*

Red, white, and blue are the colors of our flag.
He was working too hard, getting too little sleep, and eating poorly.

You will notice that some writers do not include the comma before the *and* or the *or* at the end of a series. However, it is good practice to make a habit of including it, since your meaning will not always be clear without it. That final comma leaves no doubt in the reader's mind that the last two members of the series are to be considered separately. For instance, look at this sentence:

Orders arrived from Abraham and Straus, Lord and Taylor, Saks and Macy's.

How many stores sent orders? Abraham and Straus is one store; so is Lord and Taylor; but Saks and Macy's are separate stores. If you place a comma after "Saks," the reader knows how many stores there are.

1. When the final figures are released quotations in the New York San Francisco Chicago and St. Louis markets will be affected.
2. This stationery is available in pink blue yellow and white.
3. Professor Allen his wife and their two children came to the class play.
4. By next year our company will be selling its products in Japan Australia and the Common Market countries.
5. Al Pat and Ella represented us at the science exhibit but Bill Jack and Irene represented us at the business show.
6. When you were a student you should have read works of Dickens Emerson and Poe and seen paintings of Monet Turner and Matisse.
7. We have ordered slips staples pencils and pens from the stationery department.

Check the key on page 516. If you achieved Fair to Excellent, go on to the next activity; otherwise, review the comma rules in Chapter 3, 4, and 5. Discuss your score with your instructor.

Parallel Structure

Correlatives are *either . . . or; neither . . . nor; not only . . . but also; whether . . . or; both . . . and.*

Rule: *The elements following correlatives must be parallel.*

Not Our temporary employees are not only proficient, but also they are loyal.
But Our temporary employees are not only proficient but also loyal.

Not Either Mr. Stack wants our financial statement or a letter of recommendation.
But Mr. Stack wants either our financial statement or a letter of recommendation.

Not The treasurer's plans both worked out in theory and in practice.
But The treasurer's plans worked out both in theory and in practice.

1. The ruling of the traffic department both affects drivers and those who enforce the laws.

2. Either pay your bills now, or you will have to deal with our attorney.

3. The company not only found an excellent site for its new factory but also a good market for its products.

4. Mr. Hanson will either arrive on the early plane tomorrow or in the afternoon by train.

5. Moore's Department Store expects not only to add a furniture department but also an appliance section.

6. Under current economic conditions, we can obtain funds neither from the security markets nor the banks.

7. For an additional fee, you may obtain either a receipt showing the exact address of delivery, or you may restrict delivery of your mail to the addressee only.

Check with the key on page 516. If you achieve Fair or above, go on to the proofreading exercise. If you score below Fair, review the rules. If necessary, discuss the problem with your instructor.

Proofreading

You have been asked to proof the following material, which is to be sent out by your company, The Gardeners Publishing Company. Write your corrections in the space directly above the lines.

> Given a 13-line paragraph containing errors in spelling, punctuation, and typographical usage, correct the errors.
>
> | | |
> |---|---|
> | Excellent | 13 |
> | Good | 12 |
> | Fair | 11 |

When it comes to aquiring a skill or mastering a

new technique 1 picture is often worth more th-

an a thousand words. Hear for the first time is

an inexpensive professionaly illustrated garden-

ing reference library that abounds with visual aids—

photographs, diagrams, paintings, drawings—that

will help you achieve the easy to care for beauti-

ful garden youve always wanted. In addition, each

volume contains specially comissioned maps and

charts that brake down the United States and Canada

into zones that tell you what seeds plants trees and

shrubs you can grow in you area and when they should

be planted.

Check the key on page 516. If you achieved Fair or above, you have completed Chapter 5's Focus on Language. If you did not achieve Fair, discuss your score with your instructor.

6

THE SOCIAL-BUSINESS LETTER

In your social-business life, you will have to write many types of letters. Your business commitments usually require you to write a thank-you note from time to time. If you participate in any group activity, you may find yourself writing invitations to speakers or guests to attend your meetings, forums, receptions, dinners, conferences, sports events. Since we all manage to get at least one vacation each year, it is often necessary to write a letter reserving a hotel or motel room or a cottage by the sea. Then there are the "no" letters, particularly troublesome when they must be written to your employer or to someone in authority; the congratulatory messages; the notes of sympathy or condolence; the cancellations.

In Units 17, 18, 19, and 20, we will consider four types of social-business letters—the thank-you letter, the social-business invitation, the reservation letter, the "no" letter—and work through some problems you may encounter.

commitments: pledges; engagements

condolence: expression of sympathy

cancellations

UNIT 17   THE THANK-YOU LETTER

Your performance objective for Unit 17 is:

Given the social-business situation in which you are to thank a person,

You will compose an effective thank-you letter that (1) gets to the point immediately, (2) uses natural language, (3) contains only necessary information, and (4) sounds genuine.

One of the most abused forms of communication is the thank-you letter. Many people write because they have to, not because they want to. They hide behind hypocritical phrases and weary expressions. The real gem of a thank-you letter is the one that is truthful.

Here is a situation in which you have to write a thank-you note to your host and hostess. The faculty adviser of the Business-Management Club, Professor Caleb Ross, invited you, as president, and the other members of the club's executive council to his home for dinner, which

hypocritical: false

council: assembly

Note use of collective noun as plural—"group were"—since members are acting as individuals.

flamboyant: *showy*

was to be followed by a council meeting. Professor and Mrs. Ross were very gracious, and the group were made to feel very much at home. After dinner, the council planned the term's activities, which would be presented to the membership for consideration at the first club meeting. As president of the club, you face the double responsibility of expressing both your own appreciation and that of the council.

However, each member of the council will also write his or her own note. Bill Fischer wrote his that very night. It was late, and he was tired; but he had enjoyed the dinner and wanted to say so. In his usual flamboyant way, he dashed off this note:

October 9, 19--

Professor Richard Ross, Adviser
The Business-Management Club
5 Campus Court
Trenton, NJ 08638

Dear Prof. Ross:

Here I am, home after a full day. This was completely different from my usual -- I had dinner at your home.

Thanks loads for the swell dinner. It was a real treat not to have to eat in the cafeteria, where I would of eaten otherwise.

I hope that I and the other club members will get another invite from you again some time.

Truly yours,

Bill Fischer

Bill Fischer

Spell out numbers up to and including ten.

Spell out "Professor."

Avoid slang: "loads," "swell," "invite."

"Would have" is correct.

Sometime is one word when it means "at another time."
Use a more up-to-date closing.

brash: *bold and rash*

Professor Ross appreciated this letter from Bill—so few students remember to say thank you. But Bill seemed much more interested in the food than in the company, saying in effect that anything was better than eating in the cafeteria. And he was certainly brash in asking to be invited again. Can you see the amusement on Professor Ross's face as he read the last sentence?

If Bill had given a little more thought to his host and hostess and had corrected his language and form, the thank-you note would have looked something like this:

Dear Professor Ross:

Thank you very much for inviting me to your
home tonight. It was a real treat for all of us
to have dinner with you and Mrs. Ross.

I am glad that I was elected to office in the
Business-Management Club and that I am helping
to plan the year's activities. What a first
meeting!

                    Sincerely yours,

Angie Jewkes was a timorous writer. She tried to write her letter three
times, but she just couldn't get started. Finally, she asked an older
friend to help her. When she finished, Angie was so overwhelmed by
the strangeness of the language that she couldn't believe she had written
it. (Neither could Professor Ross.)

timorous: fearful and
timid
overwhelmed: overcome

Dear Professor Ross:

May I take this opportunity to express my
sincere appreciation for the very enjoyable
repast I and the other members of the executive
council had at your home yesterday. I was indeed
pleased to have been invited to your home.

This occasion afforded the members of the council the opportunity to become better acquainted
with one another and to give further consideration to the development of a worthwhile program
for our club for the forthcoming term.

Let me express again my deep gratitude for a
very fine evening.

                    Respectfully yours,

*Avoid wordy or outmoded
expressions and those that
sound insincere.*

*Again, watch that outdated
closing.*

Angie wrote her thank-you note without delay—an important point to
remember. Her letter was polite; she got to the point at once; she closed
with an extra thank-you. But she forgot to be natural. Her language
depicted not the vital woman of the twentieth century but the old-
fashioned stereotype of the nineteenth. Let's ask Angie a question:
What would you say to Professor Ross if you met him on campus? Her
answer:

depicted: portrayed
stereotype: conventional
mental image

"Professor Ross, thank you so much for that wonderful evening we had at your home. Will you tell Mrs. Ross how much we enjoyed it? It was great of you to have the executive council. We did so much and had such a good time doing it that we feel we can't miss this year."

adapted: changed to fit

If Angie had written her letter in these terms, it not only would have sounded like her but would have left the impression that she really did enjoy herself. Note how she could have adapted her verbal expression to the written form:

Dear Professor Ross:

Thank you very much for the wonderful evening we had at your home last Tuesday. Please tell Mrs. Ross how much we enjoyed it.

It was very thoughtful of you to have the first meeting of our executive council at your home. We accomplished so much and had such a good time doing it that we feel this will be a very successful year.

Thanks again, Professor Ross.

Sincerely yours,

Now it's your turn. How will you start that letter? How can you tell Professor Ross how much you appreciate what he has done? How can you thank his wife? You start four times:

Thank you very much . . .

We want to thank you sincerely . . .

Many thanks . . .

Our sincere thanks . . .

Since you are writing for the whole committee as well as for yourself, you decide to use the last idea—and also to mention Mrs. Ross in the first sentence:

Our sincere thanks to you and Mrs. Ross for the dinner meeting you planned for our executive council on Tuesday. We certainly enjoyed ourselves. You made us feel very much a part of this college.

In the second paragraph, you want to mention the council meeting. This is easy, because the members of the group were glowing as they left Professor Ross's home, saying such things as: "What a program!" "The kids will love it!" "To think that we could really get him as a speaker!" So you write easily:

> This council is proud of the proposal for the year's activities and is especially impressed with the stature of the speakers you suggested. Your guidance and advice were of tremendous help. We cannot wait to present the proposal to the members next week. This looks like a great year!

Use active voice: "helped greatly."

The last paragraph is yours personally:

> I want to add my own personal thank you, Professor Ross, for inviting me to your home and for doing so much to make our club successful.

Use direct address.

You type your letter on stationery bearing the college seal, using the formal style of official-business correspondence. You remember that the inside address of an official-business letter comes at the end. Of course, you make an extra carbon for the club's files, and you always make one for your personal file. You are happy to sign your name to this letter, which you send through the intracollege mail.

stationery: *remember, not* stationary

    There are numerous occasions that call for a letter of appreciation—a gift, the return of a lost article, a speech, the attendance of a famous guest at a reception, the participation of a panelist, a letter of recommendation. Remember to get to the point immediately, to be natural, to say no more than is necessary, and to be sure that your thank-you sounds genuine.

intracollege: within the college
numerous: many

    Try Skills Activity 35 to evaluate two thank-you letters and to compose four letters of your own in social-business situations calling for thank-you's.

SKILLS ACTIVITY 35

1. Lupe Leon has applied for a summer job as a lifeguard at the town beach. Her neighbor has written a complimentary letter of reference about her character and her reliability. Lupe shows you the letter she has written to her neighbor to thank him for his help. Can you suggest any improvements?

Dear Mr Robbins

It has come to my attention that your letter of reference on my behalf has been partly instrumental in me acquiring the lifeguard position at Reese Beach.

Therefore, I would like to take this opportunity to say "Thank you" for helping me get the summer job. It means that I will be able to help my parents pay my college tuition for the coming year.

You may be sure that I will perform my duties in a manner which will justify the excellent reference you gave me.

Thanking you again, I remain

Yours sincerely,

Lupe Leon

Lupe Leon

Given a thank-you letter with errors, identify the errors and write your improvements above each time.

Excellent	*11-13*
Good	*9-10*
Fair	*7-8*

Name_____ Date_____

Check the key on page 516. If you achieved Fair or above, skip 2, below, and go on to 3. If you need an extra drill, try the problem below.

2. After seeing the name of your former classmate, Richard Thorne, on the Dean's List, you have written a letter to congratulate him on his achievement. Richard has written you the following thank-you letter.

```
Dear _____


May I extend my appreciation to you for your

very thoughtful missive regarding my achievement

in having my name on the Dean's list.


Needless to say, I am proud of my grades. I

expect to continue doing well at college and

than move on to graduate school where I will

work for an advanced degree.


I hope you are doing as well in your studies as

I am. Thanks for remembering me.

                            Your friend
```

Check the key on page 516. If you achieved Fair or above, go on to the next items. If you did not achieve Fair or above, discuss the problem with your instructor.

In problems 3–6, you will compose four thank-you letters.

3. On a recent Sunday afternoon, your car broke down on a busy highway. Hundreds of people passed you before a man stopped to help. He would accept no money for his help. You noticed his name and address on an envelope in his car. Write him a letter to tell how much you appreciated his help, especially when so many people paid no heed to your trouble.

4. You had written to the ABX Company to ask if they would allow you to visit their offices to study their administrative procedures. They permitted the visit, and you learned many things that were especially helpful in preparing a report for your management class. Write to thank ABX for their cooperation.

Given a short thank-you letter with errors, identify the errors and suggest improvements.

Excellent	*8*
Good	*7*
Fair	*6*

Given four business situations in which thank-you letters should be written, compose effective letters giving special consideration to (1) getting to the point immediately, (2) using natural language, (3) including only necessary information, and (4) sounding genuine.

Peer judgment of your instructor's evaluation:

Effective letter including given number of points:

Excellent	*4*
Good	*3*
Fair	*2*

5. You have borrowed Maria's tape recorder for your party, and your brother is returning it to her. Write a letter for him to take along to thank Maria for the use of the machine.

6. You bought a set of records that were broken in transit. When you wrote to the company to report the loss, they immediately sent you a duplicate set plus an extra record because of your original disappointment. Don't you think it would be nice to write a brief thank-you note to the company? What would you write?

If you achieved Fair to Excellent, you have finished the unit. If you fell below Fair, discuss your score with your instructor before going on to Unit 18.

UNIT 18 THE SOCIAL-BUSINESS INVITATION

Your performance objective for this unit is:

Given the situations in which a college president and a state senator are to be guests at a social-business function,

You will compose effective letters of invitation that use correct form, include all the facts, spotlight the reader, and clearly state the purpose of the social-business affair.

As you become more involved in group activity, you will be inviting speakers to meetings, guests to receptions, dignitaries to conventions. Just as party invitations include basic points of information for your guests—purpose, date, time, place, host and hostess—so your written social-business invitations must include such data.

dignitaries: people holding high positions

data: facts or figures

As secretary of the fraternity, you are asked to write to the president of the college, James Wells, and his wife to invite them to attend the annual Christmas banquet on December 18 as guests of honor of the fraternity. It's to be a gala affair—the national officers will attend, and this year your fraternity is to be presented with the National Service Award for service to the college, the community, and the national office of the fraternity. It is important that the president of the college be present at the ceremonies.

You compose the letter shown in Figure 6-1 with the help and counsel of your fraternity's adviser. Then, after getting Walter's signature and addressing a legal-size envelope, you deliver the invitation personally to the president's secretary.

counsel

The executive board and the national officers give you another job. They want you to invite a state senator, who is an alumnus of Kensington and a Phi Nu member, to be the guest speaker. How do you address a state senator? Your reference manual shows the following:

alumnus: male graduate (plural: alumni)

Address	Possible salutations
The Honorable James Perez The State Senate Albany, NY 12209	Sir: Dear Senator Perez: My dear Mr. Perez:

You know that you want to get to the point immediately, but you must be formal with a state senator. Four openings suggest themselves:

Please be our guest speaker.

Will you please be our banquet speaker.

It would be a special honor for us in Phi
Nu . . .

You would be honoring us in Phi Nu in a special
way by addressing the twenty-fifth annual
Holiday Banquet on Saturday, December 18, in the
Starlight Room of the Hotel Madison, Santa
Barbara.

Kensington City College

BETA CHAPTER

FRATERNITY

128 Martindale Road
Kensington City, California 95402

November 21, 19--

President and Mrs. James A. Wells
Kensington City College

Dear President and Mrs. Wells:

Beta Chapter of the Phi Nu Fraternity cordially invites you to
be our guests of honor at the annual Holiday Banquet on
Saturday, the eighteenth of December, in the Starlight Room of
the Hotel Madison, at seven o'clock in the evening. It would
mean a great deal to us in Phi Nu to have you with us on this
evening.

This year, our chapter has been named to receive the National
Service Award. The presentation will be made at the banquet
by the national officers of Phi Nu. Representatives of other
chapters are expected to attend, and many of our alumni are
returning.

We are proud to bring this honor to Kensington, and we hope
that you will be able to be with us on the eighteenth to share
our success.

Sincerely yours,

Walter R. Furst
President, Beta Chapter

Figure 6-1
A Formal Request

You adopt the last choice; but the sentence is too long, and you must shorten it. By placing a period after "18" you can include the rest of the information in the next sentence:

adopt: take as one's own

```
The banquet will be held in the Starlight Room
of the Hotel Madison, Santa Barbara, at seven
o'clock.
```

In order to give the senator freedom to speak on any topic, you write:

```
We will be happy to have you choose the topic
of your address.
```

If the senator will consent to be the banquet speaker, it will ensure the success of the banquet and add to the prestige of your fraternity. You really mean it when you say:

prestige: renown

```
It would be a special privilege to present our
outstanding Phi Nu alumnus on this occasion. Our
chapter has been named to receive the National
Service Award. This represents outstanding ser-
vice to the college, to the community, and to
the nation. The national officers will make the
presentation following the address, and they
wish you to participate in the ceremonies.
```

You have used outstanding *twice in this paragraph. Check a thesaurus or dictionary for a synonym.*

The final paragraph should reiterate your request:

reiterate: repeat

```
We hope that you will be our banquet speaker on
this occasion, for that would make our evening
a certain success.
```

Mention the date again for emphasis.

When you show the letter to Walter, he approves it with only a few suggestions for change. Then, using your fraternity stationery, you type very carefully the letter shown in Figure 6–2. When you are ready to mail it, you hesitate—should you include a self-addressed, stamped envelope to ensure an answer? The president's secretary responds: "That would be an affront to the senator. He will use his own stationery and matching envelope to reply."

affront: insult

In Skills Activity 36 you will check your ability to improve a written invitation and to compose five letters inviting guests and speakers to attend social-business functions.

Kensington City College

BETA CHAPTER

FRATERNITY
128 Martindale Road
Kensington City, California 95402

November 22, 19--

Dear Senator Winner:

You would be honoring us in Phi Nu in a special way by
addressing the twenty-fifth annual Holiday Banquet on Saturday,
December 18. The banquet will be held in the Starlight Room
of the Hotel Madison, Santa Barbara, at seven o'clock. We
will be happy to have you choose the topic of your address.

It would be a special privilege to present our foremost
alumnus on this occasion. Our chapter has been named to
receive the National Service Award this year. It represents
outstanding service to the college, to the community, and to
the nation. The national officers plan to make the presentation following the address, and they would like you to participate in the ceremonies.

We hope that you will be our banquet speaker on the 18th. It
would make our evening a certain success.

                    Respectfully yours,

                    Michael Scriber

                    Michael Scriber
                    Secretary

Senator David G. Winner
The State Senate
Sacramento, CA 95825

Figure 6-2
A Social-Business Invitation

SKILLS ACTIVITY 36

1. Your friend, Julio Ramos, has recently been elected president of the Hispanic Society at your college. Julio asks you to comment on the following letter, which he plans to send to the Spanish consular office asking for a speaker to discuss how business is conducted between the United States and Spain. Refer to this checklist, and write your suggestions above the lines of the letter. (You may assume that Julio wrote the letter on Hispanic Society letterhead, which included the name and address of the college.)

1. Correct letter arrangement?
2. Correct spelling and punctuation?
3. Name of the consul? Correct address? Appropriate salutation and closing?
4. Inclusion of all essentials?
5. Omission of unnecessary material?
6. Inclusion of amenities?

March 4th, 19--

Consul of Spain

150 E. 58th St.

New York, N.Y.

Sir

I am now the President of the Hispanic Society at Brown Community College. I have discussed with my members what program we should follow during the semester. Therefore we have decided to devote a meeting to the study of Hispanic culture. Another meeting will be to talk about how business relations are conducted with Spain.

> Given an invitation with numerous inadequacies, list suggestions for improvement.
>
> Excellent 17–20
> Good 14–16
> Fair 12–13

Name_____ Date_____

I would like you to come to the meeting dealing
with business on Thursday, April 4th, in Room
115.

Thank you for your affirmative answer to this
invitation. If you wish any further information
about the program you can get in touch with me
at the above address.

> Yours respectfully,
>
> *Julio Ramos*
>
> Julio Ramos
>
> President

Given five social-business situations requiring written invitations, compose five effective letters that (1) use correct style, (2) include all the facts, (3) spotlight the reader, and (4) clearly state the purpose of the social-business function.

Peer judgment or your instructor's evaluation:

A letter in good form meeting the given guidelines:

Excellent all guidelines
Good guidelines 2, 3, 4
Fair guidelines 2, 4

Check the key on page 516. If you achieved Fair or above, go on to the next problem. If you are below Fair, note differences with key, and review this unit. Discuss any problems with your instructor.

2. You are in charge of arranging programs for the Economics Club. The club members have been reading about the problems people encounter in arranging mortgage loans to buy new homes. You have decided to invite Mrs. Regina Coburn, manager of the mortgage department at Factory National Bank, to speak on the topic, "What Causes High Mortgage Rates?" The meeting will take place on Thursday, February 26, from 12 noon to 1 p.m. in Room 239, Main Building. Ask Mrs. Coburn to join you and the Faculty Adviser, Professor Cutts, her former economics professor, for luncheon following her talk.

3. Invite Mr. Peter Bergen of Bergen & Hamilton Associates to address the Economics Club and their parents on "Building Your Investment Portfolio." The Stock Exchange has listed him as one of their speakers. Give him a choice of two dates: March 5 or March 12. The time is from 7 to 9 p.m. Invite him to remain for the reception following his address.

4. Invite the Dean of Students to attend a symposium on "The Common Market" at which Dr. Rudolph Maylor, a noted economist from another university, will speak and lead a follow-up discussion. Ask the dean to say a few words of welcome in behalf of the administration of the college. The meeting is scheduled for March 27, from 12 to 2 p.m., in Room 945.

5. As secretary of the senior class, invite the members of the faculty who have been designated by the Senior Council as guests of the class to the Senior Prom on Saturday, June 11, in the Grand Ballroom of the Winchester Arms, Beverly Hills, at nine o'clock.

6. Invite the members of the student council of another university to cooperate with your college in a leadership conference to be held at Camp Holmes on March 28, 29, and 30. The student council should invite up to 25 of its members to participate. The cost of the conference is $60 a person, which includes dormitory facilities, meals, and transportation by bus. Top-level speakers and counselors have accepted invitations to work with the students at this conference. The deadline for reservations is March 1, but if the college wishes to participate, the secretary of the student council must answer by February 15.

Now rewrite the letter in problem 1, using your suggestions for improvement. Ask your instructor to evaluate your letter. If you achieved Fair or above, you have completed Unit 18. If you achieved below Fair, review and discuss problems with your instructor.

UNIT 19   THE RESERVATION LETTER

Your performance objectives for this unit are:

Given the problems of writing to reserve a room, to rent a car, and to cancel a reservation,

You will compose effective written reservation requests that include the seven key points for reservation letters (see below), and also cancellation letters that include an apology and an explanation in clear, precise language.

Making a Reservation

The bus was delayed by the storm—not just an hour or two, but four hours. When the four girls trudged into the ski lodge, they were fatigued and cold; but they expected warm, comfortable rooms that had been reserved by telephone two weeks before. The night clerk looked nonplussed. There were no rooms reserved for them—in fact, there were no rooms available in the lodge. What had happened? The telephone reservation had not been recorded.

trudged: walked wearily

While it is occasionally necessary to make a last-minute reservation by telephone or telegraph, it is safer to write; and you should know how to compose your own communication for this purpose. The reservation letter is an official record, and a confirmation assures you that your reservation will be waiting when you arrive.

Remember, a letter is an official record.

Once again, follow the simple rule: Be brief and right to the point, and be precise. You cannot assume that your reader knows what you want. If you write simply "Please reserve a room for me on April 22," don't be surprised to find yourself in a luxury room that you do not need and cannot afford. *You* know what you want, and you must state it clearly.

Where will you stay when you are in another city? There are a number of excellent directories in which you may find complete hotel information. When you are employed in an office, you will probably have access to the *Hotel Red Book*, which is published annually by the American Hotel Association. Regional directories published by the American Automobile Association also supply listings and ratings of hotels and motels. Several excellent guides, such as the *Guide Michelin*, list hotel accommodations in foreign countries. These directories indicate the number of rooms, the rates, and whether (in the case of a hotel) it is operated on the European or American plan. (Under the European plan, the rate represents the cost of the room only; under the American plan, the rate includes the cost of your meals as well as the cost of the room.)

access: opportunity to obtain or make use of

When you make a reservation by mail, these points should guide you:

1. *Kind of room.* If you want a room with air conditioning, cross ventilation, or television, you must say so. If the location of the room makes a difference to you (overlooking the lake, on a certain floor, near an exit), be sure to put that in the letter, too.

to
too

2. *Type of accommodations.* You should state whether you want twin beds or a double bed and, especially in foreign countries, the lavatory facilities you want.

accommodations: lodgings

3. *Approximate rate.* Tell how much you wish to pay for your room. Naturally, you should use common sense in quoting a rate that would

be commensurate with the type of accommodations and location you have requested. Requesting a room for two on the sixteenth floor, with shower and a view of the ocean, but insisting that this room cost no more than $16.50 is ludicrous.

4. *Number of persons in your party.* If there are children in the group, it is advisable to mention this fact also and to tell their ages.

5. *Date and probable time of your arrival.* You might also indicate your method of travel because of possible delays in transportation at certain times. If there is any likelihood of delay, be sure to ask that the reservation be held for you until you arrive.

6. *Length of stay.* Tell the reservations clerk how long you expect to stay so that another person can receive the room when you leave.

7. *Request for confirmation.* A confirmation of your reservation may be especially helpful to you in a city where hotel rooms are at a premium, such as Washington, D.C., during the Easter holidays.

The message below is short but complete enough to enable the room clerk at the Hotel Elizabeth to make a reservation for this student:

*In simplified style the
salutation and closing
would be omitted.*

exceed: go beyond; surpass

```
                              12 Kingston Drive
                              Pensacola, FL  32506
                              December 15, 19--

Airmail

Hotel Elizabeth
Ste Adele
Montreal, Quebec

Attention Room Clerk

Ladies and Gentlemen:

Please reserve a single room with shower, at a
rate not to exceed $20 for the night of Thurs-
day, January 2.

I am scheduled to arrive in Montreal on Canada
Airways Flight 128, at 4 p.m. on that day.
Please hold my room until I arrive.

Please confirm this reservation.

                              Sincerely yours,

                              John Q. Walker
                              John Q. Walker
```

John was careful enough to send the reservation airmail so that he could be sure of receiving the confirmation before his trip.

Now let's plan a vacation with Carol and Anne. They wish to spend a one-week vacation at a winter resort. After reading the following ad, they have decided to make a reservation at Red Maples:

resort: place for rest or recreation; also, as a verb, to use as a means; to turn to for help

---

Red Maples Is the Place for You!
SPECIAL WINTER VACATIONS!

$68 per week for each person, including meals. Fun and rest await you! Olympic-size heated pool. Skiing, skating, tobogganing, dancing nightly, indoor tennis courts. Excellent food. Write: Red Maples, Box T, Mapletown, NY 10550.

---

skiing

Carol wrote this letter and asked Anne to check it before she typed it in final form:

```
                              567 Locust Street
                              Neva, Pa.
                              Dec. 28, 19--


Red Maples
Box T
Mapletown, N.Y.

Dear Sir:

I have read your ad in the Sunday paper. Please
reserve a room for me and my friend Anne Martini
for a week's stay beginning the second week in
January, the 22nd.

Our school closes on Jan. 22 and we are looking
forward to enjoying the many activities you
listed in your ad.

Let me know if you wish a deposit.

                    Cordially,

                    Carol Giles

                    Carol Giles
```

Would you make any changes in this letter?

Note use of possessive.

Having just completed a course in writing business letters, Anne was able to make the following suggestions for improving the letter:

Write out abbreviations.

Include the zip code in the return address and the inside address.

Use the correct salutation: "Ladies and Gentlemen."

Get to the point in the first sentence: "Please reserve a room with twin beds and bath for Anne Martini and me."

Be explicit as to dates: "for a week's stay, from January 22 to 29."

explicit: clear; plainly expressed

Omit the second paragraph; it isn't necessary.

Refer to the ad and the name of the newspaper in which you read it when you state the cost of the room and meals for each person.

Ask for a confirmation—just to be sure.

Use correct closing: "Sincerely yours."

Following these suggestions, Carol rewrote the letter:

> 567 Locust Street
> Neva, PA 19133
> December 28, 19--
>
> Red Maples
> Box T
> Mapletown, NY 10550
>
> Ladies and Gentlemen:
>
> Please reserve a room with twin beds and bath for Anne Martini and me for a week's stay, from January 22 to January 29.
>
> According to the advertisement in today's Inquirer, the room rate, including meals, is $68 per week for each individual. Is it necessary to send a deposit before we arrive?
>
> Please confirm this reservation.
>
> Sincerely yours,
>
> *Carol Giles*
>
> Carol Giles

Underline names of newspapers and magazines.

Another type of reservation you can make by mail is one for renting a car. Russell planned to fly from San Francisco to Chicago. He wished to rent a car for a week, and the following advertisement caught his attention:

> **BUDGET RENTAL SYSTEM**
>
> A Corsair costs only $10 a day and 10 cents a mile. You buy only the gas you use. Our cars are equipped with automatic transmission, radio, seat belts, and heater, and they are covered by proper insurance. Airport pickup service is available at no extra charge.

Use figures with cents.

Why did Russell's message cause the Budget Rental agent so much trouble?

```
               672 Hollywood Court
               San Francisco, CA  94112

     Budget Rental System
     35 E. Wacker Drive
     Chicago, IL  60601

     Sirs:

     I want to rent a Corsair as advertised in a
     recent issue of The Far Horizons.

     I shall arrive at O'Hare Airport at 3 p.m. on
     Omega Airlines Flight 628. I should like the car
     to be delivered to the airport. The car will be
     driven for a week and will be returned to the
     airport on March 2nd at 2 p.m.

     My Hatton Bank credit-card number is A560-331.
     I have a California driver's license No. 061-
     2347.

                    Very truly yours,

                    Russell Warren

                    Russell Warren
```

Include date.

Spell out "East."

Use "Ladies and Gentlemen."

Omit "nd" when date follows the month.

license

You were right if you noted that Russell omitted the date of his arrival at the airport. What date should the car be ready for him at the airport? Will he arrive on February 23 or 24? If he had written a slightly different second paragraph, Russell would have found his car waiting for him when he arrived in Chicago.

Always double check dates.

```
     I shall arrive at O'Hare Airport on February 24,
     at 3 p.m., on Omega Airlines Flight 628. Please
     have a car ready for me at the airport. I will
```

drive it for seven days, February 24--March 2,
and will return it to the airport on March 2
at 2 p.m.

Canceling a Reservation

Sometimes you find it necessary to cancel a reservation you made for a room or for a trip. Courtesy dictates that you write a letter as soon as you learn you cannot keep that reservation.

preceding: going before *(Remember how to spell this word?)*

Let's take the preceding reservation made by Carol Giles at Red Maples. Carol sent the reservation on December 28. On January 2, she learned that she and Anne were required to attend a special school conference on January 23, 24, and 25. She wrote to Red Maples immediately:

If possible, give a reason for your cancellation.

```
                                 567 Locust Street
                                 Neva, PA  19133
                                 January 2, 19--


Red Maples
Box T
Mapletown, NY  10550

Ladies and Gentlemen:

Please cancel my reservation of December 28 for
a room with twin beds and bath for Anne Martini
and myself for the week of January 22 to January
29.

I am sorry that we cannot come to Red Maples as
we had planned. It is now necessary for us to
attend a special college conference from January
23 to 25.

I hope this cancellation does not cause you
any inconvenience.

                                 Sincerely yours,

                                 Carol Giles

                                 Carol Giles
```

In writing letters either making or canceling a reservation, use clear, precise language. Keep your letters short and to the point. If you are making the reservation, request a confirmation. Then your vacation can be a pleasure, not a fiasco.

fiasco: complete failure

Check your ability to write reservation letters by completing Skills Activity 37.

SKILLS ACTIVITY 37

1. On June 17, the Glacier Lodge received three requests for a room
reservation for the week of August 15. Only one room is available
for that week. To whom would you give the reservation?

June 15, 19--

Glacier Lodge
Glacier, Montana 59063

Sir:

I want a double room with bath for the week of
Aug. 15th. Since I will be traveling on the 15th
I may not arrive until late in the day but I
will expect you to hold the room.

Thank you for your assistance.

Truly yours,

Rod Wilcox

Rod Wilcox

> Given three letters re-
> questing a reservation,
> choose the best letter
> and list five reasons for
> your choice.
>
> Excellent   5
> Good   4
> Fair   3

150 Lowell Avenue
Youngstown, OH 44512
June 15, 19--

Glacier Lodge
Glacier, MT 59063

Ladies and Gentlemen:

Please reserve a double room with bath for the
week August 15 through 21. I understand that the
room rate, European plan, is $40 a day.

Please confirm this reservation.

Sincerely,

Jane Franklin

Jane Franklin

Name_____ Date_____

Box 185
Painted Post, NY
June 15th, 19--

Glacier Lodge

Ladies and Gentlemen:

I am planning a trip through Montana and I would
like to spend a week at Glacier Lodge so that I
could travel around beautiful Glacier national
park. Therefore, I would like to reserve a
double room with bath for the week when I will
be at Glacier. This will be the week of Aug.
15th. What will the room rate be?

Thanking you in advance for handling this reservation.

Very truly yours,

Mike Baker

Mike Baker

1. _____
2. _____
3. _____
4. _____
5. _____

Check the key on page 517. Note differences before going on to the
next problem. Discuss major differences with your instructor.

Given three social-business situations which call for a reservation letter, write three correct letters that effectively include the seven key points (page 227).

Peer judgment or instructor's evaluation:

Excellent	7
Good	6
Fair	5

2. On your next visit to New York during the Christmas holidays, you want to dine at the Top of the Sixes Restaurant, overlooking midtown at 666 Fifth Avenue. Write a letter making a dinner reservation for six on December 28 at 7 p.m. Your group would like to sit by a window for a good view of the city.

3. You are a member of Future Business Leaders of America. The organization is holding its annual regional convention at the Drake Hotel at 357 Longhorn Street, Missoula, Montana 05201, on November 26 and 27. Write to reserve a room at the Drake for the nights of November 25 and 26. Identify your organization and ask for the convention rates.

4. Assume that you are a secretary of the Accounting Club at your school. At the beginning of the term, it is necessary to reserve a room to use for your club meetings throughout the term. Write a message to the dean's office to reserve Room 432 for weekly meetings every Monday between the hours of 1 and 2 p.m.

If you achieved Fair to Excellent on all three letters, go on to the next problem. If you scored below Fair, review and discuss your problems with the instructor.

5. Correct the following letter. You will find many mistakes.

```
                              587 1 Ave.

                              Seattle, Wash.

                              Nov. 1st, '76
```

```
Hotel Summers

587 Broadway

New York, N.Y.
```

> Given a reservation request with many errors, correct the errors in the space provided.
>
> Excellent   19-20
> Good   17-18
> Fair   15-16

```
Dear Mr. Summers


Your confirmation of a room reservation was

received by me last week. Since then I have

found it desirable to change the dates of my

stay in New York from Nov. 16-18 to Nov. 25-27.

The same kind of accomodations can be reserved

for Nov. 25-27 as you had all ready reserved for

the 16-18.

                    Respectfully,
```

Check with key on page 517. If you achieved Fair to Excellent, you are ready for the next unit. If you scored below Fair, note your errors, and discuss your problems with the instructor

Name _____ *Date* _____

UNIT 20 THE "NO" LETTER

Your performance objective for this unit is:

Given the problem of saying "no" to a request,

You will answer immediately with an effective letter of refusal which gives a clear and valid excuse, expresses regret, and contains an apology.

Difficult as the letter of refusal may be to compose, it must be written. Your knowledge of human nature and your ability to use language will help you. Remember to think in terms of your reader. A refusal is always difficult to accept. The first reaction of the recipient is "why?" If the reader of a "no" letter does not get an acceptable answer to this question, you may never get another invitation or request from him or her.

Here is one "sticky" situation in which Mary Jo Elting is enmeshed. As a part-time clerk in a law office, she received an invitation to be the senior attorney's guest at an important political meeting at which the 25 people in the office were expected to be present. She was first excited to have been included and then totally dismayed when she realized that it coincided with her sister's engagement party. She discussed the problem with the attorney's secretary and was even more distressed when the secretary said, "Mr. Styles doesn't like it when people refuse." She needed this job for the next semester, but she had to say no. Keeping her job depended on how tactfully she wrote that letter.

enmeshed: entangled

This is one time she did not want to get to the point in the first sentence. The second sentence, however, had to state the facts. Mary Jo typed the following letter:

December 1, 19--

Edmond J. Styles, Esq.
Styles, Bridges, and Brown
1600 Michigan Avenue
Chicago, IL 60616

Dear Mr. Styles:

Thank you very much for inviting me to attend the Mayor's Conference on Urban Affairs on December 19. Unfortunately, my sister's engagement dinner is taking place that same evening, and I must be there.

I know the importance of this conference and am very sorry that I cannot attend. Please accept my apologies.

Sincerely yours,

Mary Jo Elting

Mary Jo Elting

"Esq."—a courtesy title often is used for lawyers—is always abbreviated (see Chapter 2).

fabrications: deceptions;
also the act of constructing
or manufacturing
appendectomy: operation
to remove appendix

procrastination: delay

Her letter was simple, but she hoped Mr. Styles would understand that she really was sorry she had to miss the meeting. He did; she kept her job.

Whatever you do, don't get involved in fabrications designed to impress an employer or supervisor with the gravity of the situation that caused your refusal. One supervisor remarked, "That's the second appendectomy Joe's mother has had in six months—she's making medical history." Six months before, the worker had written a note to a representative in another city using this excuse, and it had been reported to his present supervisor. So it backfired the second time.

Another temptation to avoid is procrastination. Since "no" letters are unpleasant, you put them off until tomorrow. This makes the letter more difficult to write and puts the reader in an antagonistic frame of mind. Think of the hostess who receives a refusal on the day of her dinner party—or the chairman of a panel discussion who receives a note just before the meeting saying: "Sorry I am no longer able to speak at the panel discussion on 'Automation and the Job Market' this afternoon."

When you write a letter of refusal, you show your concern for the reader by (1) answering immediately, (2) giving a clear and valid excuse, (3) expressing regret, and (4) apologizing.

Can you successfully apply the four elements listed above to composing the letter of refusal? Try Skills Activity 38.

SKILLS ACTIVITY 38

1. Which of the following letters would you send to say that the Business Club cannot join the Business Management Leadership Conference?

   a. On behalf of the Business Club of Clearcrest College, I must say "no" to your invitation to attend the Business Management Leadership Conference this year. Our student council failed to vote funds for the conference and our members do not wish to go on a fundraising drive now to get the money to finance our group. If you could subsidize the club, we could attend.

   b. Thank you for inviting the Business Club to attend the Business Management Leadership Conference. I am sorry, however, that we cannot attend this excellent meeting because our student council failed to vote funds for our club. Because the members understand the importance of such a conference, they are planning a fundraising drive to send a group to next year's meeting. Won't you please invite us for next year's conference?

   c. The Business Club regrets that it cannot take part in the Business Management Leadership Conference. Our student council did not vote funds for such an activity, and we cannot afford to spend our own money. Thanks, anyway, for your invitation.

> Given three letters of refusal, select the most effective letter and list four valid reasons for its effectiveness.
>
> | | |
> |---|---|
> | Excellent | 4 |
> | Good | 3 |
> | Fair | 2 |

_____

_____

_____

_____

Check the key on page 517. Note differences and reasons why before preceeding to problem 2. Discuss any disagreements with your instructor.

2. As secretary, send regrets that the Cap-It Bowling Club cannot participate in the Capital City Tournament because you are already completely scheduled in the County Tournament this year.

3. Refuse the invitation to speak on the TV panel "What's Your Responsibility as a College Student?" on Sunday, December 16, at 4 p.m. You will be attending a leadership conference. Suggest that the vice-president of your club, Mr. Fred Bates, can take your place.

4. The student council asks your organization, the Pan-Hellenic Association, to sponsor the toy drive for the local hospital. Your executive committee's reaction is that this toy drive should be sponsored by the executive councils of all houseplans and clubs as well as by the

> Given four situations in which letters of refusal must be written, compose the letters in good form with emphasis on (1) answering immediately, (2) giving a clear and valid excuse, (3) expressing regret, (4) apologizing.
>
> A grammatical letter in good form including given number of points according to peer judgment or your instructor's evaluation:
>
> | | |
> |---|---|
> | Excellent | 4 |
> | Good | 3 |
> | Fair | 2 |

Name_____ Date_____

Pan-Hellenic Association. Write to the council explaining that Pan-Hellenic will not sponsor it alone.

5. You receive a written invitation to join the office bowling team, which meets on Tuesdays from 6:30 to 9:30 p.m. Write a note explaining that you attend classes on Tuesday and Thursday evenings from 6:10 to 9:45 p.m. and so cannot join the team.

If you score Fair to Excellent, go on to the Summary. If you fall below Fair, review and discuss your problems with your instructor.

SUMMARY

In the case of each of the social-business letters we have studied in this chapter, certain specific ideas have been advanced, to help you become adept in applying the principles of writing business letters.

When you must write a thank-you letter, overcome your inertia—do it at once. Get to the point in the first sentence, and follow through with language that develops your thoughts naturally. Make the tone of your letter sound genuine. There is no need to write a lengthy letter; the fact that you write to say "thank you" is important.

In a social-business invitation, exercise care when you mention places, dates, and times. Too many embarrassing situations have arisen as a result of errors in matching days with dates or as a result of neglecting to include specific times and places. Take a little extra time to verify your information. Write so that your reader gets the impression that he or she is really important and really wanted. If you remember to explain the purpose of the affair and why the reader is being invited, you increase your chances of getting an acceptance.

In your reservation letter, you must have precise data. These data include dates of arrival and departure, number in your party, type of accommodation, rates you will pay. For your own protection, request a confirmation of your reservation, and carry that letter of confirmation with you. You wouldn't be happy if you arrived at a hotel, after a long day of travel, only to find you had no room because your letter had not arrived.

If you find it necessary to cancel a reservation, have the courtesy to write a letter giving the precise details necessary for the reservations clerk to locate the record and make the cancellation. Be sure to apologize and, if possible, to give a reason for your cancellation.

When you encounter the unpleasant task of writing a letter of refusal, do not delay your answer. Keep your letter straightforward and factual. Instead of beating around the bush, come out with your refusal honestly and clearly. Again, remember the amenities; say you are sorry.

Notice that the basic principles of letter writing apply regardless of the type of letter you write. Type all your letters neatly and with correct letter style. Organize your thinking before you write. Use up-to-date language, "talk" your letter, be grammatically correct. Let your letters answer completely the problems they are meant to solve.

You are now ready for Focus on Language. In this chapter, more than 40 spelling and vocabulary words were spotlighted. These pages will enable you to check your ability to spell and use these words. You will also continue with your work on agreement of subject and verb, the use of the comma, capitalization, and proofreading.

adept: skilled
inertia: sluggishness; inactivity

FOCUS ON LANGUAGE

Spelling

One word is misspelled in each of the following groups of words. In the space, write the correct spelling of the misspelled word.

1. commitment   exceed   preceed   access   _____

2. appendectomy   supersede   condolence   commited   _____

3. advisable   lisense   hypocritical   fiasco   _____

4. accomodations   cancellations   proceed   stationery   _____

5. explicit   trudged   data   numberous   _____

6. adept   access   incured   counsel   _____

7. intra-college   stereotype   dignitaries   skiing   _____

> Given seven groups of words in which one word is misspelled in each group, write each misspelled word correctly.
>
> Excellent   7
> Good   6
> Fair   5

Check the key on page 517. Be sure you can spell without hesitation every one of the 28 words in this problem. If you are a poor speller, have someone read each word to you so that you may write it or type it. Recheck your spelling. Repeat the procedure until you can spell every word correctly.

Vocabulary

Circle the letter of the best definition for each underscored word.

1. explicit instructions   a. vague   b. difficult   c. clear   d. exciting
2. letter of condolence   a. sympathy   b. job   c. congratulations   d. promotion
3. hypocritical person   a. honest   b. timorous   c. outgoing   d. deceitful
4. resort to trickery   a. travel   b. use as a means   c. try   d. demand
5. trudge through the jungle   a. walk briskly   b. race along   c. tramp wearily   d. plow
6. prestige of the presidency   a. importance   b. usefulness   c. name   d. need

> Given 18 vocabulary words spotlighted in the chapter, identify the correct meaning for each.
>
> Excellent   17–18
> Good   15–16
> Fair   13–14

Name_____ Date_____

7. <u>ludicrous</u> statement   a. interesting   b. enjoyable   c. loose
   d. ridiculous

8. <u>flamboyant</u> behavior   a. good   b. showy   c. wise   d. overwhelming

9. supplies <u>commensurate</u> with demand   a. proportionate   b. uneven
   c. unequal   d. commendable

10. <u>fabrication</u> of an aircraft   a. sale   b. purchase   c. manufacture
    d. marketing

11. <u>procrastination</u> in paying taxes   a. speed   b. enjoyment
    c. disagreeableness   d. delay

12. <u>depicted</u> objects of everyday life   a. told about   b. portrayed
    c. thought   d. looked at

13. <u>reiterate</u> political slogans   a. repeat   b. indicate   c. enjoy
    d. look at

14. <u>affront</u> to a friend   a. honor   b. forgiveness   c. offer of money.
    d. open insult

15. <u>brash</u> and ignorant people   a. loud   b. benevolent   c. mild-
    mannered   d. impudent

16. <u>enmeshed</u> in intrigue   a. entangled   b. lost   c. released   d. held

17. <u>stereotyped</u> behavior   a. unusual   b. having no originality
    c. expressing new ideas   d. useless

18. meeting of <u>dignitaries</u>   a. alumnus   b. people of low rank
    c. people of high rank   d. people with money

Check the key on page 517. Write original sentences using the words that you missed. Ask your instructor to check your work. Then go on to the next activity.

Sound-Alikes

The following sound-alikes were introduced in this chapter:

council—a group of elected or appointed people.
   The City Council votes on tax measures.

counsel—1. as a noun, means advice; or a lawyer.
   We offer counsel to all who ask.
   She acted on the advice of counsel.

   2. as a verb, means to advise.
   They will counsel him to act wisely.

adapt—to adjust to a situation or environment.
   The workers had to adapt to the frigid environment of Alaska.

adopt—to take as one's one.
   The group will adopt a new constitution.

adept—highly skilled; proficient.
   An adept tennis player will win the match.

to—1. as preposition: toward.
   She is going to the shore.

   2. as a part of the infinitive: *to go, to give, to receive*, and so on.
too—in addition; also; more than enough.
   He, too, is going to the shore.
   The investment is too large.

two—one more than one.
   Hazel and Jane, the two friends, worked on the project.

Be sure you understand the differences among them before you tackle the sentences below.

1. We have already (*adapted, adopted*) the plan to meet our particular situation.
2. The members of the (*council, counsel*) believed that the building project was far (*to, too, two*) expensive.
3. (*To, Too, Two*) many people are willing to offer (*council, counsel*), which may not always be good.
4. The firm of Johnson and Jackson acted as (*council, counsel*) for the defendant.
5. If management should (*adapt, adopt, adept*) this proposal, we should not encounter (*to, too, two*) many problems.
6. The company treasurer is (*adapt, adopt, adept*) in handling the funds so that we are never short of cash.
7. The effects of the measure that was passed by the (*council, counsel*) will be felt by the taxpayers for years to come.
8. Be sure to follow the advice of (*council, counsel*) in legal matters.

> *Given sentences containing eight sound-alikes, identify the correct word in each case.*
>
> | | |
> |---|---|
> | *Excellent* | *11* |
> | *Good* | *10* |
> | *Fair* | *9* |

Check the key on page 517. If you need more work on these Sound-Alikes, review the explanations above. Write each word you missed in a sentence. Ask your instructor to mark and to discuss any errors with you.

More on Agreement

When singular subjects are joined by *or* or *nor,* the verb should be singular. When plural subjects are so joined, the verb is plural. But what happens when one subject is singular and the other is plural?

Rule: *When a singular subject and a plural subject are joined by* or *or* nor, *the subject closer to the verb determines the number of the verb.*

   Neither the employees nor the supervisor was able to attend the meeting.
   Neither the supervisor nor the employees were able to attend the meeting.

*Name*_____ *Date*_____

Another agreement problem arises when a noun or pronoun follows a verb of being (*be, feel, taste,* etc.). Such a noun or pronoun is a *predicate nominative*; it is a complement that explains or identifies the subject.

Rule: *The verb must agree with the subject, not with the predicate nominative.*

Our main problem is writing complete reports and getting them into the mail on time.
Numerous field tests were the cause of the delay.

Let's try these sentences, using the rules above and the one you learned before on collective nouns (see Chapter 4).

(see Chapter 4)

1. Neither heat nor cold (*affect, affects*) these superior duplicating materials.
2. The jury (*was, were*) out ten minutes before it returned a verdict.
3. I believe that the central files or this office (*have, has*) the material you requested.
4. Either he or his partners (*has, have*) the right to sign checks.
5. The council (*has, have*) prepared standards of conduct for its members.
6. Neither the analysts nor the treasurer (*was, were*) able to report on the company's progress.
7. Either the president or the treasurer (*has, have*) an option to purchase shares of stock.
8. Her concern (*is, are*) the many people who have come to rely upon her accurate forecasts.
9. The crowd (*has, have*) cheered their hero.
10. The correspondent said that an increasing problem (*is, are*) the many reports and statistical compilations called for today.

Check the key on page 517. If you did not achieve Fair or above, discuss your work with your instructor. If you did succeed, go on to Punctuation.

Given ten sentences using singular and plural subjects joined by or *or* nor, *underscore the correct verb.*

Excellent   10
Good   9
Fair   8

Punctuation: Comma

Rule: *Use commas to set off appositives and parenthetical phrases.*

An appositive is a noun or a group of words substituting for a noun that appears next to another noun or noun substitute and explains or identifies it.

Professor Jones, our accounting teacher, has extensive business experience.

"Our accounting teacher" is the appositive.
A parenthetical expression is a word or group of words that is not directly related to the rest of the sentence.

Our class, I believe, is the best in the college.

Apply this rule—and other comma rules you have learned—to punctuate these sentences:

Given sentences requiring commas, insert commas in the correct places.

Excellent   23-24
Good   21-22
Fair   19-20

1. Joe Nelson our star pitcher led the team to victories in 1973 1974 and 1975.

2. The college however claims no responsibility for this student's behavior.

3. You can I believe get these books at your local library.

4. Have you seen the letter from John Burns president of the Acme Company?

5. If Doris Atkins our club leader has planned a good program for the semester club membership will increase.

6. You have become acquainted no doubt with our new model now that you have had a chance to use it.

7. The class of 1967 we have heard has donated a fine record collection to the school.

8. William Harvey the agent assigned to the case has prepared a lengthy report on his findings.

9. The club roster composed of Bill Nally Jack Smith Gene Ramos and ten other boys has been submitted to the adviser.

10. We shall consequently ask you to come to the office to discuss the statement.

Check the key on page 518. If you need more work on the use of commas, review. If you achieved Fair or above, go on to Capitalization.

Capitalization

Pay careful attention to rules for capitalization. Many writers tend to capitalize too often. Unless you can apply a definite principle that calls for capitalization, do not capitalize. Here is one principle:

Rule: *Capitalize all proper nouns* (that is, names of particular persons, places, or things: days of the week, months, political parties, governmental bodies and departments, historical events and periods, geographical names, buildings, and so on).

Empire State Building; Middle Ages; U.S. Department of Commerce; Middle East; Battle of Bunker Hill

Do not confuse proper nouns with the general (generic) uses of the same words.

U.S. Post Office Department; neighborhood post office
Austin High School; the district high school
President Keeler; when Mr. Keeler was president
Congress intervened; to appoint a congress

*Name*_____ *Date*_____

1. The democrats are a majority in the house of representatives.
2. The department of state has an office in chicago, illinois.
3. The students in high school will draw up a constitution for their student government.
4. The st. louis chamber of commerce has its office in the tower building.
5. The supreme court will make its decision known on monday, june 10.
6. Two major parties in the United States are the democratic and republican parties.
7. When Mr. Johnson was president, the term great society became well known.
8. The government printing office in Washington is probably the largest publisher in the world.
9. The union oil company of california held its shareowners' meeting on April 24.
10. The bicentennial commission was organized to coordinate plans for the celebration of the 200th anniversary.

Check the key on page 518. If you need more work on capitalization, discuss your problem with your instructor. If you scored Fair or above, go on to Proofreading.

Proofreading

Before sending the following material to prospective customers, proofread the paragraphs submitted by your typist. How many errors can you find?

Dear insurance prospect

Can less than 9¢ day provide you with extensive insurance protection. Yes it can. A cheque for a substashal ammount could be payed to your family in the event of acidental death.

You would be covered 24 hrs.a day, 365 days a year-near your home or anywhere in the world-at work or at play. Theres no age limit for you and no medical exam is required to become ensured.

Is there a need for this protection. Take a

look at statitics from the national safety

council. In our country there's an accident

al death every five minutes; its the leading

cause of deth for those under 45, and one of

the leading causes for all ages. With risks

like these, doesnt it make cents to have this

valuable insurance

Check the key on page 518. If you succeeded, you are ready for Chapter 7. If you did not achieve Fair or above, discuss the problem with your instructor.

*Name*_____ *Date*_____

7

THE PERSONAL-BUSINESS LETTER

Business activity is becoming more and more a part of our personal lives. We are concerned daily with such personal-business matters as insurance, sales taxes, Medicare, charge accounts, checking and savings accounts, bank statements, orders, cancellations, merchandise returns and credits, buy and sell orders of stocks and bonds, brokers' fees. To handle these matters, this chapter will help you develop proficiency in writing—

merchandise

proficiency: expertness

Unit 21   The Order Letter

Unit 22   The Letter of Inquiry

Unit 23   The Letter of Transmittal

Unit 24   Claim Letters

Written communication will enable you to keep your personal-business life functioning smoothly.

UNIT 21   THE ORDER LETTER

Your performance objective for this unit are:

Given the problem of ordering materials,

You will write correct order letters that follow these guidelines: (1) clearly identify the objects ordered; (2) specifically itemize costs and show calculations; (3) follow correct business procedures in method of payment; (4) thank the company for processing the order.

Have you looked through a mail-order catalog or a department-store sales brochure lately? Check any mail-order form (see Figure 7–1). You must supply detailed information for each item ordered: catalog number, quantity, article, color and size, unit price, and total price. A chart gives you the shipping charges you are expected to enclose with your order. Sales taxes must also be added to the cost.

Figure 7–1
An Order Form

When you write an order letter, it, too, must contain all this information. Nothing can be left to the imagination. State your method of payment, such as check, money order, stamps. Be sure to mention the exact price, and show your calculations, including sales taxes and shipping charges. Watch the price quotations. Such terms as "f.o.b." after a price may mean a big difference in cost. The automobile listed at "$3,400, f.o.b. Detroit," costs much more on the West Coast. "F.o.b." means "free on board"; therefore, "f.o.b. Detroit" means that the buyer must pay freight charges from Detroit to the point of destination.

Here is an order that was processed immediately. It was exact and could easily be filled:

In typing "f.o.b.," use lower-case letters. Notice that you don't space between the letters.

processed: subjected to routine procedure

```
                    19 Moreno Street
                    Palo Alto, CA  94303

                    January 14, 19--

Chestnut Hill Sports Shop
Six Chestnut Hill Lane
San Francisco, CA  94107


Please send me the following equipment and
charge my account:

Catalog                      Unit
 Number   Quantity Description Cost    Total

  3189       1     No. 100 reel
                     for right-
                     handers   $28.95 $28.95

  3191       2     Spools for
                     No. 100
                     reel       2.50   5.00

                     Total           $33.95

Since I am leaving on vacation on January 28,
please rush this order. Thank you.

                    Mark Murphy
                    Mark Murphy
```

Mark decides to omit the salutation and closing, using a type of simplified style.

When several sets of numbers, items, and prices are given, tabular form is clearer than writing the information in sentences.

Mark had already established his credit with the Chestnut Hill Sports Shop. There wasn't a tax in his area, and there were no shipping charges for goods delivered within 20 miles of the shop. Notice that he included just enough information to get that rush delivery, and he remembered to say thank you.

there

The order below received much slower service because it was not clear and was therefore difficult to fill—and because the credit standing of the buyer had not been established.

January 19, 19--

Masters Brothers
15 High Water Street
Sacramento, CA 95823

Gentlemen:

I am interested in the stove you advertised in the paper last Sunday. I would like it in white with the oven attached. The price was about $240.

Can you deliver this stove next Friday? I am enclosing my check in the amount of $240.

Sincerely yours,

Joanna Burns

Joanna Burns

Fortunately, an alert mail clerk did not discard Ms. Burns's envelope before he had written her return address on the letter. The order department, however, was not happy with the letter. What stove? Three stoves had been advertised in the Sunday papers, ranging in price from $225 to $265. Not one was listed at $240. All the stoves had ovens—one overhead, one below the burners, one to the right of the burners.

The credit department also had to do extra and unnecessary checking. The advertisements in every Sunday paper were checked. Every one included the statement, "Shipping charges of $10 are not included in the quoted price." Installation charges of $24 were also listed; yet Ms. Burns made no mention of this either. In addition, since Masters Brothers did not know Ms. Burns, they hesitated to accept her personal check. Before sending any stove, they would have to wait until the bank cleared the check.

Correspondence had to go back and forth before this order could be filled. Ms. Burns did not cook on her new stove that Friday!

Let's make Ms. Burns happy. We'll rewrite that order letter, following correct business procedures, and get the stove installed on Friday. The way to begin is to cut out the advertisement and keep it before you to be sure your order is exact.

228 Clove Lakes Drive
Sacramento, CA 95838
January 19, 19--

Masters Brothers
15 High Water Street
Sacramento, CA 95823

Gentlemen:

Please send me the Kelsey Range, No. 2264,
advertised in the Sunday Times, page 32. I
would like it in white porcelain. This is the
stove with four burners, two storage drawers
below the burners, and an oven and broiler to
the right of the burners.

Here is my certified check for $259 to cover
the following:

Cost of Kelsey Range, No.
  2264, in white porcelain $225
Shipping charges   10
Installation charges   24

    Total $259

Your shipping department told me this morning
that this stove can be delivered this Friday
and installed by your licensed electrician at
that time. I will be expecting the delivery on
Friday, January 23.

Thank you.

                    Sincerely yours,

                    Joanna Burns

                    Joanna Burns

Enclosure
   Certified check, $259

porcelain: hard, white ceramic ware

Have your bank certify your personal check. This means the bank has set aside the amount on the face of the check for payment.

In writing the order letter, you must (1) clearly identify the objects ordered, (2) specifically itemize costs and show calculations (verifying all figures), (3) follow correct business procedures in method of payment, and (4) thank the company for processing the order.

itemize: list by items

Skills Activity 39 will give you a chance to check your ability to handle letters of request.

SKILLS ACTIVITY 39

A. The Business Club has planned to raise funds by selling greeting cards. The president of the club has seen this ad:

> ### GREETING CARDS!
>
> *Make $25 dollars!* Easy for you or your school or club to sell 100 boxes of designer Christmas cards. Send for samples on approval. Carmine Cards, Box 1527, New York, NY   10001

Given three letters of request of varying degrees of effectiveness, identify the most effective and give four valid reasons.

Excellent   4
Good   3
Fair   2

Three members of the club have submitted letters to request the cards.

1.

Vilma Jones wrote this letter:

We have seen your ad in the Guide about designer Christmas cards, samples of which you will offer on approval. Our Business Club at Allen Community College is looking for ways to raise cash to send several delegates to the New England Conference in the spring.

Therefore, would you be good enough to send us samples on approval so we can see whether these cards could easily be sold by our group. If we go ahead with our selling drive, the 50 members of our club should be able to sell at least 300 boxes of the cards.

We'll be looking forward to receiving the cards.

2.

Bill Kelin wrote as follows:

Send the Business Club of Allen Community College the special designer Christmas Cards on approval. We may want to sell them for fund raising.

Name_____ Date_____

3.

Leslie Stone wrote:

> Please send samples on approval of the designer Christmas cards you advertised in the Guide to the Business Club of Allen Community College. Our club needs to raise money to send delegates to the New England Conference in the spring, and these cards should help us earn the needed cash.

The most effective letter is _____ because:

1. _____

2. _____

3. _____

4. _____

Check the key on page 518. If you were able to achieve Fair or above, go on to B. If you scored below Fair, check differences with the key and discuss problems with your instructor.

B. Now consider some order letters.

Given three situations requiring order letters, compose three letters that are grammatically correct and adhere to the principles of letter writing and the four guidelines for writing order letters (page 000).

A grammatically correct letter meeting given number of guidelines according to peer judgment or your instructor's evaluation:

Excellent	*4*
Good	*3*
Fair	*2*

1. The following is an excerpt from a brochure from Maple Grove, Inc., 183 Main Street, St. Johnsbury, VT 05819

> Order your pure Vermont Maple Candy now! Maple Grove, Inc., produces the finest maple-sugar candies in the world. Five gallons of maple sap are boiled to make just one gallon of pure syrup. Then we "boil down" 2½ gallons of this pure maple syrup to make just one 8-ounce box of delicious candy, which sells for only $1.25 a box.
>
> If you are looking for a creamy, melt-in-your-mouth candy treat, order a good supply of Maple Sugar Candy now. Price of $1.25 per box includes shipping charges.

Order a box of Maple Sugar Candy for yourself and a box for a friend. You will pay with a postal money order.

2. You wish to have a good outline for a review of economics, and you decide on *Outline of Economics* by Chenault and Smith. Since your college bookstore doesn't have a copy, you must write to Rock Publishing Co., Ludlow, VT 05149 for a copy. The book costs $7.50.

3. Father's Day is coming shortly, and you wish to order a gold-plated tie clasp for your father. Write a letter to order the tie clasp advertised below.

LOG-DESIGN TIE CLASP

Our own exclusive design.

14K gold — $24.95
Sterling silver — $9.95
Gold plated — $3.50

CRAFTSMEN JEWELERS
41 Clapham Street
Brooklyn, NY 11226

Mail orders accepted; no C.O.D.
Price includes federal tax. In New York,
add 8% sales tax; for shipment, add 25¢
postage and handling.

If you achieved Fair or above, go on to C. If you scored below Fair, review, noting differences expressed by your peers or your instructor.

C. Correct the following letter which was received by Waxgiser Vitamin Supplies.

Dear Sirs:

I have been ordering my vitamins and prescription drugs from you for the passed 8 years. Due to the fact that you did not have the 100 mg. Vitamin C tablets the last time I wrote you I am now ordering them again.

Send me 300 mg. Vitamin C tablets. I will enclose my check for $4.75 and hope that the price hasn't changed.

You did not send me my PartyBook stamps on my previous order for $11.25. Trusting that you will send them with the new order, I am,

Respectfully yours,

Name_____ Date_____

Check the key on page 518. Note differences before going on to Unit 22.
If you scored below Fair, discuss your score with your instructor.

UNIT 22   THE LETTER OF INQUIRY

Your performance objective for Unit 22 is:

Given the problem of requesting information,

You will write effective letters of inquiry following these specific guidelines: (1) make questions explicit, (2) request particular information, (3) supply background information necessary to give the complete picture, and (4) remember to include the amenities.

The Solicited Letter

You have already seen (in Chapter 5) how to handle the simplest form of written inquiry—sending a postcard to request a report or pamphlet offered in an advertisement. But what if your request is not so simple and a postal card will not suffice? Take the following newspaper advertisement:

> For more information concerning this homeowner's insurance, write to Mr. Ralph Moskovis, Stokely Equity Corporation, Box 701, Topeka, KS 66615.

Or perhaps a radio commentator insists that you "find out more about our investment program by writing to Investments, Radio Station WRRZ, New York, New York 10026." In both cases, you must write to get more information. Because you will have several questions to ask, you must write a letter.

   Whenever you write such a letter in response to a newspaper or magazine advertisement, a radio announcement, or a television commercial, you are writing a solicited letter of inquiry. How do you go about it?   **solicited:** asked for
To answer this typical magazine advertisement, you would write a short letter.

> NEW! COMPREHENSIVE!
>
> *56-Lesson*
> *Master Correspondence Course*
> *in Advertising*
>
> Covers every phase from copy and art to market research and merchandising.
>
> Diploma awarded.
>
> Free Booklet: "Opportunities in Advertising"
>
> The Raleigh Correspondence School
> Box 228
> Hollywood, CA   90028

Your letter might read:

```
                                        666 Mylan Road
                                        Fresno, CA  93728
                                        May 22, 19--


        Raleigh Correspondence School
        Box 228
        Hollywood, CA  90028

        Gentlemen:

        Please send me the details on the cost, number
        of weeks, educational activities, and testing
        program of the Master Correspondence Course on
        Advertising that you advertised in the Retail
        Sales Management Journal of May 15.

        What type of diploma is awarded?

        I would also like to receive the free booklet
        Opportunities in Advertising.

        Thank you.

                                        Sincerely yours,

                                        Charles Richards

                                        Charles Richards
```

When you want certain information, ask for it specifically.

As you can see, Charles Richards not only requests information offered by the advertisement, but he makes certain to find out everything he wants to know by asking specific questions and requesting particular information.

The Unsolicited Letter

concise: compact; terse

The unsolicited letter of inquiry demands additional thought. It requires careful organization and the use of clear, concise language so that the reader can easily understand and answer the questions. When you write your letter of inquiry, list the questions so that they stand out, supply the background information necessary to give the reader an understanding of your problems, and give exact dates where records are concerned.

absence

Mary Lou Alpen asks your help in writing a letter to Brockton College requesting readmission as a matriculated student. She has decided to complete her college career after an absence of two years, during which time she worked as a receptionist at the Dependable Plastics Company.

You ask her to gather her data: dates of attendance, number of credits, index. Then you discuss questions concerning her status. Should she mention that her index dropped below the readmission level? Should she ask what she can do about it? You answer, "Why not? The registrar has your records. You may get some help you could not get otherwise." This is the rough draft of Mary Lou's letter:

registrar: one who keeps records

Mary Lou should review rules for comma and semi-colon:

> I left Brockton two years ago and since that time I have worked as a receptionist at Dependable Plastics Corporation. Now I know what I want to do. I want to enter the field of elementary school teaching. Therefore, I must return to college, and have decided to do this. I would like to return as a fulltime student next September.
>
> When I left college I had 56 credits. In my last term, I did very poorly because I had lost interest; my index dropped to 1.97. Will this prevent me from being readmitted? Can I do anything about this situation?
>
> Please let me know if I may be readmitted to Brockton in September.

ago; Compound sentence with commas takes a semi-colon.

and, ... time, Introductory phrase is set off by commas.

college No comma belongs between two verbs in a single clause.

college, Use comma after introductory phrase.

You make the following comments:

Get to the point in the first sentence.
Give exact dates and precise information.
List questions.
Correct the punctuation.

You and Mary Lou revise the letter in this way:

```
                    865 Roselawn Street
                    Palo Alto, CA  94306
                    June 4, 19--

Mr. John Andrews, Registrar
Brockton College
Palo Alto, CA  94301

Dear Mr. Andrews:

I am applying for readmission to Brockton in
September as a matriculated student for the fall
term. Please send me the readmission form I must
complete.

I entered Brockton as a freshman student in
September 1972 and completed my sophomore year
```

sophomore

in June 1974. At that time I accepted a position as receptionist at the Dependable Plastics Company. I now plan to become an elementary-school teacher. To do this, I must complete my college education.

In June 1974, I had earned a total of 56 credits. During my last term, my index fell to 1.97. According to the catalog, an index of 2.0 is required for readmission.

May I be admitted as a matriculated student on a limited program?

Can I file an appeal asking for this consideration?

If not, may I take summer courses to raise my index to the required 2.0 by September? Or should I take evening courses during the fall term in order to be considered for January matriculation?

I hope you can suggest some way for me to be admitted as a matriculated student. Thank you for your help.

Sincerely yours,

Mary Lou Alpen

Mary Lou Alpen

The registrar answered quickly and without difficulty:

waiver: the giving up of a right or claim

Here is the Readmission Application you must complete. Attach an appeal letter, addressed to the Committee on Academic Standing, requesting a waiver of the 2.0 index in your case. Be sure to give all details.

And the registrar closed the letter, "Good luck."

The letter of inquiry must be explicit in its questions (listing them), must supply the background information necessary to give a complete picture, and must include those important words *please* and *thank you.*

Test your skill with letters of inquiry by trying Skills Activity 40.

SKILLS ACTIVITY 40

1. As a member of the Home Economics Club, Sharon has been asked to write to the Dewey Fabric Company, 35 Forest Drive, Peoria, IL 36501, to request a donation of fabrics so the club members can make dresses for 50 children in a nearby home. Here is the letter Sharon wrote. Help her improve her letter by writing above the lines.

362 Burns Ave.

Peoria, Ill.

Oct. 21st, 19--

Dewey Fabric Company

35 Forest Dr.

Peoria, Ill. 36501

Dear Mr. Dewey,

Each year during the holiday season, the Home

Economics Club of Brooke college donates cloth-

ing to the children of the Berkshire Home.

Therefore we will expect your usual annual gift

of fabrics so we can get started on our sewing

project by Nov. 4th to make clothes for the

childrn.

Thanking you in advance,

                    Cordially,

Name_____ Date_____

To check your ability to find the errors in this letter, check the key on page 518. Ask your instructor to evaluate your suggested improvements.

check the key on page 518.

2. Your bowling club is planning to hold its annual dinner at Lund's Restaurant on October 27. Arrangements must be made for no fewer than 25 and not more than 40 persons. Write a letter to Mr. J. K. Lawlor, manager of Lund's. Ask for sample menus as well as for prices. The dinner should be scheduled for 7:30 p.m., and your club will want the room until midnight.

3. You have heard about a book called *They Signed for Us.* You know neither the author's name nor the publisher. The book tells the story of the signers of the Declaration of Independence. Write a letter to the Stern Bookstore in your town to find out if it is available and what its price is.

4. You wish to open a charge account with Burchill's Department Store. Write a letter to ask if you are eligible for a charge account and how you should proceed.

5. You have been shopping for a Finetone transistor radio. Write to the manufacturer in New York to ask for the name of a dealer in your area so that you can buy a Finetone.

If you have scored Good or above on three of the four letters, go on to Unit 23. If you did not succeed, discuss your score with the instructor, and review this unit.

Given four situations which call for letters of inquiry, compose letters that are grammatically correct and in good form that (1) ask explicit questions, (2) request particular information, (3) supply information to complete the picture, and (4) include the amenities.

A grammatically correct letter meeting the given number of guidelines according to peer judgment or your instructor's evaluation:

Excellent	*3-4*
Good	*2*

UNIT 23 THE LETTER OF TRANSMITTAL

Your performance objectives for this unit are:

Given the situation in which you are required to send an article to another person or business,

You will write a correct letter of transmittal that is courteous, well organized, and brief; that identifies enclosures; and that calls the reader's attention to specifics; and

You will select the best postal and delivery service available.

When you mail checks, applications, reports, or other items, write a short covering letter or letter of transmittal—and be sure to keep a copy. The letter tells the reader what you sent and why; the copy is your record of what you sent, to whom you sent it, when you sent it, and the address to which you mailed it.

transmittal: passing from one to another

Recently Ms. Petersen had to mail her endowment policy to the main office of the insurance company. After she had spoken with her broker, she decided to request the cash value of her policy, which, including the interest, came to $10,350. The company was willing to mail her a check upon receipt of the policy. Would you simply put the policy in an envelope and mail it? Ms. Petersen did not; she enclosed a short letter.

endowment: a type of insurance; donation or gift

```
                            485 Eighth Avenue
                            Denver, CO  80239
                            February 2, 19--

Registered Mail

The Acme Insurance Company
Attention Mr. John Winston, Manager
500 Wall Street
New York, NY  10002

Gentlemen:

As you requested, I am sending you my endowment
policy, AF145376, which was paid up on January
31, 1976.

Please send me a check for the amount of the
endowment, plus interest. This should come to
$10,350.

Thank you.

                    Sincerely yours,

                    Joanna E. Peterson

                    Joanna E. Peterson

Enclosure
   Policy AF145376
```

indemnified: guaranteed against loss

Ms. Petersen wasn't taking any chances with the regular mail service; she sent the policy with the letter of transmittal by registered mail and asked for a return receipt. Not only did she have proof that she had mailed the policy, but she would be indemnified if it were lost. And her return receipt would show that the insurance company had received the envelope. When mailing valuables, contracts, deeds, policies, or cash, send them by first-class, registered mail. (Only first-class mail can be registered.)

When you are sending an ordinary package, however, you should use parcel post and attach your letter of transmittal to the outside of the package. This method enables you to pay the fourth-class rate for the package, insuring it if you wish, and to pay the first-class rate for the letter only. In addition, the receiver of the package can locate the letter easily.

biannual: Is this the same as "biennial"?

Jim Johnson knew he had to write a covering letter for his club's biannual report. Here is his letter:

July 10, 19--

Mr. John Finley, Adviser
Committee on Student Activities

Dear Mr. Finley:

I am enclosing herewith the biannual report of the Accounting Club. This report shows very clearly that our club has so far had a success- ful year socially and financially. We shall continue to try to do well in the months ahead.

Sincerely yours,

James Johnson

James Johnson
Secretary

Enclosure

Would your judgment of this letter include these points? Jim, you're old-fashioned! Change that first sentence to: "Here is the biannual report of the Accounting Club." Do you want to attract Mr. Finley's attention to the major accomplishments of the club? Do you want him to notice the financial status of the club? Then refer to these in your letter of transmittal.

On page 5, you will see a description of the
five major social and educational activities the
club has sponsored this year. Every one of them
has been successful.

You will note on page 8 that our financial
statement shows we are solvent. We have a
current balance of $50 in the treasury.

As adviser for all student activities, Mr. Finley and his staff were particularly helpful to the club. Shouldn't Jim thank him in the last paragraph?

Thank you, Mr. Finley, for the help you have
given us in making this year a successful one so
far. We expect the rest of the year to be even
better.

Here is another letter of transmittal you may have to write. The local department store reminded Roseann that she had not paid her last bill for $17. She had completely forgotten the bill and, in fact, had misplaced it. She wanted to pay immediately. Could she put the check in an envelope and mail it? Some people do, and the department store must decipher the signature, look up the account, check the address, and hope that they are crediting the correct account.

Roseann decided to write. With great effort she composed the following letter:

> 482 11 Street
> Waco, TX 76701
> March 15, 19--

Huxley's Department Store
585 Fairview Avenue
Waco, TX 76708

Ladies and Gentlemen:

Here is my check for $17.00 in payment of my
invoice of Feb. 3rd.

Apparently I <u>inadvertently</u> misplaced or overlooked the original statement, so I did not
send my check sooner.

I <u>beg to apologize</u> for the delay in sending my
check. <u>Assuring you that</u> this will not happen
in the future, I remain,

> Sincerely yours,

> *Roseann Blaine*
> Roseann Blaine

Add attention line.

*Omit decimal and ciphers:
$17.
"Statement," not "in-
voice."
"February 3."*

*Second paragraph is un-
necessary.*

*Underlined words and
phrases are hackneyed or
unnecessary.*

Enclosure line is missing.

formerly: before

Although Roseann's language was formerly commonly used, it is now out of date. If Roseann made the necessary corrections, updated the language, and eliminated the extraneous information, this is the short, efficient letter she would send with her check:

482 11 Street
Waco, TX 76701
March 15, 19--

Huxley's Department Store
Attention Accounting Department
585 Fairview Avenue
Waco, TX 76708

Gentlemen:

Here is my check for $17 in payment of my statement of February 3.

I am sorry for the delay.

Sincerely yours,

Roseann Blaine

Roseann Blaine

Enclosure
    Check, $17

The letter of transmittal marks you as a courteous and well-organized person. It identifies the enclosure and calls the reader's attention to specifics. Keep the letter short and to the point, and be sure to use the correct postal or delivery service to safeguard the item you are sending. Also, keep your own copy; it becomes your record.

Turn to Skills Activity 41 to apply the principles of writing letters of transmittal.

SKILLS ACTIVITY 41

1. Three students in Economics 315 failed to complete their term reports before the holidays. Professor Nolan agreed to accept the reports if they were mailed to him before December 27. He received the reports with these letters of transmittal.

From Roy Revere

> "Better late than never," is the old saying. So here's my report. Have a Happy New Year!

From Janice Butler

> Here is my report on Monetary Policies of the Federal Reserve System in the Seventies for Eco. 315.
>
> Thank you, Professor Nolan, for accepting this report after its assigned date.
>
> I hope you have a happy and prosperous New Year.

From Maria Alcorta

> Herewith is my report on Monetary Policies of the Federal Reserve System in the Seventies for Eco. 315.
>
> My paper was delayed because I was waiting for the latest figures from Jane Irwin of the Federal Reserve Bank of St. Louis. I think you will agree that these figures added depth to my research.
>
> Thank you for allowing me extra time on my report. Have a happy holiday.

> *Given three letters of transmittal of varying degrees of effectiveness, choose the most effective letter and list reasons.*
>
> | | |
> |---|---|
> | *Excellent* | *3* |
> | *Good* | *2* |
> | *Fair* | *1* |

The most effective letter is _____ for these reasons:

_____

_____

_____

Name_____ Date_____

Check with the key on page 518. Do you agree? Note the reasons for the choice. Discuss differences with a committee of other students or with your instructor.

Given personal-business situations in which letters of transmittal are to be written, compose three correct letters that (1) indicate correct postal and delivery service; (2) are courteous, well organized, and brief; (3) identify enclosures; and (4) call the reader's attention to specifics when appropriate.

Grammatically correct letter in good form that meets the given number of guidelines, according to peer judgment or your instructor's evaluation:

Excellent   4
Good   3
Fair   2

2. Assume that you have secured a reservation at Teepee Lodge for the Thanksgiving holidays. The Lodge has requested a deposit of $25. Write a letter of transmittal to send with your check covering the deposit.

3. You have been clipping newspaper and magazine articles on the effects of automation on office employment. Now that you have five good articles, you wish to send them to a new acquaintance who is writing a paper on the subject. Write a letter to accompany the articles.

4. Your club has drawn up its social calendar for the coming semester. You have written a brief article about it that you would like to have published in your school paper. Write a covering letter to send to the editor, asking him to publish your club news.

If you achieved Fair to Excellent on two of the three letters, you are ready for Unit 24. If you did not succeed in writing acceptable letters, review and discuss difficulties with your instructor.

UNIT 24 CLAIM LETTERS

Your performance objectives for Unit 24 are:

Given the problem of requesting an adjustment,

You will write correct claim letters by applying these guidelines: (1) clearly identify the problem, (2) carefully describe the product, (3) make positive suggestions for settling the claim, and (4) be courteous.

"Wow!" The adjustment clerk exclaimed, "This woman must be furious!" He had just read a letter from an irate customer who was still waiting on January 5 for the Christmas gift she had ordered for her husband on December 5.

irate: angry

He did not criticize her for being angry. But, unless her letter helped her to get the anger out of her system, it served little purpose. It did not get the package to her on time. A telephone call on December 24 might have done more, for the store might then have sent it out by special messenger.

Why do we write the claim letter? We want to correct an error, to get a satisfactory explanation of a charge, to obtain better service. Emotion helps little in these circumstances. What is needed?

Clear thinking in identifying the problem or problems.
Simple language in describing the claim or claims.
Constructive suggestions.
Courtesy.

Think positively. When you ask for an adjustment of a claim, you are giving the businessperson a chance to correct an error. For example, you may find that a record you ordered has arrived in damaged condition. The reputable seller of that record would have no objection to your writing a claim letter; it may help to improve the company's method of shipping goods. The seller would prefer to have you complain directly so that an adjustment can be made rather than to have you become a dissatisfied customer. A retail firm wants to improve the image presented to its customers.

reputable: having a good reputation; honorable

dissatisfied

Here is a case in which a claim letter should be written. Sandy's father had purchased 100 shares of common stock in the Safeguard Company. The company had been paying quarterly dividends of 20 cents a share on its stock. On April 15, Sandy's father noticed that he hadn't received his dividends since the previous September. Because Sandy was taking a course in correspondence, he asked her to write a letter to find out what was wrong; he even promised to share the dividends with her when the check arrived. Sandy asked Gary and Diane to help compose the letter. Diane wrote:

**common stock
dividends**

```
    Sirs:

    My father bought some stock in your company.
    He has not received money from you since last
    September. Because he knows that your business
    is good, he should have received some money.

    Please send his interest at once.

                    Truly yours,
```

Outmoded salutation.

Vague terms: "some stock," "money," "business is good," "some money."

Use "dividends," not "interest."

Outdated closing.

Diane did not clearly identify the problem. Sandy was surprised to see the incorrect use of the word "interest," and she substituted "dividend." Although she used "please," Diane's tone was too imperious.

Gary's suggestion was better:

imperious: domineering; arrogant

Outdated salutation.

Note commas for appositive.

Eliminate decimal and ciphers: $20.

Gentlemen:

My father, Samuel Stone, is the owner of 100 shares of common stock in Safeguard Company. He received dividends amounting to $20.00 in September but has not received any checks since then. Apparently there has been some error, because I have checked the stock page of the newspaper and know that dividends have been paid by your company.

Please look into this matter as soon as possible.

                                    Sincerely yours,

Gary identified Sandy's father by name, making it easier for the company's treasurer to locate the shares. He also listed the number of shares Samuel Stone owned, the amount of the last dividend check, and the month that check was received. Sandy would type $20, omitting the decimal and ciphers, would omit the unnecessary third sentence and the tired phrase "look into this matter as soon as possible." In fact, Sandy's letter was clear, concise, courteous, and constructive:

Ladies and Gentlemen:

Explicit information.

My father, Samuel Stone, owns 100 shares of Safeguard Company stock, certificate number 0413007. He has not received dividends since last September. (The September check was for $20.)

I understand Safeguard paid dividends in December and in March.

Polite and constructive.

Will you please check to see why my father has not received his regular dividends?

                                    Sincerely yours,

Let's take the case of two unhappy customers, Jack Leonard and his friend, Ralph Sherry. They ordered a set of two walkie-talkies at $37.95

from the Mitsi Electric Corporation. The company advertised that they would receive audible transmission up to five miles. Both Jack and Ralph were disappointed when they tried to use their set. Jack wrote this letter and showed it to Ralph before mailing it:

audible: can be heard
their

> What kind of a company are you? The walkie-talkie set you sent me and my friend doesn't have a reception of one mile, and you advertised it as having a reception of five miles.
>
> My friend and I paid $37.95 for this stupid set, and we want you to tell us what you do to get a reception of five miles--use a megaphone?
>
> I plan to report you to the Better Business Bureau for misrepresentation.

Ralph didn't like the tone of Jack's letter and said that he would write the letter using a positive approach. After all, the walkie-talkie might not have been working correctly. He thought that a suggestion for settling the claim might be a good idea. Jack agreed with his friend that this letter was more constructive:

> Ladies and Gentlemen:
>
> Will you please tell me how I can get my 56X walkie-talkie set to transmit at a range of five miles? My friend and I have not been able to get any reception beyond a one-mile limit. Does this mean that the set is defective? Is it possible that the buildings in this area are interfering with the reception?
>
> If necessary, my friend and I will buy extra parts to ensure five-mile reception. However, if you feel that we cannot successfully operate the 56X in this area, please tell us what walkie-talkie to buy and whether you will accept the 56X in exchange. Ours was a cash purchase at $37.95, following your advertisement in the Chronicle.
>
> I hope you can help us to get the 56X to operate at a distance of five miles or to suggest a walkie-talkie that will do so.
>
> Sincerely yours,
>
> *Ralph Sherry*
>
> Ralph Sherry

ensure

Ralph's answer came at once. The sales manager of Mitsi apologized and thanked Ralph for calling the problem to the company's attention. The company offered to send a new 56X set as soon as Ralph returned the original set by parcel post. What do you think the company would have done if Jack's letter had been mailed?

Shall we try one more problem? You have a three-year subscription to *Woods and Water,* which will not expire for one more year; yet you did not receive the May and July issues. You send this letter to the company:

expire: come to an end

Remember, underscore or type in capitals the names of books, brochures, magazines, newspapers.

Ladies and Gentlemen:

My May and July issues of Woods and Water did not arrive. I have a three-year subscription to your magazine, from January 1975 through December 1977. This is the first time I have not received my copy on time.

Attached is the label I removed from the June issue. This is the name and address you have in your records, and it is correct.

Will you please send me the May and July copies of the magazine? I want to have the complete series.

Thank you.

Sincerely yours,

This is the way to get results: You identified the problem, you stated clearly just what your claim was, you were positive in offering a solution, and you were courteous.

Apply the principles of this unit in Skills Activity 42.

SKILLS ACTIVITY 42

A. Write claim letters for these situations.

1. Suppose that during the past two months you have been having problems with your mail deliveries. Mail for other people was often delivered to your home; your own mail was often delayed for no good reason. On one occasion a bill for $8.56 was not received, and you had to explain to the store why you hadn't paid the bill. Write a letter to your local postmaster, asking that your postal service be improved.

2. You have joined a record club. The first shipment is made up of four records, specially priced as an introductory offer. You sent your check when you ordered the records. When the records arrive, you find that two records are badly damaged even though the package was wrapped correctly. You know that the damage must have taken place during shipping because you were very careful when you unpacked the records. What would you write to the company?

3. You have ordered 100 sheets of stationery and matching envelopes with your name and address imprinted on them. You have received the package. Your address has been printed incorrectly on the stationery; it reads 105 Reed Avenue, but it should read 501 Reed Avenue. Write a claim letter to Thatcher Printing Company to ask them to replace the stationery.

If you achieved Fair or above on two of the three letters, note deficiencies, and go on. If you scored below Fair on more than one letter, note deficiencies, and discuss the problems with your instructor.

B. How would you improve these letters?

1.

> What kind of packing department does your company have? I have just received my Book Club copy of "Let's Go West" but it is in terrible condition. The flimsy packing was torn open and the book was badly damaged.
>
> When I pay for books I want them to look like new books.
>
> When you send me another copy of "Let's Go West" plus allowance for postage, I will return the damaged book to you. If you do not send me a new copy, I will discontinue my Book Club membership.

Given three situations in which a claim must be made, write three grammatically correct letters in good form, (1) identifying the problem, (2) clearly stating the claim, (3) offering a solution, and (4) remaining courteous.

A grammatically correct letter that meets the given number of guidelines, according to peer judgment or your instructor's evaluation:

Excellent   4
Good   3
Fair   2

Given two poorly written letters, rewrite the letters using effectively the four guidelines for claims letters.

A grammatically correct letter that meets the given number of guidelines, according to peer judgment or your instructor's evaluation:

Excellent   4
Good   3
Fair   2

Name_____ Date_____

2.   Sirs:

Last year I bought one dozen azalea bushes from
your nursery. You guaranteed that they would
grow. I guess I should have known better than to
believe a newspaper advertisement because not
one of those bushes is alive and growing this
year. Apparently you think that people will not
come back and ask for what they deserve.

I hereby demand that you send me one dozen
azalea bushes to replace those that did not
grow. Trusting that you will attend to this
matter at once, I am,

                              Truly,

If you achieved Fair or above, go on to part C. If you fell below Fair,
review the comments of your peers, and discuss difficulties with your
instructor.

C. Pete wants to help his friend, who has purchased a defective calculator. Do you think that his letter will be effective?

> *Given a letter with many
> errors in spelling, punctu-
> ation, form, and language,
> correct the errors and
> write improvements
> above the lines.*
>
> | *Excellent* | *25–26* |
> | *Good* | *22–24* |
> | *Fair* | *19–21* |

Service Division

Commodore Business Machines

Bristol, Virginia, 24201

Dear sir,

I am send you this letter with the machine which

is not operating. After I recieved the fixed

machine, MM2st, on behalf of a friend, I found

it to be totaly inoperative. The person who pur-

chased the machine is Irene Dos Santos of

portugal. On account of the fact the she is

presently not in the country, I am handeling

this case.

The machine still under waranty has the number 006149 and was shipped from your location on Mzy 29. When I retrieved the machine from the store where it was bought it did not work. I agree with the store that the machine is a "lemon" and must be replaced. We agree that one should recieve a new machine.

I therefor would appreciate hearing from your division that you are giving her her just compensation in the form of a new machine. I have complete confidence that this case will be handleled smoothly so that all parties will be happy. With my best wishes for a speedy transaction.

                    Yours truly,

                    Peter Brite

                    Peter Brite

If you achieved Fair or above, go on to the Summary. If you scored below Fair, note your errors and discuss your score with your instructor.

For those who wish extra credit: You have received an invoice from the Boro Appliance Company for the purchase of a portable TV for $139.50 and an electric iron for $20.50. You bought only the electric iron. Write a letter to accompany your check for the correct amount. Your instructor will evaluate this letter.

Name _____ *Date* _____

SUMMARY

In developing personal-business letters, apply the same principles as you do for all other letter writing. But, in addition to general principles, each type of letters has some guidelines you should follow.

Your order letter, for instance, should identify clearly the objects ordered, itemize costs and show the calculation, follow correct business procedures in the method of payment, and thank the company for processing the order.

When you write a letter of inquiry, you must list explicit questions, supply background information, and remember to say *please* and *thank you.*

Your letter of transmittal should identify the enclosure and call the reader's attention to specifics relating to the enclosure. While it is desirable to retain a copy of each letter you write, it is even more important here because you will have tangible evidence of your having sent the material along with the letter.

tangible: can be touched

The good claim letter will assure you favorable treatment. Write in a calm frame of mind, identify your problem, describe the product, make positive suggestions for settling the claim, and be courteous.

Focus on Language provides a check on the 32 spelling and vocabulary words spotlighted in this chapter, review of the use of the comma for nonessential clauses and phrases, capitalization of titles, verb agreement with relative pronouns, and a proofreading exercise.

FOCUS ON LANGUAGE

Spelling

The absense of a transmital notice caused an unfortunate delay in

prosessing the shipment of merchandice. We did not want a disatisfied

customer, but a reputible firm must take necessry precautions.

The registerar was quiet unhappy because she could not dicipher the

handwriting of the sophmore. She felt it was unecessary to prosess the

shipment of porselain.

Check the key on page 519. Note errors and drill the words which you
missed. When you have mastered them, then go on to Vocabulary.

> Given two paragraphs,
> each containing spelling
> errors, write the correct
> spelling above the errors.
>
> Excellent   7
> Good   6
> Fair   5

Vocabulary

1. proficiency   a. high level of skill   b. sluggishness   c. unskilled
   d. enough
2. process   a. believe   b. supervise   c. subject to a procedure
   d. announce
3. endowment   a. common stock   b. gift   c. foundation
   d. dividend
4. itemize   a. rationalize   b. set down as a list   c. ensure
   d. list of names
5. solicited   a. bought   b. sold   c. asked for   d. indemnified
6. concise   a. lengthy   b. compact   c. superfluous   d. inexpensive
7. absence   a. attendance   b. being present   c. being away
   d. sensible
8. waiver   a. voluntary giving up of a right or privilege   b. moving
   back and forth   c. to be uncertain   d. falter
9. transmittal   a. passing from one to another   b. a change
   c. registration   d. book
10. solvent   a. substantial   b. having means to pay debts   c. not having
    means to pay   d. impartial
11. decipher   a. investigate   b. write   c. interpret   d. increase
12. irate   a. delighted   b. happy   c. gloomy   d. angry
13. reputable   a. dishonest   b. intelligent   c. disabled   d. honorable

> Given 18 vocabulary
> words with a choice of
> meanings, circle the letter
> of the word that is
> nearest in meaning.
>
> Excellent   17–18
> Good   15–16
> Fair   13–14

Name_____ Date_____

14. imperious a. arrogant b. emperor c. wide-ranging d. humble
15. audible a. cannot be heard b. well-known c. can be heard
    d. group at a show
16. expire a. inhale b. end c. take place d. carry out
17. tangible a. evidence b. real to the touch c. avoidable d. tangled
18. biannual a. perennial b. every year c. every two years
    d. twice a year

Check the key on page 519. Note differences. Be sure you understand meanings before you go on. If you did not achieve Fair or above, write a sentence using each word you had incorrect. Ask your instructor to evaluate your sentences and to discuss any errors with you.

Sound-Alikes

Read the following definitions before going on to the exercise on sound-alikes.

everyone (pronoun)—every person.
  Everyone is ready to leave.
every one (adjective and pronoun)—every person of a group.
  Every one of the team members is ready to leave.

  (Note: Most indefinite pronouns can be written as one or two words. When written as two words, they are usually followed by "of.")

formally—in a manner prescribed by custom or established procedure.
  The president acted formally at the commencement.
formerly—beforehand; previous.
  Formerly, she had been a member of the council.

their (pronoun)—third-person plural possessive.
  We have their materials.
there (1. adverb)—in or at that place.
  She waited there for an hour.
  (2. expletive)—There is much to do.
they're—contraction of "they are."
  They're ready to leave.

Given seven sentences with three sets of sound-alikes, underline the correct word in each case.

Excellent 7
Good 6
Fair 5

1. (*Everyone, Every one*) of the officers is responsible for an individual report.
2. (*Their, There, They're*) certain that the bill was passed and signed.
3. Mark takes more interest in his work now than he (*formally, formerly*) did.
4. They read (*their, there, they're*) assignments during the noon recess.
5. The president will (*formally, formerly*) present the new members of the faculty.

6. (*Everyone, Every one*) must meet with the dean at least once during the semester.

7. (*Formally, Formerly*), it was customary to write up a lengthy report.

If you achieved Fair or above, go on to Punctuation. If you did not achieve Fair or above, review the definitions and use each word you had incorrect in a sentence. Ask your instructor to evaluate your sentences and to discuss any errors with you.

Punctuation: Comma

Rule: *Use commas to set off nonessential clauses and nonessential phrases.* (A nonessential clause or phrase adds an additional thought to the sentence but is not necessary to the meaning of the sentence.)

Mr. Wall, who has been around the world, spoke to the members of the Business Club.

The team, hoping for a victory, played to win.

Rule: *However, when a clause or phrase is necessary to the meaning of the sentence, commas are not used.*

All students who do not attend classes regularly must report to the office.

The men and women working on that contract will receive premium pay.

1. All taxpayers who have refused to file returns will be penalized.

2. The Mayor having completed his investigation proposed a change in the charter.

3. All factories that are declared unsafe must be demolished.

4. Mr. Ruskin who was trusted by both sides came in to settle the dispute.

5. The *Wealth of Nations* written by Adam Smith has become a classic.

6. Employees who wish to participate in the new pension plan should report to the personnel division as soon as possible.

7. All contestants who answer these questions correctly will win a trip to Paris.

> *Given seven sentences with essential and non-essential clauses and phrases, punctuate them correctly.*
>
> *Excellent   7*
> *Good   6*
> *Fair   5*

Check the key on page 519. If you scored Fair or above, go on to Capitalization. If you scored below Fair, review the principles and discuss your score with your instructor.

Name _____ *Date* _____

Capitalization

Do you know which words to capitalize in titles of books, plays, musical compositions, book-length poems, paintings, ballets, newspapers, and so on? Here's the rule to follow:

Rule: *Capitalize the first word in a title, and capitalize all other words except articles* (a, an, the) *and prepositions or conjunctions of fewer than five letters.*

>   *An Analysis of Consumer Purchases*
>   *The Kitten and the Falcon*
>   *Watching the Sails*
>   *Thoughts Among Friends*

(Although in print titles are set in italics, when typing, remember to underscore them or to type them in all capitals.)

Rule: *Capitalize parts of published works* (chapters, poems within a book, articles, columns in newspapers or magazines, short stories) *according to the rule for all titles.*

(Titles of parts of works are enclosed in quotes instead of being underscored. The same is true of unpublished works, such as internal company reports or unpublished theses.)

<table>
<tr><td>

Given seven sentences in which titles are used, correctly capitalize and punctuate them.

Excellent   7
Good   6
Fair   5

</td></tr>
</table>

1. the superintendent of documents publishes the statistical abstract
2. james knox of the bureau of labor statistics wrote a book called employment opportunities in the middle west
3. professor smith's new book a history of economic thought will be published in september
4. frank sheldon from the bureau of internal revenue spoke on the topic new tax regulations affecting business
5. the winged victory is a famous statue in the louvre in paris
6. steel builds for a new era was a leading article in october's fortune magazine
7. Both the democrats and the republicans contributed to material in the congressional record.

If you were successful, go on to Pronouns. If you scored below Fair review the principles above and discuss your score with your instructor.

Pronouns

Relative pronouns—*who, whom, which,* and *that*—sometimes give trouble. The following rules will provide some help:

Rule: *The verb in a relative clause must agree in person and number with the antecedent of the relative pronoun that serves as the subject of the clause.*

>   Have you spoken with the man who was waiting for you.

"Man" is the antecedent of the relative pronoun "who"; therefore, the verb must be third person and singular—"was."

Where are the papers that were left on my desk?

The verb "were" agrees with "papers," the antecedent of "that."

Rule: *If your sentence contains the phrase* "one of the" *or* "one of those," *the antecedent of the relative pronoun is not the word one but the plural words that follow.*

One of the letters that were on my desk has disappeared.

The relative pronoun "that" agrees with "letters"; therefore, the verb is "were." Remember, however, that the subject of the *main* clause ("one has disappeared") is "one" and takes a singular verb "has." It is only the verb of the *relative* clause ("that were on my desk") that agrees with "letters." Be sure you understand this distinction before you go on to the next rule!

Rule: *When the words* "the only" *precede* "one," *as in the following sentence,* "one" *is the antecedent of the relative pronoun.*

He is *the only one* of the men who is making the survey.

You will understand this rule if you think of the meaning of the sentence. In the example for the second rule, there were "letters on the table." In this example, however, there are not "men making the survey"; there is only one man who is doing so. Therefore, the antecedent of "who" must be "one."

When you are certain you have mastered these rules, go to work on the following sentences. Choose the words that show correct agreement.

1. Secretaries who (*keeps, keep*) accurate files (*is, are*) valuable in any office.
2. One of the men who (*is, are*) attending the session (*is, are*) wanted on the telephone.
3. He presented a plan that, in our opinion, (*is, are*) the best of all the plans that (*was, were*) submitted.
4. One of the applicants who (*is, are*) eligible for promotion (*is, are*) here now.
5. Marlene is the only one of the students who (*is, are*) receiving an award.
6. "It (*is, am, are*) I who (*is, am, are*) surprised," said the teacher.
7. Our business is the only one of those companies which (*has, have*) shown a profit.

> *Given seven sentences calling for agreement of the verb and the relative pronoun, underscore the correct verbs.*
>
> *Excellent   7*
> *Good   6*
> *Fair   5*

Check the key on page 519. If you achieved Fair or above, go on to Proofreading. If you scored below Fair, review the rules. Discuss any difficulties with your instructor.

Name_____ Date_____

Proofreading

Once again, let's test our proofreading ability.

> *Given a letter that contains errors in spelling, punctuation, and language, write corrections above the errors.*
>
> *Excellent   21-23*
> *Good   18-20*
> *Fair   17-19*

Dear Deposter

We no you are intrested in getting the maximum of convient service that your bank can provide--and also in getting the highest return on you savings.

We have disigned a new account which makes one stop banking a realty at Central--and keeps the money in your savings account earning interest until you need it.

Under a new rule governing savings banks we a are now aloud to furnish you with negotiable payment orders. This is a with drawal form drawn on your account. But you can make it out to some body else-mail it to him-and she can cash it.

Central orders are a highly convenient way to pay bills of all kinds. Youll find them to be one of your best investments in todays ever changing bank seen.

Cordially,

If you achieved Fair or above, you are ready for Chapter 8. If you fell below Fair, note your errors and discuss your proofreading problems with your instructor.

8

THE APPLICATION SERIES

Among the most important communications you will ever write are those concerned with applying for a job:

The letter of application and the data sheet.

The thank-you for the interview.

The letter of acceptance or rejection of the job offer.

You have been gaining experience in writing business letters for personal reasons and have had a chance to learn to express yourself effectively. Many of the principles you have already learned can now be put to use in helping you get the job you want. You are now "selling" your working capacity to a prospective employer. Do two things: Put yourself in the reader's place, and plan your approach.

capacity: ability; skill
prospective: expected; concerned with the future

UNIT 25   DATA SHEET AND LETTER OF APPLICATION

Your performance objectives for this unit are:

Given the situation in which you are to present an assessment of yourself in applying for a position,

assessment

You will prepare a data sheet which presents your professional and pertinent personal background and which highlights your accomplishments, and

pertinent

Given the situation in which you are to mail the data sheet to a prospective employer,

You will write an effective letter of application which gets the attention of the reader in the opening sentence or sentences, which refers to specific accomplishments in your data sheet, and which requests an interview and makes it easy for the reader to contact you.

Appearance Counts

No matter what the content of your materials, here, more than ever, appearance counts. Your letter presents a picture of you. Make its appearance say good things about you. Some letters are attractive and seem to ask to be read, while others cannot pass inspection. Neatness and carefulness are important in any job; if your letter's appearance doesn't reflect these qualities, your letter may never be read.

Hint for a good start.

The person to whom you are writing is a stranger, and your letter deals with a business matter. Therefore, avoid the use of hotel or social stationery, or paper embossed with your fraternity or sorority crest, or other special stationery.

embossed: covered with a raised design

Type your letter on white bond paper of good quality in the standard 8½ × 11 size. Your envelope should match the stationery—its appearance counts, too. And the position of your letter on the sheet affects the reader's reaction. Allow enough space for margins.

Remember, of course, to place your return address in the upper right-hand corner along with the date and to include your telephone number if you can be reached by phone. Type the prospective employer's name and address in the usual position for the inside address. If you are writing a letter of application in reply to a help-wanted advertisement, use the address given in the ad. If the ad gives a box number, type the box number as the first line of the inside address:

Remember to leave two spaces before the zip code.

```
Box 245
Los Angeles, CA   90014
```

The salutation of such a letter should be "Ladies and Gentlemen."

Follow the rules for breaking up the letter into paragraphs to improve its readability.

Be sure to sign your letter with your official signature, in longhand and in ink, directly above your typed signature. No one will mistake your name if it has been typed.

Take Time to Plan

You know that your letter must pass an appearance test. Now you must do some preliminary planning so that the contents of the letter will match its attractive appearance.

preliminary: coming before the main event

A letter of application, to be complete and yet brief enough to get the reader to finish reading it, presents a difficult problem. Follow the modern practice of writing a short letter of application and attaching a data sheet, or résumé. This makes it easier for you to plan your letter and to use attractive display techniques in setting up the information on your background.

Keep the reader in mind.

One of the first things to do is a little preliminary homework to learn something about the company in which you are applying for a position —its main products and services, its position in its field, the number of its employees, its beginning salaries. If you are going to meet someone for the first time, you will find it easier if you know a little something about that person. (Of course, if you are answering an ad in which the firm is not identified, you cannot prepare in this way.)

Then do some thinking about your qualifications. Writing your letter of application and preparing your data sheet are very personal acts. The worst thing you can do is to copy a letter someone else wrote. You are selling yourself, and your letter should reflect you. Think in terms of what you have to offer. You may not have had much business experience, but you have an education. Get the exact dates of your high school and college career. List the specific courses you have taken that may be of value in the work for which you are applying. Jot down the names of the clubs you joined at school. Were you elected to an office? Did you work on committees to plan club activities? If you were in the top quarter of your class or achieved some other scholastic honor, be sure to mention it. Have you done volunteer work on charitable campaigns? Are you known in your community for your civic mindedness and assistance in community projects? If you have had business experience, tell a little about each job. With a little ingenuity, even a baby-sitting job can assume some importance.

Put down these facts one by one as they come to your mind. Then look them over and classify and organize them. Determine how you can present them in the most appealing way. Now you should be ready to prepare your data sheet.

then

charitable: generous in giving to the poor

ingenuity: cleverness; inventiveness

The Personal Data Sheet

After Angelo Novarro completed his data sheet, he said: "Here I am in compact, easy-to-read form!" That is exactly what the data sheet is. It is a factual presentation of you—your personal history, education, extracurricular activities, work experience, honors and awards, and references.

extracurricular: outside the curriculum

How should you begin? The usual way is to list first your "vital statistics"—name (including middle name), address, phone number, date and place of birth, country of citizenship, and state of health.

Now you are ready to list the relevant parts of your background. (As a rule, lists, not sentences, are used in a data sheet.) As you begin your career, education is your chief selling point, so you will list the details of your education first. Make your entries complete by including the names of educational institutions, their locations, and the dates of your graduation or attendance. Omit data concerning your elementary school.

attendance

In describing your educational background, you should list courses that are relevant to the position for which you are applying. You can mention four or five major courses and several background courses. Always list these courses by name rather than by a catalog number, which would mean nothing to the prospective employer.

Remember the reader!

Be sure to list activities during your school career that would indicate your intellectual abilities, your leadership qualities, your cooperativeness, and your ability to get along with others. For example:

```
1. "A" average in college.
2. Dean's List, 19--, 19--.
3. Elected captain of basketball team.
4. Member of Phi Beta Lambda, honorary
   business fraternity.
```

5. Member of Business and Economics Club,
   19--,19--. Elected secretary, 19--.
6. Member of college choir.
7. Tutor of business subjects, 19-- - 19--.

advisable
inverse: opposite in order
chronological: arranged
according to sequence in
time

It is advisable to enter data relating to your experience in inverse chronological order, giving the most recent first. This is the logical approach, because most people like to see what you are doing now before seeing what you've done in the past.

Although your job experience may be quite limited, do not hesitate to take advantage of any entry you can make. If you have held part-time or summer jobs, you should include them. Even though these jobs may not relate to the position for which you are now applying, they tell something about you—that you have initiative and ambition, that you accept responsibility, that you have had some experience working. That summer job will show that you were dependable, for no employer would keep you for an entire summer if you were not.

initiative: power or right
to take first steps

Perhaps you have had some military experience. You may include this under work experience, or you may give it a separate heading, depending on its nature and its importance to the job you are seeking.

We have already noted that you should list extracurricular activities. It is also well to list outside activities and organizations under the heading "Out-of-School Activities." These activities could include:

e.g.: for example

Outside sports programs—e.g., golf tournaments, baseball teams, bowling leagues, tennis clubs
4-H Club membership
Boy Scouting or Girl Scouting
Junior Chamber of Commerce
Travel experience
Hobbies

i.e.: that is

Hint for good human relations.

recommendation

verified: proved to be true
or accurate
Remember the amenities.

Every good data sheet contains at least three references. Vary yours, selecting a teacher or professor who has known you well, a former employer if possible, and at least one character reference (i.e., someone who knows you well outside of business or school). Of course, you will never list a name as reference unless you have received permission in advance from the person to use his or her name. If the person named as a reference has an official title, include it; it identifies that person and helps a prospective employer evaluate his or her recommendation. Above all be certain that all names are spelled correctly and that all addresses are verified; they must be accurate. If you should learn that one of your references has written a letter recommending you, write that person a short note of thanks.

enhance: increase, as in
quality

Now let's look at some things relating to the mechanics of the data sheet. Obviously, you want your data sheet to make an excellent appearance. Therefore, you must arrange it for attractiveness and for easy reading. If you make effective use of display techniques, you will enhance the readability of your data sheet. Keep in mind the rule about using adequate margins to provide an attractive amount of white area on the sheet. Type your main headings in capital letters, either centered or at the left margin. Minor headings can then be underlined. You can experiment with different methods of display to see which is most effective for your sheet.

```
Angelo Novarro                    Date of Birth:  March 17, 1957
999 Carson Drive                  Place of Birth: New York City
Sacramento, CA  95804             Citizenship:    United States

(916) 351-7584                    Height:  6 feet
                                  Weight:  170 pounds
                                  Health:  Excellent
```

EDUCATION

| | | Diploma |
Institution	Dates	Degree
Central High School Buffalo, NY 14213	1970-74	Commercial
Castleton Junior College Castleton, CA 95807	1974-76	A.A.S.

Major: Accounting   Scholastic Standing: 3.2 (B+)

Major Courses	Background Courses
Elementary and Advanced Accounting I, II, III, IV	Business Communications Business Law I, II
Auditing	Money and Banking
Income Tax Procedures	Economic Analysis
Cost Accounting	Marketing
Business Management	

EXTRACURRICULAR ACTIVITIES AND HONORS

Accounting Club, President (elected office) 1975-76
College Glee Club 1975-76
Phi Beta Lambda 1976 (honorary undergraduate business education
   association)
Future Business Leaders of America 1973-74
High-school valedictorian 1974

EXPERIENCE

Company	Dates	Job Duties
Bullock's Department Store Sacramento, CA 95804	September 1974 to present (part-time)	Retail selling, men's furnishings
Lane's Buffalo, NY 14213	Summers 1973- 1974	Stock clerk

REFERENCES

Professor James Devine, Economics Department, Castleton Junior College,
   Castleton, CA 95602
Mr. John Knight, Manager, Shoe Department, Lane's, 111 Main Street,
   Buffalo, NY 14213
Mr. Frank Naber, Department Manager, Men's Furnishings, Bullock's
   Department Store, 18 State Street, Sacramento, CA 95804
Mrs. Hazel Hines, 184 West School Street, Sacramento, CA 95602

Figure 8-1
Personal Data Sheet

Look over Angelo Novarro's data sheet (Figure 8–1) to see if it meets the standards you have been reading about. Angelo has seen this ad in the help-wanted section of the Sunday paper:

HELP WANTED

Junior Accountant. No experience required. Must like working with people. On-the-job training program. Retail Associates, 585 Oakland Drive, San Francisco, CA 94105.

Notice how Angelo set up his main headings so that his reader could pinpoint each item easily. Including his telephone area code was wise because he could very well live in a different area from the company's. Perhaps he could have left out his height and weight, which would probably be irrelevant for the accounting position. He used good judgment in listing the courses that related to the job and the extracurricular activities that showed him to be a leader.

There is no Skills Activity for this section. Prepare your own Data Sheet. Discuss any problems with your instructor. This is a vital part of your course. When your Data Sheet has been completed in a form that represents you, ask your instructor to evaluate it.

Your Letter to Accompany the Data Sheet

When your data sheet has been completed, you are ready to prepare an application letter. Its main function is as a letter of transmittal to accompany your data sheet.

RIGHT—AT THE START

crucial: of a critical or decisive nature

Remember to arouse interest at the beginning. The first sentence is crucial; if it gets the attention of your reader, your letter has a chance to tell the rest of its story.

Ideally, your first sentence should be direct, and it should have the "you" attitude. Since you are selling yourself when you write the letter, however, you may use the first-person pronoun. (Just be careful to avoid using "I" to begin each sentence or paragraph. A little careful planning will enable you to vary your sentences.)

Try a one-sentence summary as a beginning sentence. Here are examples of sentences that have hit the target:

Opening-sentence summary.

My three summers' experience as camp counselor qualify me for a position at Camp Cherokee this year.

I am applying for the position of stenographer that you advertised in the Los Angeles <u>Times</u> on May 20.

Now that I have had two years of office experience in addition to my formal education, I
believe that I am prepared to fill the position
of office assistant with United Supplies.

If you have learned about a position through someone whose name commands attention, use that person's name in that first sentence. Of course, you must have permission to do this. Opening with a name is effective when your reader knows the name and respects the person's judgment. Your opening might read:

Anita Farrar in the vice president's office
has told me that you will need a stenographer
in June. Since I will be graduating at that
time, I should like to apply for the position.

Or use a reference in the first sentence.

Professor Thomas Cook, my finance instructor,
has suggested that I apply for the opening in
your credit department.

Notice that it is good practice to mention the name of the specific position for which you are applying. It shows that you know what you are seeking, and it also helps the personnel staff if the firm has more than one position open.

A third method of attracting attention in your opening sentence is to ask a question. This approach carries with it the advantages of directness and simplicity; it places the applicant's qualities before the reader at once.

Here's how you can use the question technique:

Do you wish to hire a stenographer who can take
dictation at 140 words a minute and transcribe
at 30 words a minute with 95 percent accuracy?
I am the stenographer you want.

Or try opening with a question.

However, a word of caution if you use the question opening: be sure that your qualifications answer the questions you raise. How would you feel if the reader took you up on your statement and you could take only 80 words per minute and you made many errors?

Other possible ways to use a question are:

Will you call me when you need a man who is an
expert tax accountant?

Do you need a live-wire salesman? I hope I can
fit your job requirements.

Let's see how you would handle the opening sentences in Skills Activity 43.

SKILLS ACTIVITY 43

A. Which opening sentence would you choose in the following cases?

1. a. Your good friend, Doris Sparks, tells me that there's a good job open in your office.
   b. Doris Sparks has suggested that I apply for the position of business representative which is open at Burney & Company.

2. a. Because I have the qualifications specified in your January 15 ad in the *Times*, I wish to apply for the position of legal secretary.
   b. Because my training has prepared me so well, I have the qualifications you listed in your ad for a legal secretary. I am ready to begin tomorrow.

3. a. Are you looking for a top-flight accountant with a specialization in tax procedures?
   b. Don't you think that your company can use me—a top-flight accountant with excellent training in tax procedures?

4. a. Here's an applicant who can offer you three summers of field experience and now a degree in civil engineering.
   b. Now that I have had three summers' field experience in road construction and have earned my civil engineer's degree, I would like to apply for a position with Nickerson Construction Company.

5. a. I want to apply for the job you advertised in today's paper.
   b. I wish to apply for the position of administrative assistant which you advertised in today's *Voice*.

> *Given five pairs of opening sentences, select the more effective one in each case by circling the letter before the sentence.*
>
> *Excellent   5*
> *Good   4*

Check the key on page 519. If you agreed with the authors four or five times, go on to Part B. If you did not agree, discuss your selections with your instructor.

B. Your success as a writer has become well known among your friends and classmates. As job-hunting time approaches, you have received numerous requests for help in phrasing letters of application. Here are some introductory sentences written by candidates for employment.

1. *A political science major seeking a management trainee position in a bank:* Because I am interested in banks, I think I can qualify for a position advertised in *Graphic* in your management trainee program.

_____

_____

_____

> *Given weak introductory sentences for letters of application, rewrite them using the three approaches suggested.*
>
> *Peer judgment or your instructor's evaluation:*
>
> *Excellent   5*
> *Good   4*
> *Fair   3*

Name_____ Date_____

2. *Secretarial science major:* As a June graduate with a secretarial science major, I would be very happy if you would consider my application for the administrative assistant position advertised in *Graphic*.

_____

_____

_____

3. *Engineering major:* So I can implement a fine engineering education, I am thereby applying for the position of a structural engineer which you advertised in the *Herald* of 7 March.

_____

_____

_____

4. *Accounting major:* Jim Sloman, a good friend of yours, suggested that I might be qualified for an accounting position which he says is available in your firm.

_____

_____

_____

5. *Economics major:* I think I have the qualifications which you listed in your ad in the *Journal* for a research assistant. Therefore, I wish to apply for a job.

_____

_____

_____

If you achieved Fair or above, go on to part C. If you scored below Fair, rewrite the sentences; then discuss them with your instructor.

Given five opening sentences from letters applying for a position as an assistant accountant, rewrite them using the three approaches suggested.

Peer judgment or your instructor's evaluation:

Excellent	*5*
Good	*4*
Fair	*3*

C. As a prospective employer, how would you react to these opening sentences?

1. Replying to your ad in the *Times* of March 1st for a bookkeeper, I wish to apply for the position.

_____

_____

2. When I was looking through the Sunday want ads, I noticed that you are looking for a bookkeeper.

_____

_____

3. I am writing to answer your ad for a bookkeeper in the *Times* of March 1.

_____

_____

4. This is to ask you to consider my qualifications as a bookkeeper with your valued company.

_____

_____

5. Please let me have the job of bookkeeper that you had advertised in the newspaper yesterday.

_____

_____

If you achieved Fair or above, continue. If not, rewrite the sentences; then discuss them with your instructor.

THE MIDDLE PARAGRAPHS

Once you have made a good start, you will find it much easier to write the middle part of your letter. It is proper here to re-emphasize some of the specific educational qualifications and work experiences that appear in your data sheet. These are your central selling points. If you have had summer or part-time experience, be sure to mention it; for example:

Stress your strong points.

> My two summers at Lane's and my part-time work at Bullock's gave me some retail selling experience.

Call attention to any honors you have achieved:

> As you will see from my data sheet, I will be graduated from Harden College with an A.A.S. degree in June. As a student, I participated in extracurricular activities that further prepared me for a business position.

However, your letter should mention only briefly your most important qualifications. The purposes in referring to these qualifications are to send your reader to the data sheet, where full information is given, and to highlight your accomplishments.

Can you improve the middle paragraph of letters of application? Try Skills Activity 44.

SKILLS ACTIVITY 44

A. Which sentences would you select for the middle paragraph of your letter of application?

1. a. I worked for the past four summers.
   b. During the past four summers, I held a clerical position at Grant's.

2. a. As you can note in my résumé, my main interest is environmental engineering.
   b. My main interest is environmental engineering.

3. a. Although I have had no previous experience, I have taken courses which should help me in an office.
   b. I have taken courses in data processing, systems, and office supervision, which give me some background for an office position.

4. a. During the past year I held a position as a sales manager.
   b. During the past year, my responsibilities included supervising a sales force cf 15.

5. a. My fluent Spanish and French enabled me to assist arriving passengers at the International Airport.
   b. I took courses in Spanish and French so I could assist arriving passengers at the International Airport.

Check the key on page 520. If you achieved Fair or above, go on to Part B. If you did not score Fair or above, discuss the answers with your instructor.

B. Here are some sentences taken from letters written by the students we met in the previous section. Will you improve them?

1. *The political science major:* Even though I was a political science major at college, I know that I can understand bank management because I took a course in economics and one in financial institutions.

_____

_____

2. *Secretarial science major:* Courses in office administration and in administrative secretarial procedures will help me to improve your systems in your office.

_____

_____

3. *Engineering major:* I received good grades in all courses which related to engineering design.

_____

_____

4. *Accounting major:* As you can see, I worked during the past several summers.

_____

_____

5. *Economics major:* I really need the job so I can get started in my field of economic research.

_____

_____

If you achieved Fair or above, go on to The Closing Paragraph. If you did not score Fair or above, discuss your answers with your instructor.

THE CLOSING PARAGRAPH

When you come to your closing paragraph, you want to secure the desired action—getting an interview. Make it easy for the employer to reach you and to schedule the interview: Give the times you are available (e.g., Thursday after 2 p.m. and Friday after 1 p.m.), and include your telephone number. (Usually, of course, you will receive an answer by mail.)

Tell the employer how to contact you.

These sentences show all that you need to include in your final paragraph:

        Will you please give me an interview? I am free
        on Friday afternoons.

        May I come for an interview? My telephone number
        is 357-4389, and you may reach me any morning.

        Please suggest a time when you can interview me
        for this position. You can phone me at 598-7687
        any day between noon and 4 p.m.

        May I come to see you and bring samples of my
        work? I am available any weekday during business
        hours.

Be sure to be definite in requesting your interview. Endings such as the following do not hit the mark; they are weak and colorless, and they show a lack of confidence:

Be positive.

        I hope to hear from you soon.

        If you feel that I can fill the position, please
        allow me to come in for an interview.

Now check your understanding of the writing of the closing paragraph of the letter of application. Try Skills Activity 45.

The Application Series 307

SKILLS ACTIVITY 45

A. Can you identify the more effective sentence for the closing paragraph of the letter of application?

1. a. I will expect to hear from you soon.
   b. You may call me at 297–2692 to arrange for an interview.

2. a. I will bring samples of my work when I come to your office for an interview.
   b. If you will be good enough to interview me, I will bring samples of my work.

3. a. May I have an interview at your convenience?
   b. I hope you will grant me an interview soon.

4. a. If you feel that I am the person for the job, won't you grant me an interview?
   b. May I have an interview at your convenience to prove that I am the person for the job?

5. a. Hoping to hear from you soon, I remain,
   b. I am available for an interview at your convenience.

Check the key on page 520. If you achieved Fair or above, go on to Part B. If you did not, discuss your answers with your instructor.

Given five pairs of sentences that are used in the final paragraph of letters of application, select the more effective sentence in each pair.

Excellent 5
Good 4
Fair 3

B. Are you satisfied with these closing paragraphs?

1. Now that you have read my letter, I know you will want me in your management training program. All you need to do now is call me at 372-1220 and tell me when you want to see me.

_____

_____

2. I would like to have an interview whenever you get a chance. Then we can talk over any questions you may wish to ask me.

_____

_____

3. By interviewing me, you will have a chance to ask me about my ideas on modern road construction.

_____

_____

Given sentences from the closing paragraphs in letters of application, rewrite them keeping a positive tone, including a definite request for an interview, making it easy for the reader to contact the applicant, and being polite.

Peer judgment or your instructor's evaluation:

Excellent 5
Good 4
Fair 3

Name_____ Date_____

4. If I have convinced you that I am the accountant you need, I'll be available for an interview if you call me at 835-3488.

_____

_____

5. I think I have told you all I can about myself. The rest is up to you. I'll hope to hear from you soon.

_____

_____

If you achieved Fair or above, go on to the next section. If you did not, review your answers with your instructor.

THE COMPLETE LETTER

Let's return to the advertisement we read for the junior accountant's position with Retail Associates. Angelo Novarro prepared his data sheet; now let's see the letter he wrote to accompany it:

                              999 Carson Drive
                              Sacramento, CA 95804
                              July 1, 19--

Retail Associates
585 Oakland Drive
San Francisco, CA 94105

Ladies and Gentlemen:

Please consider me for the position of junior
accountant advertised in the San Francisco
Gazette of June 30.

My enclosed data sheet shows that I have had
extensive training in accounting and business
practice in high school and college. My extracurricular activities while in college included
being president of the Accounting Club for two
successive years.

While your position does not require business
experience, my part-time and summer jobs at
Lane's and Bullock's have given me an opportunity to deal with people and to learn something about the retail business.

May I come for an interview at your convenience?
You can reach me by calling my home any time
during the day. My telephone number there is
351-7584.

                              Sincerely yours,

                              Angelo Novarro

                              Angelo Novarro

Enclosure
  Data Sheet

Refer to the specific job.

Mention important achievements.

successive: consecutive

Note any relevant experience.

Be positive, and make response easy.

Do you agree that Angelo's letter was a good one? What about the following letters sent in by job applicants? If you were an employer, would you interview these two young ladies on the basis of their letters? The letters were in answer to an advertisement for a secretary with good skills and a willingness to assume responsibility.

```
                                      123 Middle Avenue
                                      Baltimore, MD   20782
                                      May 15, 19--

The Kipling Company
1776 H Street, N.W.
Washington, D.C.   20006

Dear Sir:

When I was reading the Sunday paper yesterday,
I noticed that you have advertised for a secre-
tary with good skills. I should like to be con-
sidered an applicant for the job.

I had some business courses in high school and I
continued to study business at college. I found
my studies at school very interesting so I think
I should enjoy a secretary's job in business.

I trust that you will grant me an interview so
that we can talk about the job.

                           Yours truly,

                           Marie Melinda

                           Marie Melinda
```

Proper salutation?

Too many I's in first and second paragraphs.

"Some" is vague. Commas needed between independent clauses.

"I trust" is both old-fashioned and presumptuous.

Proper closing?

strive: make earnest effort

Would Marie get an interview? Or could she have made her letter more effective? We suggest that Marie study her rules on the use of the comma and on letter mechanics and that she strive for a more modern, businesslike tone. Let's vitalize her letter.

First, let's delete the opening sentences and replace them with:

```
Please consider me for the secretarial position
you advertised in Sunday's Gazette.
```

Notice that this is a more direct approach and uses fewer words.

You will agree that Marie's second paragraph is vague, but that's easy to correct:

I had two years of stenography and typewriting
in high school and majored in the executive
secretarial program in college. The A.A.S.
degree included 32 credits of liberal-arts
courses and 30 credits of business-background
and career courses. My educational background
prepares me for a position as a secretary.

For her final paragraph, Marie would have done better if she had ended
something like this:

May I have an interview? You can call me at my
home at any time. My phone number is 751-3227.

Marie made no mention of having prepared a data sheet. The omission
could cost her the job.

Here is Francine's letter for the same job. She, too, seems to have
forgotten a data sheet.

A data sheet is essential.

454 Crane Avenue
Baltimore, MD 20782
May 15, 19--

The Kipling Company
1776 H Street, N.W.
Washington, D.C. 20006

Ladies and Gentlemen:

You are looking for a highly-skilled secretary
aren't you? I am willing to work for you including the assuming of responsibility that you
mentioned in your advertisement.

Wordy

My steno speed is 140 words per minute and
that's no fooling. I can transcribe at 30 words
per minute. You must admit that few of your
employees can achieve those rates. I haven't had
any business experience and I'm anxious to get
started. I did work in the playgrounds during
the summer, however.

Slang

Negative

Disorganized

When I come in for an interview I will demonstrate my skills.

Presumptuous

Sincerely,

Francine Simpson

Francine Simpson

*Can you find any punctu-
ation mistakes in this
letter?*

It looks as if Francine is hardly the bashful type! Couldn't she have toned down her letter to make herself sound more professional without losing sight of the fact that she has skills? (She claims she has speed; what do you think of her accuracy?)

Let's see what we can do with Francine's letter. We'll follow her ideas of opening with a question.

> Are you looking for a stenographer who can take dictation at 140 words a minute and transcribe accurately three letters with carbons in twenty minutes? I have those skills, and I am eager to obtain the stenographic job you advertised in yesterday's Gazette.
>
> My experience includes a vacation job as a play-ground supervisor, as you will see on my enclosed data sheet. As part of this job, I organized sports events and tournaments.
>
> May I have an interview so that you can go over my qualifications with me? If you wish, you may call me at my home, 761-1696, any time during the day.

tournaments: contests involving a number of competitions

Apply your knowledge to the complete letter of application in Skills Activity 46.

SKILLS ACTIVITY 46

A. Sue Barnes has written the following letter applying for a position as a legal secretary. She asks you to offer some constructive criticism before she mails the letter.

I am writing this letter in answer to your ad which I saw in the <u>Journal</u> looking for a good legal secretary.

I think I am the person who you are seeking because I will be completeing my AAS in legal secretarial work in June and I will be ready for a permanent job. As you will observe from my enclosed data sheet, I had excellent grades in all my courses related to legal work. I was also president of the Student Activities Comittee for the passed 2 semester. I think my part time legal experience is also good.

I will be looking forward to hearing from you. I can be reached at your convenience. Just call me at 390-1776.

> Given a letter of application that needs some revision, rewrite the letter correcting all errors and (1) making the opening paragraph more effective, (2) rewriting the second paragraph stressing the reader's point of view and stating specifics, and (3) rewriting the last paragraph, again stressing the reader's point of view.
>
> A correct letter meeting the given guidelines, according to peer judgment or your instructor's evaluation:
>
> | | |
> |---|---|
> | Excellent | 3 (rewritten letter meets all three guidelines) |
> | Good | 2 (rewritten letter meets only two of the three guidelines) |

If your rating is Good or Excellent, go on to Part B. If it is below Good, discuss the problem with your instructor.

Name _____ *Date* _____

B. Sue Barnes has been offered the legal secretarial position (only after your help, of course). She has told Al Moran to come to you for help in writing his letter. Here is Al's letter.

Given a letter of application that needs revision, rewrite the letter correcting all errors and (1) making the opening paragraph more effective, (2) rewriting the second paragraph stressing the reader's point of view and stating specifics, and (3) rewriting the last paragraph, again stressing the reader's point of view.

A correct letter meeting the given guidelines, according to peer judgment or your instructor's evaluation:

Excellent	*3 (rewritten letter meets all three guidelines)*
Good	*2 (rewritten letter meets only two of the three guidelines)*

I notice in today's issue of the <u>Journal</u> that you are seeking a top-flight assistant programmer. I am hereby applying for the position now that I am academically prepared to enter the world of employment.

I have inclosed my data sheet on which I would like you to note especially that I have held part-time jobs involving programming for the past three years. Because I like this type of work, I majored in Data Processing at my college from which I will receive my degree in June.

If you want to interview me, I can then tell you more about myself. I can be reached at 382-1078 after 11 a.m. Thank you for your consideration of my application.

_____

_____

_____

_____

_____

_____

_____

_____

_____

_____

_____

_____

_____

If your rating is below Good, discuss your letter with your instructor. If you have succeeded, go on to Part C.

C. Select and clip from a newspaper an advertisement for a position which you believe you are qualified to fill. Write the letter of application to go with the data sheet you prepared.

_____
_____
_____
_____
_____
_____
_____
_____
_____
_____
_____
_____

If your rating is below Fair, discuss your letter with your instructor. If you have succeeded, go on to the next unit.

UNIT 26 THE LETTER OF THANKS FOR AN INTERVIEW

Your performance objective for this unit is:

Given the situation in which you as an applicant have completed an interview,

You will write a correct letter thanking the interviewer for the interview by (1) focusing on the reader's point of view, (2) stating specifics, and (3) keeping it brief.

You have had the interview—a full hour session with the prospective employer. Will you now wait to see what happens? Have you completed your letter writing? One more short letter to thank your prospective employer for the interview may be the one that proves to be the clincher; it brings you back to the interviewer's mind in clear focus. This little extra effort puts you out in front.

The letter below is all that is needed:

```
                        999 Carson Drive
                        Sacramento, CA  95804
                        July 8, 19--


Mr. Lester Barnes
Retail Associates
585 Oakland Drive
San Francisco, CA  94105

Dear Mr. Barnes:

Thank you for granting me an interview
yesterday.

I am very much interested in the position of
junior accountant with Retail Associates. I
appreciate the careful consideration you are
giving my application.

                    Sincerely yours,

                    Angelo Novarro

                    Angelo Novarro
```

Be very brief and to the point.

Taking note of names is important.

Notice that Angelo was alert enough to remember the name of the man who conducted the interview.

Try Skills Activity 47 to apply your knowledge of the thank-you letter to the job application series.

SKILLS ACTIVITY 47

1. Debbie Andrews has been interviewed for a position as administrative assistant at Moore's Engineering Associates. She has thoughtfully written a thank-you letter. She asks for your advice before she mails the letter.

Given two letters thanking an interviewer for an interview, rewrite them (1) focusing on the reader's point of view, (2) stating specifics, and (3) keeping them brief.

A correct letter that meets the given number of guidelines according to peer judgment or your instructor's evaluation:

Excellent   3
Good   2

> Thank you, Ms. Singleton, for interviewing me yesterday, 5/10/76, for the job at Moore's.
>
> I sure want the job because it sounds like a real challenge. I'll be waiting to get your affirmative response to my application.

_____

_____

_____

_____

_____

_____

_____

_____

2. Debbie has also had an interview with Deskcon. After listening to your advice on her first letter, she writes this note to Deskcon. She asks you once again to check it over with her.

> Thank you, Miss Baxter, for interviewing me for the position of administrative assistant at Deskcon.
>
> I am really anxious to work at your company because of the many fringe benefits offered to employees. That four-week payed vacation sounds wonderful--it will give me time to travel or relax during the summer.
>
> I can be reached at 671-9645.

_Name_____ _Date_____

_____

_____

_____

_____

_____

_____

_____

_____

_____

If you achieved Good or Excellent on the two letters, go on to Unit 27. If you were not successful, discuss the problem with your instructor.

UNIT 27 THE LETTER OF ACCEPTANCE OR REJECTION

Your performance objective for this unit is:

Given situations in which you are to inform an employer of the acceptance or rejection of a job offer,

You will write letters of acceptance or rejection that are prompt, brief, courteous, and complete.

Finally it came—the letter that said, "You are invited to join our staff." You have been waiting for this job offer, and you are ready to answer it immediately.

Respond promptly.

```
                        108 East Washington Street
                        Indianapolis, IN  46209
                        July 15, 19--

Economy Finance Company
187 Capehart Drive
Indianapolis, IN  46207

Dear Mr. Urfer:

I am happy to accept the position of credit
investigator at a weekly salary of $175.

As you requested, I will report to Mr. Harold
Ewen in the Personnel Department on July 19 at
9 a.m.

Thank you for giving me this opportunity to
work in your company.

                   Sincerely yours,

                   Jane Ball
                   Jane Ball
```

Did you note Jane's mistakes? (She addresses a person in her salutation, but fails to include his full name and title in the inside address.)

Suppose that when the letter offering you a position arrives, you have already accepted another job. Will you disregard the offer you don't accept? Or will you keep your good name by writing to say that you cannot accept the position? It takes just a few minutes to write:

Be courteous enough to inform the company of your refusal.

Thank you for offering me the position of credit investigator with Economy Finance. Because I accepted a position with another company yesterday, I must refuse your offer.

I am pleased that your firm considered me for the position.

To see how well you can write a letter of acceptance or rejection, try Skills Activity 48.

SKILLS ACTIVITY 48

A. Gene Martinez has been offered positions at several companies. He writes this letter and asks you to offer suggestions for improving it.

> Thank you for offering me the position as sales representative at Walker Plastics. I am happy to except your kind offer.
>
> In accordance with your request, I will report to Ms. Walker in two weeks to begin my career.
>
> I know you will be glad you excepted me.

_____

_____

_____

_____

_____

_____

Given a letter accepting a position that was written by a weak letter writer, rewrite it (1) correcting all errors, (2) using modern language, (3) including all facts, and (4) keeping it brief.

A letter meeting the given number of guidelines, according to peer judgment or your instructor's evaluation:

Excellent   4
Good   3

If you succeeded, go on to Part B; otherwise rewrite the letter and discuss it with your instructor.

B. Gene wants to keep his options open, so he writes these letters turning down a job offer. Which one should he mail?

Given two letters rejecting a job offer, select the more effective letter and list the reasons for your choice.

1. Thank you, Mr. Somers, for offering me the sales representative position with Tomar Supplies. However, your offer came a day too late. I have excepted another job.

   If I can't get along well where I am now to work, I'll get in touch with you again. You may still have a good job open.

2. Thank you, Mr. Somers, for offering me the position of sales representative with Tomar Supplies. However, I have already accepted another position. I appreciate the time you have given me in explaining your business and the opportunities available in it.

_____

_____

_____

_____

_____

_____

Check the key on page 520. Be sure you understand the reasons why the letter was selected. Go on to the Summary.

SUMMARY

When you apply in writing for a position, you must plan your approach to include a short letter of application and a well-designed personal data sheet. In presenting your materials, you must realize that no matter how outstanding your qualifications may be, the appearance of your letter and data sheet will either enhance or detract from them.

Plan ahead while you are still in school. Collect the information for your data sheet. When you apply for your first job, you must be able to present a professionally typed, complete data sheet. It includes your name, address, telephone number (including area code), education, extracurricular activities, work experience, community activities, and names and addresses of the references whom you have asked to recommend you for the position.

Your brief letter of application accompanies the data sheet. It should refer to your strongest qualifications and to the specific position for which you are applying. In this letter, you should request an interview and give the times you are available for that interview.

Your writing a thank-you note for the interview may be the "extra" that gets the job for you. And, because you are a professional person, you will write one additional letter—the acceptance or rejection of the job offer.

Each phase of your job application becomes part of your file. Each one contributes to your obtaining the position or strengthens the employer's evaluation of you.

Now apply what you have learned about communications in the application series to problems involving your applying for a position. Try Skills Activity 49.

SKILLS ACTIVITY 49

Can you handle these cases in the applications series?

1. Your friend has told you about a position that will be open with her company in two months. Assume that this is the type of position you will be seeking at that time. Write a letter to apply for it, mentioning the name of the person who told you about it. Be sure to include your data sheet.

2. Assume that you have had an interview in answer to your letter in the preceding situation. Ms. Carmen DeLuca, the interviewer, said she would let you know about the position. Write a follow-up letter to thank her for the interview.

3. After a week's wait, you have been offered the job for which you applied. In the meantime, you have received another offer by a dynamic new company. Write letters to each of the two companies accepting or rejecting its job offer.

4. Read the help-wanted ads in your Sunday paper. Find an ad that appeals to you and that refers to a position you can fill. Write a letter of application and enclose your data sheet.

   You are now ready for Focus on Language, in which you will review 35 spelling and vocabulary words, three comma rules, and two rules of capitalization.

> Given cases which involve different steps in applying for a position, write correct letters that meet the criteria for each kind of letter.
>
> Letters 1 and 4 should meet the guidelines for Skills Activity 46; letter 2, the guidelines for Skills Activity 47; letter 3, the guidelines for Skills Activity 48, according to peer judgment or your instructor's evaluation.

FOCUS ON LANGUAGE

Spelling

A. 1. charit___ble

2. advis___ble

3. attend___nce

4. reco___endation

5. extracurricul___r

6. su___essive

7. init___ative

Check the key on page 520. If you did not achieve Excellent or Good, check the spelling of the words in which you made mistakes. Drill them until you are sure you know them. Then go on to B.

B. These words are not in this chapter, but they are troublesome.

1. lik___ble

2. elig___ble

3. permiss___ble

4. sim___lar

5. diction___ry

6. sep___rately

7. superintend___nt

Check the key on page 520. If you did not achieve Excellent or Good, drill the words you missed until you have mastered them. Then go on to Vocabulary.

Vocabulary

Following the list of words, you will find 11 sentences. Fill each blank space with the word from the list that most aptly fits the meaning of the sentences.

capacity	prospective	embossed
preliminary	ingenuity	extracurricular
inverse	chronological	verified
enhance	proven	strive
initiative	crucial	tournament

1. The personnel manager spoke briefly to the _____ employees.

2. Some readers prefer us to enter data relating to education in _____ order and to experience in _____ order.

3. This pronouncement, "In God we trust," is _____ on our coins.

4. Our engineers do not feel that this small calculator has the _____ to handle difficult problems.

Name_____ Date_____

5. We shall make _____ arrangements before making the final decision.

6. The committee was organized to do an entirely new job, and so was compelled to use creative _____.

7. Becoming involved in too many _____ activities can adversely affect one's grades.

8. On this job you will be evaluated on your _____.

9. He has been _____ correct.

10. _____ to win the matches in the _____.

11. It is _____ to the success of the mission.

Check the key on page 521. If you achieved Fair to Excellent, go on to Sound-Alikes. If you did not succeed, review the vocabulary throughout the chapter. Use each word you had incorrect in a sentence. Ask your instructor to evaluate the sentences and to discuss any errors with you.

Sound-Alikes

Here are three pairs of sound-alikes that can cause you problems in the office if you do not know them. Study the definitions. When you understand them, try the sentences to see if you can use the correct word.

attendants—plural of attendant; those who are present; those who attend.
   The garage attendants will park the cars.
attendance—The act of being present; an audience.
   The attendance at the game is disappointing.
passed (verb)—moved on.
   The car passed the traffic light.
past (adjective)—at a former time;
      (noun)—former time.
   She is past president of the Camera Club.
   In the past we studied the classics.

than—when; as; or if compared with
   The Empire State Building is taller than the Chrysler Building.
then—at that time; soon or immediately after.
   He then went to the office.

> *Given sentences which require the choice of the correct sound-alike, select the word that will make the sentence meaningful.*
>
> *Excellent   7*
> *Good   6*

1. His (*attendance, attendants*) at the meeting was compulsory.

2. The company reported higher earnings for this year (*than, then*) for last year.

3. The (*passed, past*) quarter has been disappointing for the Acme Company.

4. Prepare your personal data sheet; (*than, then*) mail it to our personnel office.

5. The company's sales have long since (*passed, past*) the billion-dollar mark.

6. We shall ask the (*attendance, attendants*) to record the number of people in (*attendance, attendants*) at the rally.

7. Your (*attendance, attendants*) is requested in the chairman's office.

Check the key on page 521. If you achieved Excellent or Good, go on to Punctuation. If you did not, review the definitions.

Punctuation: Comma

Rule: *Place a comma before a short direct quotation.*

The supervisor said, "Type two copies of this letter."

Rule: *Use a comma to separate introductory words, such as* yes, no, *and* well, *from the rest of the sentence.*

Yes, your car should be at the garage tomorrow.
Well, you have finally completed the job.

Rule: *Use a comma to set off words in direct address.*

Tony, will you check these figures for us.
Yes, Mr. Perkins, we have received approval of your loan request.

Use these rules—and others you have learned—to help you punctuate these sentences correctly:

1. No we do not intend to change our methods

2. Mr Cerone asked "Have you filed your return?"

3. Yes Mr Wise we have a subscription in your name

4. Do you plan to attend the conference in June Mr Peters

5. "Well we have reached our profit goal of $500000" he reported "and sooner than we'd anticipated"

6. All students who arrive late will fail the course.

7. Mr. Birns said "Yes you may leave now"

> *Given sentences with introductory words, direct address, and a short quotation, punctuate correctly.*
>
> | | |
> |---|---|
> | *Excellent* | 7 |
> | *Good* | 6 |
> | *Fair* | 5 |

Check the key on page 521. If you achieved Fair to Excellent, go on to Capitalization. If you did not achieve Fair, discuss your score with your instructor.

Name_____ Date_____

Capitalization

Rule: *Capitalize the first word of a sentence within a sentence.*

Your letter of March 15 read, "We will send our check for $25 immediately."

This is our proposal: If you pay within five days, you may take the discount.

Rule: *Capitalize points of the compass when they indicate specific geographical areas.*

When you have driven 3,000 miles west, you will be in the Far West.

1. mr ansell said, "we expect to relocate our office in the south."

2. members of the federal reserve board are studying banking conditions in the far east.

3. frank perotti pondered this question: how can we increase earnings by 20 percent?

4. drive east for 25 miles, then north for 15 miles.

5. "have you read 'middle management and computers,'" mr. drew asked, "in this month's issue of *dun's review*?"

6. ms. lopez asked, "have we enough stock on hand?"

7. Throughout history the middle east has been a problem area.

Check the key on page 521. If you achieved Fair to Excellent, go on to Chapter 9.

Given sentences with errors in capitalization, correct the space above each word.

Excellent	7
Good	6
Fair	5

III

WRITING
ON THE
JOB

9

THE INTEROFFICE MEMORANDUM

Your developing career has recently led you to accept a fulltime position as the head of the mail department in a small manufacturing plant. Two men and one woman work under you to effect the rapid delivery of the incoming mail and the servicing of the outgoing mail of the departments in your division.

effect: bring about

In this position, you will use the interoffice memorandum to communicate effectively and efficiently with other personnel in your company. You will focus on its use in the following situations:

Unit 28   Forms for the Recurring Situation and for Avoiding Errors

Unit 29   Directives and Transmittals

UNIT 28   FORMS FOR THE RECURRING SITUATION AND FOR AVOIDING ERRORS

Your performance objective for Unit 28 is:

Given the situation in which you act as the head of the mail department and face problems that recur and errors that arise from unclear directions,

recur: happen repeatedly

You will write appropriate communications in the form of interoffice memoranda that will save time and maintain efficiency in the office situation.

The Memorandum for the Recurring Situation

During that first week on the job, you and your assistants formulated this breakdown of the duties involved in processing incoming mail: time-stamping and dating, checking the envelope for notations not listed on the letter, noting differences of date of letter and postmark date, confirming inclusion of all enclosures by checkmark on the letter, sorting, and delivery. You worked as a team; and it was, therefore, obvious to all of you that interruptions in the work flow prevented rapid delivery of the incoming mail. When Joe would say, "Another one!" it meant that

formulated: stated in a systematic way

some piece of mail needed special attention, such as a note to a secretary explaining that the enclosure had not been included. With an average of 1500 pieces of mail coming through the division weekly, it was not unusual for each of the team to leave the group to type a letter to a secretary more than once each morning. If friendly, garrulous Joe types the note, it takes some time for him to complete it.

garrulous: habitually talking

                                              January 28, 19--

Ms. Rosemary Ramiriz
Secretary to Mr. John Breen
Accounting Department

Dear Ms. Ramiriz:

I have checked the attached letter again and
again, but I cannot find the enclosure. They
must have forgotten to put it in the envelope.

Perhaps they have already found it and will
mail it out immediately. As soon as the next
mail comes in, I will see if this company has
mailed anything and open it right away. If it
is the check, I will deliver it to you at once.

I am sorry this has happened and hope that you
will not have this trouble again.

                                 Sincerely yours,

                                 Joseph Adams

                                 Joseph Adams
                                 Mail Room

Incorrect use of pronoun "they"; no antecedent is given.

When Ms. Ramiriz read that note, she smiled; but she thought, "Joe must have a lot of extra time to write a note like this for a common error." She also mused: "What's the matter with the mail department? This is no way to handle this error."

Morton's cryptic note would have been more efficient if it had not become separated accidentally from the letter:

cryptic: puzzling

                                              January 30, 19--

     Ms. Aloise:

     Missing--the enclosure

                                 Morton Micheals

Ms. Aloise was annoyed when she found the 3 X 5 card unattached to a letter and without any reference information. Her remark typifies the reaction of business people to errors or inefficiency: "What's going on in the mail department!" You notice that she did not question, "What's the matter with Morton Micheals?" As head of the department, you must bear the responsibility for the procedures used in your department.

typifies: serves as a usual example of

bear: carry; take

To resolve the problem and to save time, you consider placing the word *Missing* in red next to the enclosure notation. But further marking the letters may bring objections from the addressee, so you decide to use a form. Since it will be addressed to another member of the company, you prepare an interoffice memorandum in which you can provide blank spaces for specific information.

Use blanks to make a general form suitable for specific occasions.

Just as the notes of Joe and Morton represented not them but the department, so your note must show the efficiency of your department and its willingness to serve. What information is necessary? Three specifics must be referred to: the date of the letter, the name of the sender of the letter, and the missing enclosure.

You prepare the following memo form and ask the duplicating department to run 500 copies for you:

```
              BUELL PRODUCTS CORPORATION
              Special Services Division

                              MAIL DEPARTMENT
                              Ext. 291

    DATE:

    TO:

    FROM:

    SUBJECT:

    The attached letter from _____

    _____, dated _____,

    did not contain the enclosure _____

    _____.
```

Note that the interoffice memo does not have a signature or complimentary close; it is direct and simple.

Length of blanks should suit information to be filled in.

Notice the difference from Joe's unprofessional letter. There is no reason to say that the letter was checked again and again. Are your procedures so inefficient that you could have lost the enclosure? The department to which the letter is routed may surmise that the sender had forgotten to put it in the envelope and will handle the problem after that.

surmise: guess

The memorandum form that you have prepared includes all the needed information and states its purpose in one sentence. It is a simple solution that will keep your department running smoothly.

The Memorandum to Avoid Errors

A few days later, the importance of writing instructions was forcefully brought to your attention by this news story:

> Herbert McHugh, a mail-room employee of Thewes and Company, a large brokerage house, was instructed by his supervisor to take the proxies of ABC Company from the Thewes mail room to the company's Shareowners' Relations Department—the unit responsible for relaying the proxies. On envelopes containing the proxies were the initials "SOR." Because of the initials the employee thought he had been told to take the material to the paper-shredding machine. The shredder made small pieces of the proxies in a few minutes.
>
> With the loss of 2800 proxies representing 400,000 shares of stock, Thewes and Company suffered considerable embarrassment and extra expense. The brokerage firm sent telegrams to the ABC shareholders asking them to call in their votes by phone and charge the phone bill to Thewes. The ABC shareholders' meeting was postponed indefinitely.

Verbal instructions can be misunderstood.

The mail-room employee resigned, but the major error was not his; it was the lack of explicit written directions.

occurrence

To prevent the occurrence of this type of error in your department, you immediately prepare a delivery slip in the form of an interoffice memorandum.

Include all information. (Time is important in delivery.)

Initials place responsibility for the instructions.

Notice the receipt.

```
              BUELL PRODUCTS CORPORATION
                Special Services Division

                               MAIL DEPARTMENT
                               Ext. 291

        DATE:                  TIME:

        TO:

        FROM:

        SUBJECT:

        Deliver to _____, Room _____.

        Special instructions: _____

        _____

                              Initials _____

        Received by _____

        Date _____   Time _____
```

Your memorandum provides short, simple, written directions that cannot be misunderstood and that can be referred to for confirmation. It also requires the signature of the recipient. As in all effective business communications, its purpose is immediately clear; all necessary information is included; irrelevant details are excluded; and the proper form is followed.

confirmation: proof

   Can you successfully write interoffice memoranda to handle office problems and to prevent errors? Try Skills Activity 50.

SKILLS ACTIVITY 50

A. How would you handle the following situations?

1. Al Rizzo has charge of room assignments at your college. At the beginning of the semester, there are numerous room changes because of schedule changes, added courses, dropped courses, and other reasons. Mr. Rizzo asks you, as his assistant, to design an interoffice memorandum to be sent to teachers and chairpersons asking them to report any room changes they have made for their courses.

2. Andy Andersen, a long-time employee, has been transferred to the Milan office of your company. He is scheduled to leave for Milan on August 11. You feel that it would be appropriate for his co-workers to have a farewell dinner in his honor. Assume that you have an estimate from the Peacock Club for a complete meal for $6.25 including gratuities. Write a memorandum to Andersen's co-workers inviting them to the dinner on August 1. The charge of $7.00 will include a gift for Mr. Andersen.

3. You are employed in the safety division of your company. There have been many accidents in the factory; several of them have been serious enough to be reported in the local newspaper. The company has always taken pride in its safety record, and it has consistently been ahead of other companies in its field in installing the latest safety devices. Your superior feels that some of the foremen and supervisors have probably become negligent in enforcing safety regulations among their workers. You are asked to compose a memorandum to call all foremen and department heads to a meeting to be held on Friday, March 18, at 5 p.m., in the company cafeteria. Your superior wants to discuss the matter of safety with the foremen and department heads. You might ask them to be prepared to offer suggestions for improving the safety record.

If you achieved Fair or above on two of the three memoranda, go on to B. If you did not score Fair or above, rewrite the unsatisfactory memoranda and ask your instructor to evaluate them. Discuss any problems with your instructor.

B. After Verna Waters had spoken to the Accounting Club of your college, her employer asked her to write him a brief memorandum to tell what she had discussed at the meeting.

Given three situations requiring the response of co-workers, for each situation compose a correct memorandum that (1) clearly states its purpose, (2) includes all the needed information, and (3) makes it easy to respond.

A correct memorandum meeting the given guidelines, according to peer judgment or your instructor's evaluation:

Excellent	*3*
Good	*2*
Fair	*1*

Read Verna's memo and correct it.

MOUNTAIN OFFICE EQUIPMENT

Interoffice Memo

DATE   Feb. 29th, 19--

TO   John Rogge

FROM   Verna Waters

SUBJECT   Talk to Accounting Club, 2/25

Dear Mr. Rogge

I thank you for giving me time off from work to speak to the Accounting Club of Hillsdale Community College. Hear are some of things I spoke about.

I told the students why I thought they should study business subjects. I told them that they would be certain of getting a job when they graduated college if they studied business courses.

I listed the following courses which I felt helped me on my first job:

            Business Law 1 & 2

            Accounting 1,2,& 3

            Office Management

            Economics 1

I feel that this liason between business and the community college should prove effective.

                    Cordially,

C. Gisa Cordero visited the local business-machine exposition where she was favorably impressed with the RCS electric typewriter. She is using a 15-year old manual typewriter in her office. Gisa had worked on two versions of a memo which she will give to her employer. Which of these memos should she send to Ms. Atwell?

As you know, I am still using a 15 year old manual typewriter to type legal papers. Considering the type of work we do here, it is totally unrealistic to expect good typescript from such an antiquated machine even though I am an excellent typist.

Therefore I would suggest that you purchase a new RCS electric typewriter such as I have just seen demonstrated at the business exposition. The machine will cost only $475 after a $25 allowance for our old typewriter.

If you approve the purchase, let me know and I will contact the RCS salesperson to order the machine.

Here's an idea which should help us produce better work in our office--the purchase of an electric typewriter. I have just visited the business exposition, and I think that an RCS typewriter would be perfect for our office.

Our 15-year-old manual typewriter is no longer adequate for the multiple carbon copies we need for legal work. Also, it no longer produces even-shaded letters. The cost of a complete overhaul for our old machine would be about a hundred dollars. The new RCS electric typewriter would cost $475 after a $25 allowance for our old machine. The RCS has an unconditional one-year guarantee. With good care, it should give us years of trouble-free service. The energy consumption is minimal.

Won't you please consider purchasing an RCS for our office? If you are interested, I can contact the salesperson to give us a trial machine to see the superior type of work which an electric typewriter can turn out.

_____

_____

_____

_____

Check the key on page 521. Note the reasons. If you do not agree, discuss the problem with your instructor. If you would like to work on a more difficult problem, try D. If not, go on to Unit 29.

ADVANCED CREDIT

D. Joe Blaine has been asked to write a memorandum to tell about the course in office management that he had taken at company expense. The company wanted to know about the content of the course to see whether it would be advisable to send a group of employees to take it. Here is Joe's memo. What do you think about it? Explain your ideas in detail; then rewrite the memorandum.

```
DATE      Jan. 20th, 19--

TO        Gertrude Stone

FROM      Joseph Blaine

SUBJECT   Office Mgt. 62.34


I took the course in office management at State
College during the semester from September to
January. The course was offered at 6 p.m. until
7:15 p.m. on Tuesday nights. Because I felt it
necessary to have a good dinner before attending
class, I usually came in a little late but other
students told me that I really didn't miss any-
thing during the first quarter-hour or so.
Because I had to rush to get to school, I
couldn't pay as much attention to the lectures
as I would have liked.

Professor Victor Merrill lectured during most of
the hour. Since the course was one in office
management, he spoke about automation, corres-
pondence techniques, filing, etc. It was a good
course. I think that it would be good for the
rest of our people to be able to take it.
```

Ask your instructor to evaluate your ideas and the rewritten memorandum and to discuss the evaluation with you.

UNIT 29 DIRECTIVES AND TRANSMITTALS

Your performance objectives for Unit 29 are:

Given the situation in which you, as head of the mail department, must issue general directions to your co-workers,

You will compose a directive that is well organized, complete, clearly stated, objective, and polite, and

You will write a memorandum of transmittal to be sent with the directive to co-workers.

THE DIRECTIVE

Your next problem is the effective servicing of the outgoing mail. No matter how many times you have mentioned to the secretaries and the office clerks that letters would get much more rapid delivery if they were ready for the 2 p.m. mail pickup, the volume of mail at the 4 p.m. pickup is still double that of the earlier one. Moreover, the secretaries, stenographers, and typists type the special mail services in different ways. Other annoying deterrents to rapid service—such as sealing the flaps, stuffing enclosures in the business-size envelope instead of using the legal-size envelope, or omitting the name of the sender at the top of the printed return address—interrupt the flow of operations. Following office procedure, you discuss the ways of handling the problem with Ms. Graves, the office manager, who is your immediate supervisor. She suggests that you send a directive to the employees of the Special Services Division, spelling out the exact procedures you recommend and requesting their cooperation.

directive: order or regulation

You came to the office manager with a few problems. However, your directive must include *all* the regulations and procedures for outgoing mail. You plan to include these items:

Mail-pickup service
Special mailing services
Bulk mailings
Typed envelopes
Enclosures
Mailing under separate cover.

Now that you have organized your thinking, let's work on the language you would use in writing a directive. Your directive should be definite, factual. As its name implies, it gives directions, and directions must be short and clearly stated so that no ambiguity can cloud the reader's understanding. For example, look at the following paragraph:

factual: pertaining to facts

```
Although it is sometimes possible to use the
business-size envelope when you are enclosing
small cards or forms, it is advisable to use
the larger or legal-size envelope, referred to
as the No. 10 envelope, when making other enclo-
sures. You will want to use the large manila
envelope for bulkier enclosures.
```

Vague terms: "sometimes,"
"other enclosures,"
"bulkier."
Passive: "it is advisable."
Judgmental: "you will want."

Now see how a few improvements can clarify the instructions.

Please use the No. 10 (legal-size) envelope when enclosing five pages or fewer. Use the manila envelope for enclosures of more than five pages. To enclose small cards or half-sheet forms, you may use the No. 6 (business-size) envelope.

Use colon and cyphers (10:00) when minutes appear in the list (as 11:30).

There is no reason to write a directive if you allow exceptions to the stated procedures. Use an objective and impersonal tone in your directive, and make the language work for you. For example, the passive voice is useful for achieving an impersonal tone:

Outgoing mail will be picked up at 10:00 a.m., 11:30 a.m., 1:30 p.m., and 4:30 p.m.

conform: in agreement with
cited: referred to as authority

Reading this, a clerical worker is unlikely to ask you to pick up a particular piece of mail at 10:15 a.m. or at 4:45 p.m. Rather, he or she will conform to the factual statement of procedure cited in the directive; it is impersonal and objective. You use this objective approach in the following directive:

BUELL PRODUCTS CORPORATION
Special Services Division

MAIL DEPARTMENT   Joseph DeNise
Ext. 291   Head

February 17, 19--

OUTGOING-MAIL PROCEDURES

Spell out numbers at the beginning of a sentence. Hyphenate all numbers from twenty-one to ninety-nine.

<u>Schedule</u>: Twenty-five pickup centers have been set up in all the departments of the Special Services Division. All outgoing and interoffice communications will be collected twice in the morning and twice in the afternoon at the following times:

a.m.	p.m.
10:00	1:30
11:30	4:30

The two morning pickups will be delivered to the post office at 11:30 a.m. and at 1:30 p.m. respectively, and the afternoon mail collections will reach the post office at 2:30 p.m. and 5:00 p.m. respectively.

respectively: singly in the order shown

Use headings for clarity.

<u>The Typed Envelope</u>: In order to facilitate work

in the Mail Department, please use the following
procedures in typing envelopes:

Give the complete address, including
the zip code. (See form 105A, attached,
for state abbreviations and zip codes
of the major cities in the United
States.) Type the names of foreign
countries in all capitals and underscore.

Type the name and department of the
sender above the printed return address on the envelope. Metered mail
must be charged to a department.

Type special mailing notations on the
right side of the envelope, just
below the position of the stamps or
meter indicia. These notations include:
Special Delivery, Certified Mail,
Registered Mail.

Leave the flap of the envelope open.
Let our stamping and sealing machine
do the work.

Type in all capitals a notation
for second-, third-, or fourth-
class mail below the place of the
stamps or meter indicia. If you use
a label for a package, place the
notation at the upper right of
the label.

Attached samples: The attached samples show the
correct way of addressing envelopes.

Special Services: Your Mail Department will keep
receipts for special services, such as registered, insured, or certified mail. "Return
Receipt Requested" notices will be sent to the
individual department requesting such service.

Bulk Mailings: Notify the Mail Department at
least five working days before the mailing is to
be sent, so that your mailing receives the
attention it requires.

PLEASE HELP US TO HELP YOU GET EFFICIENT MAIL
SERVICE!

Notice parallel construction of this list—each item begins with a verb.

Note instructions for foreign addresses.

In a series of hyphenated words with a common base, use a hyphen after the first element of each word, and write the base after the last word only.

Remember the amenities.

The Memorandum of Transmittal

You cannot mail your directive without a covering memorandum. To get the members of the Special Services Division to follow the procedures outlined in the directive, you must write a memo that will provoke their interest in knowing what you have written and obtain their cooperation in following the procedures. To do so, your memo must show them how they benefit by these procedures.

How will you start? You consider three possible beginnings:

Keep the reader in mind.

> Please read the attached directive carefully, and follow the procedures outlined there so that we may service your mail rapidly.

> The Mail Department needs your help!

> Do your letters just miss the last post-office delivery to the terminal? Are you spending time needlessly and delaying your letters by sealing your envelopes? Your letters deserve rapid delivery. The attached directive will tell you how to get them on their way.

You decide on the last approach, and you follow it with:

> Please read this directive on Outgoing Mail Procedures. By following the procedures and meeting pickup deadlines, you enable us to assure you of efficient mail service. Call us at any time for help with your special mailing problems. Our thanks for your cooperation.

assure: promise
"Assure you" is outdated; use "give you."

The last two sentences do not concern procedures; put them in a separate paragraph.

approbation: approval
worthwhile: of enough value to repay the energy spent

You type the memorandum and the directive in good form for your supervisor's approval. That pat on the back and the smile of approbation make all the effort you put into this project worthwhile. The office manager predicts success for your department and for you.

Let's put your knowledge of the directive to work. Try Skills Activity 51.

SKILLS ACTIVITY 51

A. How would you handle the following situations?

1. Gerry Meyer is an assistant in the Dean's office at your college. He has noticed that club members and other individuals are placing notices of club meetings, job opportunities, rentals of summer and winter homes, dance lessons, etc., on department and division bulletin boards. Mr. Meyer asks you to write a directive to be posted on each bulletin board and to be sent to all club officers.

   This directive will specify the size and type of notices which may be posted; it will state that all such notices must be stamped with the date and your initials of approval; it will also note that club notices must be removed within one day after an event takes place; it will mention that unapproved notices will be removed at once from a bulletin board.

2. Your supervisor has noticed that employees are taking an unusual amount of time during coffee breaks. Company policy allows a break of 15 minutes in the morning and a break of 15 minutes in the afternoon. Coffee and pastry are served at the employees' desks. Most of the employees are going from one desk to another and are taking about a half-hour on each coffee break. You are asked to write a directive to be posted where all employees will be sure to see it. Restate the company policy—a 15-minute break at 10 a.m. and a 15-minute break at 3 p.m. Employees are to remain at their desks so that communications will not be disrupted during the coffee breaks.

3. Business people who call your company continually claim that they have difficulty in reaching the office they are calling. Since the telephone company has recently updated your telephone-communications system, the office manager feels that telephone privileges are being abused. The manager asks you to write a directive to be sent to all employees to restate the rules on telephone usage. You should incorporate these ideas into your communication:

   Necessary local personal calls are allowed without charge. Personal long-distance calls are charged for, and the employee is expected to notify the operator when such calls are made.

   Employees are to keep personal calls to a minimum because they tie up the lines and interfere with the conduct of business. Personal calls should come through either before 9:30 a.m. or after 4:30 p.m.

   Employees should dial their own numbers, avoid asking the operator to look up numbers, and keep a list of frequently called business numbers on their desks.

> Given three situations in which general directions must be given to co-workers, compose correct directives that are (1) organized, (2) complete, (3) objective, (4) clear, and (5) polite.
>
> Peer judgment or your instructor's evaluation:
>
> | | |
> |---|---|
> | Excellent | 5 |
> | Good | 4 |
> | Fair | 3 |

If you achieved Fair or above on two of the three directives, go on to problem B. If not, discuss your answers with your instructor.

Name_____ Date_____

B. Secretaries at Intertype Corporation have been making excessive use of Mailgrams. They feel that their messages will be received the next day, but they are completely overlooking the high cost of the services.

You are asked to write a directive to explain the purpose of Mailgram service and to indicate when the service should be used.

Here is your first attempt. Will you send the directive on to the affected offices? Or will you do more work to improve it?

Given a short directive that needs improvement, rewrite it according to the guidelines in part A.

Peer judgment or your instructor's evaluation:

Excellent	*5*
Good	*4*
Fair	*3*

MAILGRAMS

When and How to Use Them

Definition. Mailgram is Western Union's high impact electronic mail. It is delivered with the next regular mail, usually the day after it's sent, sometimes the same day.

How to Use It. Simply call Western Union. Within seconds it is routed electronically to a U.S. Post Office near your addressee. There it's placed in a special blue and white envelope for delivery in the next day's mail. It can be sent for a small fraction of the cost of a telegram and probably less than most long distance calls. It can be less than the cost of a special delivery letter.

When to Use It. It should be used only when one wishes to have rapid delivery combined with a brief written record. It should be short, usually no more than 65 words. It is not a substitute for first-class letters. Study the attached list showing comparative costs for messages of different lengths of special delivery and Mailgram services to different locations.

Did you remember to compose the memorandum of transmittal?

Always use the correct service for your special type of message.

If you have achieved Fair or above, review the chapter by reading the Summary. You may either go on to Focus on Language or attempt a more difficult project for advanced credit. If you scored below Fair on this directive and letter, discuss any problems with your instructor.

Advanced Credit

C. Many employees have been working overtime at premium rates, and management has questioned the necessity for this expense. A careful investigation shows that people have been delaying some tasks until late in the day to earn overtime pay. You are asked to write a directive to make the rules on overtime work more stringent. You will incorporate these points into your directive:

The company will no longer permit employees to work after office hours unless they secure approval in advance from the director of their department.

The company has set a 35-hour general workweek. Hourly employees who have approval to work overtime will receive the regular hourly rate up to 40 hours and the time-and-a-half rate after 40 hours. Under no circumstances may an employee work more than 45 hours a week.

Ask your instructor to evaluate your directive and to discuss the evaluation with you.

SUMMARY

In a business office, your communication does not represent only you— it represents your department, your division, your company. Any error or inefficiency is not an individual's but the department's. An overly friendly, verbose letter detracts from the professional stature of the writer and the professional image of the department. The effectiveness of your communications redounds to your department's credit.

verbose: wordy

redounds: has an effect, as by reaction

For the *recurring situation*, use a form that provides blanks for references to specifics. When these are to be used within the office, follow the style of the interoffice communication. Include: *Date, To, From,* and *Subject* in the heading.

To ensure *correct understanding* and *follow-through* on directions, the person issuing them should put them in writing. Remember the plight of the mailroom employee who misunderstood the directions for delivery of the proxies and took them to the shredder.

ensure: make certain

When *general directions* are to be provided for a number of workers, the office or central agency providing the service issues a directive. The directive must be:

1. *Well organized.* Presentation, including major and minor headings and run-in headings, shows the whole picture. Tabulations are useful in listings.
2. *Complete.* All components of the operation must be included.
3. *Clearly stated.* Short, simple statements and exact words and phrases ensure correct follow-through of directions and avoid subjective interpretation by the reader.
4. *Objective.* Procedures are impersonal. The passive voice lends this tone to the directive.
5. *Polite.* The "please" may never be forgotten.

The directive is not addressed to any one individual, nor is it signed. Therefore, a *letter of transmittal* (in this case an interoffice memorandum) must accompany the directive to enlist the interest and cooperation of the reader in following the procedures.

In Focus on Language you will cover vocabulary and spelling words, including three sets of sound-alikes, the semicolon, capitalization of titles preceding names and titles in inside addresses and on envelopes, case of pronouns, and a proofreading exercise.

FOCUS ON LANGUAGE

Spelling

1. a. pertinent   b. worth while   c. embarrass   d. acknowledge _____

2. a. tipify   b. library   c. independent   d. exaggerate _____

3. a. preference   b. inference   c. occurence   d. reference _____

4. a. believe   b. siege   c. seize   d. recieve _____

5. a. confirm   b. conform   c. reform   d. asure _____

6. a. extravagance   b. benefit   c. expence   d. existence _____

7. a. busness   b. bulletin   c. athlete   d. already _____

> *Given seven groups of four words in which there is one error in each group, identify and correctly spell the misspelled words.*
>
> | | |
> |---|---|
> | *Excellent* | *7* |
> | *Good* | *6* |
> | *Fair* | *5* |

Check the key on page 521. If you achieved Fair or above, go on to Vocabulary. If you are a poor speller, have someone read the words as you write them. Check your spelling again.

Vocabulary

1. effect   a. bring about   b. act upon   c. move emotionally   d. think about
2. formulated   a. originated   b. planned   c. stated exactly   d. engaged
3. garrulous   a. habitually laughing   b. habitually talking   c. jocular   d. serious
4. cryptic   a. openminded   b. chaotic   c. puzzling   d. lengthy
5. typify   a. designate   b. locate   c. think deeply   d. be an example of
6. bear   a. support   b. expose   c. hunt   d. plan
7. surmise   a. realize   b. surprise   c. surface   d. guess
8. confirmation   a. proof   b. organized   c. vote   d. game
9. directive   a. fringe benefit   b. regulation   c. insurance   d. premium
10. factual   a. hazy   b. careless   c. based on fact   d. efficient
11. assure   a. entangle   b. withdraw   c. relate   d. promise
12. approbation   a. denial   b. approval   c. appreciate   d. guaranty
13. verbose   a. wordy   b. cryptic   c. short   d. interesting
14. redound   a. rebound   b. turn away   c. have an effect   d. reward

> *Given 14 words spotlighted in Chapter 9, select the best meaning for each from four choices by circling the letter.*
>
> | | |
> |---|---|
> | *Excellent* | *14* |
> | *Good* | *12-13* |
> | *Fair* | *10-11* |

Check the key on page 522. If you scored below Fair, review the meanings of the words you missed. Write original sentences using words you missed. Ask your instructor to evaluate your sentences and to discuss any errors with you.

Name _____ *Date* _____

Sound-Alikes

Review the following definitions carefully before trying the problems below.

respectively—singly or severally considered; singly in the order designated.

The scholarship, loving cup, and citation went to Bill, Mary, and Sue, respectively.

respectfully—marked by or showing respect.

The audience respectfully stood at attention during the playing of the national anthem.

cite—to bring forward as proof; to quote as authority; to summon to appear in court.

The judge will cite the defendant.

We can cite several authors to support our view.

sight—act of seeing; that which is seen.

The Rockies are a beautiful sight.

site—place or location; plot of ground set aside for some specific use.

The site of the new building is on Fifth Street.

assure—to make something certain; to promise.

She assured me that my vacation would not be postponed.

ensure—to make sure or secure.

Registering the letter will ensure its delivery.

insure—protect against loss or risk.

Some states require car owners to insure their vehicles.

Given sentences using three sets of sound-alikes, underscore the correct word in each sentence.

Excellent	7
Good	6
Fair	5

---

1. He spoke (*respectively, respectfully*) about his superiors.
2. The engineers have surveyed the (*cite, sight, site*) for the new dormitory and have (*assured, ensured, insured*) the administration that the space is adequate.
3. If anyone disagrees with you, you may (*cite, sight, site*) the procedures outlined in the manual.
4. The first and second meetings will be held with Mr. Jackson and Ms. Brown (*respectively, respectfully*).
5. Please (*cite, sight, site*) him the clause in the contract that (*ensures, insures, assures*) his protection.
6. You can (*cite, sight, site*) the parade from each building on the square.
7. He (*respectfully, respectively*) requested to see the (*cite, site, sight*) of the new building.

Check the key on page 522. If you scored Fair or above, go on to Punctuation. If you scored below Fair, review the definitions of the words you missed and use each word in a sentence. Ask your instructor to evaluate the sentences and to discuss any errors with you.

Punctuation: Semicolon

The semicolon is a much stronger slowdown signal than the comma.

Rule: *Use a semicolon to separate independent clauses of a compound sentence when these clauses are not joined by a coordinating conjunction.*

The game will be played this morning; the results will be known by noon.

Many analysts worked on these figures; however, Mr. Jones received credit for the work.

See how easy it is to punctuate these sentences:

1. Register for your courses here then pay your fees at the business office.
2. The new engine is economical it is designed to use diesel fuel.
3. You must study thoughtfully otherwise you cannot succeed.
4. The date was July 10 1967 the place was Seattle Washington.
5. The books arrived on time but the bookstore was slow in displaying them.
6. Weather influences spending hence it affects our business.
7. We worked hard however we did not work intelligently.

> *Given sentences with separate independent clauses not joined by a conjunction and with missing commas, punctuate correctly.*
>
> | | |
> |---|---|
> | *Excellent* | 7 |
> | *Good* | 6 |
> | *Fair* | 5 |

If you achieved Fair or above, go on to Capitalization. If you did not achieve Fair or above, review the rules and discuss problems with your instructor.

Capitalization

Rule: *Capitalize a person's title when it precedes the name. Do not use capitals when the name precedes the title or when the title stands alone.* (Exceptions to the latter rule are sometimes made in very formal writing, and a few titles are always capitalized—such as "the President of the United States.")

Doctor Smith; President Cross; Chairman McManus; Senator Jones; Bureau Director Atkins.

James Ashmore, president of General Chambers; Albert Watson, the company doctor; the senator from Maine.

Note: Capitalize all titles, whether they precede or follow the name, when you type an inside address or an envelope.

Rule: *Capitalize names of specific courses or departments, but do not capitalize fields of knowledge (except languages).*

the Economics Department; Marketing 101; a course in French; studying geography and English history

Rule: *Do not capitalize the names of the seasons.*

*Name*_____ *Date*_____

Given sentences that use titles, capitalize the necessary words.

Excellent	7
Good	6
Fair	5

Apply the capitalization rules to correct these sentences:

1. mr. raymond ewen, president of ewen electronics, will address the senior class during the spring semester.
2. general george gates stated, "we shall fly to rome early friday morning."
3. the secretary read the minutes of the fall meeting.
4. john eggert, the mayor of springdale, spoke with secretary connors.
5. marvin slade, president of the alpine ski club, has promoted winter sports.
6. the professor said, "you should register for courses in economics, science, english, and history. I would recommend history 701 and economics 4 as a beginning."
7. a purchasing department orders the supplies; the supply department only distributes them.

If you achieved Fair or above, go on to Pronouns. If you did not achieve Fair or above, review the rules and discuss the problem with your instructor.

Pronouns

Watch the case of pronouns carefully. Take the pronoun *he*, for example. *He* is the nominative case and is used when the pronoun is the subject of a clause. *Him* is the objective case of this pronoun and is used when the pronoun is the object of a verb or a preposition. The third case is the possessive—*his*—and is used, of course, to show possession.

Most writers have little difficulty using the proper case of such pronouns as *he, she*, and *you*. But the case of the relative pronoun *who* is sometimes confused. *Who* is the nominative case; *whom* is the objective case; and *whose* is the possessive. Let's concentrate on the difference between *who* and *whom*, which usually gives the trouble.

Rule: *The case of a pronoun depends on its function in the clause.*

Speak to the man who is at the desk.
He is the student whom I met at the game.

In the first sentence, *who* is the subject of the clause "who is at the desk." In the second sentence, *whom* is the object of the verb *met*—"I met whom." Notice that in "I met whom" we have inverted the clause in order to place the subject (*I*) first, the verb (*met*) next, and the object (*whom*) last. Inverting the clause is an easy way to find out if your pronoun is a subject or an object.

The objective case is also used in this sentence:

There is the boy to whom I gave the ticket.

Here the pronoun is the object of the preposition *to*, so we use the objective case, *whom*.

Now try your hand at picking the correct pronoun in each of the sentences below. Remember to look for the subject and object of the clause—and don't be confused by intervening words or phrases.

1. Write letters to the many applicants (*who, whom*) we plan to interview on Saturday.
2. James Andrews is the man (*who, whom*), you may remember, was chosen chairman of the committee last year.
3. Tell me if it is he (*who, whom*) the company should employ.
4. (*Who, Whom*) did you speak with when you telephoned the office yesterday?
5. Janet Moore is the person (*who, whom*) dreams up these singing commercials.
6. Here are several people to (*who, whom*) you can sell your product.
7. Have you spoken with the person (*who, whom*) they elected to the presidency?

If you achieved Fair or above, go on to Proofreading. If you did not achieve Fair or above, review the rules and discuss the problem with your instructor.

Proofreading

Mr. E. L. Jefferson, chairman of the Johnson and Marsh Company, has written the following memorandum of transmittal to be given to all new employees of the company. Because the person who transcribed the memo is a new employee, he asks you to check over the memo to see that it is written in correct form and that it contains no typographical or spelling errors.

JOHNSON AND MARSH COMPANY

Insurance Underwriters

To: New members of the staff of Johnson

          and March

From: E. L. Jefferson, chairman

Date: Oct. 10th, 19--

Subject: Welcome

Name_____ Date_____

Its my pleasure to wellcome you, as a new employe, to the staff of Johnson and Marsh. You will soon become aquainted with many of fine men and woman who, over the years, have found J&M a pleasent and rewarding place to work. I am confident that thease experiencedsupervisers and co-workers will make every effort to help you achieve a prompt and happy adjustment to your new job.

To help you get off to a good start, we have prepared the enclosed brochure giving you a brief history of the firm and a description of the present scope and character of our busness. The brochure is also a convient source of helpful information about our personal policies and facilities. I hope you will read it carefully. If you should wish to get additional information about any of the subjects discussed I am sure that you immediate superviser will be glad to help you—either by drawing on his or her own knowlege and exprience or by referring you to the appropriate person with our organization. In closeing allow me to extend to you my sincere good wishes for success and happiness in your new career at Johnson and Marsh.

Check the key on page 522. If you achieved Fair or above, you are ready for Chapter 10. If you scored below Fair, discuss problems with your instructor.

10

CLAIM AND ADJUSTMENT LETTERS

After a year as head of the mail department, you saw a classified advertisement describing an opening in the claims and adjustment department of a department store. Because you felt that the position offered opportunities and challenges, you applied. The job is yours.

In this position, you will use business communications to answer the claims of customers. You will make decisions concerning adjustments. Four units are provided to consider the situations you will face on this job:

Unit 30   The Problem and the Solution
Unit 31   When the Fault Is Yours
Unit 32   When the Fault Is Your Customer's
Unit 33   The Preadjustment Letter

UNIT 30   THE PROBLEM AND THE SOLUTION

Your performance objective for this unit is:

Given the problem of responding to a customer who makes a claim against your company,

You will write a letter that will maintain goodwill and ensure repeat orders by being positive; by using clear, exact language; by spotlighting the reader; and by entering the reader's world.

The Problem

At your first orientation meeting, the manager identifies the two major objectives of the Claims and Adjustment Department: to build goodwill and to get repeat orders.

One way to build goodwill would be to give the customer what is demanded whether or not the claim is justified. But every time you pay an unjustified claim, you add to the cost of the product or service of your company. This cost is ultimately reflected in higher prices, which will surely not bring repeat orders. Even the customer who was the re-

orientation: having to do with a program introducing one to a new job, school, environment, etc.

recipient: one who receives

cipient of the adjustment would quickly go to another department store to buy at lower prices. Not only are you asking your other customers to pay for the mistakes of the customer who receives the adjustment, but you are projecting an image of weakness for your company. What respect do you receive from individuals who get what they want from you by deception or by unwarranted demands? Very little! The image you project for your company when you write an adjustment letter should be one of integrity and fair play.

What will you do with this claim?

unwarranted: having no justification or support

```
Gentlemen:

I am returning this dress, priced at $29.95,
which was purchased two months ago. The color
has faded and the fabric has shrunk so that the
dress does not fit. I am very displeased with
this dress.

Please credit my account for $29.95.

                    Yours truly,

                    Mary James
```

You know you must answer the letter speedily. The usual procedure in substantiating a claim of this type is to return the dress to the manufacturer for tests, which will take at least five days. In the meantime, how would you satisfy the customer? Would you send her this postcard?

substantiating: establishing the truth of

```
Your complaint has been received. Your returned
purchase has been sent to the manufacturer for
tests. You will have to wait until the results
come in.
```

You can see that this message violates several principles of good business communication. What should you do instead?

Be positive: Avoid the use of the word "complaint."

Use clear, exact language: What returned purchase? What tests? When will the results be known?

Spotlight the reader instead of the problem: This communication implies that the testing is the important thing.

Enter the reader's world: You shouldn't be demanding that the reader accept your terms.

accept: take willingly

In addition, do not use a postcard; it detracts from the importance of the situation. A postcard is generally used for information such as:

"Your rug will be delivered on Friday, February 10." When you wish to develop rapport and understanding, when you are discussing a difficult matter, as you are in the adjustment letter, give your customer the courtesy of a letter, no matter how short it is. This note would give the customer an understanding of how you were handling her claim:

rapport (pronounce ra-por'): agreement; accord; harmony

> Dear Ms. James:
>
> We are sorry that you were displeased with the dress you bought from us.
>
> The dress has been returned to the manufacturer, who will test the fabric for shrinkage and fading. The tests will take one week.
>
> Thank you for telling us about your problem. You will hear from us as soon as we receive the manufacturer's report.
>
> Sincerely yours,

When you completed this letter, you showed it to Mr. Levin, the manager, who complimented you on this interim solution. He then made an educated guess that the dress had been washed, contrary to the instructions on the label. If this were true, how would you answer the letter?

interim: an intervening or temporary period of time
educated guess: a guess based on experience

The Solution

Based on Mr. Levin's appraisal, you compose a second letter to Ms. James explaining to her satisfaction why you cannot accept her claim. After writing this letter, you again ask for guidance from Mr. Levin.

guidance: advice

> We cannot grant your request for a credit of $29.95 for the dress you returned to us on February 2. According to the manufacturer, you did not follow directions for cleaning--you washed the dress. This caused the fading and shrinkage of the fabric.
>
> Unfortunately, our company policy does not permit us to make the adjustment when the customer is at fault.

The manager asks whether you checked with the Dress Department to see if the "Dry Clean Only" label was conspicuous enough on the dress. He points out that if the label was not prominently displayed, Helen Angers, the Dress Department manager, might agree to send Ms. James a new dress. That would make your letter much easier to write.

Next, your manager asks you to reread your letter. Does it build good-

Check for any way your company might have been at fault.
conspicuous: easily seen

will for the store? Will Ms. James want to buy there again? Or will your letter antagonize her? You agree that your letter could be improved. Since the Claims and Adjustment Department is giving a short in-service training program and you will not have the final report from the factory for a week, the manager suggests that you attend before rewriting your letter to Ms. James.

A POSITIVE APPROACH

accede: agree; consent
lose: not *loose*

At the first session of the training program, the speaker, Professor Kathleen Kerk, emphasizes the importance of keeping the customer satisfied. Whether you accede to a claim or refuse to make an adjustment, she explains, you don't want to lose the customer's goodwill. Of course, you will be courteous and pleasant; to minimize the unpleasantness of the situation, you should also be positive.

The speaker hands out the following list of negative words and phrases that you should avoid:

Antagonistic

```
Your complaint; your error; you neglected; you
say, state, or claim; you assert; we refuse;
you have not followed directions; you misused.
```

Belittling

```
We are willing to allow you; we are at a loss to
know; we are surprised to hear; we cannot under-
stand; we are disappointed to hear; you failed
to state; you would not want us to.
```

Doubtful

```
It will never happen again; you can be sure;
yours was the first complaint we ever had.
```

Let's see how you would handle some problems in adjustment letters. Try Skills Activity 52.

SKILLS ACTIVITY 52

A. Comment on these opening sentences from adjustment letters.

1. We are sorry that we cannot accept the return of the blouse that you bought on August 5. _____

_____

2. You are certainly being unfair to us when you insinuate that we tried to put something over on you by sending you a defective lamp. _____

_____

3. We cannot understand how the records could have been broken as you claim in your letter of March 10. _____

_____

4. Our service representative will be at your house Wednesday morning to be sure that your new Cine movie projector gives you good service.

_____

_____

5. In answer to your letter expressing dissatisfaction with your dictating machine, I wish to state that we stand behind anything we sell. _____

_____

6. Your complaint that the woolen fabrics we sold you are defective is under consideration. _____

_____

7. We are sorry your June 5 order did not arrive. A duplicate of this order is now on its way to you. _____

_____

Check the key on page 522. How closely do you agree with the authors' answers? Discuss major disagreements with your instructor. Now try the next problem.

B. Comment on these statements granting or refusing credit.

1. Although we are not at fault, we are willing to accept return of the lamp shade. _____

_____

2. You are such a good customer, we find it difficult not to grant your request. But, as you know, Gordon's policy has always been "no returns on sale items." We hope you will understand. _____

_____

3. Since the delay in delivery was not our fault, we cannot accept the responsibility for your loss. _____

_____

4. We shall be willing to exchange the machine in order to retain you as a valued customer. _____

_____

5. We will make this concession to you, even though it is much more than should be expected under the circumstances. _____

_____

6. Since we advised you to be home to accept the delivery, you must pay the additional delivery fee or face suit. _____

_____

7. Mr. Pedro of our Service Department will be at your home on Monday, June 10, at 2 p.m. or 7 p.m. to assemble your table. Please let us know which is more convenient. We are sorry that this difficulty arose. _____

_____

Check the key on page 522. How closely do you agree with the authors? Discuss disagreements with your instructor. Now go on to Unit 31.

UNIT 31   WHEN THE FAULT IS YOURS

Your performance objective for this unit is:

Given the problem of responding to a claim against your company when your company is at fault,

You will write a letter that accepts responsibility for and apologizes for the error, that explains the error to the customer's satisfaction, that makes the adjustment with a positive tone, that maintains good relations with a smooth closing.

The second session of the training program deals with writing a letter to rectify a mistake your company made. When the fault is yours, you are told to be honest and accept responsibility for your errors—don't try to deny them. Admit your mistake, and you will earn your customers' respect and understanding; try to cover up or shift the blame, and you will only irritate them.

rectify: correct

The Beginning

How should you begin? You remember from the previous day's lesson that it is important to be positive. How can you write about your mistake, your defective product, or your deficient service so as to leave a positive impression? When the group is asked to compare the following opening paragraphs, you can see the value of an apology.

deficient: lacking some essential; imperfect

We do not know how a mistake was made on your monthly statement.

Of course your monthly statement should be free of errors, and we are sorry that yours was not.

We have received your letter of June 8, in which you tell us that you received a damaged copy of Day's Long Summer.

A carefully packaged copy of Day's Long Summer is already on its way to you to replace your damaged copy. We're sorry that the back cover was crushed.

We have checked your allegation that the sales clerks in the camera department treated you rudely.

Thank you for telling us about your experience with the sales clerks in our camera department. Our apologies.

We cannot understand how there could be something wrong with your new Transo Radio.

We can understand how disappointed you must have been when your new Transo Radio did not work.

Because we have recently computerized our billing, your complaint about a bill being in error surprises us.

We're sorry. We have recently computerized our billing, but errors still slip in.

Your claim that your mail doesn't arrive in time to enable you to take a discount is being looked into at once.

You have every reason to be disturbed about your bills' arriving late, especially when it affects your taking a discount.

It's hardly possible that your luggage could have been damaged on our New York to Lisbon flight, No. 136, on June 10.

Please accept our apology for the damage to your luggage on our New York to Lisbon flight, No. 136, on June 10.

An apology clears the air.

In each case, you see the advantage of admitting your mistake and expressing your regret. You know that when someone says to you, "I'm sorry" or "I apologize," the sting is taken out of your complaint. Professor Kerk now turns to your next steps—to tell the customer what adjustment you will make and to explain the reasons for the error. These two steps, she says, may be interchanged, depending on the individual situation.

The Explanation

Be sure, the speaker cautions, to check carefully the reasons for the complaint, since you must satisfy the customer with your explanation. Here are some ideas for explaining why something has gone wrong:

A good explanation is logical and simple. It is not too elaborate, and it doesn't merely make excuses.

Much as we should like to do so, it is impractical for us to make a thorough inspection of every book that leaves our shipping room. We are glad to replace the ten copies.

Please excuse us during this transition period. Our computerized billing system will be straightened out this month. We know that you could not have placed 469 telephone calls a day from your home. Our computer must have confused you with a giant corporation. When human beings make mistakes, they can be serious; but when computers make them, they're astronomical.

Our new luggage-handling system has proved to be far more efficient than the system we had previously. But you know that it is impossible for any system to be 100 percent perfect. We have been working continuously to reduce the number of incidents in which damage occurs.

inconvenienced: troubled

The reorganization of our local post office has caused some delays in handling outgoing mail. We hope conditions will improve shortly because they have inconvenienced us as well as our customers.

Is "handled" hyphenated correctly? Check your dictionary.

During the rush season, many packages were handled by temporary employees. Although we paid the highest wage rates in the industry, we still found it difficult to get responsible employees in this tight labor market.

The Decision

You must tell your customer what adjustment you will make. You note this point: When the fault lies with you, the answer must be in the affirmative. Sentences such as these can be used to make the adjustment:

> You need not pay anything now. Just retain this statement until we send you a corrected bill.

> Please hold the defective radio for pickup. When your new Transo Radio arrives, the Union Parcel delivery man will pick up the one you have.

> Please have your luggage repaired. Then send us your receipted bill, and you will receive reimbursement immediately.

> You are correct. The price of the No. 5 electric toaster is $21.95, not $24.95. Please disregard the original invoice, and pay $21.95 on the enclosed corrected invoice.

invoice: list of merchandise sent, including price

> Because the outgoing mail was behind schedule last month, we have extended the discount period two days. You will therefore be credited with the full discount.

The Closing

As with all other letters that you write, you want your adjustment letter to come to a smooth finish. Professor Kerk gives you these examples:

> Thank you for writing to us about your luggage. We appreciate our passengers' comments and suggestions, for this is the way we can improve our service to them. Please plan your future business and pleasure trips with Amair.

> Please write us whenever you are not satisfied with our accommodations. We are here to serve you.

> When our computer has been thoroughly debugged, you will benefit from the improved billing practices that automation makes possible.

thoroughly: completely

> Thank you for telling us about this packaging problem. With our new procedures, including the required ten-day training program, I am sure your future orders, even during the rush season, will be handled smoothly.

> No matter how large our company becomes, we will never outgrow a personal interest in our customers' problems.

Try Skills Activity 53 to see if you can write the adjustment letter when the fault is yours.

SKILLS ACTIVITY 53

Given a problem in which the claim against your company is justified, compose a response that (1) accepts responsibility and apologizes for the error, (2) explains the error to the customer's satisfaction, (3) is positive, and (4) maintains good relations with a smooth closing.

Peer judgment or your instructor's evaluation:

Excellent   4
Good   3

You are employed at Harris Sporting Shop. It is April 1. Mr. Flannigan, a steady mail-order customer, has written to tell you that a casting reel he bought in January has no spool. He had not opened the package when he purchased the reel because he planned to keep it packaged until the end of March, when the trout season was to open. Naturally he was disappointed that he could not use his new spinning reel. Write an adjustment letter to solve this problem. Your letter might tell Mr. Flannigan that you are sending a spinning reel by special delivery. Be sure to tell him how sorry you are about his misfortune.

If you succeeded in achieving Fair or above on this letter, go on to Unit 32. If you did not score Fair or above, discuss your problem with your instructor, then rewrite the letter. Ask your instructor to evaluate it and to consider your readiness for the next unit.

UNIT 32 WHEN THE FAULT IS YOUR CUSTOMER'S

Your performance objective for this unit is:

Given the problem of responding to a claim against your company when your company is not at fault,

You will compose a response that opens on a point of agreement; that explains the facts tactfully; that makes an adjustment granting a claim, either wholly or partially, with a positive tone; or that refuses an adjustment tactfully with attention to the individual complainant; and that closes affirmatively.

The subject of the third session of the training program is the more difficult problem of answering a claim resulting from a customer's error. Professor Kerk has the following things to say:

Customers may misunderstand the terms of a guarantee; they may take the wrong number from a catalog when they place an order; they may take a cash discount beyond the discount period; they may misuse the product. There are many other ways in which the buyer may be at fault. Your watchword here is *tact.* You must do all you can to retain the customer's business. Although each case should stand on its own merits, you must not point the finger of accusation at the buyer. Put yourself in his or her place: How would you feel if you were to receive the letter?

Above all, be tactful.

The Beginning

The first sentence must be friendly; don't come out fighting. The best way to begin is to find an area of agreement with your buyer. Here are some possibilities:

Start with something positive.

    We can readily appreciate your disappointment in
    not receiving your new silk dress in time for
    Saturday's wedding reception.

    We are sorry that we sent you the wrong book on
    your order of April 5.

    We agree with you that you want color when you
    buy a color TV.

    Thank you for writing us so frankly about our
    handling of your orders.

The Explanation

Now get to the facts. An explanation of what has happened will then lead into an explanation of your decision. Use tact when you place responsibility. Here is a place where the passive voice is helpful; it can be used to minimize the personal aspect of the buyer's mistake. "A mistake might have been made" sounds better than "you made a mistake."
Compare these statements:

Take advantage of the passive voice.
minimize: reduce to the smallest degree

Harsh	Smoother
Evidently you did not read the terms of the contract.	Because it is possible that the terms of the contract were misunderstood, will you please reread them carefully?
You must have read the catalog incorrectly when you copied the price.	The catalog may have been misread. The left column shows the price of one stamp, whereas the right column shows the price for the plate block that you ordered.
You mailed your order to us too late for us to get the dress to you on time.	Your order was received on Saturday. Thus, your dress could not go out until Monday morning.
You didn't follow our advice to get a new color antenna when we originally installed the set. We did not guarantee good color reception under those circumstances.	If a color antenna had been installed when your set was delivered, reception would be excellent. I believe our serviceman recommended at that time that you change your antenna.
When you purchased your linoleum, we advised you to buy Tufguard because of your heavy traffic from outdoors.	As we mentioned, Tufguard is the only linoleum guaranteed to resist the heavy traffic of muddy and icy feet. Your linoleum can be protected, however, by "Hardiwaxing" once a week.
Our testing department reveals that you have washed the jacket in hot water, even though the label clearly reads "Dry Clean Only."	Our testing department reports that the jacket must have been washed in hot water. The cleaning-instructions tag and the label reading "Dry Clean Only" must have escaped your notice.
You didn't consider the size of your walk and garage when you ordered the snow thrower.	Yes, our No. 2 snow thrower takes care of the country estate of hundreds of feet, acres in fact. You will find our No. 15 more suitable for your 100-foot drive and walk. It is small enough to be stored next to your car in the garage.

The Decision

After you have explained to the customer why something has gone wrong, a question remains: Will you make an adjustment?

If the decision is yours to make, you must naturally consider the type of mistake the customer has made. (At this point in the lecture, you remember Ms. James's complaint. Did she just ignore the "Dry Clean Only" label, or was it so inconspicuous that she might reasonably have missed it?) You must also consider the kind of merchandise and its cost. (You might be willing to replace a $25 dress but not a $350 coat.) Another consideration is whether the claim seems to be honest or whether it is spurious and the customer merely hopes to take advantage of you. A favorable adjustment will keep a customer's good will; but, after weighing all the considerations, you may have to take the more difficult path of refusing to make the adjustment.

spurious: not genuine; false

The favorable adjustment. When you act to grant a claim, either wholly or partially, do it with a smile, not a grudging attitude.

> Because you have not yet used your snow thrower, we will gladly exchange it for a smaller model that will better fit your needs. Just have it ready to return when our trucker delivers your new model No. 15.

> Although we cannot replace your linoleum, we are sending you a trial sample of Hardiwax, which will give your floors a tough-as-iron finish. If you use Hardiwax according to instructions, your problem should be alleviated.

alleviated: relieved; made lighter

> Although a color antenna costs $60 at any time other than when the TV set is delivered, we will install your color TV antenna for the low price of $45 if you want it. Then you'll get 100 percent color enjoyment.

> Certainly, you may return the dress to us. We do not want you to keep a dress you cannot use. Instead, why not order something for spring? Our newest styles have just arrived. If you order now, you will have your spring clothes on hand in ample time for the new season.

ample: more than enough

Saying no. Sometimes you have to say no. It is easy to say, "Company policy prevents us from allowing your claim." But this makes your company an impersonal behemoth that does not consider the customer as an individual. Make customers feel that their complaints are important and that they have received individual evaluation. Compare these ideas for refusals:

behemoth: something of monstrous size or power.

Your guarantee has expired, so we will not repair your clock without further charge.	Because the guarantee expired two years ago, we must charge for repairs on your clock.
You must mail us $5.80 or return the plate block at once.	If you wish to keep the plate block, please send us your check for $5.80 to cover the difference between what you have already paid and the actual cost.

Because the garment was not cleaned according to instructions, it is impossible to allow your claim.

Terms of sale read 2/10, n/30. Company policy dictates that we must adhere strictly to the terms; we cannot favor some customers at the expense of others.

We should like to send you a new jacket; but, since the cleaning instructions were written so clearly, we cannot do so.

In fairness to all our customers, we must maintain a consistent policy on discounts. Of course, we want you to take advantage of our discount policy, but we can grant a discount only when the invoice is paid within the discount period.

The Closing

End your letter on a positive note. If you have refused to make an adjustment, don't close by referring to the complaint. You don't want to leave your reader with that thought. These statements assure an affirmative ending:

qualified: competent

If you want a new color TV antenna, just mail the enclosed card. Our qualified serviceman will come to install your antenna whenever you wish.

Pack the dress carefully, and return it to us. When it arrives, we shall credit your account.

I am glad you wrote to us, because it will avoid any future misunderstanding about our discount policy.

We hope you will get many years of excellent service from your Atlas snow thrower.

When you give an honest, open explanation and a fair adjustment to a claim, you keep your customer's goodwill and respect.

The Final Product

The factory report came in on Ms. James's complaint.

Shrinkage and fading were caused by washing dress. Labeling instructions warn against washing.

visible: able to be seen

Mr. Levin's educated guess proved correct. Now that you are coming to the end of the training course, you feel capable of rewriting that letter to Ms. James. First, you check with Helen Angers in the Dress Department. She feels that perhaps the label was not as visible as it should have been. She agrees to send Ms. James a new dress and says she plans to revise the department's labeling policy.

Then you write the following letter:

Dear Ms. James:

The Glamour Dress Company found the culprits--
soap and water. Your dress fabric must be dry
cleaned only. Because of your experience, we are
adding another label--a large blue one, attached
to the sleeve, that urges:

>   "Please don't wash me. I can't stand
>   soap and water!"

Of course, we will continue to use the label we
have been using in the neckline.

Although we cannot credit your account, we can
send you a new dress. It is on its way to you;
we hope you will enjoy it.

We are sorry that you had this problem with your
dress. Thanks for writing us about it.

>   Sincerely yours,

culprits: those guilty of an offense

You are pleased with this letter—and so is your supervisor.

When the fault is your customer's, you will find it more difficult to write the adjustment letter. Try it in Skills Activity 54.

SKILLS ACTIVITY 54

A. In the following cases, you are asked to write a response to your customer's complaints when the fault is the customer's.

1. You are employed by Peers Camera Company. Morris Sheperd, a customer in another city, ordered 50 inexpensive cameras, which you sent out by freight—your usual method of shipping. The customer has written a letter to complain that he did not receive the cameras in time for a giveaway he had planned for his special sale days. He had not told you about wanting fast shipment or about a date when he needed the cameras. How would you handle his complaint?

2. A mail-order customer, Olive Hansen, ordered an "as is" coat from a Grassman's ad. She now writes that she wants to return the coat because it has a slight defect. You must refuse her request. Write the letter to tell Grassman's part of the story, but try to keep her good will.

3. You are employed by Colorlabs, which processes film. You have received several complaints from Mr. Ritter about the way in which his films have been processed. He asks for new film because of your poor work. On two previous occasions you have told Mr. Ritter that his camera must be defective. You ask him again to have it checked. You might say that you do not wish him to send more film for processing unless he has his camera checked, because he is wasting his money.

If you achieved Fair or above on two of the above letters, you may go on to the next problem. If you did not score Fair or above on at least two letters, discuss your scores with your instructor. Rewrite two of the three letters and ask your instructor to evaluate them.

B. Rewrite this adjustment letter.

```
We are surprised to receive your letter of com-
plaint of January 12. While you had requested
Gemex tires on your new car, your dealer gave
you Royax tires because all cars of that model
come factory-equipped with Royax tires--the best
that money can buy.

Now for your specific complaint about Royax
tires. Because you had your mind made up for
another brand, you probably looked for weak-
nesses in Royax tires. You claim that they cause
a thumping action when you reach a speed of 60
miles an hour. Are you sure that your wheels are
balanced correctly? Are you sure that the tires
are inflated properly?
```

We are willing to make some concessions to you.
Instead of going to your car dealer, drive to
James Kent, your nearest Royax dealer. He will
check your tires thoroughly. If there is something wrong with the tires, he will give you a
pro rata allowance toward the purchase of a set
of new tires. In other words, you will pay only
for the mileage you already have on your tires.

If you follow Mr. Kent's instructions, you will
never have to write another letter of complaint
to us.

If you achieved Fair or above on this letter, go on to Unit 33. If you
scored below Fair, discuss your score with your instructor before continuing.

UNIT 33   THE PREADJUSTMENT LETTER

Your performance objective for this unit is:

*Given a problem in which an action by the company will result in
future complaints and requests for explanations,*

*You will forestall such complaints and requests for information by
writing the preadjustment letter.*

The final session of the in-service training program opened with this
question: Is there any way to prevent future claim letters? The speaker
cited the case of a major utility that had increased its charges for electricity. This company took the precaution to enclose the following letter
with each utility bill that was mailed. You might call this a "preadjustment" letter, because the company obviously hoped to forestall the
receipt of thousands of telephone calls and complaint letters asking for
an adjustment on the bill.

forestall: hold off; prevent
in advance

Dear Customer:

We would love to keep electricity rates at the
1970 level, if somebody would tell us where to
buy fuel, copper cable, trucks, iron pipe,
switching panels, rubber gloves, and the like at
1970 prices.

And, while we're at it, we would also like to
find a way to roll back our taxes. Today, Consumers Power is paying the highest local and
state taxes ever imposed on a power company. For
1976 these taxes will total some $155 million

on our electricity business alone--an increase of $64 million since 1970.

We realize that everybody has to pay taxes. Taxes are part and parcel of doing business these days. It's also a fact that taxes, like any other operating expense, must be paid out of the money we receive for our services. When taxes, along with fuel costs keep going up, there comes a time when rates have to go up, too.

So, recently, electricity rates were moderately increased--an increase that was absolutely necessary to ensure a continuation of the reliable electrical service our customers must have.

CONSUMERS POWER COMPANY

Check your ability to write the preadjustment letter in Skills Activity 55.

SKILLS ACTIVITY 55

Given a case in which a preadjustment letter would prevent a complaint, compose an effective letter that (1) accepts responsibility for the action, (2) explains the error to the customer's satisfaction, (3) is positive, and (4) maintains good relations with a smooth closing.

Peer judgment or your instructor's evaluation:

Excellent 4
Good 3
Fair 2

Professor Gonzalez, a teacher of Hispanic studies, has been receiving complimentary copies of *Hispanic Culture* for the past five years. The Hispanic Publishing Company can no longer send complimentary copies because of the drastic increase in printing and mailing costs. As circulation manager for the company, you write Professor Gonzalez that the company can offer him a special low-cost educator's rate of $5 a year, which just covers the cost of printing and mailing. Encourage him to subscribe under these terms.

If you achieved Fair or above, you are ready for the Summary. If you scored below Fair, discuss your score with the instructor; then rewrite the letter and ask your instructor to evaluate it.

SUMMARY

When you write your adjustment letters in answer to customers' claims, direct your efforts toward developing good will. You expect to keep your customer satisfied by granting the adjustment gracefully or by refusing it tactfully.

Answer claim letters immediately. When the fault is yours, admit the error, accept responsibility for the mistake, and apologize. Avoid negative expressions that seem to convey your displeasure at being taken to task by the customer. Naturally, your answer to a justified claim letter is that you will gladly make the adjustment for the customer.

Your problem in writing the adjustment letter is more difficult to solve when the customer is at fault. Your company's integrity must be maintained by refusing unwarranted demands, but the customer's demands must be given serious consideration. Show the customer that your company has given the complaint a personal evaluation but that it cannot accede to the request. Fair and impartial decisions based on policy win your customer's respect for the company.

In all your adjustment letters, use forthright, positive language that tells your customer that you stand behind your product and your service.

You have completed the four units in Chapter 10. Discuss any problems of your success on these four units with your instructor. At this time you can move on to Focus on Language. You will review vocabulary and spelling words, the use of the semicolon, the use of nominative and possessive cases of pronouns, the rules for writing numbers, and a proofreading exercise.

FOCUS ON LANGUAGE

Spelling

Helen requires your guidence. She wants to forstall any complaints by writing a letter that covers throughly all the recomendations that have been made. In the prosess, she'd like to emphasize the visable improvements that have all ready been made. She does not want any customer inconvienced.

> Given a paragraph containing misspelled words, underscore the errors and write the correct spelling of each directly above it.
>
> Excellent   8
> Good   7
> Fair   6

Be sure you can spell correctly each of the words in the above paragraph. Don't be happy with even one misspelling. If you scored below Fair, try again after reviewing your errors.

Vocabulary

1. When you (*accept, except*) your job with Acme, we shall (*expect, except*) you to attend (a *graduation*, an *orientation*) meeting to acquaint you with your duties.
2. We shall ask the (*donor, recipient*) of the award to write a brief thank-you note.
3. Because the merchandise was thoroughly inspected, the seller felt that the buyer's complaint was (*justified, unwarranted*).
4. The company offered (*substantiating, useless*) evidence to prove its claim.
5. There was perfect (enmity, rapport) between the two good friends.
6. The (*guidance, principal's*) office assists students in choosing careers.
7. His colorful clothes made him look (*conspicuous, inconspicuous*).
8. Please (*accede, exceed*) to the customer's request by accepting return of the merchandise.
9. We shall try to (*deny, rectify*) the mistake made by our salesperson.
10. Because of your (*deficient, efficient*) service we have been unable to meet our commitments.
11. Will you please submit your (*directive, invoice*) listing the supplies we ordered?
12. Now that the engine has been checked (*poorly, thoroughly*), we feel it is safe to drive.
13. The banker tried to (*maximize, minimize*) his losses so his statement would show some profit.

> Given pairs of words in which one in each pair is correct, identify the correct word by underlining it.
>
> Excellent   22-23
> Good   19-21
> Fair   17-18

*Name*_____ *Date*_____

14. This coin store has never sold any (*genuine, spurious*) coins to its customers.

15. His actions have (*abbreviated, alleviated*) the burden of carrying too much inventory.

16. We have (*ample, insufficient*) evidence to arrive at a correct decision.

17. The excellent safety record of the airline is evidence that they employ (*qualified, unqualified*) mechanics.

18. On a clear night, some earth-orbiting satellites may be (*invisible, visible*).

19. The ranger told the campers that two bear cubs were the (*culprits, victims*) who stole their food.

20. While awaiting the report, the manager issued (*an interim, a final*) statement.

21. The corporation is not a (*behemoth, victim*) that crushes the individual's spirit.

Check the key on page 522. If you achieved Fair or above, go on to Sound-Alikes. If you scored below Fair, review the definitions in the chapter margins. Use each word you had incorrect in a sentence. Ask your instructor to evaluate your sentences and to discuss any errors with you.

Sound-Alikes

Review the following definitions carefully before trying the sentences below.

accept—to receive with favor, willingness or consent
    We are happy to accept a price reduction.
except—aside from; otherwise than
    Everyone except Mr. Barnes stayed in the office.

lose—to part with, as by accident or negligence
    He will lose his money if he does not deposit it in the bank.
loose—not fastened or confined.
    Because of a loose wire, the car failed to start.

Given seven sentences with eight pairs of sound-alikes, underline the correct word.

Excellent	8
Good	7
Fair	6

1. Please (*accept, except*) my apology for sending you the wrong package.

2. After the label became (*lose, loose*), it must have dropped to the floor.

3. You may expect to (*lose, loose*) the respect of your customers when you do not write honestly.

4. It became an (*accepted, excepted*) way to handle such complaints.

5. All members of the sales team (*accept, except*) the sales manager are expected to attend the meeting.

6. We left instructions to set the dogs (*lose, loose*), but John was afraid he'd (*lose, loose*) track of them.
7. If the company continues to (*loose, lose*) money, it may soon become insolvent.

Check the key on page 523. If you achieved Fair or above, go on to Pronouns. If you did not, review the definitions of any words you had incorrect. Use these words in sentences and ask your instructor to evaluate them and to discuss any errors with you.

Pronouns

Remember our discussion of cases of pronouns in Chapter 9? Here are two more rules for the correct use of case:

Rule: *Use the nominative case of a pronoun when it is used as a predicate pronoun.*

It is he who will make the decisions.
It is she at the door.

Note: Although usage has made it acceptable to use "it's me," "it's him," and so on, in speaking, you should always use the nominative case in writing.

Rule: *Use the possessive case of a pronoun when it modifies a gerund.* (A gerund is the *ing* form of a verb when it is used as a noun.)

I oppose your accepting the blame for something you did not do.
His paying the bill restored his credit standing.

1. Before we can go ahead, your approval of (*our, us*) signing the paper will be needed.
2. The president says that it is (*I, me*) whom you should blame.
3. The winner of the award was probably Mr. Baker or (*I, me*).
4. There can be no agreement between (*he, him*) and (*I, me*)
5. Type two copies for the president and (*I, me*), who I know will need them.
6. There is no possibility of (*me, my*) changing my mind.
7. Do you object to (*us, our*) working on the project with you?

> *Given seven sentences in which the nominative, objective, or possessive cases of pronouns are to be selected, circle the correct case in each.*
>
> | | |
> |---|---|
> | *Excellent* | 7 |
> | *Good* | 6 |
> | *Fair* | 5 |

If you achieved Fair or above, go on to the next problem. If you scored below Fair, review the rules and the examples and discuss any problems with your instructor.

Name_____ Date_____

Punctuation: Semicolon

Rule: *Use a semicolon in place of the usual comma before the coordinating conjunction in a compound sentence when the clauses are long or already contain commas.*

Professor Allen taught marketing, statistics, and finance; but his specialty was monetary theory.

Rule: *Use semicolons between items in a series when one or more of the items contains commas.*

Our club speakers were John Evans, a former student; Ronald Duggan, a financial analyst; and Sylvia Lerner, a fashion designer.
While on the tour, they learned something about shipbuilding; studied the lumber, fur, and copper trade of the region; and attended an industrial-planning meeting.

Note: Use a semicolon only between equivalent items—to separate clauses from clauses, for example, or phrases from phrases. A semicolon should *not* be used to separate a clause from a phrase or an independent clause from a dependent one, even if the items are long or contain commas.

Correct the punctuation of the following sentences.

1. There were two members from Chicago, Illinois, four from Boston, Massachusetts, twelve from Spokane, Washington, and one from Anchorage, Alaska.
2. Ms. Edgar can teach French, Spanish and Italian and Mr. Burke can teach history, economics and economic geography.
3. The first meeting of our club will be held on Monday January 8, and the second meeting will be held on Thursday February 1.
4. Rule your paper, write your name at the top, and number the lines from one to ten.
5. Although we went to the brunch, the rally, and the game; we were still going strong in the evening.
6. Sally was reading, Babs was playing the piano, and Joan was taking a nap.
7. The situation is serious, therefore we shall appropriate funds.

Check the key on page 523. If you achieved Fair or above, move on to Numbers. If you scored below Fair, reread the rules and examples and discuss your score with your instructor.

Given seven sentences in which semicolons and other punctuation should be inserted, punctuate these sentences correctly.

Excellent 7
Good 6
Fair 5

Numbers

Rules for handling numbers vary with the type of writing you are doing. If you pick up three or four books, you will probably find that their number styles differ. However, in any particular piece of writing, the treatment of numbers must be consistent. The rules we have been giving you in the marginal notations of this book are those generally followed in business correspondence, and you should learn to use them.

Rule: *Spell out numbers one through ten; write numbers larger than ten in figures.*

There are ten men on the squad.
He spoke for 45 minutes.

Rule: *All numbers in a group should be expressed in figures. But, if a sentence contains two series of numbers running concurrently, express one series in words and the other in figures for clarity.*

Order 28 chairs, 6 tables, and 5 lamps.
Two players scored 3 runs; three players scored 2 runs; and one player scored 1 run.

Rule: *If your sentence begins with a number, write out the number.*

Sixty courses are offered in this department, and no other department offers more than 35.

Note: If the number requires more than two words, it is better to reword the sentence than to have to write out that number. "There are 365 days in a year" is better than "Three hundred sixty-five days make a year."

1. 47 salesmen attended the 3 meetings. _____

   _____

2. The Appliance Department sold 30 radios in April, 25 in May, and only six in June. _____

   _____

3. After you have read these 10 letters, will you make some suggestions?

   _____

   _____

4. We shall open our new Hartford store in twenty-five days. _____

   _____

5. Five firms employed 15 clerks, and 3 firms are willing to employ 12 more. _____

   _____

6. Tour 12B takes nine days, but Tour 13A takes 7 days. _____

   _____

7. There are only 8 days remaining until the end of the tax year. _____

   _____

> *Given seven sentences using numbers, write the sentences correctly.*
>
> | | |
> |---|---|
> | *Excellent* | 7 |
> | *Good* | 6 |
> | *Fair* | 5 |

Check key on page 523. If you achieved Fair or above, go on to Proofreading. If you scored below Fair, review the rules. Discuss your score with your instructor.

Name _____ *Date* _____

Proofreading

Your typist has placed the following letter on your desk for your signature. You decide to read the letter before signing. How many mistakes can you find?

June 10th, 19--

Miss Carmen Mendez

Box 137

Mayville, Wisconsin 53050

Dear Mrs. Mendes:

You will be pleased to no, I am sure, that your defective camera cannot only be repaired but can be returned to you within 1 week. Naturally, their will be no charge for the the service because your camera is still covered by the waranty.

Because you plan to use you're camera on a safari, may I suggest that you consider bying a telescopic lens which can be mounted quickly for long range shots in the game parks. I have all ready set 3 of these high quality lenses a side for you to examine when you come in to get your camera.

I am sorry, Miss Mendez, that youve been inconvenienced by having a defective camera. But I know that you repaired camera will serve you well on your safari along with the

2 rolls of complementary color film well give you for you

trouble.

            Cordially,

            Claire Browne

            Claire Browne

            Service Department

ef

Check the key on page 523. If you achieved Fair or above, you are ready for Chapter 11. If you scored below Fair, discuss your score with your instructor.

----

*Name*_____ *Date*_____

11

THE CREDIT LETTER

You have been with the TRK Textile Company for six months and are considered a permanent employee. As part of management's policy of maintaining flexibility of personnel, you are assigned to a training program, which will take you to a different department every two weeks for the next two months.

flexibility: the ability to adapt to change

Your assignment for the next two weeks takes you to the credit department. On your way to work that first morning, your friend Ralph says, "I spent all last night paying bills. I had to send out 25 checks to settle monthly accounts for telephone, gas, electricity, drugs, milk, groceries, department-store purchases, gasoline, and . . . and . . . ." Ralph and his wife had made many purchases on credit during the month. Because they were good risks, they had a good credit standing. Businesspeople were willing to supply them with many goods and services and to wait until the end of the month for payment.

Credit cards and charge accounts are familiar services of business. They enable customers—both individuals and businesses—to "buy now and pay later." Although this requires more record-keeping and clerical work for the seller, it enables customers to buy more and higher quality merchandise. Actually, therefore, the merchant sells more and makes more profit.

The value of credit

How does the businessperson know that a customer is a good risk and that payment will be made at the end of the month? Does everyone who wants a charge account get one? When you walk into the credit department that day, you have a number of questions you would like answered. One of the first is: How does a credit manager decide to accept or reject an application for a charge account?

Who gets credit?

You will find the answers to this question and learn how to cope with problems in writing credit letters in the following units:

Unit 34 The Introductory Letter
     35 The Three C's of Credit
     36 The Request for Credit Reference
     37 The Letter to Refuse Credit
     38 Other Credit Letters

UNIT 34   THE INTRODUCTORY LETTER

Your performance objectives for this unit are:

Given the problem of responding to a request for credit that has been approved,

You will write a correct letter extending credit that includes a welcome to the new account, an explanation of the terms of sale, a thank you, an offer for continued service, and an invitation for future service.

Given the problem of responding to a request for credit that is incomplete,

You will write a letter delaying the decision on extending credit and including conditions under which you can ship immediately; company terms; request for credit references; financial statement and bank reference; and a statement maintaining goodwill.

When the Account Can Be Opened

Your immediate supervisor for these two weeks is the assistant credit manager for the manufacturing division, Ms. Wood. You work with her and her secretary. This order awaits the approval of the credit department before the goods can be shipped:

```
TRK Textile Company
Attention Order Department
356 Fifth Avenue
New York, NY  10002

Gentlemen:

Please ship me the following items from your
brochure No. 5704:

Cat.                                Unit
 No.   Units   Description         Price     Ext.
 35X   2       Long fiber
       bolts      cotton,
                  white         $ 40.00   $ 80.00
 15W   3       Italian
       bolts      silk,
                  pink           120.00    360.00
 18W   2       Chambray,
       bolts      navy blue       80.00    160.00
                                          $600.00

Will you please fill this order on open account
according to your regular trade terms.

For credit information, you may refer to:

    Millgert Textiles
    548 Fifth Avenue
    New York, NY  10016
```

"Open account" means granting of credit without requiring security.

```
     Millis Mills, Inc.
     364 River Road
     Pawtucket, RI  04218

     Burling Mills, Inc.
     101 Travis Boulevard
     Raleigh, NC  27609

     Factory Point Bank
     28 Main Street
     Middlebury, VT  05753

     Also, here is an audited copy of our latest
     financial statement for your consideration. We
     can report our Dun & Bradstreet rating as C+ 1.

     We would like to stock your textiles for our
     regular retail trade.

                      Sincerely yours,

                      John S. Kilduff
                      President
```

audited: examined for accuracy by accountants

What does Mr. Kilduff include in his letter to make the processing of his order an easy job?

Specific information—catalog number, units, description, unit price, total price
Names and addresses of references, including his bank
His latest financial statement
The company's Dun & Bradstreet rating

Dun & Bradstreet, an outstanding credit-rating organization, publishes credit ratings of businesses that have been evaluated. The C+ 1 rating means that Kilduff's estimated financial strength is between $125,000 and $200,000 and that he is reliable and quick in paying his bills. Many companies are willing to grant credit solely on the basis of a favorable D & B rating.

solely: only

In making a judgment as to the reliability of this company, Ms. Wood looks at the D & B rating. Her secretary checks the current volume of D & B to be sure tht Kilduff's statement is accurate. Although Ms. Wood will check Kilduff's references and financial statement later, she has sufficient information to open an account for the Kilduff Fabric Center in the interim. So she tells you to see that the order is filled and to write a letter in her name to Mr. Kilduff.

interim: meantime

What will the letter contain? You make this list:

A welcome to Mr. Kilduff as a credit customer
An explanation of the terms of sale—2/10, n/30—encouraging prompt
    payment
A thank you
An offer of continued service
An invitation for future orders

Here is the letter you write, and here, too, are Ms. Wood's marginal comments:

Avoid passive.

The fabrics that you ordered--as listed on the enclosed invoice--have been shipped by UPS. They should reach you by Saturday.

Use specific date.

Use active voice to establish relationship.

The amount of the bill, $600, has been charged to your account with TRK.

Don't make assumptions.

While we have yet to check the credit references you gave us, we have rushed your order to you because of your fine credit rating with Dun & Bradstreet. We know that your suppliers will assure us of your good integrity.

"Good integrity" is redundant.

Long-winded and redundant.

It is our policy to offer the regular trade terms of 2/10, n/30. These terms apply to all orders including your present order. Therefore, you can save $12 if you pay your account in full by February 10; the full amount of the invoice will be due by March 2.

Insulting; reader can figure this out.

You will be delighted with the excellent service our company offers its dealers. Orders are filled promptly and efficiently. You and your customers are never kept waiting if it should be necessary for you to send a special order.

Unnecessary boasting; omit this paragraph.

Be specific: When will he visit? What is his name?

Our sales representative will visit you regularly. Now that he is on the road in New England, we shall ask him to call on you. He will be able to offer you many excellent ideas for promoting TRK fabrics.

Ms. Wood has also noticed a major oversight: You did not welcome Mr. Kilduff as a new customer.

You must rewrite your letter to incorporate these comments, reorganize the ideas to achieve a smooth flowing communication. Figure 11-1 shows the letter you finally submit for Ms. Wood's signature.

When Further Information Is Needed

Another order arrived at the office that day, from Bleak & Company. The writer, Mr. Bleak, did not mention credit references, nor did he en-

(212) 475-1125

T R K

Manufacturers and Distributors of Fine Fabrics

356 Fifth Avenue, New York, New York 10002

February 1, 19--

Mr. John S. Kilduff
President
Kilduff Fabric Center
111 Marcher Street
Cambridge, Massachusetts 02138

Dear Mr. Kilduff:

Your order for our fabrics will reach you on Monday, February
5, via UPS. We have charged your bill for $600 to your new open
account with us. Our terms are 2/10, n/30.

Thank you for including your references and your Dun & Bradstreet rating.

Our sales representative for the New England district, Mr.
Kenneth Miller, will visit you every three months. Now that he
is in Boston, we shall ask him to call on you. Let him help you
with the free TRK displays for your window.

Thank you for ordering TRK fabrics. You will be the first to
offer these fine imports in Cambridge.

                                    Sincerely yours,

                                    Jane T. Wood

                                    Jane T. Wood
                                    Assistant Credit Manager
                                    Manufacturing Division

sbt

Figure 11-1
A Preliminary Granting
of Credit

close a financial statement. Ms. Wood would not extend credit immediately—she was unwilling to take the risk of sending an order to an unknown buyer. Bleak & Company may become one of TRK's best customers, but only if you answer that order letter tactfully and intelligently. What must you tell Mr. Bleak?

Remember to be tactful.

Conditions under which you can ship immediately
Company terms
Requests for credit references, financial statement, bank reference
Statement of goodwill

Here is your first draft:

Can you see what's wrong with this letter?

Thank you for your letter of January 26, in which you order $200 worth of TRK fabrics.

Our regular credit terms are 2/10, n/30. These terms apply on all orders after you have had a credit clearance. As an astute businessman, you will appreciate the value of paying your bills within the discount period.

astute: shrewd; keen

Since we have not done business with you previously, it will be necessary for you to send us credit references. Don't forget to list the names and addresses on the enclosed credit application form. You also neglected to send us a copy of your latest financial statement.

C.O.D. ("cash on delivery") is typed in capitals with periods but no space between initials.

The only way we can service your order would be to send it C.O.D. As you know, it will take a long time to check your credit references after we receive them.

If you wish us to send the fabrics immediately, let us know. We can't ship them until we hear from you.

You decide that the letter is too wordy, doesn't get to the point immediately, and is negative and somewhat patronizing. You rewrite it as follows:

Dear Mr. Bleak:

Your TRK fabrics can be sent immediately if you will allow us to send them C.O.D. Please call us collect, and we will ship that day. If you would prefer to receive only a partial shipment now, we'll hold the balance of your order until your account can be opened.

partial: not complete

Please complete the enclosed credit application
form so that we can evaluate your account quickly. This is part of our routine credit procedure.

Thank you for your order. We hope that by next
month you will be one of our credit customers
who will enjoy our 2/10, n/30 terms.

                              Sincerely yours,

It is wise to mention that your credit check is routine and not a questioning of this customer's reliability.

This letter gets right to the point, is positive in tone, and includes conditions under which you can ship immediately, and a statement maintaining good will. In completing the credit application form that is enclosed with the letter, the customer will be asked to furnish credit references, bank references, and financial statements, so there is no need to include these requests in the letter.

   To give yourself the opportunity to write the introductory letter granting credit or delaying credit, try Skills Activity 56.

SKILLS ACTIVITY 56

*Given two poorly written
letters granting credit
or delaying credit, re-
write the letters granting
credit to include (1) a
welcome and thank you
to the new account,
(2) an explanation of
the terms of sale, (3) an
offer of continued serv-
ice, and (4) an invitation
for future service.*

*Rewrite the letters delaying
credit to include (1) conditions under which you
can ship immediately,
(2) company terms,
(3) request for credit references, financial state-
ment, and bank refer-
ences, and (4) a statement
maintaining goodwill.*

*Peer group judgment or
instructor's evaluation for
each letter:*

Excellent	*4*
Good	*3*
Fair	*2*

1. As a beginner in the credit department of Pioneer Paper Products, Ted Nichols is asked to submit to his supervisor for approval any letters granting credit. He has written the following letter to Business World, Inc. Can you help Ted improve his letter so that it will be accepted by his supervisor?

> Your welcome order of May 1 has been received, but it will be impossible to service it until we have some further needed information from you.
>
> Since we do not find your name among our list of customers past or present, we are asking you to send us copies of your financial statements for the passed three years as well as names of three business and banking references whom we can contact as regards your credit-worthiness. Also please complete the enclosed credit application blank.
>
> However, we are happy to tell you that your order can be shipped as soon as you let us know whether it can be sent C.O.D. Of course, we will also ship at once if you remit your check immediately.
>
> To save time, why not let us service your order C.O.D. so you can have the opportunity of selling superior and quick-selling Pioneer Paper Products.

2. Here is another letter written by Ted covering a situation in which Morris Stationers, Inc., has ordered bond paper, envelopes, and index cards from Pioneer Paper Products. Morris has had no previous business with Pioneer. Will you please help Ted with this one?

> We are glad to see that your expanding business will be selling Pioneer Paper Products. The clasp envelopes you ordered have already been shipped and should reach you before the opening of your new store in New London.
>
> Your bill for $150, as per the enclosed invoice, has been charged to your new account with Pioneer. Our trade terms are the usual 2/10, n/30. You as an experienced businessperson

know, of course, that you may therefore remit
$147 to us if you pay within 10 days of this
invoice. Most of our customers prefer to take
advantage of this discount privilege; we hope
you will too--it's to your advantage.

Congratulations on expanding your business
and congratulations, too, on selecting our fine
line of Pioneer Paper Products.

If you achieved Fair or above on 1 and 2, go on to Unit 35. If you did
not achieve Fair or above on these problems, rewrite the letters. Ask
your instructor to evaluate your rewritten letters, and, if necessary, to
discuss ways in which you can improve.

*Name*_____ *Date*_____

UNIT 35   THE THREE C'S OF CREDIT

Your performance objective for this unit is:

Given the problem of determining what information is necessary in a credit request,

You will include questions on the character, capital, and capacity of the credit applicant.

assesses: evaluates

After receiving your letter, Mr. Bleak returned his credit-application form. You are now asked to write to the references he listed, while another member of the department assesses Bleak's financial statement. What information will you need from these references? And what does the department hope to learn from the financial statement?

Remember, on your first day in this office, you were wondering: How does a credit manager decide to accept or reject an application for a charge account? Ms. Wood now introduces you to the "three C's of credit"—character, capital, capacity. They determine whether credit will be granted.

Character

She explains that although you will check all three C's, character is the most important element, the one that money cannot buy. No matter how much capital or capacity an individual may have, they are as nothing if that person lacks honesty and a sense of fairness. You remember when your friend Velma Harris asked you to lend her $10 until the following week. You knew that Velma had a very small allowance and had never saved any money. But you knew, too that Velma was trustworthy and could be relied upon under any conditions. So you gave the loan to your friend.

Capital

indebtedness: money owed

The second item, capital, Ms. Wood continues, concerns how much money the firm has and how that money is being used. For instance, what is the extent of Bleak & Company's indebtedness? Does it have money readily available to meet its day-to-day and month-to-month needs? Does it make efficient use of its money through investment and expansion? Is the company making a profit? Is it in a growing industry?

One of the first steps in assessing a firm's financial position is to contact its bank. (If you have ever filled out an application for a charge account or some other type of credit, you remember that the form asked for the name of your bank.) Although a bank will not normally reveal how much money is in a customer's account, it will give the credit office its estimate of the customer's credit reliability and will specify whether the account is one of long standing. And the existence of a bank account is itself some (though not sufficient) evidence that the customer has money on hand to pay for his purchases.

reliability: dependability
specify: state

A second source of information about Mr. Bleak's capital is the references he gave. They, too, will be asked to give their evaluation of the firm's position.

However, the credit office will obtain most of its capital information from Bleak & Company's financial statement. When Ms. Wood assigns one of her assistants to study it, she will expect answers to such questions as these.

What are Bleak & Company's assets? (What does the company own? What is the monetary value of those possessions?)

assets

What are the company's liabilities? (How much does Bleak & Company owe? To whom?)

liabilities

Which are short-term debts? (How much will have to be paid in the next year?) And which are long-term ones?

What is the owner's equity in the business? (How much is left for the owner after the company's liabilities are subtracted from its assets—that is, after all its debts are paid?)

equity

How liquid are the company's assets? (How much of its assets can be turned into cash quickly to pay its bills?)

liquid

Ms. Wood has just used a number of terms that are new to you. You are curious to learn more, so you ask her to show you Bleak's financial statement and to tell you a little about it.

curious

She is pleased by your interest and begins by explaining that businesses have two major financial statements; first, the income statement, which presents a summary of revenues and expenses of the business for a specified accounting period; second, the balance sheet (what you are interested in now), which presents a picture of a company's position at a given time.

On the balance sheet (Figure 11–2) assets are listed on the left side, liabilities and the owner's equity on the right. The statement is called a "balance sheet" because the two sides must always be equal. In other words, everything that the business owns must equal the debts it owes plus what the owner has invested or retained in the business. (The owner here is Mr. Bleak; the owners of a corporation are its shareholders.)

What balances on a balance sheet?

The assets are normally listed in order of decreasing liquidity—that is, first cash, then items (such as receivables and inventory) that are easily turned into cash, and finally those items (such as plant and equipment) that are difficult to turn into cash. Similarly, on the liabilities side, current (or short-term) liabilities—those that will require cash for payment soonest—are listed first, and longer-term debts are listed next. The

Remember, from the list above, what liquid means?

```
                Statement of Financial Condition
                      December 31, 19--

         Assets                          Liabilities

Cash               $ 9,276    Accounts payable        $12,022
Accounts receivable  11,721   Reserve for taxes         3,041
Inventory            48,294
                              Current liabilities     $15,063
   Current assets   $69,291
                              Long-term bank loan       18,500
Plant and equipment
   after reserves for            Total liabilities      33,563
   depreciation      21,481
Goodwill                  1   Owner's equity
                              William Bleak             57,210
   Total assets     $90,773
                                 Total liabilities
                                 and owner's
                                 equity               $90,773
```

Figure 11–2
Bleak & Company's
Balance Sheet

owner's claims are listed last, since the owner can claim this money only after other debts have been paid.

TRK will apply a wide variety of tests to Bleak & Company's financial statement, Ms. Wood explains. And to do this properly, her staff had to take a special course in analyzing financial statements and evaluating the results. The aim of this analysis, of course, is to learn enough about Bleak's position to determine if his business is financially sound.

Capacity

critical: most important

This brings Ms. Wood to the third of the three C's of credit—capacity. The critical question is: Will Bleak & Company be a healthy, profitable firm in the years ahead? To find that answer, she must take account not only of Mr. Bleak's character and his company's financial situation, but of his capacity—his business sense. Does he manage his business well? Is his an expanding company in an expanding industry? Do his past judgments augur well for the future? And so on.

augur: prophesy

In evaluating Mr. Bleak's capacity, Ms. Wood will be helped by the answers from Bleak's references and by her own staff's research on the customers, location, and history of Bleak & Company.

Let's put your understanding to work in the credit reference requests in Unit 36.

UNIT 36   THE REQUEST FOR CREDIT REFERENCE

Your performance objective for this unit is:

Given the problem of getting the information necessary to establish a customer's credit,

You will write an effective letter requesting all relevant information and asking for personal evaluations of specific characteristics.

You now turn to your job of writing to Mr. Bleak's references with a good idea of what you want to know from them. Before you begin, you jot down these ideas:

How long have you known Mr. Bleak?
What is your opinion of his character and reliability?
Have you ever granted him credit, and if so, what was your experience with him?
Do you have any information about his financial condition?
Would you rely on his business judgment?

What to ask the reference.

To make it easy for the references to answer your questions and for the credit officer at TRK to organize their replies, you decide to draw up a form to enclose with your letter.

```
                    Credit Reference Form


         Name:         Bleak & Company
         Address:      1010 Orchard Street
                       St. Louis, MO  63130
```

1. How many years have you done business with this firm? _____

2. Have you extended them credit? _____ If so, on what terms? _____

3. What is the highest credit you have extended this company? _____

4. What amount do they currently owe? _____

5. What is their usual speed of payment?

   Within discount   Within net
     period _____   period _____
              Number of months _____

6. Please give your estimate of the company's reliability.

7. What is your opinion of the owner's character and ability?

8. Can you provide any information about the firm's present financial status and its prospects?

Submitted by: _____
      Title: _____

Remember, in form letters, leave space after questions in accordance with the probable length of the answer.

Now you turn to the letter:

Please give us your opinion of Bleak & Company, 1010 Orchard Street, St. Louis, Missouri. Mr. William Bleak has given us your name as a credit reference.

We at TRK would like to extend credit to this company. By filling out the enclosed form, you will give us the information we need to do so.

We have included a stamped, self-addressed envelope for your convenience. Of course, we will consider your reply completely confidential.

Our thanks for your help.

Note: Letter is brief, to the point, and courteous.

In looking over your work, you are satisfied that the letter is courteous and to the point and that the form requests all the information the credit department will need.

Put your understanding to work in writing the credit reference letter. Try Skills Activity 57.

SKILLS ACTIVITY 57

1. Linda Butler has been assigned the task of contacting references for companies requesting credit with Acme Optical Company. She has composed the following letter. Please rewrite Linda's letter to show her how she can improve her work.

> We want you to write a letter of reference for Berkshire Opticians who have given us your name as a credit reference. Since you probably have had business dealings with the aforesaid named company, you should be able to fill in the enclosed form and perhaps add any other comments you may wish.
>
> We will not divulge your information to anyone. Thank you for your help.

2. You are the assistant credit manager of Raynhem's Grocery Supplies. You are asked to check the references that have been given you by Frank Seewalk's Supermarket, which wishes to purchase supplies from you on credit. Mr. Seewalk has recently moved his business from the city to the suburbs. His references are Delgardo Wholesale Grocers, Inc., and Union National Bank. Supply addresses and other necessary details, and set up your letters.

If you achieved Fair or above on these two problems, go on to Unit 37. If you scored less than Fair on these letters, review the unit and rewrite the letters. Ask your instructor to evaluate them and to discuss any ratings below Fair on these rewritten letters.

> Given two problems which require requests for credit information, write effective letters that include (1) name and address of applicant for credit; (2) statement of applicant's permission to request information; (3) request for the following information either in the letter or on an enclosed form: (a) length of time reference has known applicant, (b) opinion of character and reliability, (c) credit record, (d) financial condition, (e) evaluation of business judgment, (f) statement on confidentiality; and (4) thank you.
>
> Peer judgment or your instructor's evaluation for each letter.
>
> | Excellent | 4 |
> | Good | 3 |
> | Fair | 2 |

Name_____ Date_____

UNIT 37   THE LETTER TO REFUSE CREDIT

Your performance objective for this unit is:

Given the situation in which you must respond to a customer who has been refused credit,

You will write an effective letter that (1) softens the negative with a positive suggestion, (2) explains the reasons for the refusal but includes the favorable aspects, (3) expresses regret, (4) assures the applicant of complete and full consideration, (5) thanks the applicant for applying, and (6) offers service as a cash customer.

We must be realistic—all references do not send favorable replies, and all analyses of financial statements are not favorable. Sometimes it is necessary to refuse credit.

What does Ms. Wood do in such circumstances? Does she turn away the business abruptly? Does she say no and leave it at that? The company does not want to lose a sale; if possible, it wants to keep the customer's business although on a cash basis. How does Ms. Wood try to accomplish this?

She explains the following: It is always difficult for a prospective customer to accept a refusal. Therefore, the credit officer must be persuasive and tactful. It helps to soften the negative answer with some positive suggestion—perhaps that the order can be shipped C.O.D. or that credit may be extended when the customer's financial situation improves. An explanation of the reasons for refusal is imperative, and it should be as complete and specific as it can be. Whenever possible, this explanation should mention the favorable aspects of the credit investigation before proceeding to the unsatisfactory ones. If such information is confidential, the letter must convince the customer that the application was given full and serious consideration and that the decision was not taken lightly.

Ms. Wood gives you the file of Gordon Shoppes, Inc. Mr. Gordon had sent in an order and had requested credit. An investigation of his references and financial statement had resulted in a decision not to grant him credit. Your job is to inform him of this decision.

First, you review the file, noting that Mr. Gordon's references are very complimentary but that the application was turned down because of a poor capital situation. After some thought, you write:

abruptly: suddenly

Be as positive as possible.

imperative: essential

Positive opening.

vouch for: give proof of
acumen: keenness; quickness of insight

Good qualities mentioned first, followed by specific explanation and positive suggestion.

Dear Mr. Gordon:

Thank you for your order and for your consideration in enclosing credit information.

Your references vouch for your fine character and business acumen. But the current ratio of your company--1:1--does not permit us to extend credit now. Your order--or a smaller one--can be filled immediately, however, if you will accept C.O.D. shipment. Just telephone us collect.

We hope that improved business conditions this
spring will enable you to increase your company's liquidity. Please apply again when your
current ratio improves.

We look forward to the time when we can open an
account for you. Meanwhile, please allow us to
serve you as a cash or C.O.D. customer.

                    Sincerely yours,

Tactful effort to persuade customer to accept cash terms.

Can you write an effective letter that refuses credit but maintains good-will? Try Skills Activity 58.

SKILLS ACTIVITY 58

1. Wilfredo Goya is employed in the credit department of Plaza Electrical Wholesalers. The Herz Appliance Company has ordered supplies on credit. Herz's financial statement shows a poor current ratio (a comparison of a company's current assets in relation to its current liabilities); therefore, Plaza must refuse credit. Wilfredo writes the following refusal. Won't you rewrite it with him to project a better image for his company?

> Thank you, Mr. Herz, for your valued order of June 10th. It would be on its way to you now except for some problem which we have noted in your last financial statement.
>
> It is the policy of Plaza to refuse credit applicants whose current assets-to-liabilities ratio falls below 2 to 1. Since you have only a 1 to 1 ratio, it is impossible for us to extend credit now.
>
> On the other hand, Mr. Herz, we recommend that you let us send your order C.O.D. Our quality merchandise will move off your shelves quickly so that you will find your business improving to the point where you once again can apply for and probably receive credit.

2. Wilfredo finds it necessary to turn down another potential credit customer. He asks you again to work with him on his final draft.

> Plaza sincerely appreciates your interest in an account with us.
>
> After receiving your credit references, we find it impossible to grant you credit at this time. However, we do invite you to become one of the many retailers who save on Plaza's cash discount prices. By doing so, you will receive the same courtesy, quality merchandise, and fair prices we give to all our customers.
>
> For your convenience our latest catalog is being enclosed. Peruse it carefully; then place your cash orders with Plaza.

Given three credit-refusal letters that need improvement, rewrite the letters so that they include the six points required for effective letters refusing credit.

Peer judgment or your instructor's evaluation:

Excellent	5-6
Good	4
Fair	3

Name_____ Date_____

3. Plaza feels that Wilfredo's correspondence has been improving (you've really helped him!), so he is given another assignment involving a credit refusal. If Wilfredo doesn't have your help, will Plaza still feel that he has improved?

> Plaza is happy that you have asked to buy on
> credit.
>
> We have examined your financial statements and
> have contacted your references as you suggested.
> The information we now have on hand indicates
> that we can serve you only as a cash customer.
> Remember, however, that cash buying at Plaza
> really helps your business because of our dis-
> count policy for cash customers.
>
> Plaza hopes that after you have examined the
> enclosed catalog, you will place your cash
> orders and reap the discount savings with us.

If you achieve Fair or above on two of the three problems, you may wish to try Problem 4, the advanced credit problem. If you did not achieve Fair on at least two letters, review the unit, rewrite the letters, and ask your instructor to evaluate them.

4. Advanced Credit Problem. Read and correct the following letter, rewriting as necessary. Watch for all types of errors.

> We are sorry to inform you that it will be
> impossible to grant you credit. Apparently you
> thought that we would not check your references
> and would open an account for you without ques-
> tion. As a business man, don't you realize that
> when it takes you six or seven months to pay
> bills it will effect your reputation as a credit
> risk? We would be naive to grant credit under
> such circumstances.
>
> Naturally we have no objection to you buying for
> cash. Inclose your check with all orders and as
> soon as the check has cleared banking channels,
> the order will be shipped. It will pay you to
> buy from us because our merchandise is a profit-
> able line for anyone to carry.

Ask your instructor to evaluate your answer and to discuss the evaluation with you.

UNIT 38   OTHER CREDIT LETTERS

Given the problem of applying principles of credit in communicating with the individual customers,

You will write correct letters that grant, delay, or refuse credit and letters that request credit information from references concerning the individual consumer.

and

Given the problem of encouraging credit customers and of maintaining the goodwill of credit customers,

You will write letters to individual consumers suggesting applying for credit, and

You will write letters to individual credit customers in appreciation of their good standing.

During the past few days, you have seen several letters requesting credit; you have observed how these applications are handled; and you have even had the opportunity to write some acceptances, some refusals, and some requests for references.

Ms. Wood now mentions several other types of credit letters, among them the letter to attract new credit customers, the letter of thanks to paying customers, and the letter granting or refusing credit to a retail customer.

Credit for the Consumer

Extending individual credit, Ms. Wood explains, involves substantially the same procedures and problems as granting credit to business firms. There are differences, however, because you are evaluating an individual and not a company. For instance, an individual does not provide a balance sheet, but he or she is often requested to list any large debts—such as a bank loan. And applicants for credit must divulge their source of income—where they work and what job they hold there. Usually they are asked to put down their salary also. Reference letters also differ for the individual, but only slightly.

divulge: tell

The similarities and differences between granting credit to businesses and extending it to individuals are brought home to you the following day. You arrive at Nayles Hardware Store, where you sometimes help out on Saturdays, to find Mr. Nayles scrutinizing a credit application from a new customer—Mr. John Stillwell. Since you have now had a little experience with credit letters, you offer to write to Mr. Stillwell's references. Here is your letter:

scrutinizing: examining carefully

Please give us a credit reference on Mr. John Stillwell of 56 Frost Pond Street, Great Neck, New York. He has listed your name as a reference.

Your answers to the questions below will enable us to decide upon Mr. Stillwell's application

Can you see how this letter differs from the reference request on a business firm? Compare it to the reference form and letter on page 399.

for an account. A return envelope is enclosed for your convenience.

Of course, any information you give us will be strictly confidential.

1. For how long a period has he had an account with you?

   _____

2. How extensive is his business with you?

   _____

3. What is the highest credit you extended to him?

   _____

4. How promptly does he usually pay his bills?

   _____

5. Does he owe anything now?

   _____

6. What is your estimate of his character and reliability?

Thank you for your cooperation. We shall be happy to reciprocate at any time.

reciprocate: to do or feel in return. It is appropriate to offer *reciprocity* to large companies that may request similar references from your company.

Simple as the letter is, it will elicit information that will give Mr. Nayles a basis for accepting or rejecting Mr. Stillwell's request for credit. After Mr. Nayles receives favorable replies concerning Mr. Stillwell's credit history, he quickly sends this communication:

Mr. Stillwell . . .

   We welcome your credit business.

   Please come in tomorrow and charge your purchases.

A Note of Thanks

Continuing to apply what you learned at TRK, you suggest to Mr. Nayles that he make use of one more type of letter—the note of thanks. Nearly all people who have credit cards or charge accounts pay their bills promptly. In too many cases, they are the forgotten ones. Such reliable people should occasionally receive a note of appreciation from the company that has issued credit. This type of letter adds to the company's image; it does not really have to be written, but it serves to develop and maintain goodwill. The individuals who neglect to pay their debts receive attention; the persons who pay should receive at least an occasional thank you.

Mr. Nayles likes your idea and makes a list of his good customers, to whom you send this brief note:

promptly

There are many ways to remember the amenities.

```
Thank you for making such good use of your
Nayles charge account. It is a pleasure to do
business with someone who pays bills so promptly.

Customers like you are an asset to any company,
and we want to let you know that we appreciate
you.
```

Be sure to have each letter typed individually.

Try Skills Activity 59 to check your ability to apply the principles of writing credit letters to the individual consumer.

SKILLS ACTIVITY 59

The Heaslip Fuel Oil Company wants to thank Mr. and Mrs. Herbert Meyer for opening an account and to restate its credit policy. The following letter has been written as a first draft.

Given an ineffective letter welcoming an individual consumer as a charge customer, rewrite the letter in good language so that it includes (1) a welcome, (2) an explanation of terms, (3) a thank you, (4) an offer for continued service, and (5) an invitation for future service.

Peer judgment or your instructor's evaluation:

Excellent	*5*
Good	*4*
Fair	*3*

We duly appreciate your fine charge account, which you opened with us recently. So that there will be no misunderstandings, we want to tell you what your responsibilities are when you have an account.

You will receive your statement at the end of each month. This statement will list your purchases during the month and the final balance. If you make payment on said balance within ten days after a receipt of the statement, you may deduct a discount of 2 percent. Be sure that you do not deduct the discount if you pay at any time after the ten days. The full amount of said balance is due by the end of the month following the date of the invoice.

If you achieved Fair or above, try the next problem for advanced credit. If you did not succeed, discuss the matter with your instructor.

ADVANCED CREDIT PROBLEM

As a follow-up to the preceding problem, compose a form letter that can be sent to those who open accounts with Heaslip Fuel Oil Company. Express your appreciation for the business. Mention that a statement is sent at the end of the month; payment may be made at any time during the following month. Mention once again the 5 percent value of the trading stamps.

Ask your instructor to evaluate your response to this problem and to discuss the evaluation with you.

SUMMARY

The widespread use of credit in today's business affairs cannot be ignored. Therefore, let your correspondence with prospective credit customers help attract a greater volume of business rather than deflect it to your competitors.

deflect: turn away

When you first grant credit to buyers of your product, be sure to extend a welcome to them. Explain the terms of sale, offer quick and efficient service for now and for future business, and thank them for buying from you. When new customers wish to buy on credit but have neglected to supply you with names of references or with financial data, you must handle them tactfully. Thank them for their order, suggest that they pay cash until an account can be opened, and ask them to complete an application for credit so they may be entitled to an account—being sure to make it clear that this is routine procedure.

Before granting credit to a new customer, consider the three C's: the customer's character, capital, and capacity. Examine a financial statement, and ask for information and judgments from the customer's credit references.

Letters written to credit references should be accompanied by easy-to-complete forms that pinpoint the specific information you want. In your letter, tell the reader that you will keep the information confidential.

If you must refuse credit, try to be positive. Offer some suggestions so that the customer will be willing to be a cash customer until he or she is qualified to receive credit.

Consumer credit is playing an ever greater role in business. Usually you must write to banks and other references to see whether the individual is a good credit risk. Here, too, provide an easy form. Also, offer reciprocity, and emphasize the confidential nature of the information.

reciprocity: action returning one favor for another; mutual exchange

Be sure also, from time to time, to write a letter that gives words of praise and thanks to those customers who avail themselves of credit and who make their payments regularly.

Now you are ready for Focus on Language. You will review vocabulary and spelling words spotlighted in the chapter, the use of quotation marks, the use of numbers in percentages and amounts of money, and a way to correct the common error of misplaced modifiers. You will also try another proofreading exercise to check your ability to put your new knowledge to work.

FOCUS ON LANGUAGE

Spelling

1. Write the noun form for each of the following words.

   curious   reliable   indebted   reciprocal

   _____   _____   _____   _____

If you achieved Good or above, go on to the next problem. If you did not achieve Good or Excellent, discuss your score with your instructor.

2. Correct any spelling errors in this paragraph by writing the correct spelling above the lines.

```
John insisted that the error was partialy his

fault, since he had failed to spesify the terms.

But Mr. Winckler answered abruply that the re-

sponsability was soley his. It was his, Mr.

Winckler's, job to assess the referrences of

each firm and to do so promply.
```

Check the key on page 524. Rate yourself. Be sure you can spell every word. If you are a poor speller, ask someone to read every word spotlighted in the chapter as you write them. Check your spelling. At the end of this chapter, have someone read the words you spelled incorrectly as you again write them. Keep a list of the words you still misspelled. Continue the process until you can spell correctly all of the words spotlighted in the chapter.

Vocabulary

1. flexibility a. rigidity b. adaptability c. usability d. strength
2. audited a. looked b. examined c. reached d. read
3. solely a. few b. only c. many d. sorrowful
4. interim a. increase b. internal c. meantime d. overdue
5. astute a. sluggish b. useful c. shrewd d. lost
6. partial a. incomplete b. complete c. particle d. perilous
7. assesses a. evaluates b. speaks c. listens d. changes
8. indebtedness a. money owned b. money in bank c. money owed
   d. money paid
9. specify a. sing b. recant c. state d. precise

*Name*_____ *Date*_____

10. curious   a. available   b. interested   c. uninterested   d. inquisitive
11. equity   a. debt   b. dividend   c. ownership   d. interest
12. critical   a. unusual   b. important   c. analytical   d. common
13. augur   a. phophesy   b. tool   c. relate   d. listen
14. abruptly   a. slowly   b. aptly   c. truly   d. suddenly
15. imperative   a. improved   b. essential   c. needless   d. improved
16. acumen   a. acupuncture   b. dullness   c. keenness   d. accurate
17. vouch   a. prove   b. relate   c. ask   d. vote
18. divulge   a. react   b. ask   c. tell   d. divert
19. scrutinizing   a. talking   b. conducting   c. realizing   d. examining
20. deflect   a. turn away   b. submit   c. endeavor   d. react
21. reciprocity   a. game   b. park   c. home   d. mutual exchange

Check the key on page 524. If you achieved Fair or above, go on to Punctuation. If you scored below Fair, review the definitions in the chapter margins; then try this exercise again.

Punctuation: Quotation Marks

Rule: *Use quotation marks to enclose a direct quotation; to set off words and phrases used in a special sense; to enclose titles of chapters, poems, magazine articles, and works of art.*

Mr. North said, "There will be a staff meeting at noon."
Your letter said, "I will mail my check on November 1."
The blind man could "see" the child's face with his fingers.
This selection is taken from an article entitled "How to Win."

Rule: *Place quotation marks after periods and commas and before colons and semicolons. If a question mark or exclamation point punctuates only the quotation, it precedes the quotation marks; if it punctuates an entire sentence that includes more than the quotation, it follows the quotation marks.*

"I believe," said Charles, "that Mr. Andrews is right."
Mrs. Phillips asked, "Have your read my latest book?"
What did you mean when you said, "This is some problem"?
She said, "It's okay to proceed"; he repeated, "Okay to proceed."

Rule: *Use single quotation marks for quoted material that falls within material already enclosed by quotation marks.*

"In my article 'Mountains to Climb,'" said Mr. White, "I have written about my experiences in the Alps."

Punctuate the following sentences correctly.

1. Knowledge of correct usage is an asset to anyones writing said Miss Knox

> *Given sentences using direct quotations and quotations within a quotation, punctuate correctly.*
>
> | | |
> |---|---|
> | Excellent | 7 |
> | Good | 6 |
> | Fair | 5 |

2. Professor Edgar asked Have you read the chapter Applying for Consumer Credit

3. The new spring fashions said the designer will appeal to the young people

4. Da Vincis great painting Mona Lisa is priceless

5. Buy now and pay later is a slogan frequently used in soliciting credit accounts

6. Look out shouted the driver

7. He said One good turn deserves another; he himself did not follow that principle

Check the key on page 524. Rate yourself. If you achieved Fair or above, go on to Numbers. Be sure to note how to correct your errors. If you fell below Fair, review. Discuss problems with your instructor.

Numbers

Writing would be simpler if all handbooks agreed on correct usage of numbers where percents and money are concerned. Whichever handbook you use, be consistent. Here is how we feel about it.

Rule: *Use figures for percentages, regardless of the amount.*

6 percent; 25 percent; 4½ percent

Note: Although financial institutions usually use the percent sign (%), the word *percent* is written out in most business correspondence.

Rule: *Generally use figures for money, regardless of the amount. Be consistent within a single context.*

When cents only are used, write:

5 cents; 92 cents

When dollars only are used, do not use decimal point and cyphers:

$2, $265; $2000

When dollars and cents are used, write:

$.15; $2.00; $4.78; $249.24

When all amounts are in millions or billions, write:

$10 million; $1 billion; $3½ billion; $9.7 million

Isolated small or round numbers may be written out, as:

I wouldn't give two cents for that idea.
There are a hundred reasons for the change.

Use the number rules you have learned to correct these sentences:

Name_____ Date_____

1. Interest of four percent would yield forty dollars on a principal of $1,000.00.

2. Mail $.75 in coin to the Superintendent of Documents for the 5 pamphlets.

3. Here is twenty-five cents for the purchase of the five-cent stamps.

4. Sales of Magna Corporation have declined from $2,500,000 last year to $2,000,000 this year.

5. He paid $6 for the paper, $4.31 for the envelopes, and $10 for the stamps.

6. There was more than a thousand dollars in that sale.

7. The company's net profit was over 4 million dollars.

Check the key on page 524. Rate yourself. If you achieved Fair or above, go on to the next problem. If you did not score Fair or above, review and try the exercise again. Discuss your answers with your instructor.

Misplaced Modifiers

One of the most common errors in writing is the dangling verb phrase. (A verb phrase is one containing a gerund, participle, or infinitive.)

Rule: *A verb phrase occurring at the beginning of a sentence must be followed immediately by the subject of the sentence.* (A verb phrase at the beginning of a sentence *always* modifies the subject of that sentence; so be sure you choose the right subject!)

Not: Being sure of your answer, the ticket is enclosed.
But: Being sure of your answer, we are enclosing the ticket.

(The *ticket* isn't sure of the answer; we are.)

There are several ways to avoid a dangling phrase. You can change the position of the phrase so that it will be near the word it should modify. (Notice that the introductory phrase in the first sentence no longer modifies the subject of the sentence.)

Not: To become well informed, the habit of reading good newspapers and magazines will help you.
But: The habit of reading good newspapers and magazines will help you to become well informed.

You can also change the sentence so that the word that the phrase modifies becomes the subject.

To become well informed, you should develop the habit of reading good newspapers and magazines.

A third way is to change the phrase into a subordinate clause.

If you wish to become well informed, the habit of reading good newspapers and magazines will help you.

Now try your skill at correcting the following sentences.

1. Before rejecting these designs, we suggest that you compare them other plans.

2. Relying on his ability to react quickly in emergencies, the car picked up speed.

3. Already filled with students, the visitors could find no place in the auditorium.

4. Referring to your letter of March 13, your complaint was ill advised.

5. Having sent the incorrect invoice to you, be assured that we will adjust it at once.

6. Lying on the desk, you will find a copy of the employee-evaluation chart.

7. After discussing the proposal, a vote was taken.

> *Given sentences in which there are dangling phrases, rewrite the sentences correctly.*
>
> | | |
> |---|---|
> | *Excellent* | *7* |
> | *Good* | *6* |
> | *Fair* | *5* |

Check the key on page 524. Rate yourself. If you achieved Fair or above, go on to Proofreading. If you did not score Fair or above, review the rules and examples and try rewriting the sentences again. Discuss answers with your instructor.

Name_____ Date_____

Proofreading

Correct the errors in this letter by writing above them.

Jones & Hicks

65 Woodlawn Ave.

Hartford, Conneticut   14756

Attention Mr. R. G. Heseltine

Dear Mr. Heseltine:

We have recieved from the Eastern Division the lay-out drawings to completed the set which is allready in the hands of the F.I.A.. We are enclosing 3 copies of Drawing E-16-7 and 4 copies of Drawing C-16-4 for the office lay-out. Drawing # 2 has been superceded by Drawing #6.

The writer understands from the Eastern Division that the men in Boston, have been in contact with F.I.A. and that progress have been made.

Very truly yours

I. A. Wrede

I. A. Wrede

Treas.

Check the key on page 524. If you achieved Fair or above on the language errors and Good or above on the writing errors, you have finished Chapter 11.

12

THE SALES LETTER

Your next assignment is in the advertising department. In your preliminary meeting with Mr. Roedel, the manager of this advertising department, you glean these facts: the department utilizes the usual communications media—television, telephone, radio, newspapers, magazines—in its sales campaigns. It also relies on bulk mailings of sales letters.

glean: to collect by patient effort

media: means or agencies

You will gain an understanding of the problems of writing sales letters in the four units of this chapter:

Unit 39   Getting Your Letter Read
Unit 40   Selling the Product or Service
Unit 41   Clinching the Sale
Unit 42   Following Up

UNIT 39   GETTING YOUR LETTER READ

Your performance objective for this unit is:

Given the problem of getting the customer's attention in the opening sentence of the sales letter,

You will use six techniques in writing opening sentences that get the customer to read the letter.

Know Your Market

You are quick to ask the manager how he decides which medium to use. He explains that the most important criterion is what audience the company wants to reach. To sell a product through advertising, you must know your market—your customers. If, for example, the objective of a sales campaign is to attract retailers for the company's wholesale division, an ad in one of the trade magazines would be a good choice. On the other hand, a newspaper or radio advertisement would probably be the most effective and least costly way to inform the general public of a sale in the company's department store. But, to reach a specific

prior: coming before in time

group of individuals, TRK often uses the personal touch of the sales letter. For example, charge customers are usually given prior notice of certain sales in department stores; for that purpose a written communication to each person on the list will bring a greater response than would an ad in the newspaper.

TRK is currently working on a campaign to attract new charge customers. After some consideration, the advertising department decided to use the sales-letter technique, on the premise that the personal touch of an individual letter would help to bring new customers to the company.

premise: proposition serving as grounds for a conclusion; assumption

In showing you how this program is being developed, Mr. Roedel explains some of the fundamentals of bulk mailing. Here, too, the key requirement is knowing the market. For example, if you were trying to sell jewelry priced at $5000 or more, it would be senseless to send a direct-mail piece to everybody listed in the city directory, since the great majority of people couldn't afford such expensive merchandise.

potential: possible but not actual

For TRK's present mailing program, a list of potential customers has been obtained from a company that supplies such lists, but an important clerical operation is needed before the list is used. The names of persons who already have charge accounts with TRK must be eliminated. Think how quickly you would puncture a customer's ego if you sent a form letter inviting him or her to open a charge account when he or she had had one for years!

Meanwhile, the manager's assistant, Mr. Jaspers, is at work composing the sales letter. This is the heart of the campaign, and it requires careful thought. You are now turned over to Mr. Jaspers, who will explain to you how he goes about writing such a letter.

The Truth Sells Best

attributes: qualities

To sell a product, he begins, you must really know its attributes and write about them truthfully. If you ask a novice what the objective of a sales letter is, he may tell you: "To sell the largest amount possible." Many companies are willing to settle for this inadequate concept, which takes the customer out of the picture and substitutes a dollar sign with the product under it. After buying a product, have you ever said, "That's the last time I'll ever buy that!" The product did not live up to the promises of the advertisers. When your sales letter presents a false picture, it will not only lose customers; it will destroy the company's name as a reputable business. True, you may make a one-time "killing," to use the jargon of the trade; but your company cannot live on past successes. The sales letter that ultimately makes money for a business is the letter that builds repeat sales. Its objectives are:

inadequate: not good enough

ultimately: in the end; finally

predilection: preference

To create customer interest in, and a predilection for, the product
To get action
To develop continuing customer demand for the product

You want a customer to say,

Quotations of three lines or more are single spaced and indented from each margin; quotation marks are omitted.

```
I always go to Atman's for my rugs. Everything
they say about their rugs is true--they do grow
in beauty, and they show no wear after years
of service.
```

Not only will she always patronize Atman's but she will convince her daughter and daughter-in-law to rely on the judgment of the company's rug department.

patronize: trade with; to be a customer

Will Your Letter Be Read?

Keeping in mind that ultimate purpose of the sales letter—to build sales—you are now ready to tackle the first problem: how to induce a prospective customer to read your sales letter. You receive many letters trying to influence you to buy something. Why do some of these letters receive a positive response from you?

induce: persuade

APPEAL TO THE CUSTOMER

Mr. Jaspers asks you to look at some excerpts from successful sales letters:

excerpts: passages taken from written materials

> Will you be one of the 25 skiers who will win the Swiss skis at Snow Peak this Sunday, February 27? Return this card, and come to see the skiing demonstration at three o'clock. If you are there and your number is called, the Swiss Speed Skis are yours.
>
> Please listen to this record. You will hear some of the most beautifully read passages in the literary world.
>
> Here are four rugs for you to see in their full color and beauty. Just place each slide in the enclosed projector, hold it up to the light, and you will see each rug in the comfort and convenience of your own home.
>
> Please put this 10 cents toward your purchase of Tru-Blu Chrome Cleaner.

chrome: short for *chromium,* a bright, very hard metal

You can see that these paragraphs make the customer the center of attention; they talk about the product's advantages for that customer. These are the letters that are read, Mr. Jaspers tells you. And, when you compare the following paragraphs, you can readily see that customer appeal is more effective than product appeal.

Product Appeal	Customer Appeal
We are enclosing a sample of our long-lasting cold-relief pill.	Here is your long-lasting relief from cold miseries.
We wish to announce the opening of our new suburban store on October 10, in ample time for your Christmas shopping.	Your Christmas shopping this year will be easier than ever in our new store, which opens on October 10. Please join us for the opening.

We are hereby notifying you that there are spare-time employment opportunities at TRK Textile Company, located in your town.

Are you an experienced clerical worker tired of traveling, tired of fighting crowds? Are you looking for extra money? Apply at TRK Textile for a part-time clerical position.

THE ALL-IMPORTANT OPENING

Spotlighting the reader makes that reader receptive to your communication. But you realize that your opening sentence must first have enough punch to get attention. Mr. Jaspers is just coming to that; he illustrates a few techniques that the department uses:

Ask a question. To be answered, your question must interest the reader. Some letters that use the question approach begin like this:

Planning to buy a new color television?

Can you afford not to read The Weekly Review?

Remember to underline magazine titles or use all capitals.

Do you want your living-room furniture to look like new?

When was the last time you checked the tread of your tires? Have you traveled 15,000, 20,000, 25,000 miles on them?

Here are some good examples of this technique that arrived in the incoming mail this week:

Where do you want to spend your vacation?

Can your chief file clerk leave without your being worried about your files?

Do you want your employees to stand out at the next convention?

What are you doing to provide for your family's future security?

fulfills: satisfies; brings about the accomplishment of something
enlivened: made more lively or cheerful

Open with a direct statement. This method arouses interest if it solves a problem, fulfills a need, or satisfies some desire of your reader. It is one of the easiest openings for a sales letter. Use *you* in the beginning sentence. Note how the colorless openings on the left can be enlivened by appealing to the reader's interest, as in the sentences on the right.

Colorless

We are having a year-end sale on all merchandise in our bargain basement.

Appealing to Reader's Interests

Now you can save more than ever in our bargain basement at our year-end sale.

Our magazine keeps you in touch with current events for only a few pennies a day.	For only 4 cents a day, you can keep in touch with what is happening in the world today.
We want to take a few minutes to describe the perfect gift for the busy student.	Give us a few minutes to tell you about the perfect gift for the busy student you know.

Mr. Jaspers pulls three letters from the incoming mail and shows you how he would rewrite their opening sentences.

We want to tell you how you can get the new books you want at the greatest savings anywhere.	You will find the TRK Book Club the way to get the new books you want at the greatest possible savings.
Many business firms are victimized by fire every day, and most of them are seriously handicapped because they lose their records.	Every 56 minutes, 14 or more firms are victimized by fire. And 13 of these victims are seriously handicapped because they lose their records. It's 14 to 1 you, too, are inviting this tragedy.
We are writing to tell you how you can improve your filing system.	Put your records at your fingertips with Martax.

Use a courteous command. But make it positive, not negative.

Negative	Positive
Do not fail to take advantage of this money-saving offer.	Take advantage of this money-saving offer.
Don't forget to have your car checked thoroughly before you take that long summer trip.	Have your car checked thoroughly before you take that long summer trip.
Avoid waiting any longer to plan that round-the-world trip.	Plan ahead for that round-the-world trip.
Don't drive on tires that should be replaced.	For safety's sake, replace those worn tires today.
Don't postpone paying your taxes because you have no money.	Pay your taxes on time. Secure your tax loan at United.

Use a testimonial or a quotation from an eminent person. Be sure, though, that the person is someone known to your reader.

eminent: distinguished; prominent

"My trip with Arrow Tours," writes Dr. Martin Dunn, well-known neurosurgeon, "was sheer pleasure all the way. My every need was provided for."

"Thank you for your assistance in helping us to make our 1976 spring campaign such a success," writes Mr. Rickenbacker, president of the Life Insurance Company of Alabama.

Last year's winner of the Emons Award, Miss Anne Poppins, stays at the Hall Hotel whenever she visits Portland.

After 24 leading bankers looked over all makes of typewriters, they chose Fastwrite.

Charles Dickens once wrote: "It is well for a man to respect his own vocation whatever it is, and to think himself bound to uphold it, and to claim for it the respect it deserves."

This sentence was written to encourage membership in a professional organization.

topical: pertaining to a topic

Use a topical reference.

School opens soon. Come in for your back-to-school wardrobe.

Earn your tuition for your senior year. Apply at TRK for a summer job.

Easter arrives early this year. Is it too soon to talk about an outdoor pool?

Use the headline or two-line idea. Although the advertising division had not used this technique lately, these copies of incoming mail showed its effectiveness:

HURRY
Deposit money before the tenth of the month to earn interest from the first.

You asked for it . . .
    Now pack up and go . . .

What are you doing in New York?
    You could have flown to Paris this morning!

Here's a challenge . . .
    Read how First American squeezes 7.9% interest out of a 10-year 7% savings bond.

Banks usually use the % sign for percents.

Can you write the opening sentences that will get your reader's attention? Try Skills Activity 60.

SKILLS ACTIVITY 60

A. Which opening sentences will get the most attention?

1. a. Despite inflation, you'll be surprised to know how cheaply you can enjoy your vacation at Holiday View.
   b. It's that time again to plan your vacation at Holiday View.
   c. Did you know that Holiday View still offers you a splendid vacation at last year's low rates?

2. a. Here's an offer you must not turn down for that tax deadline—a hand-held calculator.
   b. Just in time for tax-return season—an inexpensive minicalculator!
   c. Be sure to read this letter about the new minicalculator before you prepare your tax return.

3. a. May we send you a free copy of *On the Slopes*?
   b. We are offering you in this letter a free copy of *On the Slopes*.
   c. *On the Slopes* is being offered free to a selected group of skiers.

4. a. Please take 30 seconds to read this letter.
   b. Wait! Take just 30 seconds to read this letter.
   c. In only 30 seconds you'll learn about a great new offer in this letter.

5. a. How can you sleep tonight when tomorrow you may have nothing to eat?
   b. Here's a plan to provide for food shortages to come.
   c. Are you planning ahead for the day when food may be scarce?

6. a. Five of the world's greatest economists will talk to you on tape.
   b. Hear five of the worlds' greatest economists on tape!
   c. Here are five of the world greatest economists on tape.

7. a. May we introduce our new camera, which takes a full-color picture in just one minute?
   b. Read on to learn about a new camera which takes a full-color picture in only one minute.
   c. Can you believe it? A full-color picture in only one minute?

8. a. Don't wait to replace those worn-out tires with Arax steel-belted radial tires.
   b. Order your new Arax steel-belted radial tires today.
   c. This is a reminder to replace your worn-out tires with Arax steel-belted radial tires.

9. a. Won't you spare just 10¢ a day to keep a child alive?
   b. Put aside just 10¢ a day to keep a child alive.
   c. Just 10¢ a day keeps a child alive.

10. a. For big building projects, you'll need detailed planning.
    b. Plan in detail for that big building project.
    c. Building macro? First you'll need micro planning.

> Given three choices of opening sentences in ten cases, circle the letter of the opening sentence that will get the most attention.
>
> Excellent   9-10
> Good   7-8
> Fair   5-6

Check the key on page 524. If you achieved Fair or above, go on to problem B. If you did not succeed, discuss your score with your instructor.

Name _____ *Date* _____

B. Can you give these opening sentences more reader appeal?

1. We are conducting an intensive sales campaign to get the public to know about the Book Club. _____

2. November 5 was a night of darkness for millions of people in the East. There was a power failure that lasted for several hours. _____

3. Can't you remember the fun you had at Lake Joy last summer? _____

4. The Mayfair Washing Machine is now available for sale at local stores. _____

5. The quality of the paper you use will affect your reader's reaction to your message. _____

6. We believe that the *Current Review* is a winner. _____

7. We have the machine for the executive who has everything but time—the Empire portable dictating machine. _____

If you achieved Fair or above, go on to the next problem. If you did not, discuss your score with your instructor.

C. Change these negative introductions to make them affirmative:

1. You don't want to waste your money when you buy tires. _____

2. Stickem was developed to prevent your plastic floor tiles from buckling and curling. _____

3. Don't you remember last December 26? Were you prepared to cope with the record snowfall? Weren't you huffing and puffing with your snow shovel while your neighbors guided their snow blowers along their walks? _____

If you achieve Fair or above on two or three problems, you are ready for Unit 40. If you did not succeed, review and rewrite two problems.
Ask your instructor to evaluate your rewritten sentences. Discuss any questions with your instructor.

UNIT 40   SELLING THE PRODUCT OR SERVICE

Your performance objective for this unit is:

Given the problem of developing the customer's desire to buy the product or service and of bringing the customer to a decision to buy,

You will write letters that show how the reader will benefit from the product or service and that use testimonials, free trials, guarantees, and facts to convince the reader to come to a decision.

Selling the Product

DEVELOP A DESIRE FOR THE PRODUCT OR SERVICE

You have caught the attention of your reader with that first sentence. Now—sell your product. Create a desire for that product, a preference for it over other items the reader may want and need, by showing how the reader will benefit from your offering. Mr. Jaspers illustrates by making the following revisions in some letters received last week:

preference: choice of one over another

Original	Revision
We can give you the type of engraving service that will satisfy all your needs.	Do you want invitations engraved? Artistic personal letterheads? Specially designed cocktail- or dinner-party invitations? Embossed calling cards?
Our hand-made shoes are beyond comparison for comfort and style.	You can walk a mile or stand on your feet for hours in style and comfort you have never known! You owe it to yourself to try our handmade, specially fitted shoes. Remember your two feet are the only ones you'll ever have.
Contemporary American Economics boasts of broad coverage of major issues by leading economists and financiers of the nation.	Let the leading economists and financiers of the nation discuss the major economic and monetary issues of our nation with you. Just let us deliver Contemporary American Economics to you each month.
Our Mary Ellen Couturier Salon is known as the most exclusive salon in this area. Of course, we make only one of a kind.	When you want an elegant original that is yours alone, come to the Mary Ellen Couturier Salon at TRK.

That evening, as you read your mail, you decide to try to improve an advertisement that you received:

Original	Revision
Our Super jets fly at the rate of 600 miles an hour at an altitude of 35,000 feet. They will take off from JFK Airport and land in London in five hours. We serve excellent cuisine and entertain with the finest and newest films. Our service includes hotel and theater reservations if you wish.	You can be in London in five hours, flying through the stratosphere at 600 miles per hour. You will enjoy a gourmet dinner and, if you wish, see one of the newest films. And when we set down in London, you will be taken directly to the hotel room we have reserved for you. Do you want tickets for the theater? We will be glad to have them waiting for you.

ENABLE THE PROSPECTIVE CUSTOMER TO COME TO A DECISION

entails: involves

unique: being the only one of its kind

The decision to buy a product entails more than bringing the customer to the point of saying, "I want that product." The customer must go one step further and say, "I am willing to pay the price asked for this product or service." Because this is an individual judgment, Mr. Jaspers points out, you should give your customer the facts, describe the unique attributes of your product or service, and explain why it is worth the asking price. Show your respect for the customer's judgment by letting him or her evaluate the facts.

Several methods may drive home the answer to the question: "Why should I buy the product?"

Present testimonials from satisfied users. How often do you ask your friend to give an opinion of a product before you buy it? It is a natural way to get a firsthand reaction from someone you know. The sales letter can use that technique. Here's how a seller of power mowers used a testimonial from a satisfied customer:

> One of your neighbors, Morris London, writes to us: "I have just acquired my Scout Lawn Mower and must say that it is a real pleasure. I just roll it out, and away we go. Imagine, no more wasting time trying to get a balky engine started."

The producer of a lawn builder uses this testimonial:

> Alley Pond Nurseries, the largest landscaper in Mansfield, writes: "We have gained more customers through using your Super-Grow Lawn Builder than by anything else we have done."

Another company, which markets electronic tape recorders, says:

> Standard Petrol Company has purchased 124 of our transistorized tape recorders so that each field engineer may record his observations on the spot.

A sporting-goods company uses the testimonials of top athletic stars to promote its products:

> Jesse Lyons, winner of the World Tennis Championship, says: "The light weight and perfect balance of my Mallory tennis racquet helped me to win in a breeze."

Offer your reader a sample, a trial use, a money-back guarantee, or some other inducement to show that the customer is not really taking a chance in buying your product. You thus give the reader an opportunity to know more about the product before making a commitment to buy. Such an appeal often pays for itself by enabling the prospect to make a quick decision.

inducement: incentive; that which causes one to act

The trial drive has been a popular method employed by some automobile dealers. The dealer may write to a selected list:

> Come in to prove to yourself that the new Master Eight handles and behaves like a luxury car at only a fraction of the price. Spend a day at the wheel of this superb car. Test its perfect steering, its Powermaster brakes, its rapid response to your every action. Be our guest.

A letter enclosing an advertisement for men's shirts includes samples of the materials from which the purchaser may choose:

> Examine these samples of the material that goes into our superior shirts. Note the fine quality of the cloth, the rich color selection, and the wrinkleproof feature of the material. Here is quality merchandise offered at special sale prices.

The book club offers a free trial:

> As an introduction, choose any 4 of the 98 best sellers or reference works listed in the enclosed bulletin. If you are not completely satisfied, you may return them within ten days without any cost or obligation on your part.

When you offer a guarantee in your letter, it becomes part of the contract of sale, so you must be definite and careful in your statements:

Take care in wording the guarantee.

> Niteguard guarantees your automatic night light for a period of one year from the date of purchase against all defects of workmanship, unless the unit has been subjected to mishandling or negligence. If you find any problems with your

night light, your money will be refunded with no
questions asked.

*Don't burden the reader
with too much data.*

Present facts based on experience with the product. But be brief; resist
the temptation to reproduce charts and tables in the letter. (If such
figures are necessary, include a separate sheet.)

In this year's Nobel Gas Run, the Supreme aver-
aged 24 miles to a gallon.

Last year, we sold 285 Warner air conditioners;
we had only one minor complaint.

Carton labeling is so easy with Speedy Marking
Systems. Anyone can produce 150 labels per
minute and can save up to 75 percent of labeling
costs.

You recall that the reason you bank at First Savings was the letter you
received stating:

First Savings has never missed a quarterly interest payment in its 125-year history. Our de-
positors have had perfect safety through six
wars and ten depressions.

And the data presented by Smythe and Norten, Stockbrokers, has you
saving money for them to invest for you:

Of the 50 stocks we recommended in 1976, one
declined slightly, five remained at the same
level, and the rest showed price increases. Can
any other service match that record?

The facts must be complete.

But your data must be complete. After all, this is an offer, and an acceptance is binding as a contract of sale. The seller, as well as the buyer, has
a right to know all the terms. The TRK Theater Club, which operates
out of the Book Division, sent this letter. It required two revisions before
all the information was included.

How would you like to have two tickets reserved
for you for a performance of the latest top
shows within one month after opening night? You
choose the night, the type of seat (orchestra,
loge, balcony), and we do the rest. You also
choose the shows you prefer from reviews you
will receive every three months.

How many shows must you attend each year? Just
four. And the cost of only $5 a year makes you a

full member of the Club. Your membership will entitle you to 50 percent reduction on the ticket price of from four to ten shows each year. You may order only two tickets for each show.

Please complete the attached card, and enclose your check in the self-addressed stamped envelope for this year's membership. If you act quickly, you will receive this week's review and can enjoy your first theater party as a member of the TRK Theater Club next week.

Spell out numbers from one to ten, but use figures for money and percents.

You are presenting the facts so that the reader can make a decision. Is this service worth the cost of membership?

You are ready to try to write messages that sell the product or service in Skills Activity 61.

SKILLS ACTIVITY 61

A. Are these sentences successful in selling the product?

1. Electric appliances

   Our year-end sale is a good time for you to take advantage of our reduced prices on our appliances.

2. Communication network

   We want to tell you that our information networks send messages between far-off locations at a speed of 128,000 miles per second. As soon as you finish sending a message, it can be received by your addressee no matter how far away he may be.

3. Travel service

   We are enclosing with this letter some of our newest brochures where you can read about independent tours and flight departures.

4. Job recruitment letter to college placement

   We are asking that the enclosed materials be disseminated to prospective graduates in order to ascertain their possible interest in beginning a career in this government service.

5. Strategy games

   We know you will agree with us that our new game, Energy Crisis, should provide many hours of entertainment for everyone who plays it and tries to arrive at a solution to the problem.

6. Private mint stamping commemorative coins

   We think that our Bicentennial commemoratives will appreciate in value as more and more people become interested in putting their funds into precious metals and coins.

If you achieved Fair or above, go on to the next unit. If you did not succeed, review, and rewrite the sentences. Ask your instructor to evaluate them. Discuss any problems you may have with this exercise with your instructor.

Name_____ Date_____

> *Given groups of three sentences, select the one in each group that best sells the product, and state the reason.*
>
> *Excellent*   6
> *Good*   5
> *Fair*   4

B. Identify the sentences that sell the product.

1. Portable calculator
   a. Your TR2 minicalculator will save you hours in preparing an accurate tax return.
   b. We feel that our TR2 will save you precious time in preparing an accurate tax return.
   c. A TR2 minicalculator is a great help in saving time in preparing an accurate tax return.

   _____ Reason: _____

2. Ski magazine
   a. Many skiers have enjoyed reading *On the Slopes* over the years.
   b. *On the Slopes* has long been the favorite magazine of ski enthusiasts.
   c. When you read *On the Slopes,* you join many other skiers in enjoying its entertaining articles.

   _____ Reason: _____

3. Camera
   a. After you take your picture, wait a minute and then you will have a full-color photo.
   b. Take the picture. After waiting just one minute, you will have a full-color photo.
   c. You snap your picture—you wait one minute—you have a full-color photo.

   _____ Reason: _____

4. Radial tires
   a. We know that you will appreciate the 40,000 miles you will get with our tires.
   b. If you drive carefully, we feel you can drive 40000 miles on these radial tires.
   c. Car owners will tell you that they have driven 40,000 trouble-free miles on Arax steel-belted radial tires.

   _____ Reason: _____

5. Architect service
   a. In recent years, we have planned some of the world's largest industrial projects.
   b. Carlton Towers and Salisbury Industrial Park are only two of the major projects planned by Paige Associates.
   c. We have been leaders in planning large industrial projects in different areas of the country.

   _____ Reason: _____

6. Book on career planning
   a. This is truly the best book ever written on planning successful careers.
   b. *Career Satisfaction* is truly the first practical, systematic approach to identifying strengths on which successful careers can be built.
   c. Here is the one book which will help you plan a successful career.

   _____ Reason: _____

Check the key on page 524. If you achieved Fair or above, go on to Unit 41. If you did not, discuss your score with your instructor.

UNIT 41   CLINCHING THE SALE

Your performance objective for this unit is:

Given the problem of clinching the sale in the closing paragraph of a sales letter,

You will urge immediate action by offering a treat or reward, suggesting a short supply, making the "be first" appeal, using the "save money" approach, or using the "prestige" persuader; and you will make it easy for the reader to act by providing a definite course of action.

If you have written well, by now you have the customer agreeing that this offer is desirable. Will you now assure a sale by making it easy for the customer to accept your offer? The customer who is just barely convinced will be lost if you do not.

Mr. Jaspers asks you to look closely at the last paragraph of the Theater Club letter. It does some important things: It tells the reader what to do next, it urges action right away, and the action it suggests is a simple one.

Urging Immediate Action

You want immediate action. Once the letter is put aside, the reader must overcome the usual inertia in taking up the matter again. How can you urge the reader to "do it now"? You have heard many of these persuaders:

inertia· inactivity

```
The first 25 customers who buy these stoves will
receive a set of copper-bottom pots to go with
them.
```
The treat or reward.

```
Open an account with us tomorrow, and choose one
of the 50 gifts on display in the lobby.
```

```
There are only 50 of these sets left. Be sure
you receive one of them by making your purchase
tomorrow.
```
The short supply.

```
Our membership is limited to 99 members. Will
you be one of them? Hurry!
```

```
Will yours be one of the first motels in your
area to install an indoor pool?
```
The "be first" appeal.

```
Yours can be the first hotel in the state to own
its own helicopter.
```

```
There are only 50 of these hearing aids in the
country. We will hold one for you.
```

```
This is a one-day sale. Don't miss the savings
we offer.
```
The "save money" approach.

```
This rug would sell anywhere else for $200 more.
Buy it before someone else does.
```

You can't afford to miss this opportunity to buy
a new Itcan Washing Machine.

By putting in your order for a new car this
month, you will receive the dealer's discount
of $125.

The "prestige" persuader.

You will be proud of your appearance in a Walt
Richman suit. Make an appointment today.

Only the most successful professional men drive
an Empire.

Suggesting What to Do and How to Do It

The reader is now ready to act, but the sales letter that does not clearly
state what the next step should be may still lose a potential customer.
The reader may not feel that your product is worth the time and money
that must be expended to get it. Therefore, you should provide the
reader with a definite course of action to follow. Mr. Jaspers proves his
point with these paragraphs:

expended: used up
Prescribe definite action.

Indefinite	Definite Action
Our electric heater will give your porch a warm even heat. Visit our Appliance Department tomorrow.	Will you complete the enclosed post-card by checking one of the following: ___Send the No. 112 heater for a three-day free trial. ___Send a representative to demonstrate the No. 112. ___Make an appointment for me to see a representative at the store at ____ on ____.
TRK Fashions will be modeled at Farseers on Friday, March 27, from 6 to 9 p.m. Please join us in the Dress Salon on the third floor.	Please return the enclosed card in the envelope provided before March 15, so that we may reserve a special place for you at our fashion show on March 27. You will receive your admission ticket on March 18.
Let us help you develop a successful investment portfolio. We have the information you need to make the right investment at the right time. Try us and see.	Call us at 971-9000 to tell us you are interested in developing an investment portfolio. We'll do the rest for you. Or, if you wish, drop in to one of our many offices, listed below.
Let us know if you're coming to the Bahamas again this year.	Just write across the enclosed self-sealing letter already addressed and stamped:

> Yes, I am coming.
>
> Check the type of reservation you want--you have first choice. You will receive your confirmation within a week, assuring you of another delightful vacation in May.

Furthermore, he continues, the action you prescribe should be as simple as the situation permits. You yourself know how easy it is to tear off a flyer at the bottom of a letter and enclose it in an envelope or to complete a postcard and drop it in the mail. Both are much easier than writing a letter, and both are much more likely to result in an acceptance. Here are some ideas for using reply enclosures:

Make the action easy.

> Just take your pencil and check your four choices on the enclosed card . . . with the understanding that you are placed under no obligation whatever. Your books will reach you in a few days.
>
> Now that you have examined the samples, fill in your selection on the handy order blank. Place the blank into the stamped and addressed envelope, and drop it into your nearest mailbox.
>
> You need send no money now. Just fill in your name and address on the special enclosed order card (postage free), and mail it to us. We'll start your subscription immediately and bill you only $2.
>
> Use the enclosed card and reply envelope to receive your free book and six months of Current Times for only $1. Mailing the card right now is really the only way to be certain that it will be done.
>
> In anticipation of your continued NYFP membership, we have enclosed your combination membership card and your 1976 dues bill.
>
> Act at once. Mail the order form NOW--before it slips your mind! It could prove to be one of the most prudent acts of your life.

prudent: showing sound judgment or practical wisdom

> Simply check the program in which you are most interested. We will send you a valuable free booklet describing the opportunities in that field.
>
> Join the thousands of smart people who save at

```
               First American. Fill in the enclosed deposit
               slip, and bring it to First American.
```

Try Skills Activity 62 to see if you can clinch the sale in your messages.

SKILLS ACTIVITY 62

A. Can you identify the most effective closing paragraphs?

1. a. Write as soon as you can to make your reservation for your vacation at Holiday View.
   b. Simply mark and return the enclosed reservation form to indicate the dates you'll be at Holiday View.
   c. Please send your reservation dates and check as soon as possible.

_____ Reason: _____

2. a. The TR2 is yours as soon as you return the enclosed order card.
   b. If you will be kind enough to return the enclosed order card, we will send the TR2 by return mail.
   c. Don't put off ordering your TR2—April is only one month away.

_____ Reason: _____

3. a. If you still want your free copy, now that you've read this letter, just mail us the enclosed card.
   b. Don't you think you'll enjoy your free copy of our magazine? Prove it by mailing the enclosed card.
   c. Put the enclosed YES card in the mail now while you're thinking about it. Your free magazine will be sent immediately at no cost or obligation.

_____ Reason: _____

4. a. Use the enclosed card to check the food selection you wish. Your package will be on its way as soon as your request reaches us.
   b. Make your decision as to the food selection you prefer. Then you can send the enclosed card to us, and we'll send your package on its way to you.
   c. Since we feel that time is running out, we are asking you to mail the enclosed card to us indicating which food selection you prefer.

_____ Reason: _____

5. a. Now that you must realize that Arax radials are the best on the market, come in and let us install them on your car.
   b. Indicate on the enclosed card when you will come to our shop to have new Arax radials installed on your car.
   c. Don't delay. Help us save your life. Call to make an appointment for installation of reliable Arax radials on your car.

_____ Reason: _____

6. a. Dial our toll-free number to arrange a consultation with one of our associates.
   b. Don't hold off your building plans any longer. Arrange for a meeting with one of our associates.

Name_____ Date_____

---

c. Since you must now be convinced that we can offer superior planning service, call to arrange an appointment with one of our associates.

_____ Reason: _____

7. a. Let us know that you want to study with us. Please send the enclosed acceptance card at once.
   b. If you study with us, you may look forward to a successful career, Mr. Armstrong. Just return the enclosed card to get started.
   c. You'll want to plan a successful career, of course, so you'd better send the enclosed card to us right away.

_____ Reason: _____

8. a. Return the enclosed request-for-information card, and we'll show you how you can restore your floors to their original beauty.
   b. If you will please return the request-for-information card, we'll show you how you can restore your floors to their original beauty.
   c. The return of the enclosed request-for-information card will result in our telling you how you can restore your floors to their original beauty.

_____ Reason: _____

9. a. We thank you for your inquiry and hope to hear from you soon.
   b. Thank you for your inquiry. May we hear from you soon?
   c. Thanking you for your inquiry and hoping to hear from you soon, we are

_____ Reason: _____

10. a. Send for your free garden guide today.
    b. If you send for your free garden guide today, you will be assured of a garden that your neighbors will envy.
    c. Have the best garden in the neighborhood. Send for your free garden guide today.

_____ Reason: _____

Check the key on page 525. If you achieved Fair or above, go on to problem B. If you did not, review; then discuss any problems with your instructor.

Given seven closing statements that need improvement, rewrite them urging immediate action and providing a definite but simple course of action for the reader to follow.

Peer judgment or your instructor's evaluation:

Excellent	*7*
Good	*6*
Fair	*5*

B. Can you improve these statements?
1. By stopping in at Harwood's any day during the month of May, you can purchase the one-minute camera at the special low introductory price of $39.95 and begin to have photographic thrills. _____

_____

2. After you have made your decision as to which book you would like to order, tell us on the enclosed card. _____

_____

3. If you want to hear these great economists discuss the major economic topics of today, mail your check with the enclosed order blank. _____

_____

_____

4. In case you feel that you might be interested in moving to Sunrise Estates, call Ms. Nelson for an on-site visit. _____

_____

_____

5. We feel that you should make your vacation plans now by sending for our free Planning Guide to Happy Holidays. _____

_____

_____

6. We'll give you ten days in which to look over this guide. By then you should know whether you want to keep it. If you don't want it, return it and there will be no obligation. _____

_____

_____

7. Just let us know if you want us to mail you a copy of the magazine.

_____

_____

_____

If you achieved Fair or above, go on to Unit 42. If you did not succeed, review; then rewrite and ask your instructor to evaluate. Discuss a grade below Fair with your instructor.

Name_____ Date_____

UNIT 42 FOLLOWING UP

Your performance objective for this unit is:

Given a situation in which the initial sales letter brought no response,

You will write the follow-up letter that (1) reminds the reader of the offer, (2) reactivates the desire to buy, (3) reactivates the decision to buy, and (4) makes the final action easy.

You think you have now heard the end of Mr. Jaspers' story, but he has one more question for you: What happens if the reader puts aside the letter and forgets, or hasn't made a decision to buy, or procrastinates? You write again, reactivating interest in your product and redeveloping the reader's preference for the product. Your main objective in the follow-up letter is to urge action. Mr. Jaspers shows you an example from his files and one from his incoming mail.

procrastinate: put off, delay

> Before we open our private sale to the public, we want each of our charge customers who is interested to view the antique and modern sale pieces. If you haven't had a chance to come in yet, please do so before Monday, March 1, the first day of the regular public sale.

> Has your secrectary enjoyed using the Speed-write? We hope so. However, the time has come to place this demonstration machine in another office. Complete the order form attached so that we may deliver your own brand new machine when we pick up the one you have.

coverage: extent to which anything is reported

Your own mail provides other examples of the follow-up sales letter.

> You will receive only two more issues of the weekly magazine <u>Week's News</u>. Then your subscription will expire. To prevent any interruption in your news coverage, please complete the enclosed card, which lists a special rate for renewals.

> We are holding a room on the ocean just for you. Before you put this letter aside, please tell us whether or not you can be with us again in May this year.

Because people are known to procrastinate, your department plans follow-up sales letters as a matter of policy. These give the customer a second chance to say yes.

You will try writing follow-up sales letters in Skills Activity 63. Now review the sales letter in the Summary before tackling that Skills Activity.

SUMMARY

The sales letter is written to sell a product or service to a specific individual or group of individuals and to develop a continuing customer demand for that product or service. In order to accomplish these objectives, the writer centers all attention on the prospective customer from the first sentence to the last.

The all-important first sentence attracts the customer's interest by such techniques as asking a question of the reader; making a direct statement that solves one of the reader's problems; fulfilling a need or satisfying a desire; using a courteous command that resolves an issue or urges care; quoting an eminent person that will make the offer attractive by association; or using a topical reference or a headline or two-line idea to snare the reader's attention.

Of course, the product or service is important—but only as it serves the reader. After you have created a preference for your product over other items, you can use several methods to bring your prospective customer to a decision to buy: presenting testimonials from satisfied users; offering samples, or trial uses, or money-back guarantees; or presenting pointed factual information.

Once the reader wants the product enough to pay the price you are asking, you must clinch the sale by getting immediate action. Make it easy to act by giving simple directions, and prove it is worthwhile to do it now by one of these persuaders: the promise of a treat or reward, the threat of a short supply, the "be first" appeal, the "save money" approach, the "prestige" persuader.

Finally, you must plan follow-up sales letters for the procrastinator. You give this customer a second chance to say yes, a second chance to benefit from the product or service the sales letter offers.

You are now ready to treat the sales letter as a whole. Try Skills Activity 63.

SKILLS ACTIVITY 63

A. Here are four effective sales letters for review.

1. The first letter went out to commercial bankers to sell them paper for their checking accounts.

> Is your check paper in the rough?
>   Or smooth as a putting green?
>
> There's almost that much difference in check papers. Starting with the worst, full of hills and valleys, you can progress right up to Johnson's Safeguard--the leading "pro" in safety papers.
>
> Safeguard has a smooth, level surface, where magnetic inks dry fast. Safeguard always plays the course at par, going through your reader-sorters without a missed stroke. You won't get rejects due to faulty paper--and rejects can cost 40 cents each.
>
> Safeguard is the safety paper that comes in white and seven colors, in your own selection of design.
>
> Send the enclosed coupon to your bank stationer for samples of Safeguard. Examine the quality and performance of this fine check paper yourself. It's the only fair way.

2. Here's a letter to the office manager:

> You're the boss. But could you ever demand that desks be kept clear of clutter? Where would your employees put all the things that clutter their desk tops and make your offices messy looking?
>
> Look at the work stations in the attached picture. All the things that permanently clutter other desk tops are in the drawers; letter trays, binder racks, form racks, card trays are inside.
>
> Thatcher Clear-Deck Desks make it easier to eliminate messy desk tops, improve work habits, and ensure greater accuracy throughout the office. Ingenious drawer facilities separate all paperwork and working tools into definite, easy-to-find groups, positioned for the greatest convenience of the user.

There's a right Clear-Deck Desk for every
office job. Each basic model can be expanded,
converted, or rearranged to fit any degree of
job specialization. Ask us to show you.

How? Phone your local Thatcher dealer; or fill
in the enclosed postage-paid card, and mail it
to us.

3. The tour operator sends this letter:

June in January? Yes, now is the time to plan
ahead for that summer tour of Europe. Begin
immediately on the enclosed planning kit.

Our tours provide all the essentials required by
Americans traveling abroad: first-class hotels;
a private bath guaranteed every night of the
tour; fully air-conditioned motorcoaches; the
services of a multilingual tour director, who is
on hand every minute of the day and night. You
will travel in true American-style comfort, in
the manner to which you are accustomed back home.

But Storey Luxury Tours provide the one feature
that other tours of Europe lack--leisure. On a
Storey tour, much of the travel in Europe is by
air and first-class rail. You do not sit for
interminable hours in a motorcoach. The result
is more time for sightseeing, shopping, explor-
ing, or just relaxing. And we have added evening
entertainment and other thoughtful extras to
your tour at no extra cost. A Storey tour is a
true vacation.

I very much hope that we may see you on one of
our tours. We promise you an experience in lei-
surely travel that you'll never forget. But
please remember that the best policy is to
reserve early.

4. The automobile dealer writes to a group like this:

Caravel--the logical step in any success story.

For years Caravel has been the overwhelming
luxury-car choice of successful professional and
businesspersons--people who recognize quality
and value and interpret it in terms of sound
investment.

Ownership of a Caravel provides a sense of satisfaction matched by no other car--the reward of

owning the finest that motoring has to offer.

Never has this been as true as it is for the new
model. Caravel's completely new styling is complemented by smoother, quieter, more agile performance. Its comforts are more luxurious than
ever. And, as you would expect, its safety features are unsurpassed.

With its famed long life and high resale value,
Caravel represents the world's soundest automobile investment--from both a personal and a
professional standpoint. Cunningham stands ready
to show you how well a Caravel accompanies accomplishment.

Call Cunningham today. We will drive a new
Caravel to your home and give you the opportunity to spend a day at the wheel of this great
car. No obligation, of course.

Check the key on page 525. If you achieved Fair or above on at least two
of the four letters, go on to the next problem. If not, discuss your difficulty in achieving this goal with your instructor.

B. Members of the circulation department of the magazine *Travel Abroad*
have presented the following letters for your acceptance. As the circulation manager of the magazine, which of the letters will you send
to your subscribers? Why?

> *Given a choice of two sales letters, identify the more effective letter and give reasons.*
>
> | | |
> |---|---|
> | *Excellent* | 4 |
> | *Good* | 3 |
> | *Fair* | 2 |

1. Would you like to order a special 25th Anniversary issue of Travel Abroad? Yes, you may order
one or more copies of a limited edition of the
Anniversary issue bound in beautiful silver-
embossed leatherette for your permanent library.

Our 25th Anniversary issue represents a mile-
stone in travel publishing. Many of our readers
will want to preserve this historic edition in
permanent bound form. You will want it for your
own library and to share with others. It makes a
unique and valuable gift for your family, your
special friends and associates, or for your
school library.

Only a limited number of this Anniversary issue
are being bound. All requests will be filled in
the order we receive them. So we urge you to use
the convenient form enclosed to place your order
today for this Special Collector's Edition of
Travel Abroad's 25th Anniversary issue.

2. Would you believe it? <u>Travel Abroad</u> is already 25 years old! To celebrate its Silver Anniversary, we have prepared a limited edition bound in beautiful silver-embossed leatherette.

In our Anniversary edition, we are reprinting many of the prize photographs which have been published over the years. We feel that our readers will want at least one copy of the special edition.

We suggest that you order it for yourself, your family, your friends and associates. We feel it should be a unique gift.

Because the 25th Anniversary issue will be a limited issue, we implore you to order today. We have enclosed a special order form, and orders will be filled as received.

_____ Reasons: _____

_____

_____

Check the key on page 525. If you selected the correct letter, achieved Fair or above, go on to C. If you scored below Fair, note differences with the key and discuss your answer with the instructor.

Given three cases which call for the writing of sales letters, write two or three effective letters that (1) use an attention-getting device, (2) arouse the reader's desire to buy the product or service, (3) convince the reader to make a decision, and (4) make it easy for the reader to act.

Peer judgment or your instructor's evaluation:

Excellent 4
Good 3
Fair 2

C. You are the manager of the Noranda Camp for boys. The proprietor asks you to write a sales letter to the parents of the boys who had spent the preceding summer at the camp. He wants the boys to return this year. Here are some ideas to include, not necessarily in order of importance:

1. Recall last season's pleasant vacation
2. New olympic-size swimming pool and recreation hall.
3. Improved playing fields
4. Same careful supervision as previously
5. Rates have remained same

D. You have been supervising a team of demonstrators of the Kelsey electric vacuum cleaner in their door-to-door selling of these vacuums. You have decided to follow up the demonstrations by sending a sales letter to give added weight to the salesman's visit. Write the letter, using these ideas:

1. Machine brushes and vacuums simultaneously
2. Inexpensive disposable dust bags
3. Machine costs $59.95, for limited time only
4. Fifty years of satisfied service
5. Unconditional guarantee for two years
6. Compact, easy to store
7. Easy to use, practically glides by itself

E. You are employed by a charter-bus company. Write a letter to be sent to ski enthusiasts to get them to sign up for trips to the ski country on weekends during the ski season. You will offer them a $10 rate for the bus transportation and two nights at the Avalanche Ski Lodge for $30.

If you achieved Fair or above on two of the three letters, go on to the next problem. If you did not, discuss your score with your instructor.

F. For those readers who did not respond to your letters in C and D, write follow-up sales letters.

If you achieved Fair or above go on to Focus on Language; if you did not, discuss your difficulties with your instructor. Then you may wish to try the following problems for advanced credit.

ADVANCED CREDIT

G. Write a sales letter to go to owners of home freezers. You want to sell them See-Safe plastic food bags, which are used in freezing foods. You might mention that the bags come in various sizes and that they can be used for meats, poultry, fruits, vegetables, and bakery goods. They are guaranteed to seal in flavor. They require no heat sealing.

H. It is early in October. Write a sales letter to be sent by the local garage and repair shop to encourage car owners to come there for their winterizing.

I. You are secretary of the Fish and Game Club. You want to increase membership in the club. From your local sporting-goods store, you have obtained a list of names of people who have fishing and hunting licenses. Write a letter to encourage them to join the Fish and Game Club.

Ask your instructor to evaluate your answers and to discuss the evaluation with you.

In Focus on Language, you will review vocabulary and spelling words; punctuation—the colon, dash, and parentheses; three more rules on the use of numbers; two more rules on misplaced modifiers; and you will have another chance to check your proofreading skill.

Given two initial sales letters to which readers did not respond, write correct follow-up letters that include the guidelines on page 443.

Peer judgment or your instructor's evaluation:

Excellent	*4*
Good	*3*
Fair	*2*

FOCUS ON LANGUAGE

Spelling

Irv was trying to gleen some information prier to his interview. He wanted to ascertain whether he could fullfill the requirements for either job. His preferrance was for the selling job, which seemed to have greater potenshal and would give him a chance for total covrage of a territory.

Check the key on page 525. If you achieved Fair or above, go on to Vocabulary. If you scored below Fair, ask someone to read the words in which you made errors, as you write them. Repeat the process until you can spell every word correctly.

> Given a paragraph with spelling errors, identify the incorrect words and spell them correctly in the space above each mis-spelled word.
>
> Excellent   6
> Good   5
> Fair   4

Vocabulary

In each of the numbered groups, two words or phrases have similar meanings. Can you identify them?

1. adaptability   news space   coverage   irritability
2. distribute   glean   glimmer   collect
3. media   people   reporters   agencies
4. after   before   prior   never
5. premise   proposition   surmise   promise
6. potential   impossible   possible   ruling
7. means   fortunes   attributes   qualities
8. sufficient   inadequate   insufficient   satisfactory
9. ultimately   lately   soon   finally
10. reference   predilection   negation   preference
11. beg   patronize   support   sell
12. excerpts   expresses   extracts   extras
13. corn   wheat   chrome   metal
14. fulfill   satisfy   rejoice   hope
15. stopped   enlivened   stimulated   slowed
16. typical   topical   pertaining to time   pertaining to a topic
17. preference   reference   choice   privilege
18. entails   involves   engages   entertains
19. many   unique   sole   genuine
20. inducement   disincentive   help   incentive

> Given 25 groups of four words in which two are synonymous, underline the synonyms in each case.
>
> Excellent   24-25
> Good   22-23
> Fair   20-21

Name_____ Date_____

21. activity   inertia   internship   inactivity
22. procrastinate   proffer   persuade   delay
23. relate   be helpful   expend   use up
24. prudent   careless   wise   provoked
25. imminent   eminent   prominent   overhung

If you achieved Fair or above, go on to Punctuation. If you did not succeed, review the vocabulary spotlighted in the chapter; then, on a separate sheet of paper, use each word you had incorrect in a sentence. Ask your instructor to evaluate your sentences and to discuss any errors with you.

Punctuation: Colon, Dash, and Parentheses

The colon, dash, and parentheses are more emphatic pauses in a sentence than the comma or semicolon. Your most frequent use of the colon in business writing will be following the salutation of a letter. You will also use it between the hour and minutes in writing the time—as, 3:30 p.m. Now let's check some other uses of the colon.

Rule: *Use a colon following an independent clause to separate it from a series or list.* (Notice that, as the second example shows, a colon is usually not used when the series or list is necessary to complete the sentence.)

Here are some traits the successful worker must possess: responsibility, loyalty, initiative, and good judgment.
Some traits the successful worker must possess are responsibility, loyalty, initiative, and good judgment.

Rule: *The colon is used to introduce a long, formal quotation—usually one that is indented and not enclosed in quotes.*

The Declaration of Independence reads:

When in the course of human events. . . .

Many times, a word, phrase, or clause breaks into the main thought of a sentence. Usually, such parenthetical expressions are set off from the sentence by commas. However, when a more abrupt break is in order, dashes are used instead.

Rule: *Use dashes to show a sudden change in a sentence or to show emphasis.*

This letter is about an important matter—your credit.
We are asking you—as we have asked before—to send your check at once.

In typing, a dash is formed by using two hyphens without spacing before, between, or after them.

Rule: *Use parentheses to enclose words, phrases, or clauses that are explanations or asides in a sentence but are not of major importance. Use parentheses also to enclose an entire sentence that is secondary to the logical flow of a paragraph.*

During the late afternoon hours (from 4 p.m. to 6 p.m.), Mr. Green will assist the trainees.

Apply these rules to the sentences below. Be sure, also, to add any other necessary punctuation.

1. We are again demonstrating as we did on several previous occasions some fine new products that have high customer appeal
2. Five important cities where we have offices are New York Chicago Los Angeles Boston and Seattle
3. The following officers have been elected for the coming term President Bill Nally treasurer Ralph Hicks secretary Irene Furman
4. Everything seems to favor his proposal the plant is operating the market is available people are ready to spend
5. Peter Roget 1779–1869 published the first edition of his Thesaurus in 1852
6. One of the distinctive features of the film a feature that appeals to many viewers is its excellent sound recording
7. My office has just purchased a typewriter a used one by the way that is the best I've ever used

> Given sentences in which the colon, dash, and parentheses, as well as other forms of punctuation, are to be inserted, punctuate the sentences correctly.
>
> Excellent   7
> Good   6
> Fair   5

Check the key on page 526. If you achieved Fair or above, go on to Numbers. If you did not succeed, review the rules above. Discuss any problems with your instructor.

Numbers

Here are some more rules for the correct use of numbers:

Rule: *When one number immediately follows another, spell out the first number and write the second in figures. However, if the second number is simpler than the first, you may spell it out and write the first in figures instead.*

Put on four 5-inch handles.
He had to adjust thirty 26-inch tires.
They ordered 352 ten-foot extensions.

Rule: *Write out approximate numbers.*

About three hundred students attended the pre-game rally.

Rule: *Express in figures numbered items, including page numbers, chapter and book numbers, policy numbers, and highway numbers.*

Now apply these rules to the following sentences.

1. The trucker drove about 40 miles to deliver 269 5-gallon cans of roofing tar.

> Given sentences in which numbers are used, write the correct forms above the lines.
>
> Excellent   7
> Good   6
> Fair   5

Name_____ Date_____

2. If you will read page 2 carefully, you will see that we ordered 5 nine-inch rollers.

3. About 300 students analyzed the paragraph on page six correctly.

4. 125 different calculations can be performed by this amazing device.

5. Drive sixty-five miles north on Interstate nine, then five miles east on the Ribbington Road.

6. Please buy 10 10-cent stamps, 8 18-cent stamps, and 5 26-cent airmail stamps.

7. Here is your new policy, Number three hundred-sixty-five. Please sign it and return it in two days.

Check the key on page 526. If you achieved Fair or above, go on to the next section. If not, review; then discuss the problem with your instructor.

Misplaced Modifiers

High on a list of sentence errors is the misplaced modifier. Words, phrases, or clauses that are misplaced may confuse or amuse your reader.

Rule: *Place modifiers as close as possible to the words they modify.*

Not: We saw the car walking on the road.
But: As we were walking along the road, we saw the car.
Not: Mr. Edgar has resigned from the presidency after having served four years to the regret of the members.
But: After serving four years, Mr. Edgar resigned from the presidency, to the regret of the members.

Certain adverbs are often misplaced, changing or obscuring completely the meaning of a sentence.

Rule: *Use special care in placing the modifiers* only, almost, nearly, also, quite, merely, actually, *and* hardly *as close as possible to the word they modify.*

Not: The case can only be settled by the court.
But: The case can be settled only by the court.
Not: We lost money almost when we did not figure costs accurately.
But: We almost lost money when we did not figure costs accurately.
Not: The company nearly sold its entire stock of furniture during the sale.
But: The company sold nearly its entire stock of furniture during the sale.

Can you identify the misplaced modifiers in the following sentences?

1. The Acme Company advertised for salesmen to market its radios that have cars. _____

Given sentences that include misplaced modifiers, rewrite the sentences correctly.

Excellent	7
Good	6
Fair	5

2. The products have been carefully packaged in plastic food wrap that you eat. _____

_____

3. Mr. Prout wrote his speech while he was flying to New York on a scrap of paper. _____

_____

4. The dealer nearly makes $200 on the sale of each car. _____

_____

5. The president is responsible alone for making the final decision. _____

_____

6. We saw the holiday parade passing through our store window. _____

_____

7. The tax statements are only due on the first of the month. _____

_____

Check the key on page 526. If you achieved Fair or above go on to Proofreading. If you did not, review the rules; then discuss your score with your instructor.

Proofreading

Oct. 16th, 19--

Mr. Bruce Smallpeice

Box 9744

   Saint Paul, Minnesota   55177

Dear Mister Smallpiece

You may try our new Shiny-Brite Car Wax at no

expence to you.

<table><tr><td>Given a letter with errors in spelling, typographical usage, grammar, and punctuation, rewrite each error correctly in the space above it.</td></tr><tr><td>Excellent 25-26
Good   23-24
Fair   21-22</td></tr></table>

Name_____ Date_____

Heres all you do. Go to you nearest Shiney-Brite
dealer. Preasent the inclosed coupon to him to
receive your free sample of Shiny Brite. This
free sample contains enough wax to give your car
the most perfect shine it has ever had--one that
will last for month's through all kinds of
wether.

After you have used Shiny-Brite this one time,
you will use it again and again.

All we ask in return for the free Sample, Mr.
Smallpeace is this. When you freinds ask how you
manage to keep your car so beautifully waxed
tell them that Shiney-Brite did the job and that
they can get that same glossy finish if they buy
Shiny-Brite for only $.98.

Sincerely,

A. R. Albrecht

A. R. Albrecht

Sales Dept.

If you achieve Fair or above, you are ready for Chapter 13. If you did
not achieve Fair or above, discuss your situation with your instructor.

13

THE COLLECTION SERIES

Your next assignment in the TRK training program is in the collection department. You will find answers to your questions and solutions to the problems you will meet in writing collection letters in the following units:

Unit 43   The Reminders

Unit 44   Appeals

Unit 45   Threat of Legal Action

Unit 46   When the Customer Explains

Unit 47   The Collection Series in Action

TRK takes a calculated risk when it sends $500 or $10,000 worth of fabrics to a customer on credit. In times of economic stress for the individual or of recession in the economy, those bills may not be paid. The collection department tries to obtain payment as soon as possible and at the same time to keep the customer's good will.

When TRK sells goods on credit, it loses the use of the money those goods represent until they are paid for. If they are not paid for by the end of the month, TRK will not have the money to pay its own bills and salaries. Even more important, it will not be able to buy new merchandise to sell to its customers the following month. TRK, like all companies, cannot continue to do business unless its dollars are constantly working for it; and every dollar that isn't collected is a dollar that does no work for TRK.

There is another reason that companies strive hard to get prompt payment from their customers. When you owe someone money or a phone call or a thank-you note, you avoid meeting that person because you feel guilty. The customers who owe money will keep their accounts dormant until they pay their bills, and inactive accounts hold profits down.

Despite the importance of prompt collections, businesses are concerned with keeping their customers' goodwill. In an effort to do so, a company may send its credit customers monthly statements for two or even three months without mentioning lack of payment. Usually, a

Why is prompt payment important to the creditor?

Keeping money working.

dormant: not active
Keeping accounts active.

457

Keeping goodwill may overbalance the need for prompt collections—to a point.
There are several possible reasons for failure to pay on time.

customer makes full payment within that time, and the embarrassment that has been avoided makes up for the time that the money has not been used.

Some customers, however, do not pay their bills within a reasonable time. Some have perhaps forgotten; others may be in financial difficulty; still others may really be trying to avoid payment. Most companies, therefore, set up a procedure for handling collection problems. During your time in the collection department at TRK, you learn the following things about your company's collection procedure.

A series of collection letters advances from gentle reminders to appeals to fair play and conscience, to insistent urgings and threats of action, and, finally, to legal action. Although the order of steps in the collection process is predetermined, the decision on when to progress from one step to the next is flexible. For instance, a customer who has always paid promptly in the past might receive several gentle reminders before being sent an appeal to fair play and conscience. But a customer who has been a problem before might receive one gentle reminder; then a strong appeal might follow directly, without an intervening appeal to fair play.

flexible: open to adjustment or change

UNIT 43   THE REMINDERS

Your performance objective for this unit is:

Given the problem of reminding customers of their overdue accounts,

You will write letters progressing from gentle to stronger reminders as initial letters in the collection process.

THE GENTLE REMINDER

Anyone can overlook an obligation. In fact, many people simply forget to pay a bill. You write your first letter as a gentle reminder that a specific sum of money is due. Here is an example of such a reminder:

Assume a simple oversight.

> In the rush and confusion of the holiday season, have you forgotten to send us your check for $55.70, which was due on November 30?

Since you are assuming, at this stage, that the only problem is one of forgetfulness, you might emphasize your confidence in the customer by suggesting that he or she consider some new merchandise you have to offer. For instance:

> Perhaps you have forgotten us. This reminder comes to ask you for your check for $72.48, which was due on March 1. A return envelope is enclosed for your convenience.
>
> We have also included some samples of our new

line of imported worsteds, which we think you'll
want to have on hand for the fall. Orders will
be filled any time after April 30.

THE STRONGER REMINDER

Should it be necessary to send a second reminder, your wording will be
a little stronger, and you will, of course, omit mention of any new
merchandise. But you must still assume that failure to pay is just an
oversight. You might send the following note:

*The second reminder is
stronger, but still friendly.*

You probably have forgotten your balance of
$55.70, which was due on November 30. Please
bring your account up to date by placing your
check in the enclosed envelope and mailing it
us today.

Test your skill with collection letters by trying Skills Activity 64.

SKILLS ACTIVITY 64

1. Luisa Garcia is studying collection procedures so that she can handle correspondence for the credit and collection department of Wood Lumber Company. She is working on writing first reminders to charge customers. Here is one she wrote to the Dufresne Construction Company. Can you help her improve it?

```
Don't forget! You owe us $125. Send check for
this overdue account at once.

We also want to let you know that our new Wood-
master Prepaneled units are now available for
sale. By ordering now, we think you can beat the
rush before the building season is in full swing.
```

2. Luisa didn't follow your advice, and her letter brought no response. Now she is ready for a second reminder. Once again, she looks to you for help.

```
Have you really forgotten that you owe us $125?
Didn't you receive my first payment reminder?
This bill is now overdue by two months and we
feel that you should pay it immediately.

This time I am enclosing an addressed, stamped
envelope so all you need to do is put your check
in it and have a clean credit slate.

Let's settle the account without further effort.
```

If you achieved Fair or above, go on to 3. If you did not, rewrite the letters again. Ask your instructor to evaluate. Discuss any problems you may have with this exercise with your instructor before continuing with problem 3.

3. Mrs. Jane Blackwell has an account with the Hall Department Store. She has had the account for six years, during which time she has been prompt in meeting all obligations. On December 15, she spent $97.50, which she charged to her account. The bill was due on January 31. On February 20, the collection manager asks you to write to Mrs. Blackwell about her overdue account. What will you write?

If you achieved Fair or above, go on to Unit 44. If you did not achieve Fair or above, rewrite the letter and ask your instructor to evaluate.

UNIT 44 APPEALS

Your performance objective for this unit is:

Given the problem of following up the unanswered initial reminder to pay an overdue account,

You will write successful follow-up collection letters that include one of the three appeals, the call for an explanation, and the insistent urging to pay now before credit standing suffers.

The reminders are based on a fact of human nature—people forget. The appeals, too, are directed to human nature—to the sense of fair play and the desire for a good reputation. If the reminders have not brought a response, you should still assume that the debtor is not dishonest, but is only delaying—perhaps because the company is in some financial trouble, or office personnel is overworked or inexperienced, or even because this person is habitually late in paying bills. The purpose of the appeal is to convince the debtor of the importance of paying your bill. There are several tacks you can take.

Your best appeal is the one that puts human nature to work for you.

habitually

tacks: courses of action

THE CREDIT-STANDING APPEAL

The first appeal might be a little stronger than a reminder, including only an additional mention of the debtor's credit standing. Here's one example:

> Please send us your check for $271.04. As your statement shows, this amount is now three months past due.
>
> You have always had a superior credit standing at TRK. We hope you will maintain this fine rating by mailing us your check today.

THE PLEA FOR FAIR PLAY

A slightly stronger approach is to make the debtors feel they should give you the same treatment they expect from their own charge customers. You have extended credit to them because you felt they could be relied upon; you have shipped merchandise immediately to cooperate with them. Therefore, they should treat you just as fairly. Your letter might read:

> As you know, you still owe us $178.90 on your March account. Yet you have not responded to our reminders, and the account is three months overdue.
>
> We must continue to pay our bills promptly, or our credit rating will be impaired. You expect your customers to meet their obligations each month, and we count on ours to do so, too.
>
> Please send us your check, and return your account to its usual fine status.

impaired: injured

THE APPEAL TO GOOD FAITH

American business runs on credit, and most American customers pay their bills. The low percentage of bad debts to total debts in the United States shows that businesses, as well as individuals, accept the responsibility for paying what they owe.

When the plea for fair play does not bring results, your next step is to stir the conscience of your customer still further. A customer making a purchase enters into a contract **enforceable** at law. However, you do not yet want to threaten legal action. Your approach is to appeal to the customer's code of business ethics, which should insist on debts being paid. This letter might bring the desired result:

enforceable

> Won't you please fulfill your part of our contract by paying your account of $750, which is now four months past due?
>
> We firmly believe that a contract is an agreement that must be kept by both sides. We have performed our part by shipping your order as soon as we received it.
>
> Please take the time right now to do your part. Send us your check for $750. Your payment will complete our contract and restore our faith in you.

The Call for an Explanation

preclude: prevent

Very often in business delinquent customers are not reluctant to pay; rather, they have met financial problems that **preclude** the outlay of cash. The straightforward debtor may volunteer an explanation before letters asking for payment have to be sent. However, a debtor may be reluctant to admit to you, the creditor, that his or her business is suffering a setback; so your initial letters are ignored.

In disregarding routine notices, debtors leave themselves and their businesses open for criticism and loss of faith. But you must give them every chance before you assume the worst. You need your money; if you receive a reply from a debtor, perhaps a payment plan can be worked out. And, if temporary financial stress is the cause of the problem, you want the customer's future business. So you do your best to open the lines of communication, to obtain an explanation.

Opening the lines of communication is the biggest step.

You might write one or more appeals before resorting to this approach, or you might include a request for an explanation in your first appeal. Here's one way to do it:

> Your shining record is about to be dimmed by its first overdue account. Will you please tell us why?
>
> After a perfect payment record of 20 years, you must be unhappy with this unpaid balance of $1,500, which is now four months past due.

Please take us, your business associates over these many years, into your confidence. If you will just explain the trouble, we can work out a schedule for meeting your commitment that will be convenient for you. This is all we ask.

Remember to suit the letter to the reader and the situation.

Of course, you can use one or more of these approaches at the appeal stage of the collection series. If you write more than one appeal letter, each should be stronger than the preceding one.

The Insistent Urging

If your appeals have brought no answer, you must become insistent. Before you threaten legal action, however, you try milder threats to bring a response.

Delinquent customers, by their action (or, rather, lack of action) jeopardize the standing of their business. You bring this fact to the customer's attention, using a more forceful tone than in the appeals letters. Your letter can read:

jeopardize: put in danger

Your business has built a reputation for service in this community. It has also earned an excellent credit rating. It seems incredible that you should risk the loss of this standing.

incredible

We cannot decide what to do. We have written you four times to ask you to pay your account of $2,300 or to write us to arrange terms for payment. Since you have not replied, we can only feel that you do not wish to cooperate with us. Therefore, unless you send us your check now, we will find it necessary to place your account on a cash basis.

Retain your good name in the community and with us. Send your check today.

Try Skills Activity 65 to see how well you can write appeals for payment and follow-up collection letters.

SKILLS ACTIVITY 65

1. Luisa Garcia's experience with Dufresne Construction Company has been disappointing. Now she must appeal to Dufresne to collect that past-due bill. Let's work with her in writing this appeal.

   This is the third reminder we are sending to ask for payment of your overdue account of $125. This bill may not seem like much to you, but it certainly affects the fine credit rating you have had with Wood Lumber Company for the passed five years.

   Send your check this week. You may want to charge merchandise next week. Thank you.

2. Luisa is anticipating further problems with Dufresne so she prepared a "fair play" appeal. Let's help her.

   Three months overdue! Yes, Mr. Dufresne, that's how long you have owed us $125 for the door you purchased on Feb. 15th.

   You needed the door quickly for a customer who had a break-in during a cold spell. We rushed it to you so your customer could save fuel and not have the pipes freeze. You were paid for your work, weren't you? How about being fair and paying us for our part of the bargain? We continue to pay our bills on time to maintain our credit standing. We would hope that you would too.

   Please send us your check and get back on a good credit basis.

3. Luisa now has decided to ask Dufresne why the overdue bill has not been paid. She tries this letter to elicit a response.

   Have you received our reminders of March 31, April 15, April 30, and May 15? We must assume that you have or the postal service would have returned them to us.

   You were always prompt in your payments in the past. We're sure you want to be now. Have problems arisen that make it temporarily difficult

to pay? If you cannot pay now, why not tell us
about it? Perhaps we can work out a way to maintain your good credit record, and you can continue to buy from us now that the construction
season is well under way.

Please get in touch with me to talk about the
bill, or, better still, enclose your check in
the amount of $125 in the addressed envelope
supplied herein.

If you achieved Good or above, go on to problem 4. If you did not,
discuss the problem with your instructor before going on.

4. Correct and retype the following letter.

We are disappointed that you have neglected to
send your check for the $98.07 due on our account
No. 358, dated July 1. It would seem to us that
you are unreasonable, and we must insist that
you comply with the terms of credit so gracious-
ly extended to you by us.

You cannot expect us to grant you special concessions when you as a businessman probably
would not do the same for your own credit
customers.

We expect payment in full at once. We are even
enclosing a self-addressed envelope in which you
can enclose same.

If you achieved Fair or above, go on to Unit 45. If you did not succeed,
discuss the problem with your instructor.

> *Given a letter which in-
> sists that payment be
> made, rewrite the letter
> by (1) using a mild
> threat, (2) pointing out
> that the business is in
> jeopardy because of the
> customer's inaction,
> (3) including all the facts
> about the account,
> (4) offering a course of
> action, and (5) making it
> easy to answer.*
>
> *Peer judgment or your
> instructor's evaluation:*
>
> | | |
> |---|---|
> | *Excellent* | *5* |
> | *Good* | *4* |
> | *Fair* | *3* |

UNIT 45   THREAT OF LEGAL ACTION

Your performance objective for this unit is:

Given the problem of finally resorting to threats to persuade a customer to pay overdue accounts,

You will write correct collection letters threatening legal action or collection-agency action.

How unpleasant it is to write this type of letter! You have finally come to the stage where legal action seems inevitable, but you will try once more.

inevitable: unavoidable

You threaten the debtor with the loss of prestige and the other difficulties that will ensue if you are forced to turn the account over to a collection agency or to an attorney. The loss of credit standing is publicized immediately by the major credit services, and it becomes impossible for the debtor to purchase on credit.

In addition, whether your firm decides to use a collection agency or an attorney, the debtor may face legal action if he or she does not pay or make some arrangement to satisfy the debt.

untenable: cannot be defended

Your letter should give a true picture of the debtor's untenable position. You are no longer interested in retaining this customer's business; you want to collect what is owed you. This case calls for clear and strong language. But the language should not be abusive; no purpose is served by a show of anger. Here is one letter you might write:

Always be polite.

                                             July 10, 19--

By using this service, you are assured that Mr. Griffin has received the notice.

Certified Mail

Mr. Walter Griffin
123 River Street
Dubuque, IA   52001

Dear Mr. Griffin:

You have had five letters asking for payment of
the $985.67 that you have owed us since January.
Not one response has come from you.

We want very much to settle this account without
involving an outside agency, but you leave us no
choice. On the twentieth of this month, just ten
days from now, we must turn over your account to
a collection agency. You know, of course, the

adverse: injurious

adverse effect this will have on your credit
standing.

Please do not force us to take this unpleasant
action. You can prevent it--and its unfortunate
consequences--by sending us partial payment of

$400 and an explanation of how you will handle
the balance. Your check must be in our hands by
July 20.

The choice lies with you.

Yours truly,

The Intransigent Debtor

If your threat brings no reply, you must follow through by turning the
case over to your collection agency. In a succinct note, you state that
the debtor's intransigence has forced you to take this step.

Dear Mr. Griffin:

We have turned over your account for $985.67 to
our collection agency. Since you have not responded to our letters to you, we had no alternative.

You will hear from the agency before the end
of this week.

We are sorry that you have forced us to take
this action.

Yours truly,

This customer is, of course, lost to your firm. But a debt must be paid.
In fairness to all your customers, you must take every step to see that
payment is received from those few debtors who refuse to pay volun-
tarily.

As you have learned by now, the collection process goes from the
simple reminder to the demand for payment and the legal action that
finally results from nonpayment. Throughout the series, it is important
to make the letters persuasive—to inject the element of self-interest by
convincing debtors that they are the ones who benefit most by paying
promptly.

Although the language of collection letters becomes more forceful
and more demanding as the series progresses, the maintenance of politeness at all stages is important. Your aim is to get the customer to pay
the bill, not to antagonize him or her. At each stage, you want to give
your debtor the benefit of the doubt insofar as your previous letters
allow.

Can you write a letter threatening legal action? Try Skills Activity 66.

SKILLS ACTIVITY 66

Given two cases in which you are to inform the intransigent debtor of legal action or collection-agency action, rewrite a letter so that it (1) is forceful, (2) includes all information, (3) maintains politeness, (4) provides the final alternative, and (5) gives the final deadline.

Peer judgment or your instructor's evaluation:

Excellent   5
Good   4
Fair   3

Given the case in which the debtor gives no response after the final threatening letter has been sent, write a letter informing the debtor that the account has been turned over to an attorney for action following these guidelines: (1) maintain forcefullness, (2) include all necessary information, (3) keep a polite tone, (4) state date by which an attorney will contact debtor.

A correct letter that meets the given number of guidelines according to your instructor's evaluation:

Excellent   4
Good   3
Fair   2

1. Mr. Wood tells Luisa that he has heard that the Dufresne Company has taken its business elsewhere. He asks her to write a letter threatening legal action. Here is her letter for your advice.

        We have all ready written you five letters ask-
        ing you to pay a small bill of $125. We cannot
        waste further time and postage expense. You
        haven't had the courtesy to answer one of our
        reminders.

        This letter is a now or never letter. Further-
        more, it has come to us that you are now dealing
        with our competitor on a cash basis. We consider
        your manner very unfair after the decent treat-
        ment we gave you. Therefore, if you do not send
        us your check for $125 by July 1st, we will turn
        your account over to a collection agency. That
        won't help your reputation in town.

        To avoid this nasty legal action, just send your
        check in the next mail. This is our final re-
        quest. Remember, July 1st is the deadline.

2. The collection department can wait no longer to get payment from Mr. Edward Carpenter on his three-month overdue charge account with Robson's Department Store. You are asked to write a letter threatening legal action.

3. One month after the threat of legal action, Mr. Carpenter still hasn't answered. You are asked to write informing him that the account has been placed in the hands of an attorney.

After discussion of your success or lack of success with your instructor, go on to Unit 46.

UNIT 46 WHEN THE CUSTOMER EXPLAINS

Your performance objective for this unit is:

Given the necessity of writing letters to customers who give an explanation of their inability to pay their bills,

You will write letters that sympathize with the debtor and that extend the deadline for payment.

Few customers require the entire collection series. A few reminders for the forgetful debtor or an appeal or two to the businessperson in straitened circumstances almost always bring about positive action. The usual answer is quick payment, for which no reply is required. But the customer who needs your indulgence in an emergency must receive a sympathetic reply to a letter like this one:

straitened: narrowed; suffering from hardship
indulgence: something granted as a favor; permission to defer payment

I need your help.

Will you please extend my credit for the $1,500 I owe on my January account?

The unusual cold weather this spring has kept our sales to a minimum. Added to this, our own charge accounts have been very sluggish, leaving us with insufficient cash to meet current accounts.

If you will bear with us, we shall make complete payment by April 15.

You are pleased that this customer, Alan Webster, has defined the problem and has offered a solution. You want to accept this solution and to thank him:

Dear Mr. Webster:

Thank you for suggesting a solution to the problem of your overdue account. Yes, we will be glad to extend your credit to April 15.

We understand that your sales have been adversely affected by the unseasonable weather and hope that by April 15 your sales will have turned upward.

Your account with us is open. Please use it.

Sincerely yours,

unseasonable

This is another way to say thanks to a good customer.

Now try Skills Activity 67.

SKILLS ACTIVITY 67

Given two responses to customers who have explained that they cannot pay their accounts now, make the letters more effective by rewriting them, (1) sympathizing with the customer, (2) extending the deadline for payment or suggesting a part-payment plan, (3) including all the account information, and (4) maintaining courtesy.

Peer judgment or your instructor's evaluation:

Excellent	*4*
Good	*3*
Fair	*2*

1. Luisa Garcia finds that few customers need more than one reminder. But occasionally she must write to someone who asks for help. She has just received a letter from Hebert Builders asking for a time extension on a bill for $765. Hebert has always paid promptly. Here is her note to Hebert. Let's help her once again.

We are sorry to learn that you are having financial problems because the high cost of money is causing a sluggish building season. We know that most contractors of single-family homes are experiencing business difficulties at this point in time.

Yes, Mr. Hebert, we will extend your bill for another month and hope that you will be in a sounder financial condition by then.

Thanking you for letting us know your problems rather than neglecting our reminder, we remain,

2. The following letter was written by one of your customers who found herself in financial difficulty. Mr. Ryder, your collection manager, asks you to write an answer to the letter. Mr. Ryder tells you that Ms. Splain has been a good customer for ten years and has never before been behind in her payments.

Thank you for filling our order for 12 Fyr Fiter alarms so quickly. We have your invoice Number 6783 dated January 31 for $276.50.

In the ten years that we have had our account with you, we have always made payments on schedule or even within the discount period. Right now, however, we find ourselves in serious financial difficulties because we had to close our store for five days when our heating system failed. The most we can pay on account now is $100. We hope that we can pay the rest of the bill by March 15.

Will you bear with us for a short time? We just want you to know why we cannot send you a check in full payment.

If you achieved Fair or above on both letters, go on to Unit 47. If you did not, discuss your problem with your instructor.

UNIT 47   THE COLLECTION SERIES IN ACTION

Your performance objective for this unit is:

Given problems in which payment of debts is to be effected,

You will write five letters—two reminders, an appeal, a request for an explanation, and a threat—in an attempt to persuade the debtor to pay.

Your friend Harold Nayles, the proprietor of Nayles Hardware Store, has had some difficulty with some of his charge customers. He lays the problem in your hands and asks you to draw up a series of collection letters that he can send to his customers when their accounts are overdue. You apply the principle of progressing gradually from the simple reminder to the last resort of turning over the account to a collection agency or an attorney.

lays

Here is the first letter, which Mr. Nayles can send after the statement has become overdue and a duplicate statement has been sent without obtaining a reaction from the debtor:

> Just in case you have forgotten to pay the
> $78.50 due on your statement of January 31, may
> we remind you that your check is already more
> than a month overdue.
>
> Please use the enclosed envelope to send us your
> check. And come in to see the new buffer for the
> Model 621 Sander you purchased last summer.

Since many of Mr. Nayles's customers are busy people who might well misplace or forget a bill, you feel that another gentle reminder is a good idea. So you write this note:

Keep the customer in mind.

> Did you forget? Nayles Hardware needs that
> $78.50. Please bring your account up to date by
> sending us your check today.

In your third letter, you decide to appeal to the customer's sense of fair play—"Do for me what you would want others to do for you." You hope that this appeal will stir delinquent customers out of their lethargy.

lethargy: inaction

> How would you feel if you did not receive your
> salary check on time? Would you say nothing and
> assume that you would get your money sometime?
> Or would you do something about it?
>
> It's the same with us. We need the money you owe
> us as much as you need your money.
>
> Please avoid the annoyance of receiving further
> correspondence by sending us your check for

$78.50, which is now three months overdue. A
return envelope in enclosed.

In your fourth letter, you feel it is time to try to elicit the debtor's
reason for delaying payment.

*Assume the best, not the
worst.*

When it is necessary to remind a customer for
the fourth time that an account is overdue,
there must be some valid reason for the delay
in payment.

You know that you have owed us $78.50 since
January 31. If you will tell us why you cannot
pay all or part of this debt now, we will try to
work out a plan that is convenient for you.

Your credit record with us has always been excellent. Why not keep it that way? Please send
us your check today, or give us an explanation
and let us work out a payment schedule.

You decide not to go beyond five letters in your series for Nayles
Hardware. In your fifth letter, then, you must threaten action, even
though you still hope to persuade.

Why haven't we heard from you? You have owed us
$78.50 since January 31--five months ago--and
you have not answered any of our correspondence
to let us know why your account is still unpaid.

We seldom need to pass an account on to our
attorney. However, if your account is not paid
within 30 days, or if no explanation is forthcoming within that time, we shall have to take
that unpleasant step.

Once again, we have enclosed a stamped, self-
addressed envelope for your check. Please us it.
Do not force us to take action that will be
detrimental to your credit standing and reputation.

detrimental: harmful

IN CLOSING

Looking back over this collection series, you can see the benefits of
the training program you have just completed. In addition to improving
your knowledge of the business, it has sharpened your organizational
ability, increased your efficiency, and developed your sense of responsibility. It has taught you to focus on the purpose of your job and to
consider the reactions of those your work will affect. The results of the

course are apparent in the growing ease with which you can express yourself and in the sharp, vital, modern communications you are now able to produce.

SUMMARY

Extending credit carries with it the burden of maintaining a careful watch over the payment of outstanding accounts. To the collection department falls the task of obtaining payment of bills as quickly as possible, while retaining the goodwill of the slow-paying customer.

Although specific collection procedures vary from company to company, there is a basic progression in the collection process. After the normal routine of sending monthly statements, you write friendly reminders to the customer to persuade him or her to pay. When necessary, a stronger appeal follows to state that the customer's credit standing may be affected by this delay in payment. Your next step is to call for fair play on the part of the debtor.

You continue to strengthen your case when you write to remind delinquent customers of their contractual obligation. If a customer cannot fulfill that contract, you request an explanation, so that you may be able to extend the term of the debt or reschedule payments.

As the need for stronger measures becomes evident, you must begin to threaten the debtor with the possibility of reporting the delinquency to a credit bureau and, finally, with turning over the account to an agency for collection.

Regardless of the anger you may feel toward nonpayers, you must show restraint in your writing. Throughout your collection series, you assume that the customer intends to pay. Your letters are polite; you try to appeal to self-interest. Remember, though, that each customer is an individual. Consider each case in the light of your experience with that person. Allow sufficient flexibility in your procedures to provide for individual cases. Don't use the same letter for the first offender as you do for the consistently negligent debtor. In each case, the individual must receive your genuine concern. Your objective is to collect and also to retain the customer's goodwill up to the final step.

Try your success in applying the collection series to problems in Skills Activity 68.

SKILLS ACTIVITY 68

Given four problems involving the progression of the collection series, write effectively the appeal letter, the insistent letter, the threat of action, the final letter describing action taken, following these guidelines: (1) guidelines for 1–3, Skills Activity 65; (2) guidelines for 4, Skills Activity 65; (3) guidelines for 1 and 2, Skills Activity 66; (4) guidelines for 3, Skills Activity 66.

Peer judgment or your instructor's evaluation of each letter:

Letter	1	2	3	4
Excellent	3	5	5	4
Good	2	4	4	3

1. Standard Tire Company has not heard anything from Mr. Boyle about his account. On November 30, you write another letter to him to try to collect.

2. By December 31, patience is wearing thin. You write to Mr. Boyle again. You might remind him that he has been slow at paying in the past and that you have always given him time to pay. However, his previous delays in paying were not so long as this. Try to be considerate but firm.

3. On February 1, you write to tell Mr. Boyle that his account will be turned over to a collection agency if he does not pay by February 20.

4. On March 1, you write your last letter to Mr. Boyle. He has not replied to any of your correspondence, so you have placed his account in the hands of Smith and French for collection.

If you achieved Good or above on these four letters, go on to Focus on Language. If you did not, discuss your score with your instructor. You will review vocabulary and spelling words, the sound-alikes lie and lay, some miscellaneous rules on writing numbers, the double negative, and redundancies.

In Focus on Language, you will have a final exercise in proofreading.

FOCUS ON LANGUAGE

Spelling

Jean had a firm committment to the law. As an attorney she felt responsable for the maintainance of the legal system, which permited a proceedure for the peaceful settlement of disputes. This morning, she was faced with a problem—an unenforcable law. The law books lay open on the desk. Whatever decision she made would jepardize the system.

> Given a paragraph with spelling errors, identify the errors and write the correct spellings above them.
>
> Excellent   7
> Good   6

Check the key on page 527. If you had even one error, review; then ask someone to read each word you spelled incorrectly while you write the word. Continue the process until you can spell these words correctly. Then go on to Vocabulary.

Vocabulary

For each of the following words which have been introduced in the previous chapter, circle the letter of the word which is closest in meaning.

> Given 17 words each followed by four choices, mark the word that is closest in meaning to the first word.
>
> Excellent   17
> Good   16
> Fair   15

1. dormant a. lying still b. active c. volatile d. suitable
2. flexible a. rigid b. changeable c. forcible d. valuable
3. habitually a. uncommonly b. usually c. frankly d. forcefully
4. impaired a. important b. aided c. hurt d. surprised
5. enforceable a. able to be forced b. able to be entered c. able to be carried out d. able to be seen
6. preclude a. prevent b. assist c. suggest d. talk
7. jeopardized a. aided b. endangered c. maintained d. improved
8. incredible a. innate b. inconsistent c. interminable d. unbelievable
9. inevitable a. avoidable b. unbelievable c. unavoidable d. inimitable
10. untenable a. unseasonable b. cannot be known c. cannot be maintained d. cannot be seen
11. adverse a. harmful b. avoidable c. reminder d. contact

Name_____ Date_____

12. succinct   a. brief   b. lengthy   c. succulent   d. confident
13. intransigence   a. cooperation   b. usefulness   c. internal
      d. stubbornness
14. straitened   a. crooked   b. even   c. reduced   d. useful
15. indulgence   a. unkind   b. forgiveness   c. listening   d. treaty
16. lethargy   a. inaction   b. speed   c. help   d. assistance
17. detrimental   a. helpful   b. harmful   c. useful   d. ideal

Rate yourself according to the key on page 527. If you achieved Fair or above, go on to Sound-Alikes. If you did not succeed, review all words spotlighted in the chapter; then try this exercise again using another sheet of paper. Review definitions of words that you now have incorrect. Use these words in sentences. Discuss these answers with your instructor.

Sound-Alikes

Here's a language problem you can easily correct by reviewing the following:

Definitions:

lie to recline, to put oneself in a horizontal position.
lay to place or put in a horizontal position.

Parts of Verb:

Present	Past	Present Perfect	Past Perfect
lie	lay	lying	lain
lay	laid	laying	laid

Use *lie* when the subject acts upon itself. This verb is an intransitive verb, since it does not need an object to complete its meaning. For example:

I lie down on the sofa.
The records have lain open on the desk all day.

Now let's look at the second verb. Review the meaning and parts of the verb above. Since this verb must have an object to complete the meaning of the sentence, it is a transitive verb. The subject of the sentence puts something or someone to rest.

Now I lay the book on the table.
I have laid the report on the attorney's desk.

Remember the bedtime prayer that little children are taught:

Now I lay me down to sleep. . .

Is this correct? Yes, it is, because the subject is the doer of the action. The verb or the action is *lay* not *lie* because the object of the action is *me*. When there is an object, use the verb *lay*.

Examples: lie/lay/lying/lain

1. I lie down every day at noon.

2. The records lay open on the top of the file cabinet all afternoon.

3. When the treasurer arrived, the completed audit was lying on his desk.

4. The mail had lain before him on the desk all morning.

lay/laid/laying/laid

1. At 8:45 a.m. every day, I lay the mail unopened on my desk.

2. The secretary laid the records on the file cabinet yesterday morning.

3. The auditor was laying the report on the desk when the treasurer arrived.

4. The assistant manager had laid the mail on the desk and left it unanswered.

Of course, there is still another meaning to lie which means knowingly to state something that is untrue.

The parts of this verb are:

lie, lied, lying, lied.
Usually the word poses no difficulty.

Another problem arises with the use of the passive voice. You will recall that the passive voice indicates that the subject is really the receiver of the action, not the doer. Therefore, when using the passive voice, use a form of lay, the transitive verb.

The material was laid aside.
My fears had been laid to rest.

Let's see if you can apply these understandings to the sentences below:

1. The attorney (*lay laid*) the brief on the desk.
2. Schedules A and B of my income tax return had (*laid lain*) in the desk overnight.
3. No professional business person (*lies lays*) work aside for pleasure.
4. Remember to keep the roles you play in life separated from each other. (*Lay Lie*) aside your personal and social behavior problems when you are on the job.
5. Management asked the employees to give their best in this crisis. Don't (*lie lay*) down on the job, they asked.
6. Disagreements were (*lain laid*) on the table for discussion.
7. Proxies were (*laying lying*) scattered over the desk.
8. The case had been (*laid lain*) to rest.
9. After giving blood, the employee was told to (*lie lay*) down for 15 minutes.
10. I found the book (*laying lying*) on the top library shelf.

> *Given sentences in which* lie *or* lay *is to be selected, underscore the correct word in each sentence.*
>
> | | |
> |---|---|
> | *Excellent* | 10 |
> | *Good* | 9 |
> | *Fair* | 8 |

Check the key on page 527. If you achieved Fair to Excellent, move on to Numbers. If you scored less than Fair, write a sentence for each sound-alike word you missed. Ask your instructor to evaluate your sentences and to discuss any errors with you.

Name_____ Date_____

Numbers

Let's bring together some miscellaneous rules about writing numbers.

Rule: *Fractions used alone are spelled out.*

 a one-fourth share; was two-thirds finished

Rule: *Write mixed numbers in figures.*

 $5\frac{1}{2}$ bushels; $7\frac{5}{8}$ gallons

Rule: *Measurements are usually written in figures.* (Show the unit of measurement only with the last figure of a series.)

 5 by 9 by 14 feet; 8 × 10 inches

Rule: *Time is designated by figures when the exact time is given with* a.m. *or* p.m. *With* o'clock, *time is usually written out.*

 1 p.m.; 2:30 a.m.; 12 noon; 12 midnight; four o'clock

Rule: *When the date follows the month, use figures; when it precedes the month, use words or figures.* (Remember that when the month is given first, use the cardinal, not the ordinal, form.)

 May 1; the 1st of May; the first of May

Now correct any mistakes in these sentences, remembering all the number rules you have learned:

Given sentences using numbers, write the correct form above each mistake.

Excellent	*7*
Good	*6*
Fair	*5*

1. He has willed ¾ of his estate to his wife and the rest to his daughter.

2. The stock of United Motors sold for five and ½, which was a drop of one and ½ points.

3. Please order fifty-five reams of letterhead stationery eight by ten inches.

4. According to this letter of June 10th, you have an appointment with Mr. Carswell at 8:00 o'clock.

5. The rug, which measures 10 feet by 14 feet, costs $50.00 and can be delivered between eight a.m. and four p.m.

6. We have one daily flight to London which leaves at twelve o'clock.

7. Put the information on three- by five-inch cards.

If you achieved Fair or above, go on to Double Negatives. If you did not, review the rules; then try the exercise again. Discuss your score with your instructor.

Double Negatives

Rule: *Use only one negative word in a sentence to express a single negative idea.*

> *Not:* I don't want none.
> *But:* I don't want any.
> *Or:* I want none.

Notice, however, that more than one negative word may be used if more than one negative idea is to be expressed.

> He neither agreed nor disagreed.
> Nobody wanted to go, so nothing happened.

Sometimes the double-negative error is made because the writer doesn't recognize one of the negative words for what it is. Remember that these words convey a negative idea by themselves:

never	scarcely	none
nothing	nobody	nowhere
barely	hardly	neither
no one		

Rewrite these sentences to eliminate all double negatives:

1. Didn't you hear nothing from the personnel manager about your promotion? _____

    _____

    _____

2. The problems had arisen so unexpectedly that scarcely nobody in the office knew what to do. _____

    _____

    _____

3. Arlene doesn't plan to go nowhere this summer for her vacation.

    _____

4. That cannot be done no longer by any member of the tax department. _____

    _____

5. None of us didn't go. _____

    _____

6. There is hardly nowhere to go. _____

    _____

> *Given sentences in which there are double negatives, rewrite them correctly.*
>
> | | |
> |---|---|
> | *Excellent* | 7 |
> | *Good* | 6 |
> | *Fair* | 5 |

Name_____ Date_____

7. Isn't there nobody who will volunteer? _____

_____

Check the key on page 527. If you were successful, go on to Redundancies. If not, review the rules and try again. Ask your instructor to evaluate your sentences and to discuss any errors with you.

Redundancies

Many writers, through carelessness, say the same thing twice—that is, they allow redundancies to creep into their writing. For example, there is no point in saying "6 a.m. in the morning," since "a.m." means "in the morning." See if you can eliminate the redundancies in these sentences:

> *Given sentences in which redundancies appear, rewrite them correctly.*
>
> *Excellent   7*
> *Good   6*
> *Fair   5*

1. Since a substantial segment of our population is moving to the suburbs of the city, we have arrived at the conclusion that new shopping centers should be erected in these areas. _____

_____

_____

2. There is another alternative that you may choose. _____

_____

3. John Blake has recently completed a biography of the life of Adam Smith. _____

_____

4. Because of the difficulty of obtaining credit at the present time, we suggest that you postpone your building program until later. _____

_____

_____

5. We hope to regain again the place we occupied among the ten first corporations in the United States. _____

_____

_____

6. If you will refer back to our letter of March 1, you will see that we explained our position quite accurately. _____

_____

_____

7. The consensus of opinion among each and every branch manager is
   that the machine has a serious defect. _____

   _____

   _____

Check the key on page 527. If you achieved Fair or above, go on to
Proofreading. If you did not, review and rewrite. Check again. Discuss
problems with your instructor.

Proofreading

Given a proofreading ex-
ercise containing errors
in spelling, punctuation,
typographical usage, and
form, correct the errors
in the space above the
lines.

Excellent   17-18
Good   15-16
Fair   13-14

August 15, 19--

Dear reader:

Saving money is, to a large estent, knowing how

to spent it wisely.

   Some times its as simple as buying summer

close in September or keeping a small night-

light on to prevent dangerous and costly acci-

dent.

Today you must place emphasize on cautious money

management. The cost of hireing such management

is self defeating to all accept those who sub-

scribe to MONEY SAVER MAGAZINE.

Use teh inclosed card to subscribe to MONEY SAVER

MAGAZINE for 6 months for only $2.

   Thank you for you interest.

Check yourself; the key is on page 527. If you achieved Fair or above,
you have completed Chapter 13. If you did not succeed, discuss the
problem with your instructor. There is one chapter left, "The Report."

Name_____ Date_____

14

THE REPORT

Since you have done well in all your assignments during your training program at TRK, the personnel manager now places you in the vice-president's office for the final two-week period. This office represents top management. Here is the hub of activity where major decisions are made—decisions that affect not only TRK but also its subsidiaries.

subsidiaries: companies that are wholly controlled by another company (singular: *subsidiary*)

You are to work with Ms. Borelli, one of the assistants to the vice-president. On her desk are many reports—proposals for new products, procedures, or services; studies dealing with personnel practices, marketing surveys; informational reports supplying facts and figures enabling management to make vital decisions. One of Ms. Borelli's major responsibilities is the reading, evaluating, and summarizing of these informal reports for the vice-president. She comments, "The well-written report is easily read and digested, and is quickly acted upon."

digested: summarized; or taken in mentally

In this chapter you will work with Ms. Borelli in—

Unit 48   Planning the Report
Unit 49   Writing the Report
Unit 50   Typing the Report

UNIT 48   PLANNING THE REPORT

Your performance objective for this unit is:

Given the problem of presenting facts for information, analysis, and/or action,

You will (1) plan a clearly organized and logical report, (2) collect data and arrange it for presentation, and (3) assemble a first draft.

TRK has recommended guidelines to its employees in the Report Writing Section of the office manual. It begins in this way:

To prepare a report that will be easily read, clearly understood, and quickly acted upon, the following procedures are recommended:

1. Clearly state the problem or topic and the aspects of it that you will discuss.

2. Make a tentative outline of what the report will cover. Decide what the major and minor points will be, and in what order you will present them. This is a good form to follow

Title

I. _____

   A. _____

      1. _____

      2. _____

   B. _____

      1. _____

      2. _____

      3. _____

   C. _____

      1. _____

      2. _____

      3. _____

      4. _____

II. _____

   A. _____

   B. _____

   C. _____

      1. _____

         a. _____

         b. _____

      2. _____

III. _____

(and so on.)

Human relations hint: If you are going outside your department or your company, remember to clear it with your supervisor.

imperative: urgently necessary

3. Consider what information you need, and collect it. Search out data from company correspondence and reports; from magazines, books, newspapers; from conference proceedings, yearbooks, minutes of meetings; from encyclopedias; and from any other written materials you think will be useful. Use company libraries and other libraries. Interview members of the firm or other persons who have information you need. If necessary, conduct surveys, and set up experiments.

However you collect the data, keep an accurate record of sources. It is imperative that your report give full credit to all sources of direct or indirect quotations, factual data, and other information. Keeping a 3 x 5 card for each source, with the information necessary for footnote or bibliography, is an effective procedure. Jot down on the card all the information you will need for your reference (title and author of book, page number, publisher, place and date of publication; or name of periodical, title and author of article, page number, date of issue; or name of person and place and date interviewed; etc. For fuller details, see Figure 14-1). The writer who, trapped by the need to hurry, does not keep complete records of sources will waste time later in searching out the source again. Further, failure to give full credit to others for their ideas, information, or statements, and thus claiming them as your own, is plagiarism, a serious offense.

4. Analyze the information you have collected. In order to do this, you will need to arrange it in whatever form is most suitable. This step will require clearly stated sentences, and perhaps also the preparation of tables, graphs, or charts. When your material is well presented, comparisons are clear, trends are obvious, conclusions can be drawn and summaries made that the reader will accept. The report writer has failed if the reader must stop to ask, "On what basis did the writer come to this conclusion?"

plagiarism: the act of passing off the ideas or words of another as one's own

analyze: to determine the nature and relationship of parts

The question mark is inside the quotation mark when the quoted material is a question.

Figure 14-1

A sample note card, showing source information.

5. Organize your information, following your outline. As you do this, be alert for changes that may be called for, and rearrange your topics and subtopics to accommodate them. Write headings and introductory, transitional, and summarizing statements; integrate them with the information you are presenting. You will now have a rough first draft. Read it critically, for completeness and logic. Make whatever adjustments are called for, even if they require collecting more data or rearranging a presentation.

accommodate: adjust to, make suitable
transitional: leading from one idea to another

Now test your knowledge of the steps in preparing a report by doing Skills Activity 69.

SKILLS ACTIVITY 69

Given the problem of planning a report with a committee, cooperate in (1) choosing a topic, (2) making a tentative outline, (3) accepting responsibility for a portion of the report, (4) collecting, organizing, and presenting information for the report, and (5) contributing to the preparation of the first draft.

Peer judgment or your instructor's evaluation, rating each factor on a scale of 0-5 (highest)

cooperation _____

responsibility _____

dependability _____

organization _____

source data _____

Form a committee of five or six. Decide on a subject for a report. Choose a subject with enough major topics so that each person can develop one. You may want to use one of the suggestions below:

Follow-up of the graduates in _____ (your major) for the past three years

Economic policies of the present administration

The status of women's rights

Emission control in automobiles

The job market in _____ (your field)—national and local

Controlling pollution of the environment

After your committee decides on a subject for your report, obtain the instructor's approval. Working together, develop a tentative outline, and assign one portion of the outline to each committee member. Each person will be responsible for planning that portion of the report, collecting data, recording sources, analyzing and organizing the information, and arranging it for presentation in a first draft. The committee will schedule meetings and deadlines for each stage of the work. Before proceeding, get your instructor's approval of your outline, assignments, scheduled meetings, and deadlines.

As each phase of the work is completed, it should be checked and evaluated by the whole committee, who may make suggestions for improvement.

If you were evaluated by your peers, submit the evaluation to your instructor. If your final evaluation on every point is 3 or above, go on to the next unit. If you did not attain this level, discuss your problems with your instructor.

UNIT 49   WRITING THE REPORT

Your performance objective for this unit is:

Given the problem of writing a final draft,

You will (1) compose an opening paragraph that gives a clear preview of the report; (2) develop the points noted in the preview; (3) summarize conclusions; and (4) use factual, impersonal language in writing a report.

The office manual contains the following guidelines for this stage of your work:

The Language of the Report

The language is important. Besides being clear and simple, it should be impersonal and businesslike. Since business reports are factual documents which rely for their effectiveness on the information they contain, the writer uses the third-person pronouns, not *I* or *you*.

Paragraph-by-Paragraph Development

An effective opening paragraph states the objective of the report and the points to be covered. If these are many, more than one paragraph may be required.

The next paragraphs develop the points listed in the preview—and no others. Any deviation from the content you have projected may confuse the reader and betray a lack of organization in your thinking. In accomplishing the objective of your report, length is not as important as orderly development and completeness. In some circumstances a report of three paragraphs may be effective: a preview paragraph, a paragraph presenting information on the issues raised, and a concluding paragraph.

deviation: noticeable departure from a standard principle or topic

In the final paragraph or paragraphs, state conclusions that have their basis in the facts presented, not in feeling, possibilities, or partial data. Make sure that your conclusions are well reasoned, accurate, and unbiased. Summarizing statements should include only the information presented and should not introduce new ideas.

Title and Headings

Choose a title that is clear and concise and that encompasses the entire report. If your report has several distinct sections, use subheadings to begin each. (Subheadings can often be taken from your outline.) A short, descriptive phrase in such a position helps the reader to follow your organization.

encompasses: encloses or contains

A Sample Report

Ms. Borelli now chooses one of the reports on her desk to show how its writer has observed these guidelines. This report[1] is being considered for publication in one of the subsidiaries' trade journals. Ms. Borelli's comments on it are shown at the side.

trade journals: professional publications concerning specific businesses or trades

---

[1] From Sidney Emerman, "Health, Politics, and the Catalytic Converter," *Mace*, Kingsborough Community College, Vol. III, No. 1 (Spring 1975). p. 5. Reprinted with permission.

Title is **succinct** (short and to the point) and complete.

catalytic: pertaining to an increase in the rate of chemical reaction
emissions: discharges into the air

The first two paragraphs clearly state the topic and indicate the points to be covered. The writer uses impersonal language. The familiar "you" is not appropriate in report writing, nor are emotion-laden words.

Subheadings and paragraph headings serve as signposts to carry the reader forward with full understanding.

In presenting information, use factual statements, not personal reflections nor subjective reasoning. The writer does not use emotional phrases such as "highly dangerous levels," nor does he frighten the reader with expressions like "possibly deadly."

HEALTH, POLITICS, AND THE CATALYTIC CONVERTER

Most 1975 American-made and foreign cars are being equipped with a new antipollution device called a catalytic converter. It cuts emissions of carbon monoxide (CO) and unburned hydrocarbon fuel (HC) to about one-fourth that of 1974 models. It, along with the trend to smaller cars, contributes to a 13.5 percent improvement in fuel economy over 1974 models. By requiring unleaded gasoline, it will lengthen the life of engine parts and lessen the bad effects of lead on people.

On the other hand, the converter adds about $150 to the cost of a new car, uses rare metals purchased in South Africa and Russia at a time of negative U.S. trade balance, and creates potentially dangerous emissions of sulfuric acid mist. The converter involves a fascinating web of chemical, engineering, economic, and political aspects.

Catalytic Converter Lowers Emissions of CO and HC

Reasons. CO directly affects people by preventing hemoglobin in the blood from carrying oxygen to body cells. Inhaling only 10 parts per million (ppm) for 8 hours lowers oxygen-carrying capacity by 2 percent.[1] This affects some people, especially those with heart trouble. But in many cities, rush-hour traffic commonly produces 8-hour averages of 20 to 30 ppm and one-hour averages of 50 to 100 ppm. Thus, Congress required a stepwise lowering of CO emission from 80 (pre-1968) to 3.4 grams per mile (by 1977) per car. Their aim was to reach a completely safe air level of CO by 1977.

HC does not affect human health directly, but chemical reactions in the air convert it to irritating by-products.

[1] J. R. Goldsmith and S. A. Landaw
Science, Vol. 162 (December 1968), p. 1352.

Congress has also required a stepwise lowering of HC emission. During 1968-1974, these reductions have been achieved by a series of engine modifications, like spark retard and air injection into exhaust ports. But these usually had the bad side effect of increasing gas consumption. The converter eliminates these fuel-wasting steps and achieves greater lowering of pollutant emissions.

Method. In the internal combustion engine, most of the fuel is completely oxidized to form harmless carbon dioxide and water. But a little is either unburned or partially burned to form CO and water. In the exhaust system, which is cooler than the combustion chamber, injection of air will cause a little HC and CO to be oxidized. If air is injected into a special muffler containing a catalyst, much more HC and CO is oxidized. A catalyst speeds up a chemical reaction without being used up itself.

Two durable metallic catalysts that efficiently help these oxidations are platinum and palladium. Each car has 2-3 grams thinly coated on pellets of aluminum oxide or on a ceramic honeycomb. The major cost is in stainless steel casing, electronic controls to protect the catalyst from backfire, and shielding to reflect away the converter's heat.[2]

Are these the "rare metals" that the writer mentions in paragraph 2 of the report? How does their purchase affect the U.S. trade balance mentioned there? This point should be followed up.

Concomitant Benefits. In order to work for 60,000 miles, catalysts must not be exposed to lead, which inactivates them (although a few gallons of leaded gasoline in an emergency use won't kill them). Use of lead-free gasoline has other benefits. Without the corrosive effect of metallic lead particles and lead chlorobromide, the spark plugs, engine oil, oil filter, and muffler will last perhaps twice as long. American Motors specifically recommended to its car owners to have spark plugs replaced every 30,000 miles for the 1975 eight-cylinder cars (with converters) or every 15,000 miles for the 1975 "sixes" and the 1973-

concomitant: accompanying

---

[2]J. P. Norbye and J. Dunne, "Catalytic Converters in the '75 Cars--Do we really need them?" Popular Science, Vol. 76 (October 1974), p. 76.

Note the transitional phrase, "On the other hand." It signals the reader that a contrasting point is coming.

ingest: take in

When authorities are cited, full source data is given in footnotes.

Each of the first three paragraphs under the heading "Concomitant Problems" presents one problem; the last paragraph explains why the third point is a problem.

74 models (no converters).

Concomitant Problems. On the other hand, emission of lead and its by-products has caused the average city dweller to have in his or her blood one-quarter of the lead level needed to cause poisoning. Many city children who spend time outdoors and ingest dirt have higher levels. Doctors at Kings County Hospital,[3] and in Chicago,[4] have correlated these higher levels with hyperactivity. Recognizing the health threat, the federal EPA (Environmental Protective Agency) has required a gradual reduction in the amount of lead allowed in leaded gasoline. To gain the benefits of no-lead and low-lead gasoline we will have to (and should be willing to) pay some costs.

To get good engine performance without the tetraethyllead (TEL) additive requires expensive shifts in oil-refining methods, passed on to the consumer as 1 or 2 cents per gallon.[5] However, the lead metal produced by breakdown of TEL in the engine has a lubricating effect on the valves and prevents wear.

Cars emit a tiny amount of sulfur dioxide, another pollutant, because gasoline contains a tiny amount of sulfur that gets oxidized along with the fuel. Cars are not a major source of this pollutant. However, the catalytic converter changes much of this sulfur dioxide into sulfur trioxide, which reacts with moisture in the air to form sulfuric acid. This parallels the catalytic method used by industry to make the acid.

In air, this acid can trigger asthmatic attacks or aggravate symptoms of chronic heart and lung disease. Most city air has too little sulfuric acid to harm anyone, but the level will increase

[3] O. David, J. Clark, and K. Voeller, "Lead and Hyperactivity," Lancet (October 28, 1972), II, p. 900.

[4] Personal telephone communication from Dr. Herbert Slutsky, Consulting Epidermiologist, Chicago, Illinois, Board of Health. Information received during a survey of state and municipal lead poisoning, conducted by the New York Scientists Committee for Public Information.

[5] J. O. Logan and C. G. Gerhold, Statement from Universal Oil Products Corporation to Presidential Task Force on Air Pollution, Washington, D.C., March 6, 1970.

as more cars with converters are in use.

Government Faces Problem of Catalytic Converter

To meet the original standards for 1977, which are tougher than the 1975-76 standards, "advanced" converters must be used, which EPA believes would be more efficient producers of sulfuric acid. Therefore, on March 5 this year, EPA announced that it would keep the 1975-76 standards for 1977 models.

That's as far as EPA may go by administrative ruling. EPA will urge Congress to legislate "softer" standards for 1978-81, delaying the original 1977 standards until 1982. EPA chief Russell Train, admitting that his agency made a mistake in pushing the catalyst approach, called the new announcement "the most unhappy" one the agency ever made.

The California and the New York Experiences

The correctness of the EPA decision was soon challenged by the California Air Resources Board (CARB). California, with the worst auto-caused smog problem, is the one state Congress allows to set tougher emission standards. Late this March, CARB proposed new standards for 1977 cars sold in that state, which require 73 percent less HC and 40 percent less CO than the EPA standard. CARB said that the danger of sulfuric acid pollution from use of advanced converters was not adequately documented; and, if danger is later proved, then protective measures would be taken. The stage is set for a legal clash between CARB and EPA, if EPA chooses to set limits on sulfuric acid emission lower than that actually emitted by California cars.

Meanwhile, EPA is measuring these emissions in the 1975 models. One study is in cooperation with the New York State Department of Environmental Conservation.[6] And EPA is supporting research on protective measures, namely removal of sulfur from gasoline to prevent sulfuric acid formation and neutralizing sul-

---

[6]New York State Environment, October 8, 1974 (published by New York State Department of Environmental Conservation, Albany, New York).

Margin notes:

that's: This contraction is too informal.

The author of the quoted phrase is named and identified.

The last sentence clearly summarizes the information in this paragraph. The first sentence in the next paragraph shows a transition to a new topic.

furic acid in the exhaust system to prevent its emission.

Even with greatly reduced emissions, it is likely that cities choked with traffic will have pollutants above the truly harmless levels. Therefore, the EPA requires each region to plan traffic reductions to achieve those harmless levels. The New York city-state plan, under Rockefeller and Lindsay, would have put tolls on East River bridges, would have limited taxi cruising, and would have required nighttime truck deliveries to improve Manhattan's air. A new "practical" plan under Wilson and Beame (and later accepted by Carey) involved parking lots for cars outside the city, with express buses running to midtown Manhattan.

> The writer's purpose in using quotation marks around "practical" is not clear. The reader does not know who is being quoted, or whether the intended meaning is ironical.

After months of study, the EPA this April rejected the city-state plan and issued orders that include these points: three inspections a year of the emission control systems of medallion taxi cabs; doubling the number of towaways of illegally parked cars to improve traffic flow; proving in practice the viability of express bus lanes, as well as "park and ride" facilities; state training of mechanics in the maintenance of emission control systems; and a state-run emission inspection system (such as New Jersey now has) for all cars by September 1978, or licensing garages to do this job by August 1976.

> Numbering these five points would have made them easier to follow.

Catalytic Converter Proves Necessary--Yes or No!

Yes, in the sense that automotive air pollutants have remained at harmful levels in many cities and the converter is the only technique most manufacturers have ready to cut emissions sharply in 1975 models.

> This heading, with the inappropriate exclamation point, would have been more effective as a question: Is the Catalytic Converter Necessary? Note that the answers are easily located, since each is the first word in the following paragraphs.

No, in the sense that the manufacturers surely would have found simpler means to cut emissions if they had started earlier on their research instead of waiting until the government forced them to comply with specific standards.

> **comply with:** to obey.

The Mazda, with a thermal reactor attached to a very polluting rotary engine, puts out less pollutants than catalytic cars.

> **less:** Better style would be "fewer pollutants." "Less" is used with singular nouns.

Still less pollutants are emitted by the Honda[7] in which ignition
starts with a fuel-rich mixture in a pre-chamber and spreads to a
fuel-lean, clean-burning mixture in the main chamber. The Honda
system is so good that it meets, and is the only car yet mass
produced that does meet, the original 1977 standards. Both Ford
and Chrysler have agreements with Honda to test the system in
heavier cars. A Chrysler vice-president calls the system "the
most promising alternative to current auto engines." The EPA and
Congress have given the auto industry until 1977 to study and use
these or other promising means to meet the tougher standards for
that year.

-----

[7]A. Q. Maisel, "From Japan--A 'Clean' Car That Saves Gas,"
Reader's Digest (December 1974), p. 100.

The source of this quotation should be given in a footnote.

The summarizing paragraphs are factual, and the writer presents both sides of the issue. The concluding sentence shows the positions of government and industry in their effort to find a solution to the problem that the report discusses.

As you worked with Ms. Borelli, you have learned a number of points for writing the business report. Let's put your understanding to work.

SKILLS ACTIVITY 70

A. Read each example below, and judge whether it is effective in the situation described. If it is, write "effective" in the space. If the example should be improved, write an improved version in the space.

1. *From an opening paragraph*: In this report I intend to prove that affirmative action programs make an enormous difference in the firms where they are tried.

_____

_____

_____

2. *From a paragraph above a table*: The figures on this matter for the last half of last year are still not available to me, but I have some estimated figures that we will have to work with for now. Here they are, for what they are worth.

_____

_____

_____

_____

3. *From an opening paragraph*: In Spring 1975, there will be 150,000 square feet allocated to classroom and lecture hall space; in Spring 1976, 300,000 square feet will be allocated for such use. This represents a fantastic increase.

_____

_____

_____

4. *From a concluding paragraph*: Legislation demands that one of the emissions from cars be reduced to 3.4 ppm by 1977. As a result, safe air levels would be reached by 1978.

_____

_____

_____

5. *From a concluding paragraph*: I expect this stock to increase in value.

_____

_____

> *Given sentences from business reports, identify sentences that are effective, and rewrite ineffective sentences to improve them.*
>
> *Peer judgment or your instructor's evaluation.*
>
> *Correct identification:*
>
> | | |
> |---|---|
> | *Excellent* | *9-10* |
> | *Good* | *7-8* |
> | *Fair* | *6* |
>
> *Correct revision:*
>
> | | |
> |---|---|
> | *Excellent* | *9-10* |
> | *Good* | *7-8* |
> | *Fair* | *6* |

Name_____ Date_____

6. *From an analysis of data presented*: This will give us the unheard-of reduction in price of 50 percent.

_____

_____

7. *A heading for a concluding paragraph*: Summary of Information that Has Been Given and a New Proposal

_____

_____

8. *From a middle paragraph*: Unemployment decline, which has continued over the past four months, indicates that the recession has bottomed and that the upturn in the economy is a fact.

_____

_____

_____

9. *From a middle paragraph*: The miraculous reversal of unemployment trends indicates that our economic troubles are over.

_____

_____

10. *An opening paragraph*: We know that, if we were to see your face as you read this quarterly report, you would be smiling. You would be smiling because your company has managed to do more than just to keep its head above water in this time of recession. You would be smiling because you can expect a dividend of 60 cents per share at the end of the second quarter, which is 10 cents more than your dividend at the end of the first quarter. Although expenses have gone up because of cost-of-living wage increases (8 percent this year) and higher fuel cost, sales have risen; and this rise, together with higher prices of our products, has enabled us to declare this dividend.

_____

_____

_____

_____

_____

_____

_____

_____

_____

_____

If you achieved Fair or above, go on to the next activity. If you did not achieve Fair, discuss the problem with your instructor.

B. Make whatever improvements you can in your segment of your committee report. If you were evaluated by your peers, submit the evaluation to your instructor. If you achieved Good or above, go on to the next unit. If you did not, discuss any problems you had with your instructor.

When all the parts of the report are ready to be put together, the committee should designate one or more of its members to go over the complete draft, making whatever changes are necessary for smoothness. The report is now ready for final typing, to be done after Unit 50 has been read.

> *Given the problem of writing a section of the report, you will use impersonal language, effective subheads, orderly development, complete data, and accurate summaries and conclusions.*
>
> *Peer judgment or your instructor's evaluation:*
>
> *Excellent   5*
> *Good   4*

UNIT 50 TYPING THE REPORT

Your performance objective for this unit is:

Given the problem of presenting the report in good form,

You will type the manuscript following the correct style for each part.

Ms. Borelli suggests that you read the office manual for the style recommended by TRK.

Spacing and Margins

Type the body of the report double-spaced. Indent each paragraph five spaces. For quoted matter of more than four lines use single spacing; indent five spaces from both margins. Single-space tabulated material, with three blank lines separating such material from the body of the manuscript.

Top margin: 2 inches (13 lines) on first page; 1 inch on all succeeding pages.
Bottom margin: at least 1 inch.
Side margins: left—1 1/2 inches; right—1 inch.

Headings

The headings and subheadings become guideposts for the reader to follow. Place them effectively by following these directions:
Main headings: Center and type in all capital letters. Triple space after this heading.
Major subheadings: Type at the left margin and underline. Begin each main word with a capital. Precede sideheadings with a triple space.
Minor subheadings: Indent and underline. Capitalize only the first word in the heading. Run in the remainder of the paragraph after the subheading. Precede by a double space.

Page Numbering

The first page is usually not numbered. Number other pages on the fourth line from the top, even with the right margin.

Documentation

documenting: supplying with citations to support what is stated

The two ways of documenting sources are supplying footnotes and a bibliography. A footnote is used within the report to give further information about a statement or quotation. A bibliography, which appears at the end of the report, lists the printed sources which you have consulted and gives complete data about them.

Footnotes

A footnote should appear on the same page as the passage to which it refers. Therefore, plan the page so that there will be room for the footnotes at the bottom. Make it easy for the readers to locate the footnote by dropping their eyes from the text to the bottom of the page.

superior figures: figures typed one-half line space above the line

Number footnotes consecutively, using superior figures. The superior figure should appear after the word or passage in the text that is being documented. No space comes between the last letter or mark of punctuation and the superior figure.

Divide the body of the report from the footnotes by a 2-inch underline typed one line after the last line of the text. Double-space after this divider line. (An easy way to remember this spacing is to think of the fraction 1/2: one space before the divider line and two spaces after it.)

Indent and type the superior figure for the footnote. No space appears between the figure and the first letter of the footnote. Single space the footnote, but double space between footnotes.

When a footnote is simply an explanatory sentence or group of sentences, it is written and punctuated in the usual way. Most footnotes cite sources for quotations, direct or indirect. These are usually books or periodicals. The following styles are correct:

First reference to a book:

[1]William A. Damerst, *Clear Technical Reports* (New York: Harcourt Brace Jovanovich, 1972), p. 79.

When you refer to a work which lists no author, follow this style:

[2]*Facts and Figures on Government Finance* (New York: Tax Foundation, Inc., 1973), p. 61.

If you refer to an article in a magazine, use this style when the author is known:

[3]Carol J. Loomis, "For the Utilities, It's a Fight for Survival," *Fortune*, Vol. XCI, No. 3 (March 1975), p. 98.

When no author is given for an article, use the following:

[4]"Does It Pay to Chase Those High Yields?" *Fortune*, Vol. XCI, No. 3 (March 1975), p. 79.

BIBLIOGRAPHY

Place all sources used in the report in an alphabetical list at the end. Alphabetize by the author's last name or, if the author is unknown, by the first word of the title (except *a, an,* and *the*). Follow these examples:

Aiken, Michael, Lewis A. Forman, and Harold L. Sheppard. *Economic Failure, Alienation, and Extremism.* Ann Arbor: University of Michigan Press, 1968.

"Eisenhower, Dwight David." *Who's Who in America*, 1966-67, IV, 612.

Facts and Figures on Government Finance. New York: Tax Foundation, Inc., 1973.

Loomis, Carol J. "For the Utilities, It's a Fight for Survival." *Fortune*, XCI, No. 3 (March, 1975), p. 98.

Report of the 59th General Motors Stockholders Meeting. Detroit: General Motors Corporation, 1967.

Wyoming State Tribune, November 29, 1970, p. 3, cols. 2-3.

Note that the names of the second and third author are not inverted.

The Title Page

All reports should have a title page. The title page of the report should include all of the needed information and should look attractive.

```
                    PROPOSED CHAPTER ON REPORT WRITING




                                Prepared by

                              Agnes Borelli
                     Assistant to the Vice-President

                              Office Staff:
                           Michael Glanzman
                             Marie Maguire
                             William Sachs
                            Valerie Tremont
                           Cheryl Wisnofski




                                               Submitted to
                              William Trask, Vice-President

                                    January 15, 19--
```

Figure 14-2.
A title page.

    Center the title of the report 14 lines from the top of the page (2 inches). Be sure the wording matches that on the first page of the report.

    Center the names of the report writer or writers approximately half way down on the page. When necessary, identify the writers.

    About 2 inches from the bottom of the page, blocked at the right-hand margin, type the words "Submitted to" followed by the name of the person to whom the report is submitted and his or her title. On the next line, type the date of submission.

The Table of Contents

Reports of ten or more pages should be bound at the left and should include a table of contents, which enables the reader to see the structure of the report at a glance.

The table of contents should follow the title page. Include in it the main headings, and major and minor subheadings, each followed by the number of the page on which it begins. Use leaders (spaced-out periods) to carry the eye to the page number. Type the leaders so that they fall under one another in straight lines.

Table of Contents

Writing the Business Report 18
    The Language of the Report 19
    Paragraph-by-Paragraph Development . . . 21
    Title and Headings 22
Typing the Report 23
    Spacing and Margins 23
    Page Numbering 24
    Documentation 25
        Footnotes 25
        Bibliography 27
    The Title Page 28
    The Table of Contents 30

Figure 14-3.
A table of contents.

The last step in submitting a report (after you have carefully proofread the final typescript) is writing the letter of transmittal. See Unit 23, pages 267-70, for guidelines.

SUMMARY

The purpose of business reports is to provide information on which management can base decisions and take action. Reports should be written and typed so that they can be read and understood easily and acted upon quickly.

The steps in planning a report are: (1) state the topic and define its limits: (2) make a tentative outline; (3) collect the information you need, keeping track of all sources; (4) analyze your material, and consider how to present it; (5) organize your material, and write a rough draft.

Once the content of the report is accurate and well organized, the writer prepares a final draft. Use language that is clear, impersonal, and businesslike: avoid *I, we,* and *you*; do not use emotion-laden words; and avoid biased or subjective judgments and observations.

The first paragraph should state the topic and preview the points to be covered. Subsequent paragraphs develop those points in logical order. Headings and subheadings can be used as signposts for the reader. The concluding paragraph should summarize the main points and introduce no new ideas.

Reports are typed according to standard rules covering spacing and margins, page numbering, documentation (footnotes and bibliography), and title page and table of contents. A letter of transmittal accompanies the final typescript.

SKILLS ACTIVITY 71

A. Here is the information you have collected on four 3 x 5 cards, while doing research in the library. List what other information you need for a footnote.

1. Bronowski, *The Ascent of Man*, Little Brown, 1975

_____

2. Lorus and Margery Milne, *The Arena of Life*, New York: 1971, pp. 194-217.

_____

3. Toledo Edison, *Quarterly Report*, June 30, 1975

_____

4. "Some Trends in Business Occupations," Herbert A. Tonne, *Journal of Business Education*, pp. 10-11.

_____

Check the key on page 528. If you achieved Good or above, go on to the next problem. If you did not, discuss any difficulties you had with your instructor.

> *Given incomplete information for four footnotes, add the necessary data and type the footnotes in correct form.*
>
> *Excellent   4*
> *Good   3*

B. These sources are to go in a bibliography. Type them in proper form and order.

Lamson, Newton, Mutual Funds Tackle Commodities, New York Times, September 7, 1975, Section 3, p. 2.

Century 21 Shorthand—Theory and Practice, by Edward L. Christensen and R. Dermont Bell, Cincinnati, South-Western Publishing Co., 1974.

Annual Salary Survey, Today's Secretary, Vol. 76, March, 1974, pages 18, 19, and 37, 38.

Manual of Data Processing by Doris Forman, Prentice-Hall, 1973, Englewood Cliffs, N. J.

> *Given information for a bibliography, type it in correct form.*
>
> *Excellent   no errors*
> *Good   1-3 errors*
> *Fair   4-5 errors*

Check your answers with the key on page 528. If you achieved Fair or above, go on to C. If you did not, discuss the problem with your instructor.

C. As a committee, type the report you have written. Be sure to use uniform typewriters. Include a title page, a table of contents, and a letter of transmittal.

Name_____ Date_____

Ask your instructor to evaluate your report. If you achieved Fair or above, go on to Focus on Language. Here you will review spelling, vocabulary, and sound-alike words, and you will apply the typographical rules for dividing words.

FOCUS ON LANGUAGE

Spelling

1. analyse _____
2. subsidiery _____
3. plagierism _____
4. accomodate _____
5. encompases _____
6. transisional _____

7. diviation _____
8. jornals _____
9. catalitic _____
10. sucinct _____
11. concommitant _____
12. emision _____

> Given 12 misspelled words, write the words correctly.
>
> Excellent   12
> Good   10-11
> Fair   9

Check the key on page 528. List the words you misspelled and ask someone to read them to you as you write them again. Repeat the process until you can spell every word correctly.

Vocabulary

1. subsidiaries   a. controlled corporations   b. dependents
   c. debits   d. junior partners
2. succinct   a. short and clear   b. imitative   c. boundless
   d. conforming
3. imperative   a. unnecessary   b. necessary   c. dependent
   d. correct
4. plagiarism   a. playwriting   b. presenting another's work as one's
   own   c. the state of being a plaintiff   d. larceny
5. analyze   a. process   b. reflect   c. determine relationship of
   parts   d. put together
6. deviation   a. creation   b. roles   c. revision   d. departure
7. ingest   a. shorten   b. take in   c. allow or favor   d. dissolve
8. concomitant   a. noisy   b. deprived   c. shallow
   d. accompanying
9. comply with   a. please   b. fail to meet   c. obey   d. greet
   warmly
10. documenting   a. completing   b. supplying data to prove or
    support   c. finding old papers   d. contesting

> Given ten words followed by definitions, circle the letter of the best definition for each.
>
> Excellent   10
> Good   9
> Fair   8

Check the key on page 528. If you achieved Fair or above, go on to Sound-Alikes. If you did not achieve Fair or above, review the definitions throughout the chapter and use each word you had incorrect in a sentence. Ask your instructor to evaluate the sentences and to discuss any errors with you.

Name_____ Date_____

Sound-Alikes

residents—those who occupy a place
residence—the place that is occupied

assistants—those who assist or give aid
assistance—the aid that is given

dependents—those who rely on others
dependence—reliance on others

raise—1. (verb) to lift something up; to bring up for consideration. Principal parts: *raise, raised, raising, raised*. (*Raise* always has an object.)
　　　2. (noun) an increase in salary
rise—1. (verb) to get up or go up. (*Rise* does not have an object.) Principle parts: *rise, rose, rising, risen*
　　　2. (noun) upward movement or ascent, as *a price rise*

Example: We have raised arguments against signing this contract.
　　　The salary raises were minimal.
　　　The Congressperson said, "I rise to speak in opposition to this motion."
　　　Some parents have risen against busing.
　　　The rise in prices continues.

> Given ten problems in sound-alikes, write the correct word in the space provided.
>
> Excellent　10
> Good　　　9
> Fair　　　8

1. _____ (*Residents, Residence*) complained of the lack of services provided by the landlord.

2. The agency provided _____ (*assistants, assistance*) to families of four whose income was below $6,000.

3. For _____ (*dependents, dependence*) of veterans, benefits are provided.

4. A national issue is our _____ (*dependence, dependents*) on oil from foreign countries.

5. The sun _____ (*rises, raises*) earlier in summer.

6. What salary _____ (*raises, rises*) do you expect?

7. The employees have _____ (*raised, risen*) against the contract.

8. The agency reported a _____ (*rise, raise*) in the consumer price index.

9. The college _____ (*assistants, assistance*) were housed close to the campus.

10. Their _____ (*residents, residence*) was built in the 1930s.

Check the key on page 528. If you achieved Fair or above, go on to the next exercise. If you did not achieve Fair or above, review the definitions and try the sentences again. Discuss any problems with your instructor.

Dividing Words

Let's review the following principles.

a. Avoid dividing words as much as possible.
b. Do not divide one-syllable words: eight, right, strength, scene, weight.
c. Divide at the syllabic break: pre-ten-tion, rec-og-nize, con-gress.
d. Do not separate suffixes of two letters: do not type bas-is, cred-it, clear-ly, certain-ty.
e. Avoid separating prefixes of two letters; do not type re-view, de-cide, en-tertain.
f. Divide between two vowels sounded separately: innocu-ous, continu-ation.
g. Keep one-vowel syllables with the preceding syllable; busi-ness, copi-ous, evi-dent.
h. Divide hyphenated words only at the hyphen: son-in-law, self-esteem, cost-of-living increase.
i. Do not divide the last word in a paragraph or the last word on a page.

Show how you would type these words if they came at the end of a line.

1. subsidiaries _____

2. proxy _____

3. rapidly _____

4. pleasure _____

5. evaluate _____

6. irresponsibly (last word in paragraph) _____

7. self-evident _____

8. caught _____

9. above-entitled (last word on the page) _____

10. entailing _____

Given ten words to be divided according to typographical usage, write each word with a hyphen at the point of division, and write the letter of the rule you have applied.

Excellent	*10*
Good	*9*
Fair	*8*

Check the key on page 528. If you achieved Fair or above, you have completed your last assignment in this text. If you did not achieve Fair or above, review and try the words again. Discuss any problems with your instructor.

You have now completed your training program and are ready for placement in your full-time position.

GOOD LUCK!

Name_____ Date_____

ANSWER KEY

CHAPTER 1

Skills Activity 1

1. Economy
2. Efficiency
3. Accuracy
4. Official Record

Skills Activity 2

Letters represent an efficient, economical, accurate, and official way to:

1. Request information and materials
2. Furnish information and materials
3. Build goodwill

Focus on Language

Spelling

it's
receives
efficient
competition
exaggerated
Cincinnati
schedule
farther

management
necessitate
suppliers
consignment
top-quality
permanent
deductible

Vocabulary

1. c. suitable
2. a. asking for payment
3. b. courtesies
4. d. preventive
5. d. violent hitting together
6. b. not perceived by touch
7. b. carelessness
8. d. influence

9. a. making possible
10. c. hidden
11. b. legal papers
12. c. confirm
13. a. satisfy
14. a. flooded
15. d. forgetfulness

its, it's

1. its
2. It's
3. its
4. It's; yours
5. it's

6. It's; theirs; ours
7. its
8. its
9. it's
10. its

further, farther

1. farther
2. further
3, 4. further, further
5. further
6, 7. further, farther
8, 9. further, farther
10. Further

Proofreading

　　　　　　　　　　　　　1　　　　　　　　　　2　　　　3
If you buy your clothes at the Smyth Store, you can not only
　　　　　　　　　　　　　　　　　4　　　　　　　　5
save money but earn valuable trading stamps as well. You will
　　　　　　　　　6　　　7　　　8　9　　　　　　10
find that shopping at Smyth's is always an interesting experience.

　　　　　　11　　　　　　　　　12　　　　　13　　　　14
At Smyth's you will find the latest styles in men's and women's

　　　　　15　　　　　16　　　　　　　　　　　　17
clothing at prices that will appeal to you. Stop in soon; we'll be

looking for you.

CHAPTER 2

Skills Activity 3

(Note: Some of the following answers may be subject to a difference of opinion.)

1. full block
2. official business
3. modified block
4. modified block
5. personal business-modified block

6. personal business-modified block
7. simplified
8. modified block
9. full block
10. interoffice memorandum

Skills Activity 4

1. Ladies and Gentlemen
2. Ladies
3. Gentlemen
4. Dear Professor Frye
5. Dear Mr. Brown
6. Dear Mrs. Eckner
7. Dear Doctor Hart
8. Dear Ms. Morton
9. Dear Reverend Starbuck
10. Ladies and Gentlemen
    or Dear Friends
    or Dear People

Skills Activity 5

1. Dear Mr. Agar:
2. Dear Harold:
3. Dear President Dewey:

4. Ladies and Gentlemen:
5. Dear Mrs. Gray:

Yours truly,
Cordially,
Respectfully yours,
  or Very truly yours,
Very truly yours,
Sincerely yours,

Skills Activity 6

1. b
2. b
3. b
4. c
5. b

Skills Activity 7

Problem 1

Current date

Mrs. Leonard Houghton
9907 Engels Drive
Bethesda, MD 21811

Dear Mrs. Houghton:

Sincerely yours,

John F. Gersten
President

eg

Problem 2

Current date

Gibbs Construction Company
Attention Mr. Alfred Charlton
735 South Jackson Street
Denver, CO 80210

Dear Friends:

Very truly yours,

Michael F. Thomas
Sales Department

gt
cc Mr. Edward Cusack

Problem 3

Current date

Ms. Frances Lockwood
1347 Shady Avenue
Pittsburgh, PA 15217

Dear Ms. Lockwood:

Order 5670

Very truly yours,

Norma Timms
Purchasing Agent

am
Enclosure
    Check $10

Problem 4

Current date

Certified Mail

Mr. Bruce Lineman, Treasurer
National Optical Company
2000 Penn Avenue
Ann Arbor, MI 48103

Dear Mr. Lineman:

Very truly yours,

Peter Knight
General Manager

fe

Problem 5

Current date

Messrs. Klein & Smith
Attorneys at Law
1545 Dickens Street
Sherman Oaks, CA 95681

Gentlemen:

Prentis v. Hill

Very truly yours,

Name

Skills Activity 8

1. Mrs. Leonard Houghton
   9907 Engels Drive
   Bethesda, MD 21811

2. Gibbs Construction Company
   Attention Mr. Alfred Charlton
   735 South Jackson Street
   Denver, CO 80210

3. Ms. Frances Lockwood
   1347 Shady Avenue
   Pittsburgh, PA 15217

4.

   CERTIFIED MAIL

   Mr. Bruce Lineman, Treasurer
   National Optical Company
   2000 Penn Avenue
   Ann Arbor, MI 48103

5. Return address needed

   Your name
   Street address
   City, State, Zip Code

   Messrs. Klein & Smith
   Attorneys at Law
   1545 Dickens Street
   Sherman Oaks, CA 95681

Skills Activity 9

1. More space needed between date and inside address
2-3 Second Avenue
4. NY
5. Ms.
6. We (flush left; not indented for full-block style)
7. embarrassed
8. maintenance
9. someone
10. a.m. (second period not needed)
11. your
12. apartment
13. enclosed
14. superintendent
15. your
16. delay
17. yours
18. AF:jb

Focus on Language

Spelling

embarrassment	occasion
omitted	complimentary
calendars	popular
preceding	Congratulations
accede	succeed
separately	supersede
courtesy	exceed
omission	correspondence

Vocabulary

1. a
2. a
3. a
4. b
5. b
6. a
7. b
8. a
9. b
10. a

Hyphenation

well-known
first-rate speech
income-tax law
postwar
money-making plans
tax collector
nonessential
reasonably intelligent
well-known
up to date

CHAPTER 3

Skills Activity 10

1. Address to which book is to be sent
2. Date of magazine
3. Name and number of course, number of credits, school where taken
4. Name of person to receive oil
5. Title and business name of person
6. Name of person owing money

Skills Activity 11

1. Delete: "our stock is now low"
2. Delete: "of various makes and colors"
   Possibly delete: "each involving three to seven cars"
3. Delete: "Marital status of supervisory personnel."
4. Delete: "as well as . . . plant."
5. Delete: First sentence.
6. Delete: First two sentences.
7. Delete: Second and third sentences.

Skills Activity 12

A. Missing: How many activities must be planned?
   Discuss by telephone: Points 2 5 6 8
   Include in letter: Points 1 4 9

B. To be added: Thank him for writing so you can clear up the problem. To be deleted: Point 1
   Ideas in logical order: 1) Thank him for writing, followed by Points 3, 5, 7, 2, 4, 6, 8, 9.

C. 1. Thank him for his interest in Valley Military Academy.
   2. Enclose brochure.
   3. Note type of curriculum.
   4. Emphasize excellent educational facilities.
   5. Note that tuition is payable in installments.
   6. Note that SAT is needed for admission.
   7. Note that school grades should also be forwarded.
   8. Invite parents and son for interview.
   9. Will guide son and parents around school.
   10. Call to make appointment.

D. 1. Refer to invoice number.
   2. Note that you have paid by check.
   3. Note date of check.
   4. Note that canceled check has been returned to you.
   5. Enclose copy of canceled check.

E.
1. Your school needs your help.
2. Old swimming pool no longer adequate.
3. New pool being planned.
4. Alumni contributions needed for construction funds.
5. Pledges can be made over a period of time.
6. All contributions are tax deductible.
7. Cite advantages of new pool—e.g., some swimmers might train for Olympics.
8. Appeal to school spirit.
9. Express appreciation for any help.
10. Will supply any additional information requested.

Skills Activity 13

1. b
2. a
3. a
4. b
5. a

6. a
7. b
8. b
9. b
10. b

Skills Activity 14

1. The shareholders' meeting will be held on Monday, March 15, at 11 a.m. in the Grange Hall, Route 35, Springfield, Ohio.
2. This year the holiday shopping season began on November 3.
3. Can you resist a coat priced at only $50?
4. We have the finest display of radios in this city.
5. The cost to repair your watch will be only $5.
6. Our metropolitan area has had Christmas sales of $535 million—the highest ever recorded in this region.
7. The issue of proxy voting will be discussed at the next meeting of the Rules Committee on October 19.
8. Your savings account at the Dollar Bank earns 6 percent interest.
9. Thank you for your order for the Rex De Luxe Stereo.
10. We expect to raise $1200 to send five boys and five girls to camp next summer.

Skills Activity 15

A.
extravagant	irrelevant	resident
independent	acceptance	acquaintance
superintendent	defendant	consistent
abundant	recurrence	inheritance

B.
calendar	counselor	vendor
mortgagor	distributor	similar
(or mortgager)	competitor	lesser (meaning less)
endeavor		lessor (a person who leases)

C.
labor	acknowledgment	judgment
theater	enclose	counselor

Skills Activity 16

A. liability (n) in accounting, an entry on a balance sheet showing the debts or obligations of a business to its creditors; an obstacle or hindrance to success

quotation (n) the act or practice of reproducing a passage or statement; the words repeated or cited

B. extraneous (adj) unrelated to the matter at hand; not germane
nominal (adj) existing in name only
novice (n) a beginner in any occupation; an inexperienced person

C. requisite (n) that which cannot be dispensed with; requirement
Fulfilling the rules of the state authorities is a requisite before the area can be helped.

requisite (adj) required by the nature of things; indispensable
The requisite courses in the program are economics and statistics.

antecedent (n) that which precedes or goes before
Look for the antecedent before you write the rest of the sentence.

antecedent (adj) going or being before
Read these antecedent chapters before commenting on the conclusions.

D. casualty: an accident (especially a fatal one); anyone hurt or killed or anything lost or destroyed.
cursory: hasty; rapid; superficial
digress: ramble; wander; turn aside
ambiguous: equivocal; doubtful; obscure
facilitate: ease
convey: transport; communicate; impart
marginal: minimal; meager
denote: point out; mark; signify
criterion: standard; rule; measure

E. get ahead: increase; progress; improve; succeed
stop (noun): delay; cessation; period; sojourn; obstruction; standstill; destination
    (verb): put an end to; delay; cease; halt; close; muffle; silence; break a habit; break off; prevent
be of use: avail; serve; suffice; do; answer or serve the purpose; inure; serve one's turn; be of advantage

Skills Activity 17

A.
1. S	5. CD
2. CD	6. CP
3. CP	7. CP
4. CP	8. S

B. 1. and   2. but   3. or   4. and   5. but

Skills Activity 18

A.
1. I believe the committee will accept your plan.
2. As soon as we receive your request, we will respond by telegram.
3. New fringe benefits will be included in the contract.
4. The plans for the next meeting must be changed.
5. A clean environment can be achieved if we all work together.
6. The profit in the quarterly statement will please the shareholders.
7. A number of people in the audience disagreed with the speaker.

B. 1. I want to take this opportunity to remind you of the annual campaign of the City College Fund, now under way, and to urge you to renew your generous support.
2. Your thoughtful response in the past has enabled the Fund to open new avenues of opportunity for our students and has provided direct financial aid for young men and women in need who would not otherwise have been able to continue their education.
3. Won't you take a moment to read it and to send your check today to the City College Fund?
4. We offer attractive rates, steady employment, and pleasant working conditions.
5. We find that the Wick Investing Corporation, incorporated under the laws of this state on June 21, 1970, filed a Certificate of Amendment on September 2, 1974, and changed its name to Mountain Equities Inc.
6. They must not only rewrite the material but must also verify the figures.
7. We can either call a general meeting next month, or assume committee responsibility for making the decision.
8. He is not only an excellent salesman but also a skilled accountant.

Skills Activity 19

1. Mr. Saxon smiled when he handed the award to Mr. James.
2. John chose law as his profession because his father is a lawyer.
3. The managers told the foremen to make the decisions.
4. The bookkeeper did not understand what the treasurer was talking about.
5. The auditor told the accountant to prepare the statements.
6. The committee request that the group meet tomorrow and consider weekly meetings thereafter is not possible.
7. Our progress is slow because the computer terminal, which is located in another building, is available only during certain hours.

Skills Activity 20

1. I saw the plane as it flew high in the sky.
2. Realizing that the report was late, I filed it with an explanation.
3. Reacting quickly to the crisis, the government increased the fuel allocation.
4. The audience listened attentively as the President opened his remarks with a question.
5. After carefully reviewing the consumer reports on refrigerators, he bought the C&D brand.
6. In answer to the letter, Ms. Miller's secretary sent the book.
7. After taking telephone messages, the secretary typed careful notes.

Skills Activity 21

First paragraph begins: "It is with great pleasure. . ."

Second paragraph begins: "Our headquarters will be at. . ."

Third paragraph begins: "Your representatives and the present senior partners, . . ."

Fourth paragraph begins: "We hope that the confidence. . ."

Focus on Language

Spelling

1. comparative
2. judgment
3. delete
4. accidentally
5. colleague
6. liaison
7. decimal
8. parallel
9. qualifying
10. consistent
11. guarantee
12. advertisement
13. copious
14. redundant
15. catalogs

Vocabulary

1. d
2. c
3. a
4. a
5. b
6. d
7. c
8. a
9. b
10. c

Sound-Alikes

1. principal
2. principal
3. effect
4. personal, affect
5. principal
6. stationery, affects
7. affect
8. personnel, principles
9. stationary
10. stationery, principal
11. principle
12. principals

Agreement

1. was
2. doesn't
3. has
4. was
5. has
6. has
7. have

Tense

1. will place
2. interviewed
3. dropped
4. has been falling
5. are rising
6. had stopped, went
7. took, interviewed
8. has made, is making

Possessives

1. children's library
2. fox's fur
3. women's hats
4. Jones's son
5. dealers' inventories
6. Simmons' boss
7. accountant's statement

Proofreading

1. privilege
2. obligation
3. past
4. affect
5. two
6. principal
7. A payment
8. your
9. fund
10. 15 percent
11. A dollar
12. unit

CHAPTER 4

Skills Activity 22

0 1. Three references to "we."
0 2. Too much emphasis on the company.
0 3. Should show how "you" can benefit; how "you" can find ideas.
0 4. Too many "I's"; bragging.
0 5. Needs "you" approach.
  6. Should indicate name of the car.
0 7. Presumptuous; let reader find out for himself.

1. Your new price list is on its way to you.
2. Be the first in your neighborhood to enjoy portable color television being introduced by the company which first produced a low-cost radio and which first produced portable television.
3. Join the thousands of people who have read *Good Times.* You, too, can benefit from its excellent suggestions and make your money stretch.
4. Please consider me for the position of junior accountant in your office. If you look at my record, you will see that I am qualified for the job.
5. The payment on your claim of March 10 has been sent to you. Feel free to call whenever you need service.
6. You will enjoy the best gas mileage, the smoothest ride, and the finest service when you drive a Toro.
7. You will surely find that your trip to Paris will be a most worthwhile experience.

Skills Activity 23

This letter only partly enters the reader's world. The following words, phrases, and sentences are inappropriate:

1-2. The two sentences in the second paragraph—beyond typical layman language.
3. "P/E ratio"—too technical; not in reader's world.
4. "We do not foresee"—indefinite
5. "Our projections indicate"—indefinite
6. "But if you are a minor"—indefinite; should state age.
7. "custodial account"—technical language; not in reader's world.

Skills Activity 24

0   1. Although delays in shipping are normal at this time of the year, we will send your order as soon as we can.
0   2. Our customers are nearly always satisfied with our products and service.
0   3. Open your account with Withers and Company. Our investment advisers have been very successful in helping people increase their funds.
0   4. When your credit standing has met our standards, you should be able to borrow $25,000 with no problems.
0   5. Our shoes outlast others in the same price range in comfort and durability.
0   6. If you apply, we shall try to offer you the type job you wish.
+   7.

Skills Activity 25

1. Please send me the travel folder you advertised in the March 20 issue of *This Week.*
2. Thank you for your order of February 20.
3. Will you please consider my application for employment?
4. Thank you for bringing your account up to date.
5. Please return the questionnaire to us by December 1 so that we can publish our findings by the end of January.
6. Please remember to order soon.
7. Your materials have now been located in another department. Please excuse the delay in sending them.

Skills Activity 26

A.
1. please find (A check for $10 is enclosed.)
2. Please be advised; within a short period of time (Your order will be shipped within a week.)
3. herewith; to which; please give your earliest attention; forward with as little delay as possible; as per shipping instructions attached (Please ship the enclosed order by air express on December 1.)
4. dated July 25th; duly; and noted (Your letter of July 25 has been received.)
5. Referring to your letter of the 5th; we beg to state; there has been no error in your statement (Your statement is correct.)
6. With reference to your letter; the tenth instant; wish to state; no interference with the affairs (In answer to your question of July 10, we can assure you that you may run your department as you wish.)
7. Thanking you in advance for your consideration; I am. . . (Thank you.)

B.
1. We goofed. (Please excuse our error. Your bill should read $50.75 rather than $15.75.)
2. have a ball (You'll really enjoy shopping at Tracey's.)
3. get with it (You'll keep up with your neighbors when you buy this new outdoor pool.)
4. rap a bit (When you interview me, you can discuss my qualifications with me.)
5. ripped off (If you feel that you have been cheated at your supermarket, call your consumer affairs advocate.)

Skills Activity 27

1. When your insurance representative discusses your automobile insurance with you, he or she can also discuss life, health, and personal property insurance.
2. Now that you have had time to consider our estimate to paint and refurnish your office, have you decided to go ahead with the work?
3. I shall discuss the problem of air pollution when I speak before your group on Monday, January 5, at 8 p.m.
4. Although we cannot bid on this job, please keep us in mind for other projects.
5. The sales report shows a greater increase in sales in the East than in the West, and a greater decrease in the North Central area than in the South Central.

Skills Activity 28

1. May I have an interview at your convenience?
2. Completing arrangements without further help from you is difficult.
   To complete arrangements without further help from you is difficult.
   Arrangements will be difficult to complete without further help from you.
   Without further help from you, it will be difficult to complete the arrangements.
   If we have no further help from you, it will be difficult to complete the arrangements.
3. Improving the company's profits was his primary duty.
   To improve the company's profits was his primary duty.
   His primary duty was to improve the company's profits.

Skills Activity 29

The "new" United States Postal Service was created by Act of Congress on July 1, 1971. As its name implies, service to the customer is basic to the founding principles of the new organization.

Many of our customers have told us they would like to know more about our services as well as our products. To meet these needs and to help you get the most for your postage, we are publishing a new Postal Information pamphlet.

Skills Activity 30

1. Inflation results in an inefficient redistribution of our national resources.
2. Do not miss this opportunity. *or* Take advantage of this opportunity.
3. I believe we should hold down costs rather than increase prices.
4. You may choose several courses.
5. This course will help her in her business writing.
6. Consider safety when installing that machine.
7. Keep communication lines open to assure success of the peace agreement.

Skills Activity 31

1. We have read your letter and shall ship the order immediately.
2. The Glenn Company has produced these fabrics for the past 75 years.
3. One of our experts will draw up your itinerary and handle all details.
4. The board considered our report but made no definite decision.
5. We noticed an error on your statement.
6. The vice-president made a careful analysis of the sales report.
7. The sales manager submitted his recommendations to the vice-president.

Skills Activity 32

1. This report recommends five preferred stocks.
2. They suggest that you add to your portfolio.
3. Have all of our purchases been confirmed?
4. Economists agree that profits have declined in the past quarter.
5. A quick reading of the income statement showed that the business had lost money in the preceding period.
6. Proofread your letters carefully because careless mistakes may cost you a profitable contract.
7. In this report I shall explain why our company lost money last year.

Focus on Language

Spelling

1. b   February
2. c   immediately
3. b   tailored
4. a   onus
5. b   benefit
6. b   benefited
7. d   rebuff

Vocabulary

1. b   evoke
2. b   benevolent
3. a   call forth
4. b   decisive
5. d   omnipresent
6. a   abrupt

7. b   variations
8. b   improve
9. c   twisted
10. d   commonplace
11. d   grows smaller
12. d   spend
13. b   avoid decision
14. c   examine
15. b   soothe

Sound-Alikes

1. compliments
2. accedes, complement
3. capital
4. complement
5. exceed, accede
6. capitol, capitals
7. complement, capitol

Agreement

1. wishes,   his
2. is   her
3. has   its
4. has
5. has
6. is
7. is
8. has
9. knows
10. Does

Punctuation

1. Since . . . correctly, you . . .
2. no punctuation
3. no punctuation
4. When . . . riding, Sam . . .
5. The case has closed, but . . .
6. no punctuation
7. If I were to go, he . . .
8. Either James went to the conference, or he . . .
9. When the economy functions smoothly, . . .
10. You may file the report on schedule, or . . .

Parallel Construction

1. Our new dacron shirts wash easily, drip dry quickly, and can be worn immediately.
2. Come join our company where pay is high, working conditions are pleasant, and success is possible.
3. The mechanics are trained in repairing all makes of domestic and foreign cars.
4. The personnel manager said that this employee is intelligent, alert, and capable.
5. Trying to get ahead in business is not necessarily succeeding in it.
6. If you would like additional copies of this report, mail the enclosed form or call by phone.
7. Professor Lowell asked her students to read the chapter, write answers to questions, and comment on the chapter.

CHAPTER 5

Skills Activity 33

A. Message 2 is most effective. It contains return address in easy-to-locate spot, offers specifics, and remembers to say thank you.
   Message 1 is least effective. It lacks return address, is not specific, and is too curt.

B. Postcard should include all starred items, and be brief and accurate.

C. Request should include all items in checklist.

Skills Activity 34

A. Message would be an interoffice memorandum.
Objectives of the memorandum are to emphasize need for maximum participation and to note seriousness of past accidents.

B.
1. Letter
2. Postcard
3. Phone
4. Letter
5. Phone
6. Letter
7. Letter
8. Letter enclosing $1 check or money order

Focus on Language

Spelling

1. ascertain, choose
2. mimeographed
3. insistent
4. received
5. supersede
6. privileged
7. chosen

Vocabulary

1. a
2. b
3. a
4. b
5. a
6. a
7. a

Sound-Alikes

1. all ready
2. discreet
3. already
4. advice, discrete
5. all ready, discreet
6. advice
7. further, discreet

Agreement

1. are
2. were
3. goes
4. is
5. is
6. is
7. are

Punctuation

1. When the final figures are released, quotations in the New York, San Francisco, Chicago, and St. Louis markets will be affected.
2. This stationery is available in pink, blue, yellow, and white.
3. Professor Allen, his wife, and their two children came to the class play.
4. By next year, our company will be selling its products in Japan, Australia, and the Common Market countries.
5. Al, Pat, and Ella represented us at the science exhibit; but Bill, Jack, and Irene represented us at the business show.
6. When you were a student, you should have read works of Dickens, Emerson, and Poe and seen paintings of Monet, Turner, and Matisse.
7. We have ordered slips, staples, pencils, and pens from the stationery department.

Parallel Structure

1. The ruling of the traffic department affects both drivers and law enforcers.
2. Either pay your bills now, or deal with our attorney.
3. The company found not only an excellent site . . . .
4. Mr. Hanson will arrive either in the morning by plane or . . . .
5. Moore's Department Store expects to add not only . . . .

6. Under current economic conditions, we can obtain funds neither from the security markets nor from the banks.
7. For an additional fee, either you may obtain a receipt showing the exact address of delivery, or you may. . . .

Proofreading

1. acquiring
2. technique, one
3. than
4. Here
5. professionally
6. easy-to-care-for
7. you've
8. commissioned
9. break
10. seeds, plants, trees, and
11. in your area

CHAPTER 6

Skills Activity 35

1. Suggestions for improvements:
   1. Insert colon after salutation.
   2. "It has come to my attention"—too roundabout. Preferable to say "I have learned" or "I have heard."
   3. "on my behalf"—old fashioned
   4. "has been partly instrumental"—unnecessary words. Preferable to say "has helped."
   5. "in me acquiring"—incorrect. Should be: "in my acquiring"
   6. "acquiring"—Check thesaurus or dictionary for better word.
   7. "position of lifeguard" preferable to "lifeguard position."
   8. "I would like to take this opportunity"—language too slow moving and old fashioned
   9. "Thank you"—quotes not needed as expression used
   10. "It means that"—be more specific.
   11. Personalize third paragraph: "You may be sure, Mr. Robbins, that . . . ."
   12. "Thanking you again"—old fashioned
   13. "I remain"—old fashioned

2. Suggestions for improvements:
   1. First sentence too long-winded. "Thank you" preferable to "May I extend my appreciation to you."
   2. "Missive" is pompous and old fashioned. Letter or note preferred.
   3. "Regarding my achievement"—pompous.
   4. "Needless to say"—then why say it? Unnecessary words.
   5. "I expect to continue doing well at college"—sounds boastful; better to say "I hope to continue etc."
   6. "than"—word misspelled; should be "then."
   7. "I hope etc."—condescending tone
   8. "Thanks for remembering me." Unnatural tone, not what one would expect from a person who closes with "Your friend."

Problems 3-6. Points to watch:
   1. Begin with "thank you"
   2. Include short statement showing how the favor helped the individual
   3. Use correct form of letter, including proper method of address, salutation, complimentary closing.

Skills Activity 36

1. Suggestions for improving Julio Ramos's letter:
   1. Delete "th" in March 4.

2. Obtain name of the Consul of Spain.
3. Delete "th" in 58 Street.
4. Write out Street.
5. Write out East.
6. Use abbreviation NY (no periods).
7. Add Zip code.
8. Use correct salutation: Dear Senor (last name):
9. Rewrite first two sentences to avoid unnecessary information.
10. Insert comma after the word "Therefore."
11. Rewrite fourth sentence to remove ambiguity: ". . . how business relations are conducted between Spain and the United States."
12. "I would like you to come"—verges on the impolite. This is an invitation, not a command.
13. Delete "th" in April 4.
14. "Thank you for your affirmative answer to this invitation"—presumptuous and pompous.
15. "If you wish any further information about the program, you. . ." Insert comma after program.
16. "at the above address"—unnecessary, since letterhead states address.
17. Indicate date when reply to invitation is needed.
18. Room 115 insufficient; also indicate name of building or campus location.
19. Specify time of meeting.
20. Check proper closing for a consular officer.

Problems 2-6. Points to watch: proper form of letter; purpose of the meeting; the amenities—please and thank you; specific time, place, day, date, and topic; direct address where possible

Skills Activity 37

1. Jane Franklin's letter is the best. Reasons:
    1. Return address is specific and correctly arranged
    2. Inside address and salutation are correct
    3. Complimentary close is appropriate
    4. Request is specific—leaves no questions
    5. Requests confirmation.

Problems 2-4. Points to watch: correct form; the amenities—please and thank you; specific dates, kind of accommodations, and rates; request for confirmation

5. Corrections on Hotel Summers letter:
    1. First
    2. Avenue
    3. Washington   or   WA
    4. Zip code following state
    5. November
    6. 1
    7. 1976
    8. No end-of-line punctuation for inside address
    9. NY
    10. Zip code following state
    11. Ladies and Gentlemen
    12. Colon following salutation to agree with comma following complimentary close
    13. Needs more than one paragraph for balance
    14. Could use active voice to thank for receiving a confirmation

15. Could use a transition word to begin second sentence
16. Write out November in all cases
17. Could write numbers in better form in dates
18. accommodations
19. already
20. Respectfully—not an appropriate closing; Sincerely preferable

Skills Activity 38

1. Letter b would be sent. Reasons:
    1. Remembers the amenities. Says thank you and remembers to ask for another invitation.
    2. States a valid reason.
    3. Uses a positive approach to plan for next year.
    4. Other letters insult the reader by implication.

Problems 2-5. Points to watch: Expression of regret; honest reason; appreciation for invitation; correct form

Focus on Language

Spelling

1. precede
2. committed
3. license
4. accommodations
5. numerous
6. incurred
7. intracollege

Vocabulary

1. c   clear
2. a   sympathy
3. d   deceitful
4. b   use as a means
5. c   tramp wearily
6. a   importance
7. d   ridiculous
8. b   showy
9. a   proportionate
10. c   manufacture
11. d   delay
12. b   portrayed
13. a   repeat
14. d   open insult
15. d   impudent
16. a   entangled
17. b   having no originality
18. c   people of high rank

Sound-Alikes

1. adapted
2. council, too
3. Too, counsel
4. counsel
5. adopt, too
6. adept
7. council
8. counsel

Proofreading

1. Insurance Prospect
2. 9 cents
3. protection?
4. check
5. substantial
6. amount
7. paid
8. accidental
9. hours
10. year—near
11. world
12. world—at
13. There's
14. examination
15. insured
16. protection?
17. statistics
18. National Safety Council
19. accidental
20. it's
21. death
22. doesn't
23. sense
24. insurance?

CHAPTER 7

Skills Activity 39

A. The most effective letter is 3 because the writer, Leslie Stone,
1. Remembered to say please.
2. Gave specifics.
3. Spoke positively about earning cash by selling.
4. Was concise, courteous, and correct.

B. Problems 1-3. Points to watch:
Remember amenities; return address and date, inside address, correct salutation, and enclosure notation.
1. Give specific details; include address of friend who is to receive candy; remember enclosure notation.
2. Name book specifically; request book to be billed or enclose check or money order.
3. Refer to date and place of ad; specify purchase; mention enclosure of check.

C. Corrections on letter:
1. Salutation incorrect. Preferable to say—"Ladies and Gentlemen:"
2. past (not passed)
3. eight
4. Because (rather than "due to the fact")
5. Insert comma after you ("last time I wrote you,")
6. Add the word "Please" before "send"
7. 100 mg. not 300 mg. and specify quantity wanted
8. I am enclosing (not "I will enclose")
9. Party Book (two words)
10. I hope (rather than "Trusting that")
11. I am,—old fashioned ending
12. Very truly yours, or Sincerely yours, preferable to Respectfully yours,

Skills Activity 40

1. Improvements in letter:
1. Avenue
2. Illinois or IL
3. Zip code
4. October
5. 21
6. Drive
7. IL
8. Ladies and Gentlemen
9. Colon (:) after salutation
10. College
11. Therefore
12. "we will expect your usual"—presumptuous
13. November
14. 4
15. children
16. Thank you.

Problems 2-5. Points to watch:

2. State problem; specify details—day, date, time, number of people; request menus with prices; inquire about the final date for making reservations.
3. Specify name of book; tell what you know about it; ask if stores can get copy; ask the price.
4. Get to point immediately.
5. Get to point immediately; mention that local stores do not have radio.

Skills Activity 41

1. Letter 3 is the most effective because:
1. Maria has added depth to her paper with original figures—a valid reason for delay.

2. Remembers to say thank you for allowing extra time.
3. Wishes the professor a happy holiday.
Note: Herewith is a poor beginning; she should say: Here is. . . .

Letter 2 is also effective. It has a personal touch in the second paragraph. Letter 1 is flippant.

Problems 2-4

2. Mention enclosure and its purpose.
3. Mention enclosure and purpose; give sources of clippings for further reference; mention point found interesting; enclosure notation at end.
4. Mention enclosure and purpose; mention that material should interest students.

Skills Activity 42

A. 1. a. State problem calmly—mail delivery erratic.
b. State specific instances of poor mail service.
c. Inquire about having own post-office box if home service cannot be improved.
d. Thank postmaster for considering the problem and solving it.
2. a. State problem concisely—two broken records.
b. Identify date and amount of specific purchase of four records.
c. Ask for replacements.
d. Remember the amenities.
3. a. Explain disappointment at receiving faulty goods.
b. Tell what the error is and enclose sample of stationery.
c. Ask that new stationery be printed with correct address at no additional cost.
d. Remember the amenities.

B. 1. a. Tone of letter nasty; delete first sentence and second paragraph.
b. Correct punctuation in second sentence of first paragraph.
c. Ask for a replacement copy as well as allowance for postage for returning defective copy.
d. Remember amenities—say "Please" and "Thank You."
2. a. Salutation and closing incorrect
b. Delete last two sentences in first paragraph and substitute a calm explanation such as: "Although I gave them proper care, the azaleas have not bloomed this year."
c. Delete final paragraph and substitute a solution such as: "Since you guaranteed the bushes, I know that you will replace them. I am enclosing a copy of my bill so that you can trace the original order quickly."
d. Remember the amenities—"Please" and "Thank you."

C. 1. Need inside return address.
2. Delete comma after Virginia.
3. Change Virginia to VA to conform to Post Office regulations.
4. Salutation incorrect—"Sir": (not sir)—but "Ladies and Gentlemen": preferable to "Dear Sir":
5. Delete comma after salutation and insert colon (:).
6. Sending (not send)
7. Received
8. Preferable to say "repaired" rather than "fixed" machine.

9. totally
10. Portugal
11. Better to say "because" (not "on account of the fact that")
12. handling
13. Insert commas after machine and warranty—"The machine, still under warranty,"
14. warranty
15. May
16. retrieved—inappropriate word
17. Insert comma after bought—". . . where it was bought,"
18. "lemon"—slang word to be avoided
19. receive
20. Insert commas after "I" and "therefore."
21. therefore
22. Insert customer's name—". . . that you are giving Ms. Dos Santos her. . ."
23. "just compensation in the form of"—too wordy, old fashioned
24. handled
25. Conclusion is an incomplete sentence.
26. Need enclosure notation.

Focus on Language

Spelling

absence   transmittal   processing   merchandise
dissatisfied   reputable   necessary

registrar   quite   decipher   sophomore   unnecessary
process   porcelain

Vocabulary

1. a   high level of skill
2. c   subject to a procedure
3. b   gift
4. b   set down as a list
5. c   asked for
6. b   compact
7. c   being away
8. a   voluntary giving up a right or privilege
9. a   passing from one to another
10. b   having means to pay debts
11. c   interpret
12. d   angry
13. d   honorable
14. a   arrogant
15. c   can be heard
16. b   end
17. b   real to the touch
18. d   twice a year

Sound-Alikes

1. Every one
2. They're
3. formerly
4. their
5. formally
6. Everyone
7. Formerly

Punctuation

1. correct
2. Mayor, . . . investigation,
3. correct
4. Ruskin, . . . sides,
5. Nations, . . . Smith,
6. correct
7. correct

Capitalization

1. The Superintendent of Documents publishes the <u>Statistical Abstract</u>.
2. James Knox of the Bureau of Labor Statistics wrote a book called, <u>Employment Opportunities in the Middle West</u>.
3. Professor Smith's new book, <u>A History of Economic Thought</u>, will be published in September.
4. Frank Sheldon from the Bureau of Internal Revenue spoke on the topic, "New Tax Regulations Affecting Business."
5. The <u>Winged Victory</u> is a famous statue in the Louvre in Paris.
6. "Steel Builds for a New Era" eas a leading article in October's <u>Fortune</u> magazine.
7. Both the Democrats and the Republicans contributed to material in the <u>Congressional Record</u>.

Pronouns

1. keep   are
2. are   is
3. is   were
4. are   is
5. is
6. is   am
7. has

Proofreading

1. Depositor
2. Colon following salutation to agree with comma following closing
3. No paragraph idention in full-block style
4. know
5. interested
6. convenient
7. re-turn
8. your savings
9. designed
10. one-stop
11. reality
12. governing savings banks,
13. we (drop "a" at end of line)
14. allowed
15. withdrawal
16. somebody
17. else—
18. him—
19. and he can
20. You'll
21. today's
22. ever—
23. scene

CHAPTER 8

Skills Activity 43

A. 1. b
   2. a
   3. a
   4. b
   5. b

B. 1. Please consider me for the position in your management trainee program, advertised in the <u>Graphic</u> on March 1.
   2. Now that I have completed my secretarial science education, I believe that I am qualified to fill the position of administrative assistant, advertised in the <u>Graphic</u> on June 15.

3. I am applying for the position of structural engineer, which you advertised in the Herald of March 7.
4. Jim Sloman has suggested that I apply for the accounting position which is now open at your firm.
5. Given past experience and education in economic research, I wish to apply for the job of research assistant, advertised in the Journal on April 18.

C. 1. I wish to apply for the position of bookkeeper advertised in the Times on March 1.
2. Please consider me for the bookkeeping position advertised in the Sunday edition of the Times.
3. I am applying for the position of bookkeeper advertised in the Times of March 1.
4. Please consider my qualifications for the bookkeeping position now open with your firm.
5. I wish to be considered for the position of bookkeeper, advertised in the Herald on May 15.

Skills Activity 44

A. 1. b   4. b
   2. a   5. a
   3. b

B. 1. As you will note on my enclosed Data Sheet, I have 16 credits in economics and financial institutions, in addition to my work in political science. These courses have given me the necessary background for understanding the banking business.
2. Courses in office administration and in administrative secretarial procedures have given me an understanding of the importance of office systems.
3. The high grades I received in my engineering design course are evidence of my interest in this field.
4. My two summers at Topps have given me valuable experience in practical accounting.
5. This position would offer me an excellent opportunity to gain experience in economic research.

Skills Activity 45

A. 1. b   4. b
   2. a   5. b
   3. a

B. 1. Please call me at 372-1220 to tell me when I may come to discuss the job with you.
2. May I come to your office to talk about my background? You may call me at 397-4857 and set the date and time at your convenience.
3. I would appreciate your granting me an interview at your convenience. Please call me at 751-4212. When we meet, you may be interested to hear my ideas on modern road construction.
4. If you are interested in considering me for the position of accountant, please call me at 835-3488 for an interview.
5. The enclosed Data Sheet will acquaint you with my educational background and work experience. I would like an opportunity to meet with you at your convenience. Please call me at 734-4224.

Skills Activity 46

A. Points to observe:
   1. Note errors: whom (not who) you are seeking; completing; committee; past; two semesters; part-time
   2. First paragraph too wordy and not specific
   3. Note the number of "I's" in second and third paragraphs.

B. Points to observe:
   1. Note errors: "hereby" and "enter the world of employment"—old fashioned; enclosed (not inclosed)
   2. First paragraph too wordy and not specific
   3. Note the number of "I's" throughout the letter

C. Follow guidelines listed on page 315.

Skills Activity 47

1. Points to observe:
   a. Note errors: write out date; "I sure want"
   b. Rewrite second paragraph to focus on reader's point of view.
   c. Letter is brief but not specific; poorly worded.

2. Points to observe:
   a. Note date of interview in first paragraph.
   b. Wrong emphasis in second paragraph. Rewrite to stress the job and your qualifications, not the fringe benefits.
   c. Third paragraph too abrupt.

Skills Activity 48

A. Points to observe in Gene's letter:
   a. Misspelled words: accept; accepted
   b. "kind offer" should be reworded—old fashioned expression
   c. Final sentence needs rewording with focus on reader.
   d. "in two weeks"—vague; state exact date.

B. Letter 2 is more effective because:
   1. Its tone is positive.
   2. It is well written.
   3. It is correct in spelling and punctuation.
   4. It focuses on the reader.

Skills Activity 49

For letters 1 and 4, see guidelines on page 313; for letter 2, see guidelines on page 319; for letter 3, see guidelines on page 323.

Focus on Language

Spelling

A. 1. charitable   5. extracurricular
   2. advisable   6. successive
   3. attendance   7. initiative
   4. recommendation

B. 1. likable   5. dictionary
   2. eligible   6. separately
   3. permissible   7. superintendent
   4. similar

Vocabulary

1. prospective
2. chronological, inverse
3. embossed
4. capacity
5. preliminary
6. ingenuity
7. extracurricular
8. initiative
9. proven
10. Strive, tournament
11. crucial

Sound-Alikes

1. attendance
2. than
3. past
4. then
5. passed
6. attendants, attendance
7. attendance

Punctuation

1. No, . . . methods.
2. Mr. Cerone asked,
3. Yes, Mr. Wise,   name.
4. June, Mr. Peters?
5. "Well, . . . $500,000," . . . reported, . . . anticipated."
6. Correct
7. said, "Yes, . . . now."

Capitalization

1. Mr. Ansell   "We. . . South."
2. Members of the Federal Reserve Board   Far East
3. Frank Perotti   How
4. Drive
5. "Have. . . 'Middle Management and Computers' " Mr. Drew   Dun's Review
6. Ms. Lopez   "Have
7. Middle East

Skills Activity 50

A. Points to watch for:

   Situation 1: a. Compose correct memo that enables teachers and chairpersons to list courses for current term, room assignments, and expected class enrollments.

   b. The form is important—make it easy for busy people to respond immediately.

   c. Remember the amenities.

   Situation 2: a. Compose a correct memo that gives precise details—date, time, charge, and place.

   b. Be sure to state purpose of dinner and that charge includes gift contribution as well as dinner.

   c. Remember the amenities.

   Situation 3: a. Compose a correct memo that clearly states its purpose.

   b. Be sure to include precise details—time and place—and ask for suggestions to improve safety.

   c. Remember the amenities.

B. Errors corrected in memo:

   1. Writing is immature.
   2. Too many I's
   3. Sentences lack variety.
   4. February
   5. 29,
   6. February 25
   7. Memo should not have salutation.
   8. Thank you
   9. Here
   10. graduated from college
   11. Accounting 1, 2, & 3 (space needed after commas)
   12. liaison

13. No complimentary closing on memo
14. All information lines should begin at same point
15. "certain of getting" is poor expression

C. Memo 2 is more effective.

   Reasons: Tone is positive; the first memo is braggy.
   Details points carefully
   Suggest trial period.

D. Point to watch for:

   1. Use correct memo form.
   2. Identify course by specific title.
   3. Demonstrate responsibility and interest.
   4. Show more positive attitude.
   5. Expand on actual course content.

Skills Activity 51

A. Points to watch for:

   Situation 1: a. Compose correct memo that explains purpose of bulletin board notices

   b. is precise in specifying details

   c. is clear on what is an acceptable notice

   d. is objective in stating what is unacceptable

   e. is courteous in tone

   Situation 2: a. Compose correct memo that restates company policy concisely

   b. explains necessity for employees observing rules regarding coffee breaks

   c. states time when coffee and pastries will be served

   d. explains objectively why employees should remain at their desks

   e. is positive in tone

   Situation 3: a. Compose correct memo that clearly states company rules on telephone usage

   b. that explains necessity for observing these rules

   c. that is positive in tone and asks for the cooperation of employees

   d. that offers assistance to employees who might have difficulty with new system

   e. that is polite yet firm

B. Suggested improvements on mailgram directive

   1. Explain when to use mailgrams before you explain how to use them.

   2. Under "How to Use It": Explain more precisely how to give message to Western Union. Avoid the pronoun "it"; substitute for clarity the Noun "mailgram."

   3. Follow guidelines listed on page 349.

Focus on Language

Spelling

1. worthwhile
2. typify
3. occurrence
4. receive
5. assure
6. expense
7. business

Vocabulary

1. a bring about
2. b planned
3. b habitually talking
4. c puzzling
5. d be an example of
6. a support
7. d guess
8. a proof
9. b regulation
10. c based on fact
11. d promise
12. b approval
13. a wordy
14. c have an effect

Sound-Alikes

1. respectfully
2. site, assured
3. cite
4. respectively
5. cite, ensures
6. sight
7. respectfully, site

Punctuation

1. here; then
2. economical; it
3. thoughtfully;
4. July 10, 1967; Seattle,
5. on time,
6. spending; hence,
7. hard; however,

Capitalization

1. Mr. Raymond Ewen   Ewen Electronics
2. General George Gates   "We   Rome   Friday
3. The
4. John Eggert,   Springdale   Secretary Connors
5. Marvin Slade,   Alpine Ski Club
6. The   "You   English   History 701   Economics 4
7. A

Pronouns

1. whom
2. who
3. whom
4. Whom
5. who
6. whom
7. whom

Proofreading

1. Johnson and Marsh
2. October
3. 10
4. Expand subject title
5. It's
6. welcome
7. employee
8. acquainted
9. delete "of" (before "fine")
10. women
11. pleasant
12. these
13. experienced supervisors
14. supervisors
15. coworkers
16. business
17. convenient
18. personnel
19. discussed,
20. your
21. supervisor
22. you—
23. knowledge
24. experience
25. within
26. closing,

CHAPTER 10

Skills Activity 52

A.

1. Ineffective. An immediate refusal without stating reason; does not spotlight the reader.
2. Ineffective. Insults the customer.
3. Ineffective. Implies that the customer is not being truthful; unbusinesslike.
4. Effective. Offers a good solution to a problem.
5. Ineffective. Sounds very old fashioned; stodgy.
6. Ineffective. Negative approach; inconclusive.
7. Effective. Regrets delay, but offers instant solution.

B.

1. Ineffective. Shows a grudging attitude.
2. Effective. States a well-known policy reason for the refusal.
3. Ineffective. Insulting to the customer; negative.
4. Ineffective. Offers an exchange but is condescending in tone and uses outdated language.
5. Ineffective. Grudging, scolding attitude toward customer.
6. Ineffective. Lecturing the customer; rash overstatement.
7. Effective. Offers a constructive solution.

Skills Activity 53

Follow guidelines for letter listed on page 368.

Skills Activity 54

A. Cases 1-3: Follow guidelines on page 374.

B. Rewrite letter, following guidelines on page 374.

Skills Activity 55

Follow guidelines on page 376.

Focus on Language

Spelling

guidance   forestall   thoroughly   recommendations
process   visible   already   inconvenienced

Vocabulary

1. accept, expect, orientation
2. recipient
3. unwarranted
4. substantiating
5. rapport
6. guidance
7. conspicuous
8. accede
9. rectify
10. deficient
11. invoice
12. thoroughly
13. minimize
14. spurious
15. alleviated
16. ample
17. qualified
18. visible
19. culprits
20. interim
21. behemoth

Sound-Alikes

1. accept
2. loose
3. lose
4. accepted
5. except
6. loose, lose
7. lose

Pronouns

1. our
2. I
3. I
4. him, me
5. me
6. my
7. our

Punctuation

1. Illinois; Massachusetts; Washington;
2. Spanish, Italian;
3. Monday, January 8; Thursday, February 1.
4. Correct
5. game,
6. Correct
7. serious; therefore,

Numbers

1. Forty-seven; three
2. 6
3. ten
4. 25
5. three
6. seven
7. eight

Proofreading

1. 10
2. WI
3. Miss
4. Mendez
5. know
6. can not only
7. one
8. there
9. delete the
10. warranty
11. No paragraph indention
12. your
13. buying
14. long-range
15. parks?
16. already
17. three
18. high-quality
19. aside
20. you've
21. your
22. safari,
23. two
24. complimentary
25. we'll
26. your

CHAPTER 11

Skills Activity 56

1. Suggestions for improving first letter:
   a. First sentence much too negative; "welcome" order is an outdated expression.
   b. First sentence in second paragraph too lengthy; past (not "passed") three years; "as regards"—old fashioned.
   c. Fourth paragraph is boastful.
2. Suggestions for improving second letter:
   a. Mention all products ordered, not just the clasp envelopes.
   b. Mention date of shipment.
   c. Since Morris had no previous business with Pioneer, you may assume that credit references and financial statement accompanied the order. Ted should mention this and thank him.
   d. Lecture on credit terms sounds a bit condescending. Be factual and to the point.

Skills Activity 57

1. Suggestions for improving Linda Butler's letter:
   a. Avoid expression "We want you"; strikes the reader as too demanding.
   b. Avoid "aforesaid named company"—an old fashioned expression.

   c. Avoid "you should be able to"—verges on insulting.
   d. Final paragraph too abrupt; needs rewording.
2. Points to watch for:
   a. Include name and address of person seeking credit.
   b. Enclose form and ask reference to complete it.
   c. Assure reference that information will be kept confidential.
   d. Offer reciprocity.

Skills Activity 58

1. Suggestions for improving Wilfredo Goya's first letter:
   a. "Valued" order of "June 10th"—old fashioned expression; delete "valued" and "th."
   b. Rewrite second sentence of first paragraph to achieve better tone.
   c. Rewrite complete second paragraph to achieve better tone.
   d. Rewrite third paragraph to avoid condescending attitude.
2. Suggestions for improving Wilfredo's second letter:
   a. In first sentence, use a more specific word than "interest."
   b. In second paragraph, be more tactful in refusing credit.
   c. In third paragraph, reword first sentence to avoid passive voice.
   d. The word "peruse" comes across as unnatural; choose a better word.
3. Suggestions for improving Wilfredo's third letter:
   a. First sentence lacks sincerity.
   b. Second paragraph lacks tact.
4. Suggestions for improving Advanced Credit problem:
   a. Tone is crude and insulting throughout.
   b. Note "businessman" is one word.
   c. Note incorrect use of the word "effect"; should be "affect."
   d. Note in first sentence of second paragraph the incorrect use of "you buying"; should be "your buying."
   e. Note the misspelled word "inclose"; should be "enclose."

Skills Activity 59

1. Suggestions for improving letter to Mr. and Mrs. Herbert Meyer from the Heaslip Fuel Oil Company:
   a. Tone of letter is insulting and commanding.
   b. The expression "duly appreciate" is old fashioned.
   c. Rewrite first paragraph (1.) to express a sincere welcome to Mr. and Mrs. Meyer as charge account customers, and (2.) to tell them that they may begin using their account at once.
   d. Rewrite second paragraph to explain statement and terms of sale factually but in a less commanding tone.
   e. Write concluding paragraph that (1.) invites customers to take full advantage of their new account, and (2.) that offers them good service.
2. Advanced Credit Problem: Follow guidelines listed on page 410.

Focus on Language

Spelling

1. curiosity
   reliability
   indebtedness
   reciprocity

2. partially; specify; abruptly; responsibility; solely; references; promptly

Vocabulary

1. b adaptability
2. b examined
3. b only
4. c meantime
5. c shrewd
6. a incomplete
7. a evaluates
8. c money owed
9. c state
10. d inquisitive
11. c ownership
12. c analytical
13. a prophesy
14. d suddenly
15. b essential
16. c keenness
17. a prove
18. c tell
19. d examining
20. a turn away
21. d mutual exchange

Punctuation

1. "Knowledge . . . anyone's writing," . . . Knox.
2. asked, "Have . . . chapter 'Applying for Consumer Credit'?"
3. "The . . . fashions," said the designer, "will . . . people."
4. Da Vinci's painting, Mona Lisa, is priceless.
5. "Buy now and pay later" is . . . accounts.
6. "Look out!" . . . driver.
7. He said, "One . . . another"; he . . . principle.

Numbers

1. 4, $40 $1,000
2. 75 cents,   five
3. 25 cents,   five 5-cent stamps.
4. $2.5 million $2 million
5. $6.00, $10.00
6. Correct
7. $4 million

Misplaced Modifiers

1. Before rejecting these designs, compare them with other plans.
2. Relying on his ability to react quickly in emergencies, the driver of the car picked up speed.
3. Because the auditorium was already filled with students, the visitors could find no place to sit.
4. Referring to your letter of March 13, we feel that you should have taken a different approach.
5. We shall adjust the incorrect invoice at once.
6. You will find a copy of the employee-evaluation chart lying on the desk.
7. After discussing the proposal, we took the vote.
(Note: Other answers may also be correct since there are several ways to rephrase a sentence to avoid a dangling phrase.)

Proofreading

1. Insert date.
2. Attention line before Woodlawn Avenue
3. Avenue
4. Connecticut (preferably CT)
5. Plural salutation
6. received
7. layout
8. complete
9. already
10. F.I.A. (delete extra period)
11. three
12. four
13. layout
14. Number 2
15. superseded
16. Number 6
17. I (not the "writer")
18. understand ("have learned" would be better terminology)
19. Boston (no comma)
20. progress has
21. yours, (insert comma to agree with colon after salutation)
22. Treasurer
23. Enclosure notation needed
24. typist's initials

CHAPTER 12

Skills Activity 60

A.
1. c
2. b
3. a
4. b
5. a
6. b
7. c
8. b
9. c
10. c

B. Rewrite sentences to focus on the reader—for example:
1. Read what membership in the Book Club can do for you.
2. Where were you on November 5 when darkness fell?
3. Remember the fun you had at Lake Joy last summer?
4. Your local dealer has a Mayfair Washing Machine waiting to be delivered to you.
5. Notice how the quality of the paper you use affects your reader's reaction.
6. Current Review wins again!
7. The executive with everything but time needs the Empire portable dictating machine.

C.
1. Get your money's worth with Arax tires.
2. Use Skickem to keep your plastic floor tiles smooth and firm. Playroom floors always keep their smart-as-new look.
3. Do you remember last December 26? Were you prepared to cope with the record snowfall? Were you huffing and puffing. . . .

Skills Activity 61

A.
1. Take advantage of reduced prices on appliances at our year-end sale.
2. RZP information networks transmit your message at the speed of light. Your message is received as soon as you send it.
3. Look over the independent tours and flight departures in our latest brochure.
4. Please distribute these career materials to your prospective graduates who may wish to begin a career in IRS.
5. Play our new game, Energy Crisis, for hours of entertainment while you solve the energy problem.
6. These Bicentennial commemoratives will increase in value as more people decide to invest their funds in precious metals and coins.

B.
1. a. Reason: Sentence focuses on prospective buyer; puts product in hands of buyer.
2. b. Reason: Sentence sells on the basis of past satisfaction.
3. c. Reason: Sentence is attention-getting and to the point.
4. c. Reason: Sentence gives testimonial to past success.
5. b. Reason: Sentence cites specific achievements that can be examined.
6. b. Reason: Sentence is specific.

Skills Activity 62

A.
1. a. Reason: Sentence is specific and to the point.
2. a. Reason: Sentence is to the point; makes it easy to order and receive quick delivery.

3. c. Reason: Sentence is direct; makes it easy to receive magazine.
4. a. Reason: Sentence is direct; shows how to speed delivery.
5. b. Reason: Sentence is specific and to the point; makes it easy to answer letter.
6. a. Reason: Sentence tells how to get quick results.
7. b. Reason: Closing is friendly; enables reader to respond quickly and easily.
8. a. Reason: Sentence indicates concisely what to do to receive information.
9. b. Reason: Closing is polite. Question calls for answer.
10. a. Reason: Sentence is direct and to the point.

Skills Activity 63

A. 1. Letter to commercial banks
   1. Attention-getting device: First two questions
   2. Reader's desire aroused: Second paragraph
   3. Writer tried to convince: Third and Fourth paragraphs
   4. Action writer urges: Concluding paragraph
2. Letter to office manager
   1. Attention-getting device: First two questions
   2. Reader's desire aroused: Second paragraph
   3. Writer tried to convince: Third and Fourth paragraphs
   4. Action writer urges: Concluding paragraph
3. Letter from tour operator
   1. Attention-getting device: First paragraph
   2. Reader's desire aroused: Second paragraph
   3. Writer tried to convince: Second and Third paragraphs
   4. Action writer urges: Concluding paragraph
4. Letter from automobile dealer
   1. Attention-getting device: First and Second paragraphs
   2. Reader's desire aroused: Third paragraph
   3. Writer tried to convince: Third and Fourth paragraphs
   4. Action writer urges: Concluding paragraph

B. Letter 1 is more effective. Reasons:
1. Letter 1 is longer; it focuses much more on the reader.
2. Letter 2 is brief but is too curt at times.
3. Letter 1 is more persuasive and enthusiastic; it projects the idea that the book described has true prestige.
4. The use of the word "implore" in concluding paragraph of Letter 2 is inappropriate; the purpose of a sales letter is to *sell*, not to *beg*.

C. In addition to including ideas listed on page 448, you will want to:
1. Check for correct letter form.
2. Arouse reader interest.
3. Develop ideas that will guide parents to make a positive decision.
Suggestions for organizing letter:
1. Open with information about new facilities.
2. Describe plans for summer activities.
3. Encourage early reservations.
4. Include cost-free, easy-to-complete form for making reservation.

D. Include items listed on page 449. In addition, be sure to:
1. Check for correct letter form.
2. Remind customer of salesman's visit and demostration.
3. Restate good features of product.
4. Develop ideas that will guide customer to make a positive decision.
5. Offer trade-in
6. Make it easy for customer to place order.

E. Include points mentioned on page 449. Also:
1. Be sure to use correct letter form.
2. Open with question asking if people want efficient transportation and assured accomodations.
3. Tell how to organize group to get benefits of trip.
4. Tell how much better for all to be together with no driving worries.
5. Make it easy to make reservations.

F. Follow-up letter to C:
1. Ask if reader has overlooked reservation form.
2. Tell that space is running out.
3. Set time limit for reserving.
4. Enclose another reservation form.
Follow-up letter to D:
1. Does reader have any questions about vacuum demonstration?
2. Reiterate strong points about product.
3. Send another order blank.

G. Advanced Credit
1. Congratulate owner of home freezer.
2. Tell how product will help him or her enjoy the freezer.
3. Describe various good features of product.
4. Provide check list to send in order.

H. 1. Open with a question: "Don't wait too long to have your car winterized?"
2. Encourage customer to come to garage while service is available without rushing.
3. Encourage customer to make appointment.

I. 1. Emphasize fellowship with membership in club.
2. Tell what activities the club has planned.
3. Tell about its facilities.
4. Make it easy to join.

Focus on Language

Spelling

glean; prior; fulfill; preference; potential; coverage

Vocabulary

1. news space — coverage
2. glean — collect
3. media — agencies
4. before — prior
5. premise — proposition
6. potential — possible
7. attributes — qualities
8. inadequate — insufficient
9. ultimately — finally
10. predilection — preference
11. patronize — support
12. excerpts — extracts

13. chrome	metal
14. fulfill	satisfy
15. enlivened	stimulated
16. topical	pertaining to a topic
17. preference	choice
18. entails	involves
19. unique	sole
20. inducement	incentive
21. inertia	inactivity
22. procrastinate	delay
23. expend	use up
24. prudent	wise
25. eminent	prominent

Punctuation

1. demonstrating—as . . . occasions— . . . appeal.
2. New York, Chicago, Los Angeles, Boston, and Seattle.
3. term: president, Bill Nally; treasurer, Ralph Hicks; secretary, Irene Furman.
4. proposal—the . . . operating; the . . . available; people . . . spend.
5. Peter Roget (1779-1869) . . . 1852.
6. film—a feature . . . viewers—is . . . recording.
7. typewriter (a used one, by the way) . . . used.

Numbers

1. forty; 269 five-gallon
2. five 9-inch
3. three hundred; page 6
4. One hundred twenty-five
5. 65 miles; Interstate 9; 5 miles
6. ten 10-cent; eight 18-cent; five 26-cent
7. No. 365.

Misplaced Modifiers

1. In order to market its radios, the Acme Company advertised for salesmen with cars.
2. The products you eat have been carefully packaged in plastic food wrap.
3. Mr. Prout wrote his speech on a scrap of paper while he was flying to New York.
4. The dealer makes nearly $200 on the sale of each car.
5. The president alone is responsible for making the final decision.
6. As we looked through our store window, we saw the holiday parade passing.
7. The tax statements are due only on the first of the month.

Proofreading

1. October
2. 16
3. no indentation on address
4. St. Paul
5. Zip abbreviation MN
6. Mr.
7. Verify correct spelling of Smallpeice
8. expense
9. Here's
10. your
11. Shiny
12. Present
13. enclosed
14. months
15. weather
16. delete "this" before "one time"
17. sample (lower case "s")
18. spelling of proper name, Smallpeice
19. your friends
20. waxed,
21. Shiny
22. 98 cents
23. Sincerely (delete comma to agree with salutation)
24. Sales Department
25. reference initials missing
26. enclosure notation missing

CHAPTER 13

Skills Activity 64

Letter 1: First paragraph needs to be rewritten. Suggested revision: "Perhaps you have forgotten that you owe $125 on last month's bill. Please take the time now to send us your check; a stamped, addressed envelope is enclosed for your convenience. If you have already mailed your check, simply ignore this reminder." Second paragraph also needs revision. Note misplaced modifier in last sentence; avoid expressions "beat the rush" and "in full swing"—both sound unbusinesslike.

Letter 2: Rewrite all three paragraphs to achieve better tone. First paragraph is insulting and condescending—e.g., "Have you really forgotten. . . ?" Second sentence is weak—e.g., "we feel . . . " is an unbusinesslike expression. Be factual, to the point, and yet polite. Second paragraph is also unbusinesslike—e.g., "This time I am enclosing . . . ." Why wasn't the envelope enclosed before? Third paragraph is too abrupt; always remember the amenities.

Letter 3: Follow guidelines listed on page 460. Adopt a friendly tone; remind customer of her fine credit reputation for past six years; suggest some possible explanations—has she been away?; mention some storewide sale to bring customer back; conclude by using direct address to thank her for being a loyal customer and how much the store values her account.

Skills Activity 65

Letter 1: Rewrite letter following guidelines listed on page 464. Avoid unbusinesslike expressions—e.g., "This bill may not seem like much to you, . . ." Also: note incorrect choice of word "passed." Avoid any flippant remarks—e.g., "You may want to charge merchandise next week."

Letter 2: Rewrite letter following guidelines listed on page 464. Be careful to observe correct form: Spell out February; delete "th" after 15. Second paragraph comes across as argumentative—e.g., "You were paid for your work, weren't you?"

Letter 3: Rewrite letter following guidelines listed on page 464. Suggestion: delete second sentence of first paragraph—it is unnecessary and rude. Second paragraph is friendly in tone and offers constructive suggestion. But second sentence—"We're sure you want to be now."—is condescending and presumptuous. In third paragraph rephrase to delete old-fashioned expression "supplied herein."

Letter 4: Rewrite letter following guidelines listed on page 465. The tone of the letter is insulting. First paragraph could be stated more briefly: "Do you realize that your account is now three months overdue? Please use the enclosed envelope to mail your check for $98.07." Second paragraph could be deleted or rephrased to mention fair treatment in less insulting tone. A brief concluding sentence—"Please settle your account now."—would be preferable to the third paragraph.

Skills Activity 66

Letter 1: Rewrite letter following guidelines on page 468. Letter should be firm but polite. Also, note Luisa's mistakes in spelling—already; in hyphenation—now-or-never letter; in dates—July 1.

Letter 2: Follow guidelines listed on page 468. Be firm, yet polite; remind customer of the factual details of his overdue account; remind customer that legal action could result if he does not settle his account by a specified date.

Letter 3: Follow guidelines listed on page 468. Be brief, factual, and forceful; maintain a polite tone; include all necessary details; be sure to emphasize when attorney will get in touch with customer.

Skills Activity 67

Letter 1: Rewrite letter following guidelines on page 470. Points to observe: Make Luisa sound more up to date; conclude letter with complete sentence—not the old-fashioned "Thanking you. . ." and "we remain."

Letter 2: Write letter to Ms. Spain:
1. Thank her for explaining her problem.
2. Express regret at her difficulties.
3. Assure her of your confidence in her ability to pay and offer the extension.
4. Extend offer to her to make further purchase.

Skills Activity 68

Letters 1-4: Follow guidelines for preceding Skills Activities. In all letters, maintain a firm yet polite tone.

Focus on Language

Spelling

commitment; responsible; maintenance; permitted procedure; unenforceable; jeopardize

Vocabulary

1. a lying still	10. c cannot be maintained
2. b changeable	11. a harmful
3. b usually	12. a brief
4. c hurt	13. d stubbornness
5. c able to be carried out	14. c reduced
6. a prevent	15. b forgiveness
7. b endangered	16. a inaction
8. d unbelievable	17. b harmful
9. c unavoidable	

Sound-Alikes

1. laid	6. lain
2. lain	7. lying
3. lays	8. laid
4. Lay	9. lie
5. lie	10. lying

Numbers

1. three-fourths
2. 5½; 1½
3. 55; 8 by 10 inches
4. June 10; eight o'clock
5. 10 by 14 feet; $50; 8 a.m. and 4 p.m.
6. 12 noon
7. 3- by 5-inch

Double Negatives

1. Didn't you hear anything?
2. scarcely anybody
3. Arlene doesn't plan to go anywhere.
4. cannot be done any longer *or* can no longer be done
5. None of us went.
6. There is hardly anywhere
7. Isn't there anybody

Redundancies

1. Since a substantial segment . . . is moving to the suburbs, we have concluded that new shopping centers should be built there.
2. There is an alternative that. . .
3. . . . biography of Adam Smith.
4. . . . obtaining credit now, we suggest that you postpone your building program.
5. We hope to regain the place we occupied among the first ten corporations.
6. If you will refer to our letter . . . our position accurately.
7. The consensus among all branch managers. . . .

Proofreading

1. August 15	10. accidents
2. Reader	11. emphasis
3. extent	12. hiring
4. spend	13. self-defeating
5. No paragraph indentation	14. except
6. Sometimes	15. use the
7. it's	16. enclosed
8. clothes	17. six months
9. night light	18. your interest

CHAPTER 14

Skills Activity 69

Follow guidelines listed on page 486.

Skills Activity 70

A. 1. Ineffective
Revision: "This report will prove that affirmative action programs make great difference in the firms that try them."
2. Ineffective
Revision: "Sales estimates for the last half of 1976 are as follows:"
3. Ineffective
Revision: "In Spring 1976, 300,000 sq. ft. of space will be allocated to classrooms and lecture halls, representing a 100 percent increase over the 150,000 feet allocated in Spring 1975."
4. Effective
5. Ineffective
Revision: "Because of the reasons stated, this stock should increase in its value."
6. Ineffective
Revision: "This plan should reduce prices by 50 percent."
7. Ineffective
Revision: "SUMMARY"

8. Effective
9. Ineffective
   Revision: "The strong reversal of unemployment trends indicates an improvement in the economy."
10. Ineffective
    Revision: "Despite the recession, XYZ Company has increased its quarterly dividend 10 cents a share to 60 cents. The increase in our sales volume, together with higher prices for our products, exceeded the increase in expenses caused by cost-of-living raises and higher fuel costs."

B. Follow guidelines listed on page 497.

Skills Activity 71

A. 1. Add complete name of author, locations of publisher, and page number.
   2. Add name of publisher.
   3. Add page number and location of company.
   4. Add volume, number, and date of periodical.

B. 1. Lamson, Newton. "Mutual Funds Tackle Commodities." New York Times, September 7, 1975, Section 3, p. 2.
   2. Christersen, Edward, and R. Dermont Bell. Century 21 Shorthand—Theory and Practice. Cincinnati, Ohio: South-Western Publishing Company, 1974.
   3. "Annual Salary Survey." Today's Secretary, Vol. 76 (March, 1974), pp. 18-19; 37-38.
   4. Forman, Doris. Manual of Data Processing. Englewood Cliffs, NJ: Prentice Hall, 1973.

Focus on Language

Spelling

1. analyze
2. subsidiary
3. plagiarism
4. accommodate
5. encompasses
6. transitional
7. deviation
8. journals
9. catalytic
10. succinct
11. concomitant
12. emission

Vocabulary

1. a   controlled corporations
2. a   short and clear
3. b   necessary
4. b   presenting another's work as one's own
5. c   determine relationship of parts
6. d   departure
7. b   take in
8. d   accompanying
9. c   obey
10. b   supplying data to prove or support

Sound-Alikes

1. Residents
2. assistance
3. dependents
4. dependence
5. rises
6. raises
7. risen
8. rise
9. assistants
10. residence

Dividing Words

1. sub-sidi-ar-ies
2. no division
3. no division
4. plea-sure
5. evalu-ate
6. no division
7. self-evident
8. no division
9. no division
10. entail-ing

INDEX

Note: *For your ready reference, entries pertaining to grammar and usage appear in italics.*